Grief Lessons

Grief Lessons

Four Plays by

Euripides

Translated by

Anne Carson

NEW YORK REVIEW BOOKS

New York

THIS IS A NEW YORK REVIEW BOOK
PUBLISHED BY THE NEW YORK REVIEW OF BOOKS
1755 Broadway, New York, NY 10019
www.nyrb.com

Library of Congress Cataloging-in-Publication Data

Euripides.
  [Selections. English. 2006]
  Grief lessons : four plays by Euripides / by Euripides ; translated and with an introduction by Anne Carson.
     p. cm.
  ISBN 1-59017-180-2 (alk. paper)
  1. Euripides—Criticism and interpretation. I. Carson, Anne. II. Title.
  PA3975.A2 2006
  822'.01—dc22
                                    2006009092

ISBN-13: 978-1-59017-180-6
ISBN-10: 1-59017-180-2

Printed in the United States of America on acid-free paper.
10 9 8 7 6 5 4 3 2

Contents

NOTE

Numbers in the margins refer to the lines of the present translation; numbers at the top right of the pages to the lines of the original Greek text.

PREFACE

Tragedy: A Curious Art Form

Why does tragedy exist? Because you are full of rage. Why are you full of rage? Because you are full of grief. Ask a headhunter why he cuts off human heads. He'll say that rage impels him and rage is born of grief. The act of severing and tossing away the victim's head enables him to throw away the anger of all his bereavements.[1] Perhaps you think this does not apply to you. Yet you recall the day your wife, driving you to your mother's funeral, turned left instead of right at the intersection and you had to scream at her so loud other drivers turned to look. When you tore off her head and threw it out the window they nodded, changed gears, drove away.

Grief and rage—you need to contain that, to put a frame around it, where it can play itself out without you or your kin having to die. There is a theory that watching unbearable stories about other people lost in grief and rage is good for you—may cleanse you of your darkness. Do you want to go down to the pits of yourself all alone? Not much. What if an actor could do it for you? Isn't that why they are called actors? They act for you. You sacrifice them to action. And this sacrifice is a mode of deepest intimacy of you with your own life. Within it you watch [yourself] act out the present or possible organization of your nature. You can be aware of your own awareness of this nature as you never are at the moment of experience. The actor, by reiterating you, sacrifices a moment of his own life in order to give you a story of yours.

1. Renato Rosaldo, "Grief and the Headhunter's Rage," *Text, Play, and Story*, edited by E. M. Bruner (Washington, D.C.: American Ethnological Society, 1984), pp. 178–195.

Curious art form, curious artist. Who was Euripides? The best short answer I've found to this is an essay by B. M. W. Knox, who says of Euripides what the Corinthians (in Thucydides) said of the Athenians, "that he was born never to live in peace with himself and to prevent the rest of mankind from doing so." Knox's essay is called "Euripides: The Poet As Prophet."[2] To be a prophet, Knox emphasizes, requires living in and looking at the present, at what is really going on around you. Out of the present the future is formed. The prophet needs a clear, dry, unshy eye that can stand aloof from explanation and comfort. Neither will be of interest to the future.

One thing that was really going on for much of Euripides' lifetime was war—relatively speaking, world war. The Peloponnesian War began 431 BC and lasted beyond Euripides' death. It brought corruption, distortion, decay and despair to society and to individual hearts. He used myths and legends connected with the Trojan War to refract his observations of this woe. Not all his plays are war plays. He was also concerned with people as people—with what it's like to be a human being in a family, in a fantasy, in a longing, in a mistake. For this exploration too he used ancient myth as a lens. Myths are stories about people who become too big for their lives temporarily, so that they crash into other lives or brush against gods. In crisis their souls are visible. To be present when that happens is Euripides' playwriting technique. His mood, as Walter Benjamin said of Proust's, is "a perfect chemical curiosity."[3]

There is in Euripides some kind of learning that is always at the boiling point. It breaks experiences open and they waste

<hr />

2. *Directions in Euripidean Criticism: A Collection of Essays*, edited by Peter Burian (Duke University Press, 1985), pp. 1–12.
3. Walter Benjamin, "The Image of Proust," *Illuminations*, edited by Hannah Arendt, translated by Harry Zohn (Schocken, 1968), pp. 203–204.

themselves, run through your fingers. Phrases don't catch them, theories don't hold them, they have no use. It is a theater of sacrifice in the true sense. Violence occurs; through violence we are intimate with some characters onstage in an exorbitant way for a brief time; that's all it is.

HERAKLES

PREFACE

Q: Will you admit this fact, that we are at a turning point?
A: If it's a fact it's not a turning point.[1]

Herakles is a two-part man. Euripides wrote for him a two-part play. It breaks down in the middle and starts over again as does he. Wrecks and recharges its own form as he wrecks and recharges his own legend. Two-part: son of both Zeus (god) and Amphitryon (man) he is immortal, *maybe*—experts disagree and he himself is not sure. Container of uncontainable physical strength, he civilizes the world by vanquishing its monsters then returns home to annihilate his own wife and children. Herakles is a creature whose relation to time is a mess: if you *might* be immortal you live in all time and no time at the same time. You end up older than your own father and more helpless than your own children. Herakles is a creature whose relation to virtue is a mess: human virtue derives from human limitation and he seems to have none; gods' virtue does not exist. Euripides places him in the midst of an awareness of all this. But awareness for Herakles is no mental event, it comes through flesh.

Herakles' flesh is a cliché. Perfect physical specimen, he cannot be beaten by any warrior, by any athlete, by any monster on the earth or under it. The question whether he can be beaten even by death remains open; it is a fact that he has gone down to Hades and come back alive: here is where the play starts. This fact becomes the turning point—the overturning point—of his cliché.

1. Maurice Blanchot, interview with himself, *La Nouvelle Revue Française*, April 1960.

How do you overturn a cliché? From inside. The first eight hundred lines of the play will bore you, they're supposed to. Euripides assembles every stereotype of a Desperate Domestic Situation and a Timely Hero's Return in order to place you at the very heart of Herakles' dilemma, which is also Euripides' dilemma: Herakles has reached the boundary of his own myth, he has come to the end of his interestingness. Now that he's finished harrowing hell, will he settle back on the recliner and watch TV for the rest of time? From Euripides' point of view, a playwright's point of view, the dilemma is practical. A man who can't die is no tragic hero. Immortality, even probable immortality, disqualifies you from playing that role. (Gods, to their eternal chagrin, are comic). For this practical dilemma Euripides' solution is simple. From inside the cliché he lets Herakles wreck not only his house, his family, his perfection, his natural past, his supernatural future, but also the tragedy itself. Into the first half of the play he packs an entire dramatic *praxis*, complete with reversals, recognitions, laments, revenge, rejoicing, suspense and death. This melodrama ends at 814. The actors leave the stage. You may think it's over and head for the door.

But if you stay you will see Herakles pull the whole house of this play down around himself, tragic conventions and all. Then from inside his *berserker furor* he has to build something absolutely new. New self, new name for the father, new definition of God. The old ones have stopped. It is as if the world broke off. Why did it break off? Because the myth ended. If you pay attention to the chorus—especially their last utterance which is very, very brief—you will hear them make a strange remark. After the murder by Herakles of his own family they respond (992ff/1020ff)*:

*Please note that the first set of figures given refers to the line numbers of the present translation, the second to those of the Greek text.

>   ... these evils here
>   belonging to the son of Zeus
>   go far beyond
>   anything in the past.
>
>   . . . .
>
>   What groaning,
>   what lament,
>   what song of death,
>   what dance of Hades
>   shall I do?

The Greek word *choros* means a dance accompanied by song, also the people who perform the dance. One of the functions of the tragic chorus is to reflect on the action of the play and try to assign it some meaning. They typically turn to the past in their search for the meaning of the present—scanning history and myth for a precedent. It was Homer who suggested we stand in time with our backs to the future, face to the past. What if a man turns around? Then the chorus will necessarily fall silent. This story has not happened before. Notice they do not dance again. Let the future begin.

As we look back from the future at this old tragedy and its (all too contemporary) brutalized and brutalizing hero, we might consider some aspects of the play and its production that are foreign to modern tastes or expectation. Nowadays we think of a play as something that happens inside a small black box with artificial lighting. The ancient theater of Dionysos at Athens could seat 12,000 to 15,000 spectators and its plays were performed in daylight, starting at dawn. The backdrop of the theatrical space (the space in a modern theater that appears when the curtains part) was formed by open air. At Athens the audience looked out on miles and miles of Aegean Sea. No curtain, very little set. Closest to the audience was a round *orchestra* ("dancing space") where the chorus performed its songs and dances; behind this, a stage building of some kind (e.g. Herakles' house) where the actors went in and out. Two *parodoi* ("side roads") permitted entrances and exits from the wings. The play's action was performed in the small area between the *orchestra* and the stage building. Violence was not presented onstage. Violent acts and death were at times audible while happening inside the stage building or narrated afterwards by an eyewitness (usually the Messenger). Occasionally the consequences of violent acts that had taken place inside were extruded onto the stage on a mechanism called the *ekkyklema* ("rolling platform") e.g. the mayhem visited by Herakles upon his family. Think tableau. In a theater of such scale, much of the audience's visual experience would have been an appreciation of tableau—a design of bodies moving or posed in space a long distance away. Hence the conceptual importance and symbolic possibilities of posture: you can read the plot of a play off the sequence of postures assumed by its characters. Up is winning, down is losing, bent is inbetween. Herakles' unlucky family is shown at first semi-prostate on the stage in supplication for their lives, then briefly upright while Herakles champions them, then strewn as corpses. Herakles himself enters gloriously upright but is soon reduced to a huddled and broken form. His task in the last third of the play is to rise from this prostration, which he does with the help of Theseus. Euripides makes clear that Herakles exits at the end leaning on his friend. Herakles' reputation in myth and legend otherwise had been that of lonehand hero. Here begins a new Heraklean posture. Meanwhile throughout the play this image of collaborative heroism is embodied, movingly, in the tableau of the chorus. They are old men; they lean on sticks or on each other. All mortals come to this.[2]

Gods remain a problem. You will hear gods' names and see their consequences rawly displayed throughout the speeches and the action. You will sympathize with the chorus who cower before them and also with Herakles who decides not to believe in them —not to believe, that is, in *the story of his own life*. Bold move. Perhaps he is a tragic hero after all.

---

2. Herakles also figured for the Greeks as a symbol of eternal youth; according to legend he ascended to Mount Olympos after death, married the goddess Hebe (Youth) and lived forever. Euripides does not introduce this strand of the myth directly for he wants to tell the story of a mortal man or at least one whose magic fails him. Yet youth and age are thematically present in every choral ode and also in certain striking mimetic gestures of the play: the rock-like weight of old age of which the chorus complain at 619/638 is realized in the rock that Athene hurls at Herakles to check his frenzy (976–979/1003–1006; cf. 1380/1397); the veil of shadow that old age feels upon its eyes at 620/641 is realized in the shadowy covering that Herakles draws over his head at the approach of Theseus (1137/1159; 1206/1216); Herakles takes Theseus as son (1384/1401) and looks forward to burying his own father (1406/1421). Time is uneasy in this play and it unsettles the cliché of heroic autonomy.

CAST OF CHARACTERS
In order of appearance

AMPHITRYON (MORTAL), *father of Herakles*
MEGARA, *wife of Herakles*
three SONS *of Herakles and Megara*
CHORUS *of old men of Thebes*
LYKOS, *usurper of Thebes*
SERVANTS *of Lykos*
HERAKLES, *son of Zeus/Amphitryon and of Alkmene*
IRIS, *messenger of the gods*
MADNESS
THESEUS, *king of Athens*
MESSENGER

The scene is set at Thebes. The stage has two side entrances and a central stage building representing the house of Herakles. Nearby is an altar of Zeus Savior where Amphitryon, Megara and the children sit as suppliants.

AMPHITRYON

Who does not know the man who shared his marriage bed
with Zeus?
Amphitryon,
son of Alkaios,
grandson of Perseus,
father of Herakles,
me!
I used to own Thebes,
where dragons' teeth sprang out of the earth like ears of corn
and lived as men.   10
Their children fill this city.
From them came Kreon, ruler of this land
and father of Megara—
wedding songs rang out
when Herakles led her to my home as his bride.
But he left Thebes behind,
left Megara, left me—
to live in that Argive city
from which I was exiled
because I committed a murder.   20
He wanted to dwell there, to ease my way back.
The price was high:

to civilize the entire world was his contract.
I wonder, did Hera have her spike in him then
or was it all just his fate?
Anyway, the task is finished now
except one last labor—
the threebodied dog must be got up from hell.
He went down there but has not come back.

According to legend   30
Dirke's husband long ago was Lykos,
despot of this sevengated city.
And it is his grandson, with the same name,
who came from Euboia, murdered Kreon and rules us now.
The city was divided, he fell upon it.
Then our kinship with Kreon turned out a bad thing.
And now that my son is down in the basement of the world,
glorious Lykos wants us dead—Herakles' children,
Herakles' wife (to quench the seed)
and me, the man of the family I guess,   40
though I'm useless and old.
Blood justice is what Lykos fears.

So I—left in the house here
to care for the children, along with their mother,
when my son went underground—
I've set us up at the altar of Zeus Savior,
built by my son to mark his victory
over the Minyans.
Here we watch and wait,
lacking everything—food, water, clothing,   50
on the bare ground,
sealed out of our house.

Who can help?
Friends disappear
or they are powerless.
This is what misfortune means
an acid test of friendship.
I wouldn't wish it on anyone.

MEGARA

Old man—you who once demolished the Taphians' city,
you who commanded an army for Thebes—   60
nothing the gods do makes sense!
I was no outcast from luck on my father's side.
He was rich and big and boasted
of his power, long spears leaping around it,
boasted of his children.
He gave me to your son,
to Herakles, a brilliant marriage.
And now all that has vanished.
You and I will die, old man,
and Herakles' little fledglings—   70
like a bird I cover them with my wings.
They fly to me asking one after another,
Where is father gone?
What is he doing?
When will he come back?
I put them off with stories.
It shocks me,
whenever the doors creak everyone jumps up
as if to run to their father's knee.
Can you ease me with hope or some way of salvation, old man? 80
I look to you.
We could never cross the border secretly,

guards are posted on every road.
Nor can we hope for salvation from friends anymore.
Whatever your thoughts,
speak them. Death is at hand.

AMPHITRYON

Daughter, I find it hard
to rattle off advice like that.
We're weak, let's play for time.

MEGARA

Wait for worse? You love the light so much?   90

AMPHITRYON

I do, I love its hopes.

MEGARA

Well yes, but there's no use expecting the impossible, old man.

AMPHITRYON

To delay evils is a kind of cure.

MEGARA

This waiting gnaws at me.

AMPHITYON

A clear path may open
out of these troubles, for you and me.
My son might come.
Be calm. Wipe their tears
and soothe them with stories,
a bit of make-believe.   100

Even catastrophes grow weary,
no wind can keep blasting all the time.
And great happiness in the end falters.
Yes, all is change.
Best to keep hoping.
Despair is the mark of a bad man.

[enter Chorus from both side entrances into orchestra]

CHORUS (*entrance song*)
Leaning on my stick I come,
   quavering my laments,
      like some old white bird—
         I am nothing but words,   110
           just a shape
              of dreams or night.
          I tremble. But my heart is full!
        O poor fatherless children,
     poor old man,
   poor mother calling out
to your husband in Hades.

Come do not tire, heavy foot, heavy leg,
   heavy burden, uphill
      like a workhorse   120
        I go.
          Take my hand,
        take my robe,
       where the foot falters.
     Old man side by side with old man—
   as our young spears once stood side by side in war,
no shame to our glorious country.

Look how the gorgon-gaze of their father
stares out of their eyes.
Bad luck is not gone from these children,   130
but neither is beauty.
O Greece! what fighters you will lose
when you lose these!

But I see Lykos coming.
Lykos, tyrant of this land.

[enter Lykos by side entrance with Servants]

LYKOS
You people!—Herakles' people,
if I may, a question:
and since I am master here,
yes! you must answer.
How long do you think to prolong life?   140
What hope do you have? What defense do you see?
Or do you believe
he will come back from Hades?
Hysteria!
You, boasting you sowed the same marriage bed as Zeus,
and you, that you married a world hero!
What was so spectacular about those "labors" of his anyway?
So he killed a water snake, or that Nemean creature—
he did it with nets, not his own hands.
Is this your claim? Is this why you think   150
his sons should escape death?
A man who got a name for courage,
though he was *nothing*—he fought animals!
No good for anything else.

Never had a shield on his arm,
never came near a spear: he used a bow!—
coward's weapon—always ready to run.
A bow is no test of a man's courage.
No—but standing fast, staring the enemy down,
facing the gash of the spear! 160
Now me,
I'm not shameless,
just cautious, old man.
I killed Kreon, her father,
I know that. I sit on his throne.
Don't want those boys
reared up as avengers on me.

AMPHITRYON

Let Zeus defend the Zeus-part of his son.
The rest is mine: Herakles,
I'll show this man knows nothing about you. 170
To hear you abused—no!
Against unspeakable charges, like cowardice,
I call the gods to witness.
I call the lightning of Zeus, the chariot of Zeus,
in which you went to shoot the giants down
and raised a cry of victory with the gods.
Go to where the centaurs live, ask them—
those monsters on four legs—ask
what man they judge the bravest: they'll say
my son! 180
Whereas, if you ask Dirphys, your own local mountain,
to praise you, she couldn't name a single deed of yours.
And then you denounce that tactical masterpiece,
the bow.

27

Listen, you'll learn something.
Your hoplite is the slave of his weapons.
If he breaks his spear he's dead.
Dead too if his comrades on either side aren't good men.
But the one who aims a bow—
world's best weapon—can shoot a thousand arrows   190
and still have some to save his life.
He stands back, wounds his enemy with invisible shots
and keeps his own body
unexposed. This is intelligent warfare,
to damage the enemy,
stay safe yourself
and don't trust to luck.
These are my views, opposed to yours—
it's an old debate.
But now,   200
why do you want to murder these children?
What have they done to you?
I grant you're smart in one way: a coward yourself,
you fear the sons of a hero.
Still,
this lies heavy on us—to die for your cowardice!
You would be the one to die,
if Zeus were just.
But let's say you're determined to take over this country—
then allow us to go into exile.   210
You should beware of violence you know,
the wind may change.
God might come round on you.
PHEU! [*cry*]
O land of Kadmos (yes I reproach you too!)
is this how you defend Herakles and his children?

28

Herakles who all alone fought off the Minyans
and let Thebes look through the eyes of freedom.
Nor can I praise Greece—Greece is a coward!
Greece should have come with fire and sword
to help these poor little birds of his,   220
in return for all he did—
he cleared the sea, he changed the world!
O little ones, they do not avail you,
not Thebes, not Greece.
You look to me, a weak old man,
a whisper of a man.
Strength left me some while back.
I tremble, I blur.
But if I were young,
still master of my body,   230
I'd bloody that fair head of his,
I'd run him out of town at the end of my spear!

CHORUS

    Slow start, good speech.

LYKOS

    Towers of words.
    I will use actions.
    Here! [*to Servants*] you—go to Helikon and you to Parnassos.
    Tell the woodsmen there to cut logs of oak.
    Bring them here, pile up wood
    around the altar and set it on fire.
    Burn these people alive! So they realize   240
    no dead man is going to rule this land.
    I am master here.
    And you defiant old men

will be groaning not just for Herakles' children
but for your own house
as it falls. Remember,
you are my slaves.

CHORUS

O sons of earth, whom Ares once sowed
with teeth ripped out of the dragon's jaw,
stand up now! Break this man's ungodly head—   250
he's no Theban. A foreigner! Evil!
You will never lord it over me.
You will not enjoy the work of my hands.
Go back where you came from,
use your arrogance there.
While I'm alive, you shall not kill Herakles' children—
he isn't buried so deep.
He did good for this land.
You ravaged it, robbed him.
Am I a troublemaker if I help a friend in need?   260
O right hand, how you long to grip the spear!
But weakness kills longing.
Else I would have stopped you calling me a slave
and we'd live happily in Thebes.
But here you strut.
This city must have lost its mind
to put up with your despotism.

MEGARA

Old men, I thank you. Friends ought to show
righteous anger on their friends' behalf.
I only hope your rage does not cause you suffering.   270
But Amphitryon,

hear me. Think.
I love my children, how could I not?
And death is awful. Yet
to strive against the necessary turn of things
is simply stupid.
Yes we must die but there is no need
to die mutilated by fire—a laughingstock to our enemies!
That's worse than death.
We owe our house a finer dignity than that.   280
You have known glory in war—unbearable
for you to die as a coward.
And my husband, whose fame needs no witness,
would prefer these children not be saved
if the price is dishonor.
It breaks a good parent's heart to see children disgraced.
I must take my husband's example.
Look,
you think your son will come back from Hades?
What dead man comes back?   290
Or do you hope to soften up Lykos?
Not likely. When your enemy is a savage, flee him.
With men of culture
you can negotiate, they have a sense of shame!
It had occurred to me
we might plead for exile for the children.
But wouldn't that be worse—
to trap them in a salvation made of abject poverty?
You know the saying, people in exile
get one day of smiling from their friends.   300
Dare death with me.
Death stands by you anyway.
I call on your greatness of soul, old man.

He who battles fate shows courage,
but the courage of a fool.
No one will ever make necessity not happen.

CHORUS

Had I strength in my arms and someone were assaulting you,
I'd stop it.
But I am nothing. Now it's your task,
Amphitryon, to thrust a way through this bad luck.   310

AMPHITRYON

Not cowardice or love of life
prevents me dying: I want to save the children of my son—
impossible as this seems.
Look! You have a sword, here's my neck—
stab me! murder me! throw me from a cliff!
But grant us one favor, king, we pray.
Kill us first, before the children.
We cannot watch that.
Unholy sight—their souls
breaking free of life   320
as they call out to us.
And the rest—if you're set on it—do it.
We haven't the strength not to die.

MEGARA

I add a prayer:
you,
grant us this alone.
Let me dress my children for death.
Open the doors (we are locked out)
and allow them this much at least of their father's wealth.

LYKOS

    It shall be so. I instruct my servants to unbar the doors.   330
    Go in and dress, I do not begrudge you clothing.
    When you are ready
    I shall hand you on to the world below.

[exit Lykos by side entrance]

MEGARA

    Children, come with me
    into your father's house.
    It is still ours in name.

AMPHITRYON

    O Zeus, in vain I shared my wife with you!
    In vain I shared my son.
    Your love is not what it seemed.
    In fact I surpass you in virtue—and you a god! A big god.   340
    Herakles' children I did not betray.
    But you—you know how to sneak into other men's beds,
    how to get whatever sex you want,
    but not how to save your own kin.
    For a god, you're an idiot. Or simply immoral.

[exit Amphitryon, Megara, children into house]

CHORUS [*first choral ode*]

    Sing sorrow! on top of joy.
    So Apollo sings
    driving the gold pick into his beautiful voicing lyre.
    And I sing
    of the man who went underground, down to the dark—   350

Herakles

whether I call him son of Zeus
or of Amphitryon.
I want to place a crown of praise upon his labors.
To sing of noble actions
is a glory for the dead.

First he cleared out the lion
from the grove of Zeus
and hooded himself
in its big yellow jaws.

Laid low the wild mountain centaurs   360
with arrows of blood,
arrows like wings—
those monsters known
to the long barren fields,
to the river,
to the farms,
to the grasslands
where they filled their hands with pine branches
and rode Thessaly down.

Shot the deer with golden horns   370
that used to ravage men,
and offered it to Artemis
who kills wild things.
Broke the mares of Diomedes,
bridling their bloody jaws,
their murder meals,
their man-eating joy—
their tables of evil.
Crossed the river Hebros

where the streams run silver,   380
working for his lord of Mykenai.

Slew Kyknos
on the Melian shore,
whose hospitality was
to chop his guests in bits.

Went west to the halls of evening,
where the Hesperides sing
and plucked a gold fruit
from apple branches.
Killed the snake with fiery scales   390
that coiled its coils there.
Sank through the sea
and set a calmness on the lives of sailors.

Drove his hand straight up through heaven
in Atlas' place
and held the starry houses of the gods
aloft all by himself.

Hunted the Amazon army
across rivers and rivers,
to the other side of a hostile sea,   400
gathering every Greek as he went—
hunting
the goldchased belt of the daughter of war.
Her wild gold spoil fell to him,
kept in Mykenai to this day.

Burned to death the thousand heads

of the deadly dog of Lerna.
Dipped his arrows in her poison
to kill threebodied Geryon.

Other races, other glories, he ran, he won.   410
Now's he sailed to Hades,
place of tears—
last of his labors.
He comes not back.
His house stands empty.
Charon waits.
The journey waits.
The children wait—
looking to you!
You, gone.   420

If only I had the power of youth
to shake my spear
and join my comrades,
I'd stand and save these children—force on force!
But as it is
I lack myself.

Here they come dressed for death,
once the sons of magnificent Herakles.
Here is his wife, pulling them along,
and the old father.   430
Oh sad pity.
I cannot restrain my tears,
my old man's tears.

[enter Megara, children, Amphitryon from house]

MEGARA

Well then where is our priest? Where is our sacrificer?
We stand ready to make our offerings to Hades.
Strange-looking death group.
Old men, mothers, children all together.
Grotesque fate.
I look on you for the last time.
I gave you birth, I reared you up, for enemies   440
to mock, outrage and murder.
PHEU! [*cry*]
All the hopes fell wrong,
the hopes we had your father and I.
He would have left you Argos when he died,
and Eurystheus' palace to rule,
with power over rich Pelasgia
and that famous lionskin that he himself
used to pull over your head.
You would be king in chariotloving Thebes,   450
possessor of all my lands,
for you were always asking him for this
and he used to play with you,
putting his big carved club into your hand.
And to you he promised Oichalia,
captured once with bow and arrows.
Three sons, three kingdoms: he had a grand design.
And I
would have chosen your brides and made you marriages
with Athens and Sparta and Thebes   460
to anchor fast your happy lives.
These things are gone.
Luck turns. Luck gave you deaths as brides,
my tears as bridal bath.

Your father's father welcomes Hades to the wedding feast—
dread father of the bride!
O little ones, which of you should I take to my heart first,
which last, or kiss, or hold?
How I wish like a bee I could gather you—
all my heartbreak for you into one teardrop.   470
O Herakles, beloved, if you hear a voice down there,
I call to you.
Your father is dying, your children are doomed, and I.
I who was once called *blessed* because of you.
Help us! Come back! Even as a shadow,
even as a dream.
They are vile men who destroy your sons.

AMPHITRYON
Make your prayers to those below, woman.
I shall spike my hand to Zeus—Zeus! if you do intend
to help us, it's almost too late!   480
But you've heard this. I waste my breath.
Death has us in its necessary grip.
Old men,
life is a small thing.
Go through it as sweetly as possible,
day into night without pain.
Time does not know how to keep our hopes safe,
but flutters off on its own business.
Look at me: I had fame, I did deeds.
Luck stripped me bare   490
as a wing to the air
in one day.
Wealth, glory—nothing is sure.
You are looking at me for the last time, old friends.

MEGARA

EA! [*scream*]
Old man! I see him! Or what am I saying!

AMPHITRYON

I don't know. I'm struck dumb.

MEGARA

Him! The one who was under the ground!
Or is it some dream in daylight—
what am I saying? What kind of dream? Am I crazy?   500
No, it is—your son, old man, no other!
Run, children, hurry, hold tight to his clothes,
don't let go!
He is no less than Zeus the Savior come to us!

[*enter Herakles from side entrance*]

HERAKLES

O house O halls O hearth of mine!
How glad I am to see you in the light!
[*cry*]
What's this. Here are my children out in front
dressed in black.
I see my wife in a crowd of men,
my father in tears—   510
what's wrong?
Woman, what is happening here?

MEGARA

O beloved!

AMPHITRYON
O light of your father!

MEGARA
You have come, you are safe, you can save us!

HERAKLES
What do you mean? Father, what is this turmoil?

MEGARA
We were lost! Old man, forgive me
if I break in.
Females are better at lament than men.
And death was on us—my children and me!   520

HERAKLES
Apollo! What a beginning!

MEGARA
My brothers are dead, my father is dead.

HERAKLES
How? What killed them?

MEGARA
Lykos. The new king here.

HERAKLES
In war? Revolution?

MEGARA
Civil war. He took power in Thebes.

HERAKLES

But why are you and my father in a terror?

MEGARA

He intended to kill us and the children.

HERAKLES

What did he fear from my sons?

MEGARA

That they one day seek to avenge Kreon.   530

HERAKLES

And why are you in funeral clothes?

MEGARA

We dressed ourselves for death.

HERAKLES

Death by violence? What horror.

MEGARA

We were all alone. We heard you were dead.

HERAKLES

You despaired of me?

MEGARA

Heralds proclaimed your death again and again.

HERAKLES

And why did you leave my house and hearth?

MEGARA

He forced us, threw your father out of bed—

HERAKLES

He had no shame, even before an old man?

MEGARA

Shame? Lykos? He stays clear of that.   540

HERAKLES

And where were my friends then?

MEGARA

Who has friends in bad times?

HERAKLES

Do they make so little of the wars I won for them?

MEGARA

I say it again, bad luck has no friends.

HERAKLES

Throw off those wreaths of death!
Look to the light! No shadows now,
it's time for me to change things!
First I'll raze this upstart tyrant's house,
cut off his unholy head
and toss it to the dogs.   550
Then all those men of Kadmos who made good off me
will fall beneath my bow of victory—
watch the arrows fly!
Until the river is thick with corpses

and the fountains run red with blood!
Who else should I defend if not wife,
sons, father? Farewell my labors!
That was all pointless.
I should have been here.
How is it heroic   560
to fight hydras and lions for Eurystheus,
while my children face death alone?
I shall never be called "Herakles the victor" again.

CHORUS

Help your family, that's the right thing.

AMPHITRYON

How like you my son, to love your friends
and hate your enemies. But don't rush in.

HERAKLES

Am I rushing in?

AMPHITRYON

Lykos has allies, desperate men,
who staged a revolution and brought this city down,
hoping to milk their fellow citizens dry.   570
Watch out!
You were seen coming in. Enemies gather.

HERAKLES

I don't care if the whole city saw me!
But I noticed a bird, a weird bird, on my way here.
Made me feel strange.
So in fact I came secretly.

43

AMPHITRYON

Good. Now go in and greet your hearth.
Let the house look on you.
Soon Lykos arrives with his murder plan.
Just wait: everything will unfold   580
around you.
Don't stir up the city, child,
until everything here is clear.

HERAKLES

Well advised. I'll go inside.
I am returned to life
from the sunless hole of Hades underground:
it would be disrespectful to the gods of my house
if I did not greet them.

AMPHITRYON

Did you really go into the house of Hades?

HERAKLES

Yes, and brought back the threeheaded dog.   590

AMPHITRYON

Did you do battle, or was it a gift?

HERAKLES

I did battle. And won because I had seen the mysteries.

AMPHITRYON

Where is the dog now—at Eurystheus' house?

Preface

In early April 1814 a new type of twin-hulled ferryboat cast off from the waterfront at New York City and proceeded across the East River to Brooklyn. The boat's progress was accompanied by an odd cacophony of noises: the splashing of paddles in the water, the rumbling of gears, the rhythmic drumming of hooves on planks, and the snorts of irritated horses. For passengers who had grown accustomed to making the 1.2-kilometer (³⁄₄ mi.) crossing in small, wet rowboats or awkward, slow-sailing scows, the sounds must have had a musical quality, for the ferry was faster, more dependable, and safer than any they had ever boarded. This miraculous new boat was propelled from shore to shore by horses who walked in a circle around the deck.

The age of equine-powered watercraft was off to a rousing start. For the next half-century, paddle-wheeled horseboats or *teamboats* would be a familiar sight at ferry crossings on the continent's lakes and rivers, and many people—merchants, farmers, migrants, and tourists—would come to depend on these reliable craft. Development of horse-powered ferries proceeded rapidly in the decades after 1814, and the introduction of two new forms of horse machinery would greatly lower the cost of ferry operations in the United States and Canada.

By the second quarter of the nineteenth century, the teamboat was unquestionably an important element in the North American transportation network, but its story has long been obscured by contemporary—and well-publicized—advances in maritime technology such as steamboats, canals, and fast-sailing packet and clipper ships. Steamboats, in particular, overshadowed horse-propelled craft: The first commercially successful steamers preceded horse ferries by seven years, and steamers were always larger, faster, more numerous, more expensive, and technologically much more complex. Moreover, they frequently exploded, burned, or sank with great losses in human life. Mundane and relatively safe ferryboats rarely made the headlines in newspapers.

There was clearly a place for horsepower alongside steam in the American transportation network, however. In the early decades of the century, steamboats were chiefly employed as long-distance conveyors up and down rivers, lakes, and bays, whereas horseboats were well suited to the traditional task of the ferryboat, carrying people and goods across narrow bodies of water. Horse ferries were confined to short- and medium-distance crossings because of the limited endurance of their equine crews, but their paddle-wheel propulsion permitted dependable service regardless of wind and current, a great advantage over earlier sailing ferryboats.

Relatively inexpensive machinery and low fuel costs allowed horse ferries to operate economically at crossings that would have been unprofitable for early steam-propelled ferries. As the nineteenth century progressed and steam machinery grew cheaper and more reliable, many ferry owners would convert to steam, but a considerable percentage of them would find it too expensive and subsequently revert to horse propulsion. Construction of horseboats and steamboats declined in the second half of the nineteenth century, as railroads expanded across the continent and became the predominant form of inland transportation. Teamboats would remain in use into the twentieth century, but only at obscure ferry crossings with meager traffic.

The inspiration for this book first appeared on the side-scan sonar printout of two New York researchers, James Kennard and Scott Hill, who were surveying the waters of Lake Champlain for shipwrecks in 1983. Kennard and Hill recognized that the well-preserved hull was probably one of the lake's little-known horse-propelled boats, and they reported their find to the Vermont Division for Historic Preservation. The following year we got our first look at the mysterious wreck in its resting place beneath 15.24 meters (50 ft.) of water during the course of a sonar survey of Lake Champlain, sponsored by the Champlain Maritime Society.

The horseboat was a haunting sight in the dim light at the bottom of the lake, the sort of wreck every diver and nautical archaeologist hopes to see at least once in a lifetime. The hull, listing over a few degrees to starboard, was partially buried in the lake floor, its old timbers eroded and weakened by nearly a century and a half of immersion. The foredeck was missing, exposing frames and other internal elements of the hull. The paired spokes of each paddle wheel, their ends worn and rounded, extended above what was left of the deck. Beneath the afterdeck could be seen the spokes of a much larger, horizontally oriented wheel, as well as iron gears and shafts crusted over with a thick layer of corrosion.

It was evident that the wreck had much to tell us about horseboats, but the process of extracting the information would not get started until 1989, when the site was formally opened to visits by divers as an "underwater preserve," or archaeological park. At this time, the Division for Historic Preservation authorized a multiyear archaeological study of the wreck and its contents to create a permanent record in the form of hull plans, a written description of the vessel, photographs, and video footage. The archaeological documentation was undertaken by the Lake Champlain Maritime Museum and the Institute of Nautical Archaeology at Texas A&M University and would require four field seasons of diving.

The initial survey of the hull in 1989 concentrated on the exposed structure: the upper portions of the sides, the deck, and especially the treadwheel-sidewheel mechanism. The measurements and sketches made in this year allowed a partial reconstruction of the propulsion mechanism and deck, but it was obvious that excavation at selected locations inside and outside the hull was necessary if we hoped to complete our analysis of the ferry. The most accessible location inside the hull was the bow, and so in the course of 1990 and 1991, seven weeks were spent systematically removing sediment, recovering artifacts, and recording every possible detail of the internal structure. Inside the bow were many artifacts that shed light on the ferry's history and daily operations. The full lengths of the stem and the stern post were also exposed and recorded in 1991 and 1992. The final season of work on the wreck was a four-week endeavor in 1992 that focused on excavating the port-side structure in the after part of the hull. The data collected during the archaeological study are presented in Part Two.

The research had a second, historical component that ran concurrently with the excavation and architectural study of the wreck. The horse ferry that sank in Burlington Bay was, like all vessels, merely one element in the great interconnected system of technology, economics, and social dynamics that comprise human cultures, in this case North American society in the nineteenth century. The archaeological study of the wreck promised to illuminate one part of the story: the design, construction, and working life of one equine-powered ferry on Lake Champlain. The historical study, we believed, would tell the rest of the story: the origins of horse-powered machinery and vessels, the circumstances that created a demand for these vessels in the United States and Canada, and, most importantly, the history of the people who designed, built, owned, worked on, and traveled on horseboats.

Finding the history of horseboats proved to be a far greater challenge than we anticipated, for there were no comprehensive sources on the subject, and relatively few on the more generalized topic of ferrying. John Perry, author of *American Ferryboats*, aptly described the problem: "One of the difficulties in writing about early American ferryboats is that few records were ever kept, and of these, not many survive. . . . those which do exist are scattered, frequently as part of collections in which ferries and ferry crossings figure merely incidentally." In other words, the everyday business of carrying people and goods back and forth over the water has seldom been considered a subject worthy of attention for its own sake.

Researching horse ferries in libraries and archives was much like panning for gold, for it was often necessary to sift through an enormous amount of irrelevant material to find a few tiny nuggets. The lack of a common terminology sometimes made it difficult to tell if references to *horse ferries* in a document meant that the ferries were powered by horses or that they were merely ferries designed to carry horses. Searching through book indexes was also perplexing: Do you look under *horses*, or *teamboats*, or *treadmill boats*, or just plain *ferries*?

Our strategy for finding references to horseboats depended greatly on accounts of travel in North America during the nineteenth century, especially accounts by European travelers, for they found this mode of crossing the water new and therefore noteworthy. Other productive sources were published histories of towns, counties, regions, and states that were located along navigable rivers and lakes; town histories published in the nineteenth century were particularly helpful because they were written in an era when prolixity was a virtue, and they often called upon the memories of people who had actually witnessed teamboats in service. Old newspaper advertisements provided "snapshots" of a ferry's hours and rates at a particular time but rarely included other information. Town and state libraries occasionally yielded bundles of original records about a horse ferry operation, but locating this material was a hit-or-miss proposition and usually occurred only after a lengthy search; the Townsend and Thomson Papers at the New York State Archives were among our most exciting finds in this regard and are extensively cited in Chapter 6.

We found that the greatest resource in our hunt for the history of horse propulsion was other researchers, some of them old friends and some of them new, who shared horseboat information they had on file, or who took the time to copy references they encountered while pursuing their own research interests. We were also frequently blessed by the kindness of strangers—librarians and historians, both professional and avocational, who responded to our out-of-the-blue requests for assistance with copies of documents and illustrations or with personal knowledge they had gained over the years. Without the contributions of these people, our knowledge of horse ferries would be poor indeed.

It is not often that an archaeologist or historian gets to write the book on an overlooked aspect of human (and in this case, equine) history, but after years of research we are reasonably confident that this volume is the first book devoted to the subject of North America's age of horse-powered boats. It also contains the first detailed description of a horse-propelled ferry that is based upon the archaeological study of a horseboat wreck. We sincerely hope that your introduction to these unusual boats will be as enjoyable as the decade that we have spent discovering their role in the daily life of nineteenth- and early twentieth-century North Americans has been to us.

Acknowledgments

The archaeological study of the Burlington Bay horse ferry wreck and the historical study of North America's horseboats were assisted by a great many individuals and institutions. It is with great pleasure that we take this opportunity to acknowledge the time, effort, information, funding, and encouragement that made these studies possible.

Much of the institutional support for the Horse Ferry Project has come from three organizations. The Vermont Division for Historic Preservation, charged with the task of protecting and studying Vermont's archaeological sites, provided direction, logistical support and funding for the field work and analysis; special recognition is due to Eric Gilbertson, Giovanna Peebles, Jane Lendway, and archaeologist David Skinas. The directors, staff, and volunteers of the Lake Champlain Maritime Museum at Basin Harbor, Vermont, have consistently supported our many archaeological endeavors on the lake, including the years of work on the horse ferry. The museum maintains and displays the ferry's artifacts and has provided thousands of schoolchildren with the chance to play the horse on a one-half-scale working replica of the boat's horizontal-treadwheel machinery. The Institute of Nautical Archaeology at Texas A&M University provided equipment and funding for the project from 1991 to 1992; many thanks are due to the institute's directors, staff, and friends, especially Ray Siegfried II, John and Ellie Stern, and Harry Kahn. Texas A&M and the University of Vermont greatly assisted our work by sponsoring archaeological field schools in 1991 and 1992.

We owe special thanks to Jon Eddy and the folks at the Waterfront Diving Center of Burlington, Vermont, who took care of our diving-equipment needs and gracefully handled the daily intrusion of our field crews. The U.S. Naval Reserve permitted us to set up a shorefront base in their Burlington facility in 1990 and 1992, and the U.S. Coast Guard did the same in 1991; both branches of the service deserve recognition for this important contribution to the project.

The archaeological study of the wreck would not have been possible without the efforts of the staff, volunteers, and students who spent weeks of their time on and under the water, patiently dredging away the silt and recording details of the horse ferry's construction. Deserving special mention are Fred Fayette, the ever-cheerful, ever-vigilant captain of the RV *Neptune*, and John Butler, who kept us all diving safely and still found time to take superb photographs of the wreck.

1989 Crew: Bryce Howell, David Skinas, James Squires, Clem Thompson, and David Andrews.

1990 Crew: David Andrews, John Butler, Erick Tichonuk, Ron Plouffe, Ed Bell, Ginny West, David Burnor, Daniel Laroche, Joseph Vicere, Fred Fayette, and Anne Cohn.

1991 Crew: John Butler, Fred Fayette, Joe Cozzi, John Fenimore, John Bratten, Tina Erwin, Tina Lessem, David Robinson, Tommy Hailey, Tray Siegfried, Bryan Lorber, Scott McLaughlin, Ned Chase, Heather Babcock, Jon Eddy, Matt Perry, Chris Porter, Erick Tichonuk, Laurie Eddy, Ron Plouffe, Pat Beck, and Scott Jenkins.

1992 Crew: John Butler, Fred Fayette, John Bratten, Joe Cozzi, David Robinson, Tray Siegfried, Elizabeth Robinson Baldwin, Alan Flanigan, Curtis Hite, Toby Brown, Lisa Denis, and Jennifer Faul.

Dr. D. L. Hamilton, founder and director of the Texas A&M University Conservation Research Lab and head of the Nautical Archaeology Graduate Program, provided space, chemicals, and equipment for conserving the horse ferry's artifacts and, together with his lab staff, Dr. Wayne Smith and Helen DeWolfe, advised and assisted the processing of the finds. Nautical Archaeology Program graduate student Tina Erwin carried out conservation and also, with the help of James Bahrke, Brian Jordan, and Erika Washburn, prepared the catalog and drawings of the artifacts. Erick

Tichonuk and Robert Barros provided additional artifact illustrations. Wood samples from the ferry wreck were identified by Dr. Roy Whitmore, professor emeritus of the University of Vermont Forestry Program. Dr. Fred Hocker of the Texas A&M Nautical Archaeology Program offered encouragement and helpful observations during the drafting of the hull plans.

The historical research on horse-powered watercraft was aided by many people, libraries, museums, and archives. Two historians deserve special recognition for their contributions: A. Peter Barranco of Montpelier, Vermont, and Morris F. Glenn of Essex, New York, and Oxford, Maryland. Chapter 7, "Mountain Teamboats," is based largely on newspaper and other sources that Peter and Morris collected in their files over the years; Chapter 5, "Barnabas Langdon," was bolstered by the research of Morris Glenn and Richard Ward of Plattsburgh, New York. We feel fortunate to have friends like these.

Other people and organizations that contributed research include the Evans Library at Texas A&M University (particularly the Interlibrary Loan Services office); Dr. Paul Huey of the New York Bureau of Historic Sites; Dr. Paul Johnston of the Division of Transportation, National Museum of American History, Smithsonian Institution; the New York State Archives; the Troy Public Library and Rensselaer County Historical Society, both of Troy, New York; the American Antiquarian Society of Worcester, Massachusetts; Katherine MacKenzie and John M. Scott of the Georgeville, Quebec Historical Society; Raymond Beecher of the Greene County Historical Society, New York; Ralph Malmgren of the Wolfeboro Historical Society, New Hampshire; Robert Sincerbeaux and the Cecil Howard Charitable Trust; Judy Wood of the U.S. Army Corps of Engineers, Savannah, Georgia District; Jean Di Marzi of Gargenville, France; University of Vermont Special Collections; Donald Shomette of Dunkirk, Maryland; Phillip Gillesse (Ontario's own "Mr. Horseboat"); the Dartmouth Heritage Museum, Dartmouth, Nova Scotia; the Umatilla County Historical Society; Lee Cox of Philadelphia, Pennsylvania; Ellen Zobrist and Judy Brock of New Haven, Missouri; Dorothy Heckmann Schrader of Hermann, Missouri; Sue Deppe and Meta Arrington of Bellevue, Iowa; Verda Corbin of Clayton, New York; Ronald and JoAnn Crisman of Peacham, Vermont; Edwin and Mary West of Townsend, Massachusetts; the Public Library of Cincinnati and Hamilton County, Ohio; the New-York Historical Society; ship modeler Harold Patten of San Rafael, California; photographer Basil Papazassiliou of Washington, D.C.; and the many graduate and undergraduate students at Texas A&M University who passed along information they discovered while researching term papers, theses, and dissertations. Special thanks are due to Anne Lessmann for her editorial assistance.

Finally, but most importantly, we gratefully acknowledge the continued support, assistance, love, and patience of Ginny B. West and Anne M. Cohn. It's probably all a coincidence, but every season of excavation on the horse ferry wreck and the completion of the manuscript was enlivened by a new arrival: Nathan Cohn (1990), Claire Crisman (1991), Genevieve Cohn (1992), and Leah Crisman (1995).

PART ONE

The History of North America's Horse-Powered Boats

1

A Brief History
of the
Animal-Powered
Machine

The idea of converting the push–pull power of animal muscle into rotary power by means of a simple machine has been around for at least several millennia; it dates so far back in antiquity, in fact, that it is impossible to properly credit the people who originated the concept. Nor can we say with any certainty where animal-powered machines were conceived, although the ancient civilizations of the Mediterranean or China, with their irrigation-based agriculture and massive stone architecture, seem likely candidates for this honor. These were, in any event, the first cultures to employ animal-powered machines on a large scale.

Whenever and wherever the animal-powered machine first appeared, it represented a significant advance in the ability of humans to generate and harness power for physically demanding or tedious jobs such as lifting heavy weights, grinding grain, and pumping water. Human and animal muscle was, furthermore, one of only three forms of power widely available prior to the age of the steam engine, the other two being water and wind.[1] Before we look at horseboats in North America, it may be useful to examine the development of the machinery that made these craft possible.

THE EARLIEST ANIMAL-POWERED MACHINES

Two types of muscle-powered rotary machinery for human and beast are known to have existed in the classical-era Mediterranean region: the internal vertical treadwheel and the capstan or windlass. The former consists of a pair of vertically oriented wheels connected by treads to form a hollow drum. A human or animal walking upon the treads inside the drum spins the tread-wheel upon its axis, thereby generating power that can be harnessed for any number of uses; the exercise wheel provided for hamsters and gerbils is the miniature modern equivalent of the ancient treadwheel. Human-powered machines of this design can be seen on Roman monuments carved during the first century A.D., and the same style of mechanism remained in common use well into the nineteenth century.[2] Over the centuries, vertical treadwheels were made to accommodate people, donkeys, goats, and dogs, but ox- or horse-powered versions appear to have been extremely rare, because of the great size, weight, and limited agility of the latter animals.[3]

The second type of early muscle-powered rotary machine, the capstan or windlass, consists of a large drum or axle—vertical for capstans and hori-zontal for windlasses—with one or more radially protruding bars. The wind-lass is worked by one or more persons standing beside the machine and turn-ing the bars by hand; though simple and relatively efficient for small lifting or pulling jobs, it is not designed for extremely heavy loads, nor can it be easily adapted for use by animals.

The capstan is powered by turning bars in a circle on the horizontal plane to revolve a vertical drum. The upright design is easily adapted for human or domestic animal use, and it has greater power-generating potential than the windlass, for it employs leg muscles instead of weaker arm muscles. The number of people or animals working a capstan can be increased by adding more bars to the machine or by lengthening the bars. Capstans built for horses are known as *horse whims* (or *horse gins* or *horse engines*). Whim-style mechanisms saw two millennia of widespread usage and were used to pro-pel the earliest versions of horse-powered watercraft.

One of the earliest recorded uses for horse-whim mechanisms was in turn-ing rotary mills, a practice first recorded in Greece around 300 B.C., which became common in Roman grain-grinding and olive-crushing mills around the first century B.C.[4] Donkey whims found at Pompeii indicate that some of these mills forced the animals to walk in an extremely tight circle, illus-trating one of the whim's drawbacks: Walking in circles day after day, espe-cially small circles, is not a healthy occupation.[5]

The notion of propelling boats by paddle wheels driven by capstan machinery was developed by Roman engineers, at least as far as the drawing-board stage. A description of a war galley propelled by oxen, dating to around A.D. 370, exists in a manuscript known as *De Rebus Bellicis;* a copy of the orig-inal illustration of the vessel provides some idea of the boat's appearance.[6] The system, as illustrated and described, depended upon pairs of oxen har-nessed to whims; the power these animals generated by walking in a circle

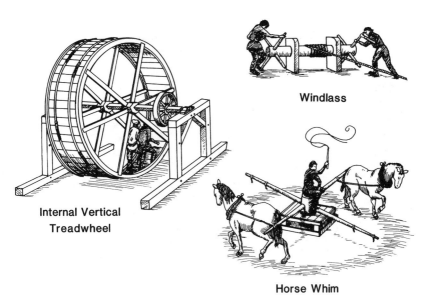

Windlass

Internal Vertical
Treadwheel

Horse Whim

Figure 1. Early forms of animal-powered machinery: the internal vertical treadwheel, the windlass, and the horse whim. Drawing by Kevin Crisman.

was transmitted, presumably by cog wheels, to a pair of side wheels. The war galley *Liburna* featured three teams of oxen rotating three pairs of paddle wheels. We do not know if such a vessel was ever actually built.[7]

The illustration and description of the Roman ox-powered boat resemble the successful horseboats of a much later era. Why was animal propulsion not widely adopted at this time? Most likely, there was just no place for such a craft in the Roman transportation system. If speed and independence from the wind were the vital factors in the propulsion of a vessel (as it was for Roman warships), then galleys propelled by oarsmen would be faster and more maneuverable. As we shall see in later chapters, animal-propelled boats are not very economical when used as long-distance conveyors; a sailing vessel could carry more cargo over longer distances at less cost and with less likelihood of mechanical breakdown. The first forays into the realm of animal-powered watercraft by the Romans did not lead to a transportation revolution, and indeed, the next recorded experiment in the field of animal propulsion would not occur until many centuries later.

ANIMAL-POWERED MACHINES, A.D. 1200–1800

The practical applications of land-based, animal-powered machines developed by the Romans clearly did not disappear during the early Middle Ages,

Figure 2. Roman ox-powered sidewheel war galley. From Singer et al., *History of Technology.*

but not much is known about the use of this equipment between the fifth and the twelfth centuries. The revitalization of engineering, industry, and commerce during the late Middle Ages and the increasing emphasis on cutting labor costs in the production of goods and services provided an ideal climate for the proliferation of animal-powered machines. Illustrations and descriptions of these devices become increasingly common after the twelfth century. The basic design of the vertical treadwheel and the horse whim did not change much from those employed by the Romans, but the arrangements of the machinery were more sophisticated and the range of uses for these machines expanded. Water wheels and windmills were also becoming common throughout Europe at this time, and though both could generate a high level of power for sustained periods, neither could match the portability and low initial costs of the animal-powered machine.

The use of animal machinery between the thirteenth and sixteenth centuries can be seen in technical manuscripts by Renaissance inventors and engineers. For example, the Mesopotamian inventor Ibn al-Razzaz al-Jazari prepared a manuscript titled *The Book of Knowledge of Ingenious Mechanical Devices* in A.D. 1204–6; in it, al-Jazari described in text and paintings a series of whim-style water pumps powered by oxen and donkeys.[8] Renaissance Italy produced a multitude of brilliant artists and engineers, including Sienese inventor Mariano Taccola, whose book *De Ingeneis,* dating to around 1433, illustrates chain pumps and hoists powered by animal-whim machinery.[9] Among the many inventions of Leonardo da Vinci from the late fifteenth and early sixteenth centuries are descriptions of a variation on the tread-wheel, the external vertical treadwheel, which consisted of an upright wheel with cleats or steps attached around the outside to provide footing for human operators.[10]

Perhaps the finest source of information on power-production technology in the late Renaissance was an exhaustive work on mining practices first published in 1556, Georgius Agricola's *De Re Metallica*. Agricola details the tools and machines common to the central European mining industry in the mid-sixteenth century. Besides several depictions of windmills and water wheels used for pumping water and processing ore, *De Re Metallica* illustrates the full range of human- and animal-powered machines in use at that time.

Vertical treadwheels and windlasses for humans and whims for horses predominate in Agricola's book, but *De Re Metallica* also featured a new type of machine that would reappear on nineteenth-century horseboats. This was the horizontal treadwheel: a revolving circular platform, similar to a phonograph turntable, upon which people or animals walk in place. The principal advantage of this arrangement was that it eliminated the whim's requirement of incessantly walking in circles. Structurally, the horizontal treadwheel was less complicated and more compact than the vertical type, although initially its design did not take advantage of gravity; this drawback was recognized at the time, and an inclined treadwheel was built to utilize gravity acting upon the operator.[11] Agricola showed a small, two-person horizontal treadwheel in service, each man gripping a fixed bar to stay in position while forcing the wheel around with his legs; cleats fastened to the top of the platform gave purchase to the operators' feet. Comparing the horizontal treadwheel with the hand-cranked windlass, Agricola noted: "This kind of machine is less fatiguing for the workman, while it raises larger loads."[12]

Examples of animal-powered machines are increasingly diverse and interesting in the seventeenth and eighteenth centuries. Europe was in the process of becoming industrialized, and the demand for *prime movers*, that is, machines that can power other machines, was constantly growing. The potential of steam as a source of power was recognized by many European inventors in the late seventeenth century, but decades of experimentation and development would be required before inexpensive, reliable steam engines would be widely available to power manufacturing and transportation.[13] Until the last quarter of the eighteenth century, water, wind, and animal muscle were still the only sources of power available for extractive industries (such as mining) and for manufacturing, agriculture, and transportation.

Water-powered mills remained the best option for manufacturing, since they generated the most power and were dependable (although sometimes seasonal), and, though expensive to build, the machinery was relatively inexpensive to operate. There were only a limited number of rivers with appro-

Figure 3. Human-
powered horizontal
treadwheel used for lift-
ing buckets from mine
shafts. From Agricola,
De Re Metallica.

priate sites for mills, however, and not all of them were located near sources of labor, raw materials, and cheap transportation. Windmills could be situated in more diverse locations, but except in particularly breezy regions, wind is not a consistent source of power. Thus, many industries during the seventeenth and eighteenth centuries, particularly the smaller ventures, had no choice but to build animal machines to power their operations.

The applications of animal-powered machines in mining operations described by Agricola in the sixteenth century continued relatively unchanged through the following two centuries. Mines and quarries for iron, lead, coal, slate, and many other types of metal ores, building stones, and minerals employed horse gins for hoisting material out of excavations, pumping water out of mines, and keeping miners supplied with fresh air.[14] Horse-powered pumps were also used in the seventeenth and eighteenth centuries for draining swamps during land reclamation projects.[15]

Animal machinery was used in all types of manufacturing enterprises. Industrial operations that relied at least partially upon horsepower included rolling mills for iron bars and sheet lead, brass founding (especially for crushing zinc ore), cloth making (including machines that assisted in the spinning, pressing, and dyeing of cloth), block making, coin minting, cardboard manufacturing, and armor production (horsepower was used to power grinders and polishers in armories).[16]

Large draft animals were not the only domesticates to find jobs in the factories, for eighteenth-century English and Scottish cloth manufacturers employed dogs on internal vertical treadwheels, dubbed "canicular mills," to grind dyes and power early weaving machines. Dogs evidently did not find this a fulfilling career, for as one observer remarked: "The dog at every recurring period of work, is painfully and almost humanly conscious, and reluctant to begin his task."[17] Canine-powered treadwheels stayed in service well into the nineteenth century.

Dependence upon animal machines in food production continued during the seventeenth and eighteenth centuries and appears to have greatly increased on farms, particularly during the second half of the 1700s. Rotary horse, ox, and donkey machines milled grain, cut chaff, ground turnips and animal feed, crushed apples to make cider, and pressed olives to extract the oil. The development of a mechanical thresher in the 1770s led to the installation of horse whims on many Scottish and English farms.[18] Colonial-era sugar plantations of the Caribbean Islands relied heavily on ox- or horse-powered mills to extract juice from cane for sugar, molasses, and rum.[19]

Thus far we have dealt only with animal-powered machines used on land, but these devices were also employed on and around the water. Horse whims and human-powered capstans and vertical treadwheels could be found at seaport docks powering cranes or careening ships to clean their bottoms, or alongside canals where they lifted ships to different levels or opened and closed lock gates.[20] Ports suffering from chronic siltation problems kept their channels open to deep-draft vessels by building rotary-chain dredgers powered by people or horses.

The first functional example of a rotary-machine-powered dredge, propelled by men walking on a pair of external vertical treadwheels, was reportedly invented in 1589 by a Dutchman, Cornelis Muys of Delft. The device proved very efficient and partially replaced earlier, less efficient methods of clearing silt.[21] In 1622 another Dutchman, Jacob Jacobssen of Haarlem, built the first dredger using a horse gin instead of human treadwheels, and thereafter these machines became a common sight in European harbors; during the eighteenth century, five three-horse machines were constantly employed in keeping Amsterdam open to shipping.[22] Horse-whim-powered dredging machines were also used in North America to clear the harbors at Philadelphia and Baltimore in the 1770s and 1790s.[23]

Interest in paddle-wheel propulsion for boats resurfaced during the Renaissance, when inventors began preparing plans—and in a few cases building prototypes—of paddle wheels and the muscle-powered rotary machines needed to turn them. One early example of a paddleboat, from a manuscript dated 1335, shows a small, double-ended boat fitted with two pairs of direct-drive, hand-cranked sidewheels.[24] The design is elementary and perfectly feasible. Its advantages for the operator over oar propulsion included a forward view and a relatively uniform cranking motion; the advantages of this system over oars in terms of effort and speed are not as clear.

Several renowned Renaissance designers, among them Mariano Taccola, Roberto Valturio, and Francesco di Giorgio included variations on the hand-cranked paddle-wheel design in their manuscripts. Between 1495 and 1500 the most famous Renaissance inventor of all, Leonardo da Vinci, also toyed on paper with direct-drive, hand-cranked paddles for boats before going on to substantially improve the mechanism by adding a large, centrally mounted flywheel (to ease the dead spot in the cranking action) and gears between the crank and paddle to increase the paddle's revolutions.[25]

The earliest known example of a European, human-powered paddleboat appeared around 1540 at Malaga, Spain; a second trial took place at Barcelona in 1543. The machinery was the brainchild of inventor Blasco de Garray, about whom little else is known. One of the vessels that underwent trials measured 200 Spanish tons, a sizable vessel for the time. It was fitted with a pair of sidewheels worked by twenty-five men; another of de Garray's paddle-wheel machines was propelled by forty men. The top speed attained by these devices was about 5.6 kilometers (3½ mi.) per hour; according to one skeptical observer, the vessels could have been propelled more easily by men using oars. De Garray's experiment showed that paddle wheels would work even on large vessels, but it also demonstrated that something more powerful than human muscle was needed.[26]

Despite the multitude of horse-powered machines used in Europe during the sixteenth and seventeenth centuries, there was a seeming reluctance on the part of inventors or their patrons to test the practicality of a horse-powered watercraft. The experiment was finally made around 1680, when Rupert, prince palatine of the Rhine, admiral, inventor, and cousin of England's King Charles II, designed and built the first horseboat known to history. Surprisingly (and disappointingly) little is known about Rupert's Thames River boat, although by all reports it was a success.

The limited descriptions of this sidewheel-equipped vessel suggest that it was fitted with a standard horse-whim mechanism, for its motive power was said to consist of "a trundle working in a wheel turned round by horses." In speed tests, Rupert's horseboat easily outdistanced a royal barge propelled by sixteen oarsmen. This boat (or one built to a similar design) was in use as a towboat at the Royal Navy's Chatham Dockyard on the Medway River in 1682; drawing 1.37 meters (4½ ft.) of water, it was powered by four to eight horses and reportedly was capable of towing the largest ships of the Royal Navy.[27] The lack of any further mention of horseboats in England at this time suggests that Rupert's prototype was considered to be merely a novelty, rather than a practical addition to the fleet of working boats on the Thames.

A second foray into the realm of animal-powered watercraft was made around 1730 by French general and adventurer Maurice, comte de Saxe. His machinery, approved by the French Academy of Science and published in

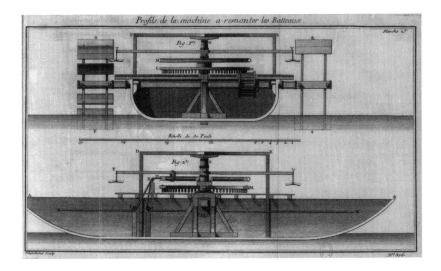

Figure 4. Section and longitudinal profile of the horse-whim-powered boat designed by Maurice, comte de Saxe (1732). Courtesy of the Bibliothèque Nationale de France.

1732 in the sixth volume of *Machines Approuvées,* was obviously based on contemporary horse-whim mechanisms. It consisted of a pair of sidewheels connected by an axle and turned by a simple arrangement of crown and lantern gears. Two or more horses, harnessed to the radial arms extending out from above the crown gear, provided the power to propel the craft. Maurice envisioned the boat being used on the Seine River to tow boats from the English Channel to Paris and claimed that the mechanism was sufficiently powerful to stem the river's currents.[28] A full-size, working prototype of this boat was apparently never built.

Although other experiments in muscle-powered vessels were made in Europe during the eighteenth century, equine-propelled watercraft failed to achieve widespread acceptance there (in spite of the many rivers, lakes, and protected bays that were well suited for the operation of this type of vessel). The technology for putting horses to work on the water certainly existed, for as we have seen, horse gins and treadwheels were quite common from the sixteenth century onward, and by the eighteenth century they were an essential part of European industry and agriculture. Prince Rupert's experiment proved that horse-powered boats worked, and the design of Maurice, comte de Saxe, was eminently practical, but neither of them made a lasting mark on English or French waterways. Why did such a seemingly useful invention as the horseboat go undeveloped?

A combination of circumstances may explain the general disinterest in these boats. By the beginning of the eighteenth century, European inventors were increasingly aware of the potential of steam as a prime mover for both industry and watercraft, and some began to focus their attention on the development of reliable steam-powered machinery. Paddle wheels for boats also continued to interest marine engineers, who examined various ways of combining steam machinery with rotary propulsion systems.[29] Dabbling with a limited power source like horses and horse machinery no doubt appeared a waste of time when such a potent force as steam was visible on the horizon.

The lack of interest in horseboats might also be attributed to the nature of European transportation, economics, and culture at this time. In most countries, well-developed road systems existed for overland travel, and many rivers had been spanned by bridges. On broader rivers, lakes and bays, ferries propelled by sails, sweeps, or poles had been operating efficiently for centuries, and the human labor necessary to work these types of ferries was relatively plentiful and cheap. Quite simply, the public demand and commercial incentive for horse-propelled boats does not appear to have existed in seventeenth- and eighteenth-century Europe. Conditions favorable for the widespread employment of floating horsepower would have to await another century and an entirely different continent.

2

The Horseboat
Comes to
North America

The geographical and cultural differences between Europe and North America in the eighteenth and early nineteenth centuries are well illustrated by the reception horseboats met with on each continent. In Europe, despite the long history and use of animal-propelled machinery, horseboats did not advance beyond a few drawings and experimental craft like Prince Rupert's creation, simply because there was no place for them in the existing transportation network, no sustained public interest, and seemingly no economic incentive to develop them.

The situation was very different on the other side of the Atlantic. Overland transportation in North America was impeded by a multitude of large rivers, lakes, and bays; the only practical way to cross them was by ferryboat. Human labor was less available and more expensive, and labor-saving devices of all sorts were welcomed by entrepreneurs; and here (as so many European tourists in America remarked) the populace always seemed to be in a hurry to get to their destinations. These circumstances were favorable for innovative ferryboats that could, with a minimum of human labor, traverse the water briskly, regardless of wind and water currents. By the end of the eighteenth century, American inventors were attempting to build such a ferry.

FERRIES AND INLAND TRANSPORTATION

Today's traveler, speeding along in air-conditioned, shock-absorbed automotive comfort on an interstate highway, can hardly be expected to appreciate how much of an impediment water was to travelers of the eighteenth and early nineteenth centuries. The inland waters of North America are spanned by bridges or tunnels; even the big rivers, the St. Lawrence, the Hudson, the Delaware, the Ohio, the Missouri, and the Mississippi, require almost no effort to cross, except possibly slowing down for a moment to toss a few coins in a toll booth collection basket. It was not always this easy.

Among the many challenges facing the colonizers of North America in the seventeenth and eighteenth centuries was the establishment of an interior transportation network of roads, bridges, and ferries. The difficulties were enormous, and the creation of new routes would advance only slowly, in fits and starts. The problem was obvious: A relatively small population was spread over a wide expanse of rugged, forested landscape. Accounts of travelers in the colonial and early national periods are nearly universal in their description of North American roadways as a slough of despond, with impossibly steep climbs and descents, protruding tree stumps, jarring corduroy roads, deep ruts, and bottomless mudholes that bogged down horses, wagons, and riders.[1]

Water, in the form of rivers, lakes, and bays, constituted one of the greatest obstacles for the overland traveler. Narrow rivers or brooks could be spanned with bridges, but the great expense and technical difficulty of building bridges over larger bodies of water left only one choice for most crossings: the ferryboat. From the earliest colonial days, these humble workingboats were essential for the movement of people, livestock, and all manner of goods.

All types and sizes of watercraft served as ferries in North America. The earliest and smallest were the bark and dugout canoes of Native Americans, as well as the planked boats of European colonists. Passage was limited to people and their goods; horses and cattle had to wade or swim across on their own. At more heavily trafficked crossings, ferry owners built shallow, flat-bottomed floating boxes, called scows or flats, to accommodate horses, wagons, or livestock. The longest crossings, over broad rivers, bays, or lakes, required substantially built ferries capable of safely navigating wide expanses of open water.

Until the early nineteenth century, the means of propulsion available to ferry owners were the same that had been used for thousands of years: wind, currents, and human labor. The selection of a propulsion system depended upon a number of factors, principally the distance the ferry was required to cross, local navigational conditions, the financial resources of the owner, and the amount of traffic at a particular crossing. For short passages over relatively protected water, ferry operators relied mostly upon paddles, oars, or poles to drive the vessel from shore to shore. This often involved back-breaking labor, especially when a boat was heavily laden or fighting strong currents. One alternative for short crossings was the cable ferry, which consisted of a boat fastened to a cable stretched across the water. On rivers with strong currents, a cable could be fixed at an angle that forced the flowing water to push the vessel from shore to shore.[2] The final option for boat propulsion, the employment of one or more masts and sails, was used at most of the lengthier ferry crossings. Sails involved less labor than rowing or poling, but crossing by sail could mean hours or even days of delay if the winds were not favorable.

The ferryboat's contribution to the economic well-being of the North American colonies (and later states and provinces) is indicated by the many references and regulations concerning ferries and ferry crossings in the public records of towns, colonial assemblies, and state or provincial governments. Lacking the wherewithal to build and operate ferries, governments or communities granted private entrepreneurs permission to establish ferries at important crossing points. In some instances a tax, in the form of an annual license or fee, was assessed on ferry owners. The owners' investment was protected by conferring exclusive ferrying rights (in other words, a monopoly) at a crossing for a certain number of years. In return, the rights of the traveling public were also theoretically guaranteed by establishment of fixed toll rates and stipulations that the ferry should be kept in good repair and promptly serve all patrons during daylight hours.[3]

Figure 5. Oar-propelled ferry crossing the Susquehanna River, circa 1811–12. Watercolor by Pavel Svinin. Courtesy of the Metropolitan Museum of Art.

Figure 6. Sloop-rigged scow ferry on Lake Champlain. Courtesy of the Lake Champlain Maritime Museum.

Ownership of a ferry concession could be a liability or an asset, depending upon the nature of the waterway, the amount of traffic, and, of course, the business acumen of the owner. Possession of rights to a heavily trafficked crossing meant full-time and highly lucrative employment for a family or a company, and these rights were jealously guarded and passed down from generation to generation. Busy ferries like these were often attended by their crews all day, and some ran on a regular, predetermined schedule.

Conversely, and more commonly, ownership of a ferry on a lightly traveled route provided only part-time employment that had to be supplemented with farming or a trade. Ferries in this category generally ran only when they were needed, which meant that travelers had to blow a horn, raise a flag, ring a bell, shout, or just patiently sit and wait until the ferry owner showed up. Indeed, some of the more marginal ferry concessions seem to have been a millstone around the neck of the proprietor, with receipts from the business barely covering the costs of building and maintenance, as well as the inconvenience of constantly being on call during daylight hours. It is hardly surprising that ferries such as these should be poorly attended and repaired.

The importance of well-maintained ferries in North America becomes strikingly apparent in the journals and memoirs of travelers who made overland journeys in the eighteenth and early nineteenth centuries. Nearly every writer had at least one memorable (often in the negative sense) encounter at a ferry crossing; some travelogues seem merely a succession of anecdotes about ferrying delays, mishaps, and assorted calamities, interspersed with hostile encounters with rude, incompetent, or intoxicated boatmen. Travelers approached the more notorious ferries with a sense of dread: They were risking their property and even their lives by crossing the water.[4]

In the decades between the Revolutionary War and the Civil War, scores of hardy European tourists explored the North American continent and then went home to write books about their adventures. Although these travelers were responding to contemporary interest in the American wilderness and American society, their accounts are a gold mine of information for archaeologists and historians. Europeans were cultural outsiders; much of what they observed was different, sometimes bizarrely so, from what they knew back home, and no detail of their experiences seemed too insignificant for comment.

Most European visitors were coming from countries with relatively well-developed networks of roads, bridges, ferries, stages, and canals, and what they found on the other side of the Atlantic seemed appallingly crude and ill managed. Travelers disdainful of all things American found in the roads and ferries further proof of an inferior people; more understanding tourists recognized the rutted roads and haphazardly run ferries as signs of a young and rapidly expanding society that was growing faster than its ability to build a good transportation system. There was universal agreement, however, that travel in this land was an ordeal. Regardless of their individual biases, these writers provide one of our best sources on ferryboating in this era.

The disregard for safety and public service that so many American ferry operators displayed was a continual source of wonderment to foreign travelers. The duc de La Rochefoucauld, journeying along the U.S.–Canadian border in 1795, concluded that the average Canadian ferry was better managed and maintained than its counterpart south of the border. "The major part of the American vessels or ferries," he observed, "are entirely left to the will and pleasure of the owners, without any public office taking the least notice of their condition, and providing for the safety of the travelers."[5]

North American ferries of the late eighteenth century are prominently featured in the journals of a French politician and savant named Moreau de St. Méry. This gentleman arrived at Norfolk, Virginia, in March 1794, with his family and a handful of other refugees fleeing the bloody revolution then sweeping through France. He remained in exile in the United States for the next five years, residing primarily in Philadelphia, during which time he kept an account of his experiences in this new and very peculiar land. St. Méry was a remarkable observer with a keen eye for every detail of American life, and during his frequent travels along the eastern seaboard, particularly in the year following his arrival, St. Méry rode on every sort of ferryboat then in existence. His experiences seem typical of the time.

Only a few days after St. Méry arrived in Virginia, he took passage across the Elizabeth River between Norfolk and Portsmouth. This first experience with American ferryboats did not impress him. The ferries were small boats designed to safely carry six to eight passengers, but the oarsmen loaded on as many as fifteen passengers per trip so that they could enjoy a longer wait on the opposite shore. On some days, St. Méry reported, the oarsmen simply abandoned their boats and hid, thereby stranding travelers on the beach.[6]

After St. Méry established his residence in Philadelphia, he frequently found occasion to take a carriage to New York, a 152-kilometer (95 mi.) journey that involved five ferry crossings. His account of one of these trips is instructive, for the route between the two cities was heavily traveled and, for that era, relatively well developed and maintained. His description of the ferries also makes it clear why North Americans would so eagerly welcome new and more reliable forms of ferryboats in the coming decades.

St. Méry began in Philadelphia by boarding a stage, which he described as "very high, long and narrow"; the drivers, he observed, "are almost always slightly drunk, [and] drive so fast that accidents are excessively common."[7] From Philadelphia the carriage started northward, paralleling the western bank of the Delaware River for 48 kilometers (30 mi.) before reaching Trenton, New Jersey. Here two ferries provided service across the river, one of which St. Méry boarded. Passengers were permitted to remain on the stage while it rolled onto the ferry, but he did not recommend it, for the slightest movement of an uneasy horse could result in a serious accident. St. Méry's conveyance was successfully loaded, but a horse stepped on the bare foot of a ferryman, "making the blood spurt" and nearly grinding off three of the poor man's toes. This misfortune delayed the ferry for fifteen minutes.

From Trenton the stage proceeded northeast through central New Jersey, rapidly passing the towns of Princeton, New Brunswick (where it crossed the Raritan River in a modest ferryboat), and Elizabethtown but not reaching the Passaic River until after dark, when the ferry had shut down for the evening. After spending the night at a nearby inn, St. Méry and his companions returned to the Passaic crossing early the next morning. The Passaic ferry was drawn back and forth by means of a cable attached to pulleys on the side of the craft. Space on the ferry was limited, and it was necessary to unhitch the two leading horses and load them separately. St. Méry complained: "We then found places as best we could; for in general . . . a public carriage and its horses are attended to first, and the passengers it carries receive no consideration whatever."[8]

A short distance beyond the Passaic was the Hackensack River, which was wider and therefore required a sail ferry. Under the best of circumstances, with a fair and steady wind, the crossing required a quarter of an hour; on this day the wind was not fair, and St. Méry found the passage "long and disagreeable," since it was necessary for the ferry to tack back and forth across the river. Making this crossing at night, St. Méry warned his readers, "was a great risk."

From the east bank of the Hackensack, the end of the journey was practically in sight, although St. Méry commented: "When all the annoyances of the ferry had been endured (and they were considerable, particularly if one arrived to take the ferry at the precise moment it was leaving, loaded with another stage, which could occasion an hour's wait on the Hackensack shore) there were still two leagues to go before reaching New York." A brief ride brought St. Méry's stage to the edge of the Hudson River where, St. Méry confided, "one is consoled by the thought that this new embarkation will also be the last."[9]

In 1794 the Paulus Hook–Manhattan crossing was served by three sail ferries, each large enough to contain two carriages and their horses, along with twenty-five passengers and two crewmen. With favorable conditions, the trip took twelve to fifteen minutes; with unfavorable winds, an hour or more; and with no wind, the wait could be indefinite. Excessively windy weather made the Hudson too dangerous to hazard in a small ferry. St. Méry thought the crossing "was far from being without danger," and he noted that it was difficult to keep the horses calm, especially if there was a swell on the river. On this particular trip, however, the Philadelphia stage's passengers arrived safely in New York, "cheerful, active, and in possession of all their limbs."[10]

The rough, haphazard state of inland transportation that St. Méry experienced in 1794 had been a cause for concern among citizens of the United States since the founding of the republic. Many of the country's leaders, including George Washington and Thomas Jefferson, advocated a national policy for internal improvements, since the growth and well-being of industry, agriculture, and trade would clearly depend upon a well-developed, low-cost system of transportation.[11] Washington, in particular, wished to ensure the long-term political integrity of the nation by creating strong economic ties between new settlements west of the Appalachian Mountains and states on the eastern seaboard. During the 1780s and 1790s many ambitious projects were proposed, and some were actually begun, to build canals, improve river navigation, upgrade roads, and span rivers with new bridges.[12] Years would pass, however, before Washington's vision of an efficient system of inland transportation began to be realized in a substantial way.

FALSE STARTS AND OBSCURE SUCCESSES:
THE EARLIEST HORSEBOATS

The same spirit of improvement that led to the building of new roads, bridges, and canals also prompted American inventors to experiment with steam engines and other machinery for propelling vessels through the water. This awakening of interest was inspired partly by the ongoing development of steam power in Europe, which by the 1780s had resulted in the introduction of an improved engine by England's James Watt. However, much of the experimentation with steamboats in the United States was carried out by an emerging class of inventors and entrepreneurs who would make their own contributions to the coming revolution in land and water transportation. It was some of these very people, the pioneers of American steam, who successfully combined horses and paddle-wheel propulsion for the first time and thereby launched North America's age of horse-powered boats. Steam- and horse-powered boats were introduced to American waterways in the late 1780s and early 1790s, but commercial success required two decades. Contrary to what one might expect, it was the mechanically complex and potentially explosive steamboat that first achieved widespread acceptance and patronage among the traveling public in 1807; horseboats would have to wait seven more years to gain the same kind of popular enthusiasm and widespread usage.

Appropriately enough, the first recorded example of an American horse-powered boat can be credited to John Fitch, who is also recognized for producing the first working steamboat in the Western Hemisphere. Fitch's story, alas, is not a happy one, for neither steamboats nor horseboats brought him fame, wealth, or contentment during his lifetime. A native of Connecticut, Fitch apprenticed in a variety of trades as a young man, including clock making, brass founding, and silversmithing, developing skills that served him well as an inventor of mechanical devices. His work as a gunsmith and merchant before and during the Revolutionary War made him, for a time, relatively wealthy. In 1785 he began experimenting with steamboats, and over the next two years he laid the foundation for his dream by organizing a steamboat company and seeking out investors, obtaining fourteen-year monopolies on steam navigation from four states, and taking on as a business partner a Philadelphia watchmaker named Henry Voight.[13]

Fitch and Voight tested their prototype steamer on the Delaware River near Philadelphia during the summer of 1787. The boat worked, even with the unwieldy arrangement of vertically suspended paddles that drove it through the water. Shortly after this promising trial, however, Fitch became mired in an all-consuming "I was first" feud with a rival steamboat inventor from Virginia, James Rumsey, and his next boat was not launched until May 1790. This vessel, named *Steamboat* by Fitch, retained the duck-leg mode of propulsion but proved much faster than the earlier version, and for the remainder of the navigation season it ran between Philadelphia and Trenton, New Jersey. Fitch's enterprise was a mechanical triumph, but in spite of speedy passages and low fares, it did not attract customers, and the boat had to be permanently laid up at the end of the year. It was the old story of the inventor being slightly ahead of his time. Unfortunately for Fitch, the American public needed time to consider the advantages and hazards of the "floating teakettle" before accepting steamboats as a reliable way to travel.

Meanwhile, the ongoing squabble over who was first to devise a practical steamboat, now involving Fitch, Rumsey, and a third inventor, Colonel John Stevens of New Jersey, led the federal government to create the Board of Patent Commissioners in 1790 (this would result in the founding of the U.S. Patent Office). The commissioners, unwilling or unable to credit only one of these men, gave all three patent rights—a bad decision that only led to more feuding and litigation. Dispirited and increasingly shunned by financial backers, Fitch never managed to bring another steamboat into regular operation.[14]

It was around this time that Fitch told Henry Voight of his concept for a double-hulled boat propelled by cattle. In Fitch's own words, Voight "took the idea and persued it," preparing plans and a description of the boat and its machinery and submitting them to the patent commissioners. A patent was issued to Voight on 10 August 1791.[15] A contemporary drawing of the Fitch–Voight creation shows a catamaran configuration: two narrow hulls fastened together with a broad platform or deck, upon which the animals could walk in a wide circle. The propulsion machinery consisted of a typical eighteenth-century horse whim, which by a precarious-looking arrangement of gears, drive shafts, and cranks powered Fitch's odd vertical-paddle apparatus at the stern.

The animal-propelled boat proved to be the catalyst for a falling-out between Fitch and Voight. At the same time that Voight drew up his patent application, he prepared an article of agreement and conveyed one-half interest in the new invention to Fitch; this division of shares made no provision, however, for investors in Fitch's transportation company, some of whom had provided money for the boat's development. Fitch later lamented: "This I confess is the most underhanded way of Dealing that I ever acted in this world, and hope I may be forgiven." The fact that the patent was issued only in Voight's name also generated a great deal of resentment. Fitch complained that Voight was "intoxicated with his pattent for the Cattle Boat," and that "had he told them [the patent commissioners] that it was solely mine he would have done himself strict justice and given me no more than my due."[16]

In 1794 Fitch convinced businessman John Nicholson of the merits of the animal-propelled boat, and after he signed over to Nicholson the greater portion of his rights to use the boat on the Delaware River, they built one at Philadelphia. The catamaran arrangement was retained for Nicholson's boat, with each hull measuring 16.76 meters (55 ft.) in length; the hulls were separated by a sufficient distance to allow four animals to walk around a crown

Figure 7. Cattle-propelled boat, patented by Henry Voight (1791). Fulton manuscript book, "Propulsion of Vessels." U.S. Patent and Trademark Office Scientific Library. Photograph by Basil Papazassiliou.

wheel 6.4 meters (21 ft.) in diameter. Horses, not cattle, were apparently the animals of choice for powering this boat. Fitch put the horseboat through its trials in the fall of 1794, during which he claimed to have made a round trip between Philadelphia and Trenton in just ten hours. One spectator who witnessed the trials at Philadelphia noted that "she appeared to get along with some reputation tho' the tide was then against her."[17] The subsequent career of this boat remains a mystery.

In April 1795 Fitch approached his old steamboat-patent rival, the wealthy and influential Colonel John Stevens of Hoboken, New Jersey, with an offer to sell him four-tenths of the patent rights for exclusive use of a horseboat on the Hudson and Raritan Rivers. Stevens ran a ferryboat line between New Jersey and New York City, and he probably looked like a good potential customer to Fitch because of his obvious interest in new forms of vessel propulsion. The colonel was indeed interested, but cautious. He asked a Philadelphia friend, Matthew Barton, to inquire about the reputation and reliability of Nicholson's boat, as well as the legal status of the patent rights. Barton obliged by calling upon Fitch's former partner Henry Voight, where, predictably, he was told that Voight was the true inventor of the craft, as well as the real owner of the patent (Barton was apparently not informed of the fifty–fifty division of interest with Fitch). His intoxication with animal-propelled boats clearly over, Voight declared that the vessel was expensive to build and operate, disputed Fitch's claim that the horseboat built for Nicholson had voyaged to Trenton and back, and concluded by calling it "an invention more to be admired for its Novelty than for any advantage that could result from it."[18]

Stevens sought more information by writing to John Nicholson to solicit his opinion of Fitch's horseboat and to verify the claims that had been made about the boat's accomplishments and patent status. The colonel also clearly stated his interest in the craft: "My reason for troubling you on this subject is that, being the proprietor of the Ferry from South Amboy to New York, if there really is a prospect of this invention being usefully applied to the propelling [of] passage boats, I might possibly be induced to take a concern in the business."[19]

Nicholson's reply to this letter may not have been favorable, or Stevens may have foreseen the possibility of being drawn into lawsuits for patent infringement. It is also possible that Stevens was simply wary of becoming involved in business dealings with a perpetually unlucky and contentious man like John Fitch. For whatever reason, he chose not to commit himself to a horseboat venture at this time, although as events would show, he did not give up on the idea of someday building a horseboat for his ferry service.

Fitch doggedly continued to hawk his horse-powered craft. In the summer of 1795 he again proposed to build Stevens a catamaran-style horseboat, or an alternative type with a single hull 19.81 meters (65 ft.) in length, 4.26 meters (14 ft.) in beam, and with a draft of 1.37 meters (4 ft., 6 in.). Propulsion would be supplied by four horses turning a 3.96-meter-(13 ft.) diameter crown wheel. "This, Sir," Fitch declared, "is as impossible of failure as that four horses would fail of drawing a wagon," and on this opinion the inventor promised to "pledge the mechanical reputation of John Fitch."[20] Several more letters in the same vein followed, some of which included estimates for the profits to be made running the boat between Albany and New York, as well as promises to have the boat built and in the water by the spring of 1796. Stevens declined all offers.

It was the end of the line for the Fitch–Voight "cattle boat" and the end of Fitch's tormented career as an inventor of mechanically propelled vessels. In 1796, out of money and out of friends, he gave up and moved to the Kentucky frontier to live on property he owned there. He attempted to drink himself into an early grave but found that whiskey worked too slowly. An overdose of opium finally ended his misery in 1798.[21]

Fitch's horseboat, like his steamboat, was a good idea slightly ahead of its time, an invention that suffered from an indifferent or suspicious public and the erratic nature of its inventor. The question of who owned the horseboat patent, and the legal confusion generated by state grants of exclusive rights to use new inventions on their waters, undoubtedly further contributed to the delay in the acceptance of these boats. Investors are rarely eager to risk their money in a new venture if there is a strong possibility of legal entanglements.

At least five horseboat inventors followed closely in Fitch's wake, although it is not clear if they were inspired by his creation or came up with the idea on their own. The U.S. Patent Office approved the applications for three horse-boats in the two decades following the Fitch–Voight boat, including a horse-powered boat designed by W. P. Sprague in 1795, a machine for horseboats by M. Crafts of Troy, New York, in 1809, and a horseboat by S. Fuller of Clark County, Indiana, in 1811.[22] Accounts of two other early experiments in animal power have been discovered, both of which offer insights into the tri-als and tribulations of creating a new form of transportation. By coincidence, both boats were built and tested in 1807.

The first of these vessels, a western river keel boat of about 40 tons, was tested on a particularly demanding pair of waterways: the Ohio and Mis-sissippi Rivers. The captain (and possibly the inventor) was a man named John Brookhart, about whom little is known, except for the fact that he was unbelievably persistent in the face of great difficulties.[23] The machinery that propelled the *Horse Boat* (as Brookhart named his craft) was powered by six horses walking in a circle on a platform above the deck. This imparted motion to two pairs of paddle wheels, one forward and one aft of the machin-ery, and drove the boat through the water at a rate of 8–9.6 kilometers (5–6 mi.) per hour. The boat reportedly averaged about 32 kilometers (20 mi.) a day when advancing upriver against powerful currents.

Brookhart clearly hoped to solve the greatest problem facing early west-ern river boatmen and merchants—that is, how to minimize the tremen-dous expense and human labor required to float goods upriver from New Orleans. The river's current and winding course precluded the use of sail-boats, and before the *Horse Boat,* there had been only a limited number of ways to navigate up the Mississippi and Ohio: paddling, rowing, and poling upstream against the flood, or more commonly, employing men to walk along the riverbanks and drag a boat with tow ropes. With high hopes and expec-tations Brookhart and his boat departed from Louisville, Kentucky, in the spring of 1807 and passed swiftly downriver, arriving in New Orleans by July of the same year.

The passage back up the river was another story. Brookhart advertised for freight in the *New Orleans Gazette* on 23 July, noting that he had room for a few tons only, the greater part of the hold already being taken up with cargo. The boat, he assured the public, was "completely fitted for the voyage." When a full cargo (mostly sugar) was secured, Brookhart departed, and his unlucky horses began the herculean task of walking the heavily laden boat upstream against the mighty flow of the Mississippi. Their progress was, to say the least, slow. By the time winter arrived, the *Horse Boat* had only reached the town of Natchez. A rumor reached New Orleans that between twelve and twenty horses had perished on the wheel and that Brookhart had been forced to abandon his project after reaching Natchez.[24]

In fact Brookhart did not give up, although the thought must have crossed his mind on more than one occasion. After overwintering at Natchez, he and his surviving horses pressed on in the spring of 1808, and by the middle of May were doggedly working their way up the Ohio River to Louisville. The rumors at New Orleans were greatly exaggerated, for at this point only seven horses had died during the voyage, and two of the original six were still alive.[25] Nevertheless, this was a high mortality rate. The cargo of sugar may have fetched a good price, but the cost of feeding and replacing horses must have bitten deeply into whatever profits were generated by the venture. No further mention of the *Horse Boat* has been found, and it seems unlikely that any more lengthy voyages were attempted. As we shall see, Brookhart was not the last to employ a horse-powered boat as a long-distance transport, and the lessons of his epic voyage would have to be relearned many times over the course of the nineteenth century.

The second horseboat venture in 1807 was more modest in its ambitions and achievements. It consisted of a screw-propeller vessel built at Providence, Rhode Island, by Jonathan Nichols, a blacksmith from Vermont, and his partner David Griere, a tailor from Nantucket. They began by constructing a scale model of their invention, and after this proved the utility of the design, they went on to construct a 12.2-meter- (40 ft.) long boat powered by four horses. On what appears to have been the boat's maiden voyage, Nichols and Griere made the trip from Providence to Pawtucket in two hours, carrying a wedding party and some Masons on an outing. On the return passage, the boat, which reportedly did not have a keel, was blown ashore by a squall but not seriously damaged. For reasons unknown, it was subsequently sold at a sheriff's sale and purchased by a Boston mechanic; he arranged a tow to Boston by a sloop, but the horseboat was cut adrift during the passage and wrecked in Buzzard's Bay, Massachussetts. The loss was total.[26]

While Brookhart, Nichols and Griere, and other inventors tinkered with their horseboat designs in 1807, a long-anticipated milestone in the development of steamboat navigation was taking place on the waters of the Hudson River. On 17 August 1807 American inventor and entrepreneur Robert Fulton piloted his celebrated *North River Steamboat* on its inaugural voyage from New York City to Albany and back, a four-day trip.[27] With this vessel and this voyage, the age of steam-powered transportation officially began. The mechanical and commercial success that the *North River* enjoyed was not the result of especially innovative machinery or a breakthrough in hull designs, but rather it was a product of Fulton's skill in combining the work of many other inventors and adding improvements of his own to create a practical, reliable steamboat. Part of the *North River*'s success might also be attributed to the American public's willingness at last to accept steamboats as a fast and relatively safe way to travel.

The steamboat was truly a revolutionary advance in marine propulsion, providing for the first time a practical alternative to human labor, winds, and currents. Steamboats brought a new measure of speed and regularity to navigation of inland waters and the high seas, and in the process created, in the minds of the public, the expectation that water transportation should no longer be restricted by tides, difficult currents, or adverse winds. The pace of travel and life for North Americans was about to speed up.

3

"We Congratulate the Public"

The Age of the
Horse-Powered Boat Begins

North America's era of horse-powered boats began and ended in the shadow of the steamboat, a fact that clearly accounts for the relative obscurity of the horseboat in the historical and pictorial record. Steamers represented something new under the sun, a technology that liberated the human race from the limitations of propulsion by wind, current, and muscle and propelled ships faster and more dependably than they had ever gone before. Beyond that, steamboats were impressive. They were large, angular, and imposing; they made loud noises, grabbed the surface of the water with a paddle-wheel grip, and lunged impetuously forward; billowing black clouds of smoke and cinders issued from their tall metal chimneys. Against this masterpiece of engineering, power, and high drama, horseboats and their more modest accomplishments could not possibly hope to compete for attention.

Steamboats may have upstaged horseboats but nevertheless must be credited with a part in our story, for they gave the nudge that started horse-propelled ferries on their way to becoming a common sight on the waterfronts of nineteenth-century North America. The influence of steamers was twofold. First, although steam engines and the paddle-wheel propulsion pointed the way to a revolution in maritime transportation in 1807, several practical limitations prevented their immediate adoption for ferrying purposes. The chief drawbacks in the early years were the scarcity, size, complexity, and expense of the steam machinery. The first three problems were soon minimized by improvements in steam machinery and the establishment of machine shops that produced boilers and engines, but the high cost of steam would remain a difficult hurdle for ferry owners to overcome. Early steamers were not practical for most ferries, unless the crossing happened to be heavily trafficked and highly lucrative. An alternative was needed, a boat with all the advantages of paddle-wheel propulsion but without the complications and expense of steam power.

Complex legal entanglements surrounding early steamboat ventures also played a role in launching the horseboat era. The legal problems stemmed from the states' practice of granting monopolies on steam navigation in their waters; the reward of a monopoly may have encouraged early inventive efforts, but it effectively strangled all competition once the technological breakthrough had been achieved. Ferry owners who hoped to capitalize on the new age of paddle-powered vessels found themselves legally prohibited from building steam ferryboats of their own. In New York City in 1814 they turned to horsepower as a practical alternative.

NEW YORK CITY: CRADLE OF THE TEAMBOAT FERRY

When Robert Fulton and his business partner Robert Livingston successfully navigated the Hudson River by steamboat in 1807, the state of New York rewarded them with a most valuable prize. By maintaining an average speed of 8 kilometers (5 mi.) per hour during the first voyage to Albany and back, the *North River Steamboat* exceeded the 6.4-kilometer- (4 mi.) per-hour requirement necessary to win a sixteen-year monopoly on steam navigation in New York. Fulton and Livingston did not rest on their laurels but continued to improve upon steamboat machinery and hull forms and to expand their passenger-carrying operations. The *North River* was followed by the *Car of Neptune* in 1809 and the *Paragon* in 1811.[1] During these early years rival steamboat ventures occasionally challenged the rights of Fulton and Livingston, but all either entered into licensing agreements with the monopoly holders and paid them a certain percentage of profits or were forced to move their steamboats to other states. Colonel John Stevens of New Jersey found himself in the latter category in 1808 when his new steamer, the *Phoenix,* built for use on the Hudson, was driven off by the monopoly and instead began a career on the Delaware River.

The New York steam monopoly was certainly a plum to be jealously guarded. In the decades after the Revolutionary War, the city of New York had surpassed Boston and Philadelphia as the leading port and commercial center in the United States. With its central location on the eastern seaboard, year-round safe anchorage, and access to the interior via the Hudson River, the city's geographical advantages promised limitless growth. The utility of the steamboat in all facets of New York's maritime activity—transporting passengers and freight, towing sailing ships, and ferryboat operations—quickly became manifest to most merchants and ship owners.

The potential of steam and paddle-wheel propulsion in New York's many ferrying enterprises was especially evident. Since the earliest Dutch settlement in the seventeenth century, ferries were essential to the region's economic vitality, for they provided the link between Manhattan Island and the surrounding countryside, namely Brooklyn and the rest of Long Island across the East River, and New Jersey across the Hudson River. New York City received much of its food and livestock via ferryboats, and most of the people traveling to and from the island did so by ferry.[2]

The rivers surrounding New York are broad and deep with strong tidal currents, conditions best suited to ferries crossing under sail (although oared boats were used here as well). When winds and tides suited, sail ferries could make the passage in a matter of minutes, but fickle winds or periods of calm could delay crossings for hours or even days. By the early nineteenth century the amount of business carried on by New York's ferries was substantial, and the disruptions of commerce and travel occasioned by erratic ferry operations were increasingly troublesome. Steamboats offered New Yorkers the tantalizing prospect of dependable, scheduled passages on their ferries.

New York's first steam-powered ferry, the first in the world, got its start on 5 February 1811 when the Common Council of New York City granted to Colonel John Stevens a lease for a ferry between the foot of Vesey Street in New York and Hoboken, New Jersey. Stevens had an unusually strong economic incentive for improving the ferry service at this locale. He had purchased most of the Hoboken land in 1784 from the state of New Jersey, and in 1804 he began an ambitious development project, platting his proposed city of Hoboken and offering lots for sale. Stevens envisioned the community as a retreat for New Yorkers, a place where weary city dwellers could enjoy a scenic country outing (he built a 1½-kilometer [1 mi.] promenade along the riverfront), or indulge in feasting, drinking, and merriment (Stevens maintained the '76 House tavern for this purpose). Obviously, fast and efficient ferrying across the river between New York and Hoboken was essential to the success of these plans.[3]

The lease that Stevens received in 1811 for a steam-powered ferry was good for fourteen years, but it was granted on the condition that Stevens have a steamboat operating at the crossing within two years. The colonel wasted no time in getting a boat, which he called *Juliana*, built and outfitted for service; by the fall of 1811 travelers taking passage across the Hudson could experience a wonderful new level of regularity and speed, for the boat made as many as sixteen round trips per day carrying an average of one hundred passengers per trip.[4]

By all accounts the *Juliana* was a smart, fast little steamer, but the vessel's career as a ferryboat was brief. Stevens's lease was approved by the Common Council of New York City, but not by the Fulton–Livingston monopoly. Stevens, a brother-in-law of Robert Livingston, initially offered to compensate Livingston and Fulton for his use of their navigational rights and was granted permission to run the boat in New York waters on the basis of an informal agreement. Fulton was under the impression that the *Juliana*'s payload would consist mainly of excursionists going on day trips to Hoboken and would not include horses, wagons, or cattle. Above all, he did not want the Hoboken ferry to compete materially with another new steam-ferry operation, the Paulus Hook Company, that was about to begin service between New York and New Jersey under a formal license from the Fulton–Livingston monopoly.

The arrangement between the monopolists and Stevens worked for only a year, then fell apart when Fulton accused Stevens of trying to entice skilled mechanics away from his machine shop, of carrying wagons and livestock on the Hoboken ferry contrary to their agreement, and of belittling Fulton's claims for original inventions in the field of steam technology. Stevens's right to navigate by steam was revoked and he was compelled to cease steamboat operations and dismantle his boat in July 1812.[5] Refusing to accept defeat and give up on paddle-propelled ferrying, Stevens turned to the mode of propulsion suggested to him twenty years earlier by John Fitch and began work on a horseboat to replace the *Juliana*.

During the same month that the *Juliana* went out of service, the Paulus Hook Company commenced ferry service over the Hudson with two Fulton-designed steamers named *York* and *Jersey*. A contemporary illustration of one of these ferries shows a catamaran design, with a pair of long, narrow hulls fastened side by side and bridged by a broad deck. The single paddle wheel revolved in the well between the two hulls. A boxlike housing on the center of the deck contained the engine and boiler, as well as compartments to shelter passengers from inclement weather. The ferry was a true double-ender, fitted with rudders at either end that allowed the vessel to change direction without having to turn around. The *York* and *Jersey* were capable of accommodating as many as eight wagons, twenty-nine horses, and four hundred passengers on their capacious decks, and whereas sail ferries could sometimes take up to three hours to make the passage, the steamers crossed the 1.6-kilometer (1 mi.) distance in fifteen to twenty minutes.[6]

John Stevens pressed ahead with his plans for a horseboat despite many distractions, which included managing his growing fleet of steamboats on the Delaware River. On 2 August 1813 he asked the Common Council of New York to alter the original ferry lease and permit him to substitute a horse-

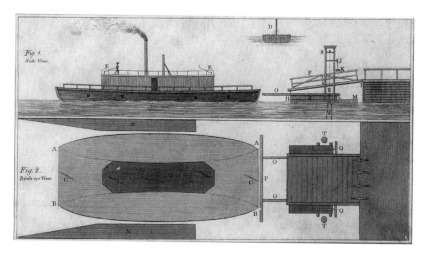

Figure 8. Fulton's steam ferryboat. Courtesy of the Peabody Essex Museum.

boat for a steamboat. Writing to his son Robert on 26 October, Stevens commented: "My operations here, in the horse-boat way, have been much retarded. The machinery, however, is in such a state of forwardness that I can count on an experiment very soon."[7]

In a subsequent letter to his son he elaborated upon his plans. The design of the vessel was quite unusual, for it was a trimaran, or three-hulled boat, with the central hull measuring 27.4 meters (90 ft.) in length by 3 meters (10 ft.) in breadth; the deck covering the hulls, 10.7 meters (35 ft.) in breadth, offered ample space for passengers, wagons, and livestock. The boat was to be fitted with whim-type machinery of Stevens's own design, with the horses revolving a 3-meter- (10 ft.) diameter horizontal crown wheel to turn two paddle wheels measuring 1.8 meters (6 ft.) wide and 3 meters (10 ft.) in diameter. Stevens determined that each orbit of the horses around their walkway would turn the paddles 8.72 times and that while underway the paddles would average about 18 revolutions a minute, "which, considering their breadth, I think will be fast enough." The design was patented in 1813.[8]

The catamaran and trimaran hulls of Fulton's steamboat and Stevens's horseboat were perceived to have certain advantages for ferrying. Locating the paddle wheels between the hulls offered a measure of protection from injury in the event of a collision with other vessels, docks, or floating obstructions such as ice and logs. Multihulled boats were extremely stable and unlikely to capsize in rough weather, and their broad decks allowed plenty of room around the steam or horse machinery in the center. The amount of deck space required by a horse-whim mechanism and its walkway drastically limited the usefulness of a single-hulled craft. There were drawbacks to multihulled ferries, however: Their size made them more expensive to build and maintain, and they were found to be somewhat slow and awkward to maneuver.[9]

John Stevens was not the only inventor working on a horseboat to compete with Fulton's steam ferryboats at New York City, and credit for launching the first commercially successful horse-propelled ferry (and consequently the age of the horseboat in North America) has been given to another man, Captain Moses Rogers of New York City. Like Stevens, Rogers had been deeply involved in steam navigation for several years, both as a steamboat captain and as a tireless promoter and builder of steamboats. Besides building his celebrated horse ferry, Rogers achieved two other firsts with new maritime technology during his brief lifetime (ca. 1779–1821): commanding the first ocean voyage of a steamer (the 1809 passage of Colonel Stevens's *Phoenix* from New York to the Delaware River), and commanding the first transatlantic crossing by a steam-engine-equipped vessel (the 1819 voyage of the ship *Savannah* from Savannah, Georgia, to Europe and back).[10]

Rogers designed and built his horseboat at the request of Rodham Bowne, owner of the sail-and-oar ferries that crossed between Catherine Street in Manhattan and the town of Brooklyn on Long Island. Bowne was reacting to a plan by Robert Fulton and his brother-in-law William Cutting to commence steam ferry service between New York and Brooklyn, a ferry that threatened to draw away much of Bowne's business. Rogers must have started work in 1813, if not earlier, for he was awarded a patent for his boat on 2 February 1814. On 3 April 1814 the Rogers horse ferry cast off from the dock at Catherine Street for the first time, on a passage that was, for horse-propelled ferries, the equivalent of the *North River Steamboat*'s first trip to Albany in 1807.[11]

The new horseboat was an instant hit with the public. Brooklyn's *Long Island Star* reported:

> On Sunday last the public were gratified by the performance of a new invented Ferry-boat, on the New-Ferry between this village and New-York. This boat was invented by *Moses Rodgers* [sic], esq. of New York. It is in some respects similar to the Paulus Hook ferry-boats, and calculated to receive waggons in the same commodious way; but the water wheel in the center is moved by *eight horses*. It crossed the river 12 times during the day, in from 8 minutes to 18 minutes each, and averaging 200 passengers each time. It makes good way against wind and tide; and promises to be an important acquisition. Another boat to go by horses is now building for that ferry, and a *steam-boat*, belonging to William Cutting and others, is nearly ready for the ferry between Brooklyn and Beekman-Slip. These great improvements cannot fail to benefit this village and the adjacent country.[12]

On 30 April the *Niles Weekly Register* published this encomium for the new boat under the heading "Progress of the arts":

> For several days past, the new ferry boat, invented by Moses Rogers, Esqr. of this city, propelled by the draught of six horses, has been plying between this city and Brooklyn, a distance of three quarters of a mile [1.2 kilometers]. On slack water she crossed in seven minutes. In one of her passages she had upwards of 300 persons on board. For short distances she answers all the valuable purposes of steam boats. We congratulate the public on this cheap and important addition to their comfort and safety.[13]

Perhaps the most pleasing aspect of this boat for Bowne and Rogers was the discovery that the horse ferry could make the crossing in about the same amount of time as Fulton and Cutting's New York–Brooklyn steam ferry, the *Nassau*.[14]

Our best pictorial evidence of an early New York whim-type catamaran ferry is a set of plans published by contemporary French naval architect Jean-Baptiste Marestier in a book titled *Memoir on Steamboats*. The boat and its designer are unfortunately not identified by Marestier, but the craft seems typical of horseboat designs of the period. The plans depict an eight-horse-powered ferry of substantial dimensions, 24 meters (79 ft.) in length and 12 meters (39 ft.) in breadth on deck; the twin hulls are each 3 meters (10 ft.) in breadth and separated by a distance of 3.3 meters (10 ft., 10 in.). According to Marestier, catamaran ferries generally had flat-bottomed hulls with tapered ends, matching descriptions of Rogers's ferryboats being "wall sided with flat bottoms sharp at both ends."[15] The ferry in the Marestier plans is equipped with two rudders, one at either end of the well between the hulls, permitting the vessel to change direction without having to turn around. A similar rudder arrangement has already been noted on Fulton's steam ferry, and Stevens would also employ double rudders on his horseboats. The deck of the ferry has a central structure with two compartments forward and aft, presumably for sheltering passengers, and a roundhouse in the center for the horse walkway and machinery.

John Stevens had his prototype trimaran ferry built and launched by the spring of 1814, and the vessel seems to have entered service between Hoboken and Manhattan not long after Rogers's Brooklyn horseboat. Stevens was pleased with his experiment and later that year reported to New York City's Committee on Ferries that the boat "answered the purposes intended as well as a steamboat." He immediately began construction of a second horse ferry. Stevens charged 12½¢ for a saddle horse, 31¢ for light carriages, and from 25¢ to 50¢ for a wagon (the price reflected whether the wagon was full or not).[16]

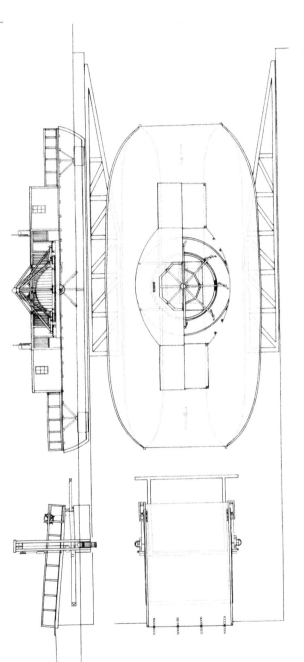

Figure 9. Catamaran–hulled ferry propelled by a centrally mounted horse-whim mechanism and paddle. Traced from a print in Marestier, *Memoir.*

The creation of new horseboat designs did not stop with Rogers and Stevens, for a third type of horseboat was introduced at New York in 1814. This boat is somewhat more mysterious, as little is known about the designer; it followed Rogers's boat by only two months, entering the water on 4 June 1814. The New York *Columbian* reported:

> This morning was launched, at the shipyard of Mr. Charles Browne, an elegant double boat, intended to ply as a ferry from Corlaers Hook to Williamsburgh, Long Island. This beautiful boat is called *Williamsburgh,* and is to be propelled by horse-power, with machinery very different from that already constructed and used in the Hoboken or Brooklyn boats, and is thought by competent judges to be very complete. She is by far the most spacious and will afford the greatest accommodation to the public, of any yet constructed—presenting to view an extensive deck of 80 feet by 42 feet wide [24.4 by 12.8 meters]. It is supposed that two or three weeks may yet be required to complete the machinery, & c. before she can be placed in her station, when hundreds will flock, to view the extensive improvements of the present day.[17]

The *Williamsburgh* began service shortly thereafter from the ferry slip at the foot of Delancy Street, crossing the East River to Long Island and providing the same regularity of service demonstrated by the Catherine Street boat. It is unfortunate that a good description of this boat's machinery has not yet turned up, for it would be interesting to see just how the mechanism differed from the Stevens and Rogers boats.

And so it began. By the summer of 1814 horseboats had proven their worth to New York ferry owners and the public alike, and ferry proprietors around the island were laying plans to build additional craft to ensure that their crossings were adequately serviced during busy periods, or whenever one ferry happened to be unavailable. For the next decade horse ferries would be a familiar sight among the harbor's shipping. It was also around this time that people began calling the vessels "teamboats," a play on the word *steamboat* that is indicative of the closely intertwined relationship between the two modes of propulsion.

Horseboats may have begun as a substitute for steamboats, but their utility and cheapness made them attractive even to companies working under a Fulton–Livingston license. The ferrying enterprise founded by Robert Fulton and William Cutting (officially known as the New York and Brooklyn Steam Ferry Boat Company), owners of the East River steamer *Nassau*, is a case in point. Under the terms of its lease with New York, this company was required to complete a second steam ferry as commodious as the first by 1819, but the operation simply could not afford to build another vessel the size of the *Nassau*. The directors therefore petitioned to build a large horseboat, citing the savings in construction and maintenance costs and service to the public that was comparable to the existing steam ferry. The potential savings for the company were impressive: The *Nassau* cost about thirty thousand dollars to build, whereas a horseboat, complete with extra horses and a stable on shore, was estimated to run about twelve thousand dollars. The city of New York agreed to the substitution on 17 December 1817.[18]

The Steam Ferry Boat Company's eight-horse ferry went into service in 1819; measuring 22.9 meters (75 ft.) in length on deck and 12.8 meters (42 ft.) in beam, the vessel was entirely sheathed with copper below the waterline to protect against wood-boring worms. The new boat was found to be a most useful addition and was thought by many to be safer in winter than the *Nassau* (unlike steam engines, horses knew enough to stop when the paddle wheel hit a large chunk of ice).[19] It was not entirely free of mishaps, however, for on one occasion a boy set off fireworks on the deck and startled the horses, causing them to violently disengage the machinery. The disabled ferry drifted downriver until it reached Governor's Island.[20]

An inventory of New York ferries in 1819 reveals the expansion of teamboats along the city's waterfront since their introduction just five years earlier. By 1819 at least eight and possibly as many as twelve horse-propelled boats churned between Manhattan and points across the Hudson and East Rivers. These included Charles Watts Jr.'s Weehawken horseboat at the Spring Street Dock; John Stevens's Hoboken trimarans (two were apparently kept in service) at the west end of Vesey Street; the Fulton–Cutting Company's horseboat that ran opposite the steamer *Nassau* from the foot of Fulton Street; Rodham Bowne's two Rogers-built catamarans operating out of the Catherine Street ferry slip; and two horseboats owned by William Hunter, William Vail, and Thomas Morrell, one of which ran from the bottom of Grand Street to Yorktown, Long Island, and the *Williamsburgh,* which ran from the east end of Delancy Street to Williamsburgh.[21] The Grand and Delancy Street crossings may each have had an additional horseboat in operation. A lease was issued in 1817 for a teamboat ferry line between Walnut Street and the Navy Yard in Brooklyn, but it is not clear if the boats were ever built.[22]

The date of yet another New York City horseboat is less certain, although it was probably running by 1817. Governor Aaron Ogden of New Jersey had commenced running the steam ferry *Seahorse* between Elizabethtown, New Jersey, and Whitehall Street in Manhattan in 1813, but like John Stevens, he was quickly barred by the Fulton–Livingston monopoly from navigating in New York waters. In order to continue business, Ogden was forced to employ a sail ferry to carry patrons from Manhattan to New Jersey waters near Ellis Island, where an exchange of passengers took place with the *Seahorse.* A more awkward way of running a ferry is hard to imagine. Ogden

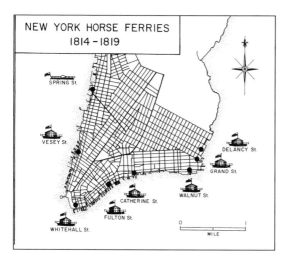

Figure 10. New York horse ferries, 1814–1819. Map by Kevin Crisman from a map in Haswell, *Reminiscences of an Octogenarian.*

later replaced the sail ferry with a horseboat called, appropriately, *Substitution.*[23]

Accounts of the early New York horse ferries often have derogatory undertones, which is not surprising, since many were written long after teamboats had passed from the Hudson and East Rivers, in a century that witnessed countless new and exciting advances in transportation. With all the benefits conferred by hindsight, late-nineteenth-century historians of New York City looked back and found horseboats to be quaint relics of a bygone era, perfect fodder for their "just look how far we've come" narratives. One old-timer, reminiscing about the New York City of 1823, described walking down a country lane called Grand Street to catch a ferry: "Grand Street Ferry was then known as the 'Hook' ferry. You would laugh at the ferry-boats of those days. They had open decks with an awning stretched over and benches around the sides, and were propelled by horse-power."[24]

Another long-time resident of New York, an artist named Banvard, chose to record his impression of a Brooklyn horseboat operation in verse:

How well I remember the horse-boat that paddled
'Cross the East River ere the advent of steam:
Sometimes the old driver the horses would straddle,
And sometimes ride round on the circling beam.

The old wheel would creak, and the driver would whistle
To force the blind horses to pull the wheel round;
And their backs were all scarr'd and stuck out in bristles,
For the driver's fierce stick their old bones would pound.

The man at the gate, in fair weather or rainy,
Stood out in the storm by the cold river-side,
With pockets capacious, to hold all the pennies:
It took just four coppers to cross o'er the tide.

The pilot, he, too, took the wind and the weather,
Perched o'er the horses, with his tiller in hand;
Sometimes would the wind and the tide fierce together
Delay him in getting his boat to the land.

Though four-horse was the power that plowed the fierce river,
Yet oft in his hurry would the passenger curse,
Though no thought would come to make a man shiver,
About the dread danger of a boiler to burst.[25]

The ferry service between Hoboken and New York took a turn for the worse in January 1817 when John Stevens made the mistake of subleasing the entire operation for the term of ten years to John, Robert, and Samuel Swartwout. The terms of the lease conferred to the Swartwouts all rights, responsibilities, and profits for running the ferry, and in return they promised to pay Stevens an annual rent of $512.25. The Common Council of New York agreed to this transfer in April, on the condition that the Swartwouts keep two eight-horse boats plying the river.[26] Stevens's decision to get out of the day-to-day management of the ferry was no doubt intended to free his time for other business ventures, but by the next year he would have cause to regret ever letting go of the business.

In 1818 the Swartwouts encountered financial difficulties, and their ferrying business was sold in a sheriff's auction to Phillip Hone of New York City. Hone's acquisition included the two horseboats, and according to an announcement issued in June, they were to depart punctually from each side of the river at every hour, starting at five o'clock in the morning and ceasing at eight o'clock in the evening. The "punctual" departures announced by Hone seem to have been empty promises, for the operation swiftly deteriorated under his ownership.[27]

At least some of the deterioration seems to have been part of a calculated effort to increase profits. Hone did not change his animals two or three times a day like most teamboat owners but instead kept the same horses plodding around the walkway for the full fifteen hours. Besides saving on the expense of several teams, the resulting snail's-pace progress of the worn-out animals contributed directly to higher sales of alcohol in the bars that Hone installed on board each ferry.[28] It was the ideal enterprise for an unscrupulous businessman: The ferry concession was a monopoly, and unfortunate people who needed to make the passage had no choice but to suffer long waits afloat and ashore.

One passenger on a Hoboken horseboat, more bemused than disgusted by the sorry state of the ferry, described his crossing thus:

> We embarked on an aquatic conveyance, called by the people of these parts a horse boat. But I am inclined to think that this novelty is a mere sham, a trick upon travelers. There are a dozen sorry nags in this contrivance, which go around in a circular walk, with halters on one end and beams at the other extremity. How this orbicular movement can promote the rectilinear advancement of this mammoth boat is to me a mystery. And as we were six hours in crossing the river, I suspect that they go and come with the tide; and that the horses are a mere catchpenny, to bring their masters the trigesimosecundal part of a dollar more on every head than the customary ferriage levied on passengers. However, the unhappy quadrupeds appeared to strain very severely, and in their hinder quarters very particularly; indeed, every sinew of the latter part seemed to be over-exerted, while the neck, head and forelegs moved glibly enough, which is certainly a natural curiosity. I account for it in this way: as the horses are all in a string, and the hinder parts of each one immediately subjected to the inspection of his follower, these noble animals draw up their anteriors from pride, and contract their posteriors from decency.[29]

Besides the aggravation of seeing Hoboken so poorly served by the Hone ferry, Stevens suffered monetary losses when excursionists stopped crossing over for liquid refreshment at his '76 House tavern on the New Jersey shore. After two years of increasing exasperation Stevens acted on 29 August 1820 by the legal formality of walking down to the Hoboken dock and declaring to the ferry master, John Van Boskerck, that he intended to repossess the ferry, on the grounds that Hone had broken the terms of the original lease agreement. Van Boskerck, as expected, refused to yield the ferry, and so Stevens commenced a lawsuit.

The quarrel over the ferry ended the following May, when Hone agreed to give up the ferry to Stevens's sons John and Robert in exchange for an undisclosed amount of money. In their joint petition to the city of New York declaring the change of ownership, Hone and Stevens also announced a momentous change in the mode of propulsion: Stevens proposed to replace the horseboats with "a very superior" steamboat. He also promised to provide a horseboat and two sailboats for a second ferry at Spring Street in New York, north of the existing crossing at Barclay Street.[30]

By 1821 both Fulton and Livingston were long dead and buried, and the ability of their heirs and lessees to maintain a monopoly on steam navigation in New York waters was being increasingly challenged by rival entrepreneurs. Stevens, who had ample resources for fighting a protracted court battle, decided to simply go ahead with his plans to run the ferry on steam and confront the monopoly directly if it attempted to stop him. His "Hoboken Steamboat Ferry Company" was incorporated on 3 November 1821, and by the following May the 29.9-meter (98- ft.) long ferry *Hoboken* began to cross the river every hour. Stevens added the steamer *Pioneer* to the Spring Street crossing in September 1823, and in April 1825, his steamer *Fairy Queen* entered into service. On 4 July 1825 Stevens retired his last horseboat, ending their decade-long reign on the Hoboken waterfront.[31]

The legal compulsion for building horseboats as substitutes for steamboats in New York ended permanently on 2 March 1824, when Chief Justice of the United States John Marshall handed down a decision in the Gibbons v. Ogden case (in which Thomas Gibbons represented challengers to the Fulton–Livingston monopoly and ex–New Jersey Governor Aaron Ogden, now a lessee of steam navigation rights, represented the monopoly). In this ruling the Supreme Court declared that individual states had no constitutional right to restrict the flow of the nation's commerce, and that henceforth all authority to regulate commerce and navigation within the United States belonged to Congress and the federal government.[32] State grants of monopolies on steam navigation were now a thing of the past.

Gibbons v. *Ogden* effectively opened all New York City ferries to steam navigation, and here, where traffic was heavy and the ferrying business immensely profitable, owners began to retire their worn-out horseboats and replace them with the latest models of steam ferryboats. The process of sidelining the teamboats was gradual and not widely advertised. In September 1826 the Williamsburgh Ferry Company petitioned the common council for permission to replace their horse ferry with a steamboat, a necessary request since steam had not been mentioned under the terms of the original concession.[33] We do not know when the last horseboat passed from New York's busy harbor, but it seems unlikely that any were in regular service after 1830.

It is somewhat ironic, although entirely predictable, that the first place to build horse-powered craft in large numbers and make them a popular form of transportation would also be among the first places to get rid of them. The Fulton–Livingston monopoly clearly played an important role in the development of the horse-powered boat by forcing creative, wealthy, and highly respected inventors like Stevens and Rogers to design and build efficient teamboats when their prior interests lay entirely in steam-powered craft. By the time the monopoly was dissolved in 1824, the vital developmental work was complete, and horse-propelled vessels could be found throughout the United States and Canada.

THE SPREAD OF HORSE-POWERED FERRIES, 1814–1820

Horseboating after 1814 conformed to a pattern typical of any new technology that has proven its practical value and moneymaking potential; namely, there was a rush of excitement, invention, and speculation. In this case the initial burst of inventive activity lasted for approximately five years. Experimentation with horse machinery and widespread use of horse ferries would continue for decades, but by 1820 some of the novelty of horse propulsion had worn off, and horseboats were increasingly regarded as a common and useful part of the inland transportation network.

In the years directly following the New York horseboat debut, American inventors, stimulated by the possibilities inherent in a cheap form of paddle-wheel propulsion, devoted considerable time to developing their ideas for horse machines and new types of horse-powered boats. Between 1814 and 1818 the U.S. Patent Office approved applications for more than a dozen machines and boats, and there were undoubtedly many other designs that reached at least the prototype stage without ever receiving a patent.[34] Nor did the success of the New York horseboats in 1814 go unnoticed by the entrepreneurial element in North America, and soon ferry owners and potential ferry owners from the United States and Canada were inquiring about the cost of building these boats and purchasing different types of horse-whim machines.

The correspondence of the Halifax Steamboat Company of Halifax, Nova Scotia, provides what may be a typical example of the research conducted by ferry companies into the relative merits of horsepower over steam. This venture was organized in 1815 by some of Halifax's leading businessmen to provide reliable ferry service between their city and the town of Dartmouth on the other side of Halifax Harbor. The name of the company clearly indicates its original intentions for the ferry's propulsion, but word of the new horseboats led to a reconsideration of steam. One of the company's directors, Richard Tremain, traveled to New York City in April 1815 to look at ferries and consult with inventors, ferry owners, and machine shops about the suitability and expense of the various designs.

Tremain reported back on 4 May after making the initial inquiries. Based on what he had seen and heard at New York, he thought the Halifax–Dartmouth boat should be a catamaran 18.3 meters (60 ft.) in length and 11.6 meters (38 ft.) in breadth, with a roundhouse in the center of the deck to contain the steam or horse machinery. Tremain was confident that a boat of these dimensions could carry four to six horses and carts on the deck as well as two hundred passengers, which was more than adequate for the estimated traffic at the Halifax crossing.[35]

Tremain went on to offer his own view on the steam-versus-horse question:

> I am of the opinion that a Boat worked by Horses (or perhaps oxen) would answer every purpose at Halifax. Horse Boats are found to answer well here where the Tide is 4 knots and upward. The expence of working them is much less here—and would probably be less with us. The first cost is much less. The machinery so simple that if out of order any Millwright or Carpenter could repair them with ease. At Halifax there is little Tide and the Horses would not find the labour hard.[36]

Probably the strongest argument in favor of horse propulsion for the Halifax ferry came in the form of three estimates from American steam engine manufacturers. Robert McQueen and Company's Columbian Foundry in New York could produce an eight-horsepower engine for $4,000, exclusive of the boiler, and arrange for a mechanic to go to Halifax and install it at the rate of $3 per day. William Somerville's City Foundry in Philadelphia offered to build a fourteen-horsepower engine (and presumably the boiler), install it, and oversee its first ten days of operation, all for the sum of $6,000. Daniel Dodd of Delaware estimated that he could produce the engine and machinery, but not the boiler, for $4,000. The boiler would cost an additional $3,000 if it were made entirely of copper, or $2,000 if it were made of wood and copper. Dodd added: "I would not, by any means, recommend wooden boilers—as I have in two or three instances, seen the experiment tried, and the results have been unfavorable." These stiff prices can be contrasted with Tremain's estimate that "the expence of machinery for a Horse Boat will not . . . exceed two to three thousand dollars."[37]

By December 1815 Richard Tremain was back in Halifax, but the directors of the company still could not decide between steam or the cheaper horse machinery. A member of the company wrote to a New York acquaintance named Henry Barclay, submitting a long list of questions and requesting that he procure a wooden model of a horseboat, adding "most of the parties interested are so ignorant of the nature of Horse Boats that you will oblige them by having the Model as Complete as possible." Among the directors of the Halifax Steamboat Company, Barclay was told, "the prevailing opinion now seems to be in favor of a Horse Boat which it is contended will cost less, and be worked at a cheaper rate than that carried by steam and less liable to accidents and expensive repairs."[38]

The reply from Barclay, dated February 1816, probably sealed the decision of the directors to proceed with a teamboat. "There is not the least doubt," he wrote, "but that a horse boat will answer your purpose infinitely better than a Steam boat—both the original expense and the management being very small in the former when compared with the latter . . . the steam engine alone will cost nearly as much as the complete boat for horses." Barclay also succinctly defined the complementary roles that teamboats and steamboats were carving out for themselves on lakes, rivers, and bays: "It is believed that horse boats will get into general use for ferries & the steamboats will be used for long passages up rivers etc."[39]

Barclay's letter was specific about what would be required to run a horse ferry business at Halifax:

> You cannot require a boat of more than fifty feet [15.2 m] long by 35 to 40 feet [10.7–12.2 m] wide, such a boat in moderate weather will go at least six mile [9.6 km] an hour & six or seven horses will be fully sufficient, she will require three men viz. one for the horses, one at the helm & one to assist in getting fast to the dock, one man will be required to attend on each side of the harbor also to make the boat fast when she arrives. Such a boat with all the necessary machinery may be built here for $4500—and there will be no difficulty in making a steamboat of it at any future period. She will draw 12 to 14 inches [30.5–35.6 cm] of water. Besides the expence of the boat however, the necessary docks or floating wharves will be a heavy expence. As your harbour is much infested with worms, composition nails or bolts & a copper bottom will be very advisable. The machinery (here) complete will cost from $800 to $1000. The horses and machinery will occupy a circular space of 25 feet [7.6 m] diameter on the deck of the boat, knowing this you can easily calculate the size you will want, if you have any idea how many passengers & carriages may require to cross at any one time. It appears very immaterial of what wood the boats are built, but pine for the decks & large beams which run entirely across both boats & extend beyond their sides, & on which the deck is laid is best, in consequence of the lightness. There will be no difficulty in getting mechanics to go to Halifax to build the boats (if necessary) but that is a very simple business, and all the machinery can be made here of the most approved materials and cheaper than with you.

Barclay went on to note that most of this information had been supplied by Moses Rogers and that Rogers had engaged a workman to build a scale model of the proposed boat. Rogers was willing to provide the Halifax Company with a complete description of the boat at no charge, provided they pay seventy-five to one hundred dollars for the model and a percentage of the ferry's profits until the expiration of the patent fourteen years hence. The percentage to be paid was one-half of profits when the ferry's income exceeded 12½ percent on the capital. "This proposition," Barclay confided, "I think you may safely accede to without much chance of paying him anything."[40]

The directors of the Steamboat Company opted for horseboat economy over steamboat glamour and appointed a committee to oversee the work. A shipbuilder from New York was hired to superintend the assembly of the twin hulls, and an order was placed, presumably with Moses Rogers, for the construction of the horse machinery. Construction of the vessel proceeded at a favorable rate, and the launching took place on 30 September 1816. Named *Sherbrooke* for the governor general of Canada, Sir John Cope Sherbrooke, Halifax's new ferry began scheduled service on 28 May 1817.

Moses Rogers's contributions to the Halifax Company's new ferry were only one aspect of his continued activities in the field of horse propulsion. Unsatisfied with the machinery on the first Brooklyn ferryboat, he made a series of modifications that were pronounced "great improvements" and then went into business supplying the increasing demand for horse ferries.[41] In early 1816 Carpenter, Lawrence, and DeWint, owners of the Hudson River ferry crossing between Newburgh and Fishkill, New York, hired Rogers to build them a boat. This vessel, called *Moses Rogers,* incorporated all of Rogers's latest innovations and received considerable publicity after it was launched in July 1816. The *Newburgh Political Index* reported on 10 August: "The teamboat *Moses Rogers,* passed from this village, on Wednesday last [8 August], to Fishkill Landing with the following load—one coach and horses, a wagon and horse, seventeen chaises and horses, one horse, and fifty passengers."[42] The *Niles Weekly Register,* always an enthusiastic supporter of American inventions and internal improvements, said of the *Moses Rogers* on 31 August: "It is thus that we may have safe, cheap, and expeditious *ferries* in places where the building of bridges is inexpedient or impracticable."[43]

We are fortunate to have a detailed description of the *Moses Rogers,* contained in a letter written in 1817 by Newburgh resident William Gardner to ferry owner John A. Thomson. The latter, proprietor of the Hudson River ferry crossing at Catskill, New York, was considering the purchase of a horseboat and had written to Gardner for an evaluation of the new boat. Gardner responded:

> I have conversed with one of our principal proprietors of the Boat now in operation here, Mr Carpenter, and have ascertained the following particulars.
>
> Her length of deck or platform is 65 feet [19.8 m], her width 42 feet [12.8 m]; she is propelled by seven horses, fed principally on cut straw and shorts. She has crossed the river in eight minutes, the distance over a mile [1.6 km]. Her time of crossing, however, varies from ten to twenty minutes, as the wind and tide is more or less in favor. She has never been compelled to lay still, in consequence of the violence of the weather, but has always crossed with apparent ease and safety, when the wind was most violent. She has taken across at one time ninety three head of cattle, besides passengers, and could have carried one hundred head. Eight two-horse waggons & teams could cross at once without unharnessing. This boat cost $6,000 but Mr. Carpenter tells me she could now be built for $5,000 or less. They were improved very much in their machinery. He is of the opinion the machinery could be put on board this boat for $1,500 or less.[44]

Figure 11. Hudson River catamaran horseboat ferry *Moses Rogers,* 1816. From Ruttenber, *History of Newburgh.*

Moses Rogers apparently used the same shipyard at Newburgh to build another, slightly larger horseboat, 21.3 meters (70 ft.) in length by 13 meters (42 ft., 6 in.) in beam, for a ferry crossing at New London, Connecticut. When he found that the boat would not be wanted for some time in New London, Rogers offered it to John Thomson of Catskill at cost (about five thousand dollars). Thomson declined the offer and would continue to employ a scow ferry until 1821, but Rogers probably had no trouble finding another buyer for the ferry.[45]

By 1818 Rogers had become deeply involved in building and testing a trans-Atlantic steamship, a dream that he realized with the historic round-trip voyage of the ship *Savannah* in 1819, and it is unlikely that he did more with horseboats after this time. And by 1818 a pathfinder like Rogers was no longer needed to promote the spread of the horse-powered ferry, for the boats were now proving their worth at crossings all over the eastern half of North America.

In addition to the horse ferries operating at New York City and the *Moses Rogers* at Newburgh, people crossing the Hudson River were served by at least two other teamboats before 1820. One of these commenced crossing between Athens and Hudson, New York, around 1816; this boat was of the standard catamaran design with a central paddle wheel and was propelled by nine horses. It was constructed by a builder named William Johnson and cost the owners of the ferry $6,000.[46] At around the same time, 1816 or early 1817, two businessmen from Albany, boatbuilder Charles Kenyon and mechanic James Rodgers, built a catamaran called *Horse's Back* for the ferry between Albany and Greenbush, New York, at a cost of $6,163.30.[47]

Besides the Halifax Steamboat Company's *Sherbrooke,* two other Canadian teamboats are known to have been in operation prior to 1820. One of them, the *Edmond,* was built at La Prairie, Quebec, in 1819 and went into operation across the St. Lawrence River between Longueuil and Montreal. The boat's machinery was built by James Rodgers of Albany, New York. Powered by ten horses and reportedly capable of carrying as many as thirty-eight carriages, the *Edmond* began regular service in July 1819 and performed admirably, crossing the river in twelve to sixteen minutes. A local paper, the *Montreal Herald*, took a pessimistic view of this new form of transportation: "Since the very successful application of steam as a navigating power has become general, we think it supercedes the use of horses in this way unless where extreme scarcity of coal renders the Employment of Steam too expensive. In the present state of affairs, we can use coals brought from Britain at a cheaper rate than we can employ horses in Boats."[48]

The third early Canadian horseboat, imaginatively named *Horse Boat,* was built in 1817 at Hampstead, New Brunswick, on the St. John River. This vessel may not have been a catamaran, for it is said to have been a side-wheeler measuring 30.5 meters (100 ft.) in length and powered by twelve horses walking around a whim-type mechanism. Owner William Peters made the oft-repeated mistake of trying to compete with steamers in the business of hauling people and freight long distances, in this case between the cities of St. John and Fredericton. Although the *Horse Boat*'s machinery seems to have performed adequately, Peters was plagued by wags on the riverbank who would shout "whoa" and temporarily stop the horses. The boat was—predictably—a financial failure and was soon retired to nearby Grand Lake and converted into living quarters for lumbermen.[49]

Farther down the eastern seaboard, south of New York, horseboats appeared at other locales in the pre–1820 period. The Delaware River between Philadelphia and Camden, New Jersey, had one as early as 1816 called *Ridgeway,* a typical catamaran-hulled ferry with a center-mounted paddle wheel propelled by eight horses. The *Ridgeway* ran from Cooper Street in Camden. A second boat, the *Washington,* went into service at the Market Street crossing not long after the *Ridgeway,* although the exact year when this vessel commenced service is not yet known.[50] Passengers traveling up and down the Potomac River between Georgetown in Washington, D.C., and Alexandria, Virginia, were served by a teamboat called *Union* in 1817.[51] Even farther south, near Charlestown, South Carolina, a horse ferry was making regular trips across the Ashley River by 1818.[52]

The use of teamboats was not confined to the eastern seaboards of the United States and Canada during these early years, for some ferry men on interior rivers purchased or fabricated horse whims and built boats to accommodate the machinery. According to one source, a "Mr. Plumb" had a horse ferry operating on the upper St. Lawrence River between Ogdensburg, New York, and Prescott, Upper Canada, in 1815.[53] At least two horse-propelled ferries were in service on the Ohio River in 1819. The first, at Cincinnati, Ohio, was mentioned by British traveler James Flint in May 1819; unfortunately, all he says of this craft is that it was "a large ferry boat, wrought by horses."[54] The second Ohio River boat in operation in 1819 was patronized by another British traveler, Adlard Welby Esq., who was similarly unforthcoming in his written description of the boat, saying only that it was "lately established" at Maysville, Kentucky.[55] Welby did, however, include a view of this ferry moored below the town; the vessel was clearly a catamaran and resembled the Newburgh ferry *Moses Rogers*.

This list of North American horse ferries known to be in service before 1820 is surely incomplete, for the economy and dependability of these boats could not have failed to attract other ferry owners. In 1816 the *Niles Weekly Register* had predicted: "We have heard a great deal about *steam* boats—but *team* boats, for passing rivers and going other short distances, appear likely to come into common use."[56] Just three years later, in 1819, the same journal could proudly report: "We have many team boats at different ferries in the United States, and at some places they are used for the conveyance of passengers and goods considerable distances."[57] The age of the horse-powered boat was off to a strong start in the United States and Canada.

European visitors to North America considered horseboats a novel form of transportation, and some advocated their widespread adoption in the Old World. German tourist Ludwig Gall, for example, thought that "on the Moselle, Saar, and other rivers, where wind cannot give power . . . teamboats that could go from Coblenz to Trier in two days, would be a great benefit."[58] Horse propulsion was, in fact, adopted by some European entrepreneurs. England, for example, had such a craft paddling between Hull and Gainesborough on the Trent River around 1818 or 1819.[59] And in Switzerland a catamaran-hulled vessel built by an American named Church went into service as a ferry and part-time excursion boat on Lake Geneva in 1825. Known as the *bateau-manège* ("treadmill boat"), or more derisively as *L'Escargot du Lac* ("Snail of the Lake"), Church's creation was not a financial success and had to be retired in 1826.[60] There were other Old World teamboats, but they do not appear to have been as numerous and popular as they were in North America.

4

Three Early
Horseboat Ventures

The wave of teamboat building that followed the successful debut of these craft at New York City in 1814 brought horse propulsion to ferry crossings throughout the North American continent. Most early teamboat ventures had two features in common: They employed whim-style machinery on twin-hulled boats, and they operated at relatively busy (and lucrative) crossings, usually near large towns or cities. The three horseboat businesses described in this chapter all employed horse whims on catamarans, but only two of them, the Halifax Teamboat Company and Samuel Wiggins's company, functioned as ferries. The third venture, William Bird's *Genius of Georgia,* was an experiment in long-distance navigation. The three operated in different corners of North America (Nova Scotia, Missouri, and Georgia), under different forms of ownership, and with different levels of profit. In these three examples we get a glimpse of the successes and failures of the earliest horseboat entrepreneurs.

THE HALIFAX TEAMBOAT COMPANY

At first glance, early-nineteenth-century Halifax, Nova Scotia, would seem an unlikely locale for a horseboat, since this maritime city is better known for its fishing schooners and sailing merchant ships. With its large, well-protected, and generally ice-free harbor, the port served as the anchor of Canadian transatlantic trade and communication. By the beginning of the

nineteenth century, however, continued settlement of the Nova Scotian hinterland around Halifax was also expanding the city's role as a center for
regional trade, and this is where a horseboat enters the picture.

The efforts of the Halifax Teamboat Company (or, as it was founded, the
"Halifax Steamboat Company") to find and build the perfect vessel for the
Halifax–Dartmouth harbor ferry have been chronicled in the preceding
chapter. As we have seen, the company puzzled for many months over
whether to build a steam- or horse-powered ferry, before finally electing to
proceed with horse propulsion because of its lower costs of building and
maintenance. The launching of the new eight-horse-powered boat *Sherbrooke*
took place in Dartmouth on 30 September 1816.[1]

A profile view of the *Sherbrooke* shows a fairly typical catamaran ferry,
with a broad deck surrounded by a low rail. A roundhouse covering the
machinery and the horses on their circular walkway rises from the center of
the deck. Passengers could take shelter in cabins fore and aft; smoke pipes
protruding from the roof of each passenger compartment are proof that the
company saw to the comfort of its customers during cold-weather crossings. The *Sherbrooke* was built to be utilitarian rather than attractive, and the
vessel can best be characterized as "houselike" in appearance, but to the
residents of Dartmouth and Halifax who needed to cross the harbor regularly, the *Sherbrooke* must have seemed an attractive vessel indeed.

The company purchased the twelve horses it would need to propel the
boat—eight to turn the whim and four in reserve—in the late spring of 1817,
and operations formally commenced on 28 May. An advertisement for the
Sherbrooke in the 27 August edition of the *Nova Scotia Royal Gazette* detailed
the ferry's daily schedule. The vessel began service at sunrise every day and
continued until one hour after sunset; crossings required about twenty minutes, and there was a pause of fifteen minutes at the end of every passage
for the horses to rest and new passengers to board, which meant that the
ferry completed a round trip in roughly one hour.

The ferry company made every effort to attract customers by providing
them with amenities such as a coffeehouse on the Dartmouth shore and a
stable where travelers could leave their horses before crossing over to
Halifax. The stable in this instance consisted of a worn-out ship's hull at
the ferry wharf. Further efforts to promote use of the new ferry included
reduced fares for cattle and carriages. The advertisement for the ferry promised the public: "Every exertion will be made to accommodate Passengers,
and to give satisfaction."[2]

During its first year of service the ferry operation was struck by an inex-
plicable tragedy: A drunken young man named Hurst boarded the *Sherbrooke*
and proceeded to stab all eight horses laboring on the walkway. The cruelty
of this act shocked Haligonians, and Hurst was tried, convicted, and sen-

Figure 12. The catamaran horseboat *Sherbrooke,* Halifax Harbor, Novia Scotia. From the collection of the Dartmouth Heritage Museum, Dartmouth, Nova Scotia.

tenced to a lengthy prison term. There is no record of restitution being paid to the company, and it seems likely that the teamboat company's directors were forced to cover the loss out of their own pockets.

Operating a major ferry like the Halifax–Dartmouth crossing with just one teamboat was not a good idea, since repairs to the boat could interrupt service for several hours or even several days. The directors of the company were well aware of this problem, and in 1817 they considered adding a second horseboat or even a steamboat, but the ferry was not making enough money to pay for such a vessel. Instead the company invested in boats propelled by hand-cranked side wheels, which were judged to be adequate for carrying passengers across the harbor when the *Sherbrooke* was out of service. This was done, and by late 1818 two small boats, nicknamed "grinders," provided a backup for the teamboat.

It is apparent from company records that the early years of the ferry were not especially lucrative, and the business was, at best, breaking even on its operating costs. By 1820 the investment in boats, horses, wharves, and related facilities totaled more than £7,460, a considerable sum of money for that time. During that same year the ferries ran up expenditures of £1,149 for horse feed, crew's wages, and other expenses, which were balanced by profits of £1,186 from passenger fares and other income. The company repeatedly petitioned the province's Royal Council and House of Assembly for subsidies on the grounds that it was providing Nova Scotia an essential service. Allowances were granted, but only for small sums of money.[3]

Like most companies suffering from financial troubles, the company also looked into ways of cutting expenses. The wages paid to the men operating the hand-cranked boats were cut, and oxen were purchased for the team-boat to see if these animals would provide more cost-effective service than horses. The oxen must have proven too slow, for horses were back on the job within a short time. The company also approved the installation of a square-rigged mast on the ferry that allowed the crew to deploy a mainsail and a topsail whenever the wind was favorable. This expedient reportedly did lessen the workload of the horses and gave the ferry "a most picturesque appearance on the water."[4]

The *Sherbrooke* continued its busy daily schedule through the 1820s; business on the line did not grow sufficiently during the course of the decade to justify building another teamboat or steamboat, and so the *Sherbrooke* remained the grande dame of the harbor's ferries. Accounts of the horse-boat's activities at this time were occasionally included in newspapers or other public records. In 1826 the *Sherbrooke* towed Samuel Cunard's new 400-ton sailing ship *Pacific* from the shipyard at Dartmouth to the Halifax side of the harbor for outfitting, and in July of the same year the teamboat carried bands, spectators, and dignitaries across the harbor to attend the opening of the Shubenacadie Canal between Lakes MicMac and Charles. A complaint regarding the ferry's management was lodged in the 20 October 1827 edition of the *Acadian Recorder* by a patron who was disgusted by the splitting and salting of fish taking place on the deck during the harbor's annual run of mackerel. Another ferry patron defended the boat's captain in the following issue, claiming that the fishing activity was "more proof of his desire to accommodate."[5]

By 1829 the *Sherbrooke* was worn out, and the directors of the ferry elected to replace the ferry with a steamer. The launch of the steam ferry *Sir Charles Ogle,* the first steamship ever built in Nova Scotia, took place on 1 January 1830. The single-hulled boat measured 32.9 meters (108 ft.) in length and 10.7 meters (35 ft.) across on the deck.[6] The *Sir Charles Ogle* seemed the harbinger of a new era of navigation for residents of Halifax, Dartmouth, and their surrounding communities, for the steamer made the crossing in seven minutes to the *Sherbrooke*'s twenty. Steam technology, it seemed, had proven its superiority over horses trudging around the whim.

The *Sherbrooke*'s horses were sold and the teamboat retired from ferrying service in early 1830. The old horseboat was used as a platform for driving dock pilings in the spring of that year, but in November it was placed on the auction block and sold for £85.[7] The hulls could not have been in the best of shape, which may account for relatively low sale price. Thus ended Halifax Harbor's fourteen-year saga of horseboating.

During the following months and years, the ferry company directors and the public must have deeply regretted the *Sherbrooke*'s retirement. The *Sir Charles Ogle* failed to live up to the early high hopes and instead wallowed in a sea of debt and calamity. In the spring of 1830 the steamer's engineer fell off the ferry dock in a drunken stupor and drowned. A lack of freshwater sources around the harbor led the new engineer to use saltwater in the boilers, a decision that resulted in clogged pipes and frequent interruptions of service while the boilers were scrubbed clean of salt deposits. And then there was the debt: The company had borrowed heavily to finance the *Sir Charles Ogle* but soon discovered that faster harbor crossings did not attract enough new business to begin to pay off the loans. Rather than finally realizing a profit from their investment, the directors found themselves shoveling more money into the operation to stave off disaster.[8] The company experienced a wave of director resignations and found its shares selling for a pittance.

The Halifax Steamboat Company, overburdened with debts and management troubles, struggled along for six years after the *Ogle*'s launch. The bleak situation finally took a turn for the better in 1836, when future steamboat magnate Samuel Cunard took over the presidency of the company and thoroughly reorganized the business, permitting the ferry to slowly climb out of its financial hole. By midcentury the operation was even moderately prosperous. The *Sir Charles Ogle*'s boiler and mechanical problems were eventually ironed out, and the boat continued in service on Halifax Harbor for the astounding term of sixty years. Taken all in all, it was a happy ending to the Halifax–Dartmouth Ferry's traumatic conversion from horsepower to steam.

THE WIGGINS FERRY AT ST. LOUIS

Two and one-half years after the launch of the Halifax Teamboat Company's *Sherbrooke,* another ferry business located half a continent away from Halifax also began its great experiment in horsepower. Samuel R. Wiggins's St. Louis–Illinois ferry across the Mississippi River commenced its horse-ferrying operations just as the first great wave of immigration and settlement swept across the midwestern regions of North America. With his first horseboat Wiggins provided the public with a faster, cheaper, and more dependable ferry service than had previously existed at St. Louis, and he laid the foundation for a ferry company that would last until the beginning of the twentieth century.

St. Louis was settled as a fur-trading post in 1764 and was governed by Spanish or French regimes until 1803, when it passed to the United States as part of the Louisiana Purchase. In the early decades of the nineteenth century St. Louis experienced prodigious growth as the fur trade expanded, settlers from the eastern United States and from Europe poured into the region, and steamboats revolutionized the navigation and trade of the Mississippi River.

The first ferry at St. Louis appeared in the late eighteenth century when Captain James Piggot, a veteran of the American Revolutionary War, was given a grant of land in the Illinois Territory by the United States Congress, a grant that included the shore opposite St. Louis. Piggot established a ferry to St. Louis in 1797, a business he ran until his death in 1799, whereupon his family, the heirs to the ferry concession, leased the operation to a succession of boatmen for the next sixteen years.[9]

In 1815 two St. Louis woolen merchants, John McKnight and Thomas Brady, purchased five-sevenths of the Piggots' rights, and Samuel R. Wiggins, a tavern keeper from Ohio, obtained a lease for the remaining two-sevenths of the ferry rights shortly thereafter. For the next few years the ferry business at St. Louis was chaotic, to say the least. The McKnight–Brady and Wiggins ferries ran in competition with one another, and two other ferrying ventures, run by John Day and Alexis Amelin, further intensified the struggle for supremacy on the St. Louis waterfront.[10]

The Mississippi was a difficult waterway for ferries. About one kilometer (or slightly more than half a mile) across at St. Louis and with a high-water velocity in its central channel of nearly 3.4 kilometers (5 mi.) per hour, the river was often choked by ice flows in the winter and early spring, and snags of floating timber threatened boats throughout the year. Early ferries were limited to crudely built and unstable river boats propelled by oars, a labor-intensive and expensive mode of propulsion. The difficulties of getting over the water were considerable, and the dangers quite real.[11]

Of all the rival ferry owners in St. Louis between 1815 and 1820, one was especially determined to succeed in the business: Samuel R. Wiggins.[12] He recognized that both the river conditions and the ever-increasing commerce of St. Louis made the crossing ideal for paddle-powered boats and that possession of such vessels would place his competitors at a great disadvantage. Wiggins petitioned the Illinois legislature for a grant of exclusive ferrying rights along 1.6 kilometers (1 mi.) of the eastern river front and in return guaranteed that he would place a paddleboat in service.

On 2 March 1819 the legislature approved the ferry rights for Wiggins, with two conditions: The boat or boats must be powered by steam or by horses, oxen, "or other four footed animals," and at least one boat had to be in service within eighteen months of the legislature's approval date.[13] If Wiggins met these conditions he would be the sole ferry proprietor along 1.6 kilometers (1 mi.) of the Illinois waterfront facing St. Louis, with the guarantee that anyone infringing the monopoly would forfeit their boat and its equipment to him. The new horseboat for the crossing, an eight-horse catamaran of unknown dimensions, was purchased in Cincinnati and brought to St. Louis in the spring of 1820.

Wiggins's competitor John Day had the same idea, and he also had a horse-boat ready to start in the ferry business in the spring of 1820. On 19 April the *St. Louis Enquirer* described the dawning of a new era in river ferrying:

> The public are congratulated on the establishment of the new ferry boats at St. Louis. Mr. Wiggins and Mr. Day have each started a boat propelled by eight horses, which make passages in a few minutes across this broad and rapid stream. The boats have cabins for the accommodation of the passengers, where they sit as comfortably as in the chamber of a hotel. Mr. Wiggins' boat is particularly elegant. By the establishment of these ferries the river is now crossed regularly and rapidly, with safety and convenience, and at a much cheaper rate than in common flats.[14]

Wiggins swiftly consolidated his hold over the city's ferries. In 1821 McKnight and Brady got out of the business, selling the five-sevenths share they owned of the Piggot ferry to John Day, who subsequently sold all of his interests to Wiggins.[15] It is not clear if Day also sold his horseboat to Wiggins, or if it was put into service at some other river crossing. In any event, by 1821 Samuel R. Wiggins's "St. Louis and Illinois Team Boat Ferry" effectively held a monopoly on all ferry transportation across the river.

Our knowledge of the Wiggins ferry's day-to-day operations in the 1820s is limited, although occasional glimpses surface in public records and travelers' accounts of St. Louis. On 16 March 1822 the company advertised in the *Enquirer* that it was paying cash for twenty "Large Sound Blind Horses," and that parties wishing to dispose of the same should apply to Mr. H. Hopkins at the ferry.[16] Blind horses were no doubt less skittish, as they could not see the water upon which they worked. In 1823 Samuel's brother William C. Wiggins took over the day-to-day management of the ferry.[17]

Despite the navigational advantages provided by horsepower and paddle wheels, running a teamboat on the Mississippi could still be a hazardous occupation. Wiggins demonstrated that he was not averse to taking risks from time to time if it meant making a little extra money, an attitude that nearly led to tragedy in January 1824. Historian Moses Meeker was among the people stranded in St. Louis that month:

> I found the Mississippi running so full of ice that neither the mails nor travelers could get over, and many persons arriving daily on each side of the river. The ice began to slacken some. Wiggin, the owner of the horse-boat, agreed to try crossing if eight hundred dollars should be made up for him for the round trip, by persons on both sides of the river. It was very soon raised, and we got over, but not without much peril to the boat and passengers. Before we landed on the Illinois side there was but one bucket left on the paddle-wheel, and that was stopped by a cake of ice. When within two rods of shore, the boat drifted

rapidly down stream upon a snag or large tree, with one end imbedded in the mud, and the other projecting above the water and floating ice; twenty feet more and all would have been lost. The ice was cleared from the wheel, and the eight horses put to their utmost speed, and the boat went ahead and was landed safely, with about two hundred passengers and about forty horses.

Meeker also got a lesson in human nature on the crossing:

It is astonishing how many people there are in times of danger that give up in despair. There were many that could do nothing but mourn their untimely fate as they imagined and made offers of money, from one dollar to five hundred, to be put on the shore safely. But the instant the boat landed, those that were most frightened were the first to leave her, without stopping to make the least acknowledgment of thanks and gratitude. Mr. Wiggin made use of every exertion that was possible for a man to make to save the boat, and when we landed, he generously called upon all of us who had assisted him in working the boat, offering to refund the money we had paid him; but all were satisfied with him, and with themselves, that they had got over safely, and that we had only done our duty, and further that we did not wish him to pay us for it.[18]

Wiggins's first horseboat was reportedly crushed by ice during the winter of 1824 (perhaps in the crossing described by Moses Meeker), and he had a new, supposedly better and larger horse ferry called *Sea Serpent* built as a replacement. Two more Wiggins teamboats, one called *Rhinoceros* and the other *Reindeer* (or, according to other sources, *Antelope*), subsequently entered into service at St. Louis.[19]

Wiggins may have enjoyed a monopoly on ferry service around St. Louis, but this did not mean that he was free to charge whatever fares he felt that passengers could afford. The state of Missouri's laws regulating ferry operations granted county courts the right to set fares, and they further stipulated that printed rates for ferriage had to be posted at the ferry wharves or on the ferry itself. In 1825 the St. Louis and Illinois Team Boat Ferry's charges for crossing were 12½¢ for a foot passenger, hog, sheep or calf, 50¢ per horse or "neat" cattle, and no fare for wagon drivers and children under age ten. A one-horse wagon cost $1.25, and a four-horse wagon, the most expensive fare, cost $2.25. Wiggins permitted all empty wagons, carts, and other vehicles to make the return trip within ten days at no charge.[20]

Despite the fact that rates were set by the courts and not by Wiggins, the idea of a transportation monopoly rankled some people in Illinois and Missouri, who voiced their complaints in the press. A sarcastic response to the complaints, printed in the 7 December 1824 edition of the *Edwardsville (Illinois) Spectator*, showed that feelings ran high on both sides of the monopoly issue:

Mr. Wiggins has been guilty in almost every instance of taking for ferriage much less than the law allows him, and of charging in some cases one-half or one-third of the legal price to those going to market and recrossing them free! He has even been known to risk the lives of passengers and loss of his boat by crossing them over floating ice.

Let every citizen voice his opinion on the good old times of crossing the Mississippi in an old keelboat. Thus every man will have the pleasure of getting to the market the best way he can![21]

During the years that Wiggins operated his horse-driven ferries, the St. Louis waterfront was the scene of a series of experiments with human-powered paddle-wheel boats, experiments that stemmed from the U.S. Army's efforts to establish fortified outposts along the western frontier. The transportation of troops and their supplies depended upon rivers, especially the Missouri River, which empties into the Mississippi just a few kilometers north of St. Louis. A lack of steamboats led the commander of the 1819 expedition, Colonel Henry Atkinson, to convert four keelboats to human-powered side-wheelers. Keelboats were long, narrow craft, 12.2–30.5 meters (40–100 ft.) in length, with pointed ends, a planked deck, and a covered passenger or cargo space amidships. They were propelled by poles, oars, sails, or most commonly when going upriver, by tow ropes pulled by men walking along the riverbanks.[22]

Atkinson's 1819 boats used a mechanism similar to the whim on Wiggins's first horseboat, a capstan turned by men walking in a circle while pushing on the bars. Labor availability and costs were not a consideration for Atkinson, because the army had plenty of soldiers and they were paid the same wages every day, whether they sat in the boat or turned its sidewheels. The boats were each fitted with two capstans and two pairs of sidewheels, and eight soldiers turned each capstan. In late spring of 1819 the first of the army's paddle-propelled keelboats was tested with a 3.2-kilometer (2 mi.) jaunt up the Mississippi and then back to St. Louis, a round-trip passage completed in thirty minutes. A loaded boat ran trials on the Missouri on 27 June and covered several kilometers without trouble. For unknown reasons Atkinson seems to have stopped using the boats later that summer and did not resume his experiment until four years later.[23]

The army relied on traditional keelboats until 1823, when a war with Native Americans along the Missouri created a demand for fast-moving boats to carry supplies and troops. This time Atkinson experimented with a large tilted wheel upon which the men walked—an inclined treadwheel—for propelling keelboats by sidewheel. These boats, too, seemed to work well, with one inclined treadwheel boat powered by twenty-four "indifferent" men going 38.4 kilometers (24 mi.) up the Mississippi from St. Louis in one day, a speed that was double the usual rate for keelboats towed from the riverbank. The army initially approved the fitting of all its keelboats with this machinery but later withdrew the order as a cost-saving measure.

The next year, 1824, Atkinson devised an entirely new mechanism that had soldiers seated like oarsmen, pumping on horizontally sliding bars that turned a gigantic vertical flywheel, which in turn spun a pair of sidewheels. The mechanism tested successfully, and in September four boats loaded with men, supplies, and equipment traveled 1,056 kilometers (660 mi.) up the Missouri from St. Louis. Nine of these boats were used in 1825, but after that year the army scaled back its operations on the upper Missouri and depended increasingly on improved versions of river steamers.[24]

By 1828 a change from horsepower to steam power was also in the works for the St. Louis and Illinois Team Boat Ferry. Protected by his monopoly and enriched by the increasing trade between Illinois and Missouri, Wiggins made the switch in motive power by building the steam ferry *St. Clair*. The new boat reportedly had a capacious deck, moved swiftly across the river, and could shuttle back and forth without having to rest worn-out horses. Two years later, in 1830, Wiggins added a second steamer, the *Ibex,* to his ferry line.[25] The teamboats were sold off, ending the decade of floating horsepower on the St. Louis waterfront.

Samuel R. Wiggins followed his teamboats into retirement. In 1832 he sold his ferrying business to a joint-stock company composed of eight investors, one of whom was the ferry's manager, William C. Wiggins. The new ferry company promptly elected William Wiggins as president, and he continued to supervise the business until his death in 1853, when he was succeeded by his son Samuel B. Wiggins.[26] The Wiggins Ferry Company, as the organization was called, grew and prospered until 1874 when a bridge was built across the Mississippi at St. Louis, but ferries would keep running at this locale until the early twentieth century.

WILLIAM BIRD AND THE *GENIUS OF GEORGIA*

For some early-nineteenth-century inventors and entrepreneurs, the limitations of animal power were not always obvious or acceptable, and during the earliest years of horseboating there was an ongoing (if somewhat muted) debate over the future of propelling boats by horses or other animals. There were extremists on both sides of the issue, from steam proponents who saw horseboats as a major step in the wrong direction, to horsepower proponents who envisioned a time when marine steam engines and boilers might be entirely replaced by horse machinery. The arguments advanced in this debate, and the experiments that were made to bolster those arguments, provide interesting case studies in the adoption, and adaptation, of a new form of technology.

An article in the July 1821 edition of the *North American Review* provides what may be a typical "pro-steam" viewpoint on animal propulsion. The author does not entirely dismiss the horseboat ("it is not our purpose to decry experiments of any kind; nor to discredit the utility of this mode of conveyance, when nothing better is to be done"), but the arguments advanced against animal propulsion are numerous and strongly stated. "This power," the writer observed, "has its limits in practice. It would be absurd to think of employing in one boat the animal force of forty horses, while it is very easy to use a steam engine of that power." The article went on to assert:

> We scarcely think it necessary to name the superior durability of engines over animals, nor the liability of the latter to sickness and death. It is obvious, that if an engine requires to be readjusted, there is meanwhile no expense for fuel, but if one or two of a set of mules are unable to perform, still the rest must be fed. Experience and interest will undoubtedly instruct and guide men in all kinds of business: nor should we have dwelt this long on this topic but from the apparent retrocession of this expedient from the great modern improvement of steam navigation.[27]

Proponents of horse machinery might have countered that "the great modern improvement of steam navigation" was meaningless if a steam engine was too expensive to purchase. Others might have pointed out that although horses did have limitations as a power source, they were at least safe: Horses did not overheat and set the boat on fire, nor did they overpressurize and violently explode.

Far on the other side of the steam-versus-horse debate were the dreamers who intended to compete successfully with steamboats in long-distance travel and perhaps even drive steam out of business. One such optimistic inventor who prophesied an early end to steam navigation was Mr. W. Hart of Baltimore. In 1819 he unveiled a model of his revolutionary new ship and began to seek out potential investors. The vessel was to measure 41.5 meters (136 ft.) in length and 7.6 meters (25 ft.) in beam, and it would advance over the water through the combined efforts of seventeen or eighteen horses. Hart was entirely confident that his "team ship" would carry twice the freight of a steamer, could be built and fitted with machinery at a fraction of the cost ($10,000 to $12,000, as opposed to $40,000 or $50,000 for a steamship), would cost less to operate ($15 per day, instead of $60 or $70), and would cruise at the same speeds (five to seven knots). "This is," Hart assured the public, "the only plan that can answer for great distances."[28] Investors must have been skeptical, for no evidence has been found of Hart's ship being built in North America.

Yet another long-distance venture, a Hudson River packet teamboat, was considered in 1818 but apparently never built. Called *Golden Fleece,* the proposed packet was to consist of a long, narrow vessel 27.4 meters (90 ft.) in length and drawing no more than 76.2 centimeters (30 in.) of water. Propelled by a team of four horses (with two back-up teams of horses standing by), the *Golden Fleece* was designed to make a two-day round-trip between New York City and Newburgh, New York. The multitude of steamers navigating the Hudson in 1818 presumably sank this idea.[29]

These experiments may never have seen the water, but there were many other boats that would attempt to compete with steam over the lengths of lakes and rivers. We have already met two of them—John Brookhart's keelboat, which voyaged upon the Ohio and Mississippi in 1807–8, and William Peters's horseboat, which began and ended its career in 1817 on the St. John River in New Brunswick.

One of the more spectacular and well-documented bids to compete directly with steamboats was made in 1820 by William Bird of Effingham County, Georgia. Bird built his boat, which he called *Genius of Georgia,* and launched her in the early spring of 1820. While the *Genius* was being fitted out with machinery in Savannah, Bird's intentions for the boat were announced in the local paper: "After satisfying the citizens of Savannah of the practibility [*sic*] of this species of boats—and prove to them by actual experiment if required, that they are equal in motion to any Steam-boat ever in [the] Savannah River . . . she will take freight for Augusta."[30]

At this time Bird also made the rather remarkable claim that he did not know that other teamboats existed in the United States until his vessel was launched; this is difficult to believe, since Moses Rogers (of New York teamboat fame) had made his historic transatlantic steamer voyage from Savannah the previous year. Bird may have professed ignorance of other horse-powered craft to avoid charges of patent infringement. In any event, his mechanism differed in some respects from other designs of the period.

The *Genius of Georgia* measured 25.9 meters (85 ft.) in length and 16.8 meters (55 ft.) in breadth on deck and had the double-hull configuration typical of the early horseboats. The principal component of the horse-whim mechanism was a gigantic horizontal wheel, 12.2 meters (40 ft.) in diameter, that turned two 5.8-meter- (19 ft.) diameter paddle wheels placed between the two hulls, one before the other. A circular platform above the horse walkway served as a deck to carry cargo and also as a shelter for the horses. The *Genius* carried an equine crew of twenty-four, harnessed two abreast when they turned the horizontal wheel.[31]

The horse walkway on Bird's boat was much larger than on most other horse-whim-equipped boats, and its 15.9-meter- (52 ft.) diameter in fact took up most of the main deck. Although this "large and fair circle" allowed the horses to work "with much ease to themselves," Bird's motives may have been practical as much as humanitarian. The distance between Savannah and

Augusta was considerably more than 160 kilometers (100 mi.), and a wide circle was probably essential if the horses were to go this distance without wearing out. Bird expected the boat to make a profit by transporting cotton on the upper deck (400 or 500 bales) and in the holds (150 bales), and by towing freight-laden riverboats.

Like any good entrepreneur, Bird began his operation by showing off his remarkable new boat, inviting members of the public on a day-long excursion downriver from Savannah. A passenger aboard the boat on that day later glowingly recounted the event in the local paper:

> It was indeed pleasing to the friends of national improvement, and must have been peculiarly so to the bosom of every genuine Georgian, to witness the laudable curiosity excited on the occasion—and it must have been still more pleasing to see that curiosity so fully gratified—The shore was crowded with ladies and gentlemen to view the Genius of Georgia, as she moved from the bridge with a number of respectable citizens on board. She was put in motion by the horses at 5 o'clock, and proceeded down the river with great majesty of movement. We might say as Byron said of another vessel:
> She walked the water like a thing of life.[32]

The first voyage from Savannah to Augusta began promisingly enough on 9 May 1820, when Bird advertised that his vessel was moored at Wayne's Wharf and was accepting consignments of freight bound for Augusta. The *Genius of Georgia* set off from the wharf just four days later, on 12 May, and began churning upriver against the current. The passage to Augusta required twelve days, nine of which were actually spent underway. At Augusta the boat took in a cargo of flour and started back down the river, a passage that took only five days, including two days spent aground on a sandbar.[33] The *Genius* made at least one more passage, and possibly several more during the summer of 1820, but after this it time disappears from the historical record.

There would be other experiments in hauling freight between ports with teamboats, but from the beginning of the horse ferry age to the end, nearly every attempt to compete directly with steam in long-distance navigation ended in failure. Like all living creatures, horses have their physical limits, and they cannot labor indefinitely nor generate the power necessary to move large vessels efficiently over long distances. North America's horses should bless the steamboat, for it probably saved countless animals from a lifetime of drudgery on the treadmill.

5

Barnabas Langdon and the Horizontal-Treadwheel Horseboat

The whim-propelled ferries of horseboating's earliest years were not without their drawbacks, some of which have already been discussed in the previous chapters. The whim mechanism and the walkway that circled it required a considerable amount of deck space, a serious handicap for a ferryboat as it is deck space that earns the profit. Rogers, Stevens, and the other inventors solved the space problem by building multihulled boats—catamarans—to accommodate the horses and propulsion machinery as well as wagons, carts, livestock, and passengers. With the catamaran design, however, owners of these boats were buying and maintaining two hulls instead of one, an expensive proposition. During the 1814–20 period horse-powered catamarans may have been cheaper than their steam equivalents, but they still represented a substantial amount of money, and many ferry owners did not have enough business at their crossing to afford the five to six thousand dollars required to purchase one of these boats.

A second problem was inherent in horse-whim machinery, one rarely mentioned in documents but which nevertheless must have concerned ferry owners for reasons both economic and humanitarian. Walking in tight circles all day was terribly hard on the horses (one early nineteenth-century inventor familiar with whims considered them "very injurious to that noble animal").[1] A reported side effect of the whim on horses was dizziness or disorientation, which caused some horses, when put out to pasture after a long spell on the walkway, to continue to walk in circles.[2] Sickness and mortality rates for animals laboring on these machines may have been higher than usual for working horses.

Clearly, there was room for improvement in horse mechanisms and horse-boats. While some inventors were tinkering with existing whim-and-catamaran ferry designs in the 1814–20 period, others struck off in a different direction, hoping to create equine machinery that was cheaper for ferry owners and easier on horses. This quest was fulfilled between 1816 and 1819, when a new form of propulsion was developed, tested, and improved, leading to an inexpensive and practical design that would soon become a common sight on North American rivers and lakes. However, the quest for a better horse-boat had its martyrs.

"AS SOON AS THE BOAT INSANITY IS OVER": CHARLES WATTS AND THE INCLINED TREADWHEEL

The machinery that would bring about the revolution in teamboating was an invention that had been around for centuries: the treadwheel. This was nothing more than a revolving circular platform or turntable, upon which one or more draft animals walked in place; instead of the horse turning in a circle, the circle turned underneath the horse. We have already seen this device in Georgius Agricola's 1556 treatise *De Re Metallica*, in the form of a horizontal treadwheel worked by men. The works of two slightly later inventors, Agostino Ramelli (1588) and Vittorio Zonca (1607), included plans for treadwheels, powered by men or oxen, that were canted to one side ("inclined" or "oblique" treadwheels).[3] The general lack of references or illustrations suggests that treadwheels were not widely employed in seventeenth- and eighteenth-century Europe and North America.

The era of treadwheel horseboating began with the submission of two patents to the U.S. Patent Office. The first, approved in October 1816, was for an "inclined horse wheel" designed by Joseph Best Robinson of Cincinnati, Ohio. Robinson's elementary device consisted of a treadwheel fitted with cog teeth beneath its lower rim to turn a lantern gear and horizontal power shaft. The second patent design, approved in October 1817, was for an "inclined power wheel" nearly identical to Robinson's patent, submitted by Moses Isaacs and John Wilbanks of Philadelphia. Both inventions had the wheel canted to one side, forcing the horses to walk uphill and thereby contribute their weight to the force that turned the wheel. The patent drawings imply that these devices were intended for use in mills or other land-based light industry.[4]

Why did the Robinson and Isaacs–Wilbanks wheels qualify for separate patents if they were so similar in design and function? The answer to this lies in the nature of contemporary U.S. patent laws. During its earliest

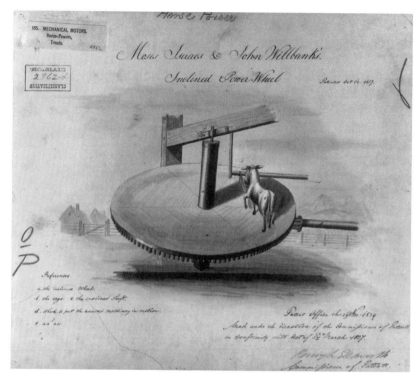

Figure 13. Moses Isaacs's and John Wilbanks's Inclined Power-Wheel, 1817. Patent drawing number 2862-x. National Archives.

decades of existence, the U.S. Patent Office operated as a small bureau within the Department of State and was given neither the means nor the authority to closely evaluate the merits of applications. The office simply issued fourteen-year patents to nearly everyone who cared to apply. Conflicts between owners of similar patents and questions of infringement were all left to the jurisdiction of the courts.[5] The system almost guaranteed strife between patent holders.

One of the inclined-treadwheel patentees, Moses Isaacs, had his eye on the market for teamboats and submitted a design to the Patent Office. The application was approved on 17 March 1818.[6] Detailed written specifications for Isaacs's horseboat have not been located, but plans for an inclined-tread-wheel vessel included in French engineer Jean-Baptiste Marestier's memoir on steamboats almost certainly illustrate Isaacs's creation (Marestier was gathering information in New York at the same time that Isaacs was building horseboats there).[7] The plans show a single-hulled vessel equipped with sidewheels and a canted treadwheel located directly beneath the sidewheel

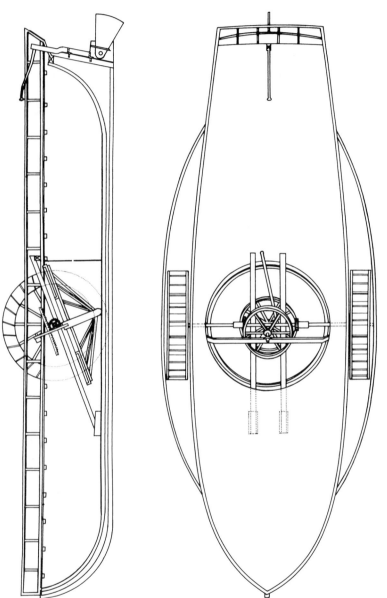

Figure 14. Inclined-treadwheel horseboat. Traced from a print in Marestier, *Memoir.*

axle. A lever extending aft from the axle allowed the operator to shift between forward and reverse. It is not clear where the horse or horses stood, but presumably the inventor had this all worked out.

Moses Isaacs's horseboat seemed the solution to problems inherent in horse-whim-equipped catamaran ferries: It required only one hull, and the horses were not forced to walk in circles. Inventing a new form of motive power was one thing; making commercial success of it was another matter altogether. The little we know about Isaacs suggests that he was a man of modest means and limited experience in the world of business, and so it is not surprising that he joined forces with someone possessing greater financial and legal knowledge, New York lawyer Charles Watts Jr. The two began working together in 1818 to promote treadwheel propulsion.

Watts's background is also somewhat obscure, but we know that his deceased father was a moderately successful merchant and cabinetmaker, and that Charles Jr.—like many Americans in the economic boom that followed the War of 1812—was attracted to large-scale, and risky, financial ventures. Watts had unsuccessfully attempted to incorporate a bank in 1818, and when that fell through he apparently decided that Isaacs's improved horseboat could make him wealthy.[8] He leaped headlong into organizing new horseboat companies and building boats to sell to other ferry owners.

One of Watts's first enterprises was the opening of a new Hudson River ferry between Manhattan Island and the rural farming town of Weehawken, New Jersey (immediately north of Hoboken). In early 1819 the city of New York granted a lease to a man named Phillip Earle for a New York–Weehawken ferry located near the foot of Canal Street for a term of fifteen years; subsequently Watts either joined Earle in a partnership or subleased the crossing. On 10 February Watts purchased from Moses Isaacs the right to use inclined-treadwheel boats, "such as has already been constructed," at the Weehawken crossing, in exchange for three thousand dollars or one-fourth of the ferry's profits.[9]

In April 1819 Watts also proposed a partnership with a "Mr. Conklins" of Poughkeepsie, New York, to operate one of Isaacs's boats at that town's Hudson River crossing. The New York lawyer offered to provide a newly built treadwheel ferry if Conklins arranged to lease docks on each side of the river, provided all the horses, and superintended the business once it was in operation. After subtracting expenses for horse feed, hire of crew, and maintenance of the boat, the remaining profits would be evenly divided. A teamboat did begin operation at Poughkeepsie in 1819 but did not include Watts or Conklins among the directors, so we can assume that their partnership failed to materialize.[10]

Watts also employed his legal training to defend Moses Isaacs's patent from infringement. The most immediate threat came from Dr. William

Thornton, superintendent of the U.S. Patent Office. On 31 March 1819 Thornton informed Watts that treadwheel patentee Joseph Robinson of Cincinnati had a prior claim to inclined treadwheels for horseboats.[11] Watts was immediately suspicious, as Thornton had previously purchased horse-boat machinery from Moses Isaacs along with a license to run it on the Potomac River, a strange acquisition if Robinson supposedly had superior patent rights. In his reply to Thornton, Watts requested copies of Robinson's patent specifications to see if they made any reference to boat propulsion.

By late May Watts's suspicions hardened into certainty that Thornton had entered into some form of horseboat patent agreement with Robinson and was now misusing his office to dispose of the competition. He had grounds for this belief because Thornton, superintendent since 1802, had a reputation for questionable practices such as issuing patents to himself and laying claim to the inventions of others. A contemporary said of the superintendent: "Not a model ever came into his office for a patent that he did not declare that he had had some impression of the same thing, and that virtually, he was a prime inventor of it."[12]

Watts, convinced of "irregularities and improper inducement" in the Patent Office, wrote to associate Nathaniel Green Pendleton in Cincinnati to request his help in extracting vital information from Joseph Robinson. Pendleton was instructed to gain the inventor's confidence and then learn everything possible about the Robinson's patent of 1816 and about the deal-ings of Superintendent Thornton. Watts wished to know details of Robinson's treadwheel patent, the nature of his agreement with Thornton, and whether Thornton had in fact backdated the grant of Robinson's patent to October 1816 in order to undermine Isaacs's patents of 1817 and 1818. Watts warned Pendleton that "the above inquiries are of a delicate nature" and were to be made "in a manner not to excite suspicion."[13]

At the same time that Watts was preparing to wage legal battle with the head of the Patent Office, he asked his associate, John D. Dickinson of Troy, New York, to investigate a new type of horseboat mentioned in the 20 May 1819 edition of the *Troy Post*. The boat appeared to have many of the same characteristics as Isaacs's treadwheel-propulsion system, and Watts was con-cerned about both patent infringement and commercial competition. He asked Dickinson to look into the matter and obtain a description of the hull, the machinery, the boat's average speed, "or any other particulars that may strike [you] as useful or explanatory."[14] Watts's concern over the Troy ferry was justified, for as we shall see, it was to prove a significant milestone in the evolution of North American horseboats.

By early June the nefarious dealings of Superintendent Thornton and the operation of the mysterious boat at Troy were, for Charles Watts, overtaken by the more immediate challenge of getting the Weehawken horseboat ferry into service. A series of invoices and receipts from June and July document his progress. On 14 June the firm of Sayre & Force submitted an invoice for $20 for the bell that would be used to announce the ferry's departure; on 20 June Mr. E. Hitchcock of New York leased dock space for the ferry at Spring Street at the rate of $100 per year; another invoice shows that a 9.1-meter-square (30 ft. sq.) wharf costing $1,056.92 was built on the New Jersey side of the river. Finally, on 24 June and 3 July, Watts paid the *New York Commercial Advertiser* $7.75 to announce the commencement of ferry service.[15]

According to Watts's newspaper advertisements, the Weehawken ferry began crossing on 27 June 1819, with four round trips every weekday. Watts emulated Colonel John Stevens in Hoboken by promoting Weehawken as a "delightful spot," the ideal resort for city dwellers on a country outing. "For boldness and variety of scenery," he promised, "this place is not exceeded by any within one hundred miles [160 km] of the city, you are at once embosomed in farms, farm houses, woodstocks, streams, valleys and hills." For excursionists with more sedentary habits, Charles Bullenger's Weehawken Hotel (advertised in the paper immediately below the ferry notice) offered "satisfaction in . . . refreshments, liquors, and attendance."[16]

The opening of the Weehawken ferry in the summer of 1819 was probably the high point of Charles Watts Jr.'s career in horseboats, for in the next twelve months he would experience a swift downhill slide in his fortunes. Watts had chosen an extraordinarily bad year to launch a new enterprise. In early 1819 the post–War of 1812 economic bubble, fueled by unsupported credit and artificially high commodity and land prices, suddenly burst. The United States was gripped by financial panic as personal fortunes dissolved overnight, banks called in loans, and widespread unemployment left workers and their families without income.[17] Many New Yorkers now had leisure time, but few had money to spend on a ferryboat excursion to Weehawken. A summary of the new ferry's expenses and receipts, prepared in early September, suggests that the business was only breaking even on operating expenses, with nothing left over to pay the considerable debt on the boat and new wharf.[18]

In the fall of 1819 Watts encountered severe pecuniary and technical difficulties with a second horseboat. He had previously entered into an agreement to build a treadwheel boat for a Philadelphia ferry company, and between July and September 1819 the hull was assembled in the yard of New York shipwright Noah Brown. The horseboat *Phoenix* was in the water and awaiting its machinery in early November, but the Philadelphia company was having trouble with its creditors (and presumably in meeting the payments for the new boat). Unpaid bills continued to pile up on Watts's desk, and by the end of 1819 he was frantically seeking money to stay solvent.[19]

Convinced that the sale of the *Phoenix* offered the only escape from his plight, Charles Watts gambled everything on its completion. The boat was towed from New York to Philadelphia, where it was subsequently damaged by ice. Watts joined the boat by February 1820 to personally oversee repairs and outfitting and to escape from bill collectors in New York. Before leaving home he handed over the deeds to his Weehawken ferryboat and real estate to Moses Isaacs, and he signed over other property, including his personal library and a horse, to his brother-in-law Henry Jones.[20] These actions were evidently intended to prevent seizure of Watts's assets by creditors.

Without money Watts found it nearly impossible to exist in Philadelphia. His requests to Isaacs for assistance brought expressions of puzzled sympathy, but no funds. On 20 February Isaacs wrote: "I have observed the contents of your letter with concern and surprise"; on 14 March he added: "I was extremely sorry to hear that you have got yourself in so much trouble as you represent"; and on 29 March: "Its astonished me a person of your note & respectability should not be able to get a loan of $200 or $300 on the boat." Isaacs pleaded his own hard luck and deteriorating health for his inability to find the money needed to complete the ferry.[21]

Watts was finally reduced to begging for loans from friends and relatives, a humiliating last resort, for though the supply of money was tight, there was no shortage of admonitions and platitudes. Watts's friend Daniel Robert of New York replied to pleas for help with a lengthy sermon on maintaining moral fiber in trying times. He advised abandoning the horseboat, returning to New York to pay off debts, and resuming the practice of law. Robert went on to comment: "Call to your mind the many instances of men who in early life sometimes by their own imprudence and sometimes by the folly or wickedness of others have been overwhelmed for a while by a tide of adverse events, but have nevertheless from native strength and energy of soul risen superior to their misfortunes." After a short temperance lecture on avoiding "the temporary oblivion of drink," Robert cautioned: "Remember that nothing but vice can ruin you and that your happiness and respectability at least, if not your fortune are yet in your hands."[22]

Perhaps the most painful correspondence came from Watts's sister in New York City, Hellen Jones. She learned of her brother's troubles through her husband Henry, and on 22 March sent word of her anxiety and bitter disappointment. "You still feel determined to try your fortune with horse boats but without success," she complained; "return . . . to the study of the Law and leave your wild imaginary schemes to some more fortunate adventurer." She concluded her letter by noting, "it is impossible for me to express on paper all I feel."[23]

By 12 May Jones had overcome her inability to express her feelings on paper and sent a letter calculated to add guilt to the already-heavy burden her brother carried. After inquiring whether or not he had abandoned his "absurd boat," she informed him that their mother was going to send him money "from her pittance." She added mournfully, "Ah! Charles, what you have not reduced her and me to[;] she ought to have been able to have looked up to you in her declining years. . . . you have disappointed us all." Jones concluded with one final barb: "I will not say too much, your own feelings must be enough[,] but why have you been so obstinate. . . . to continue so long in error is unpardonable."[24]

Watts's brother-in-law Henry Jones was more encouraging ("keep a good heart and as soon as the boat insanity is over you may return to the law"), and he promised to send money at the earliest opportunity. The news conveyed in his letters, however, was especially grim. One of Watts's principal creditors, a man from Hoboken named Van Boskirk, was filing suit and threatened to have Watts arrested. "You had better take the benefit of the act [in other words, declare bankruptcy] at once," Jones warned, "Buskirk will never release you."[25]

Perhaps equally alarming was Henry Jones's news of Moses Isaacs, who was refusing to hand over the horse and other possessions that Watts had deeded to his brother-in-law. "Isaacs . . . says you are a fool and that he had a deed and bill of sale for all your property at Weehawken. This damn scoundrel will cheat you as sure as hell. . . . you had better come on and get those papers out of his hands." Isaacs, it turned out, was also spreading the rumor through the New York business community that Watts had been arrested for his debts in Philadelphia. "Charles," Jones wrote, "everybody is surprised to find you have had anything to do with this drunken Isaacs for I was told . . . he was drunk every day and that he was letting all go to the devil."[26]

By May 1820 Watts was sinking beneath the "tide of adverse events": Sidney Wright, the foreman at Noah Brown's shipyard in New York, had repossessed the Weehawken horseboat, Van Boskirk in Hoboken was proceeding with his suit, and Watts's erstwhile friend and partner Moses Isaacs was claiming the remaining Weehawken assets. In Philadelphia Watts faced legal action by local creditors, the treadwheel machinery on the *Phoenix* could not be made to work properly, and the ferry company that contracted for the *Phoenix* threatened to sue for damages caused by the boat's detention. The last straw came in mid-May, when the *Phoenix* sank in the Delaware River.[27] Watts, finally recognizing defeat, abandoned the boat, returned home, and took the benefit of the act. In February 1821 he left New York to start over in a locale where his failure was not common knowledge.[28]

The disaster that swamped Charles Watts Jr. in 1820 also proved to be the end of Moses Isaacs's propulsion system, for the inclined treadwheel was rarely (if ever) used on horseboats after this time. The mechanism's association with a drunken inventor and a bankrupt promoter may be partly to blame, but there are also numerous hints in Watts's correspondence that the design was flawed. Installing a massive, horse-sized treadwheel at an oblique angle on a boat would have been a difficult undertaking, and it may have been impossible to keep one of these canted machines aligned properly on a flexible wooden hull. Perhaps Isaacs's invention could have won widespread acceptance if there had been time to remedy its apparent defects, but in the spring of 1819 a simpler, more mechanically reliable treadwheel design made its debut and swiftly relegated the inclined treadwheel to the scrap heap of horseboat history.

BARNABAS LANGDON'S "SINGULAR HORSE FERRY-BOAT"

In June 1819 the U.S. Patent Office approved a treadwheel-propelled horse-boat design submitted by Barnabas Langdon, then a resident of the Lake Champlain port of Whitehall, New York.[29] Langdon's solution to engineering problems inherent in the inclined treadwheel was brilliant, yet simple: Use a horizontal wheel. Two unscaled drawings of his invention, filed at the Patent Office along with Langdon's patent application, show the rudiments of the system. The treadwheel consisted of eight radial arms with a planked ring around the outside for the horse walkway; a second ring, closer to the center of the wheel, was fitted with cog teeth to turn the gear on the drive shaft.

The second patent drawing, a plan view of a boat fitted with Langdon's horizontal wheel forward of the paddle wheels, has two horses harnessed together on one side of the turntable. The power they generated by walking in place on the wheel was transmitted via a shaft fitted at each end with a lantern gear. The gear coupling between the drive shaft and paddle-wheel axle allowed the direction of the paddle wheels (and hence the direction of the boat) to be changed by shifting the lantern gear on the drive shaft from one crown wheel to the other. This forward–reverse shifting arrangement would be a standard feature on most if not all horizontal-treadwheel boats built in North America.

Many details shown on the patent drawings would be changed on the boats subsequently built to Langdon's design. Modifications included the use of cast-iron spur, bevel, and crown gears in place of obsolete wooden cog teeth and lantern gears. The cogs on the treadwheel would be replaced by a gear rack made up of contiguous sections of cast-iron teeth (why Langdon showed outmoded cogs and lantern gears on his drawing is a mystery, since cast-iron gears were available by 1819). Other significant changes included moving the treadwheel aft of the sidewheels and balancing the horses' weight by placing them on opposite sides of the wheel. In all essential elements, however, the patent drawings show the treadwheel mechanism that would be

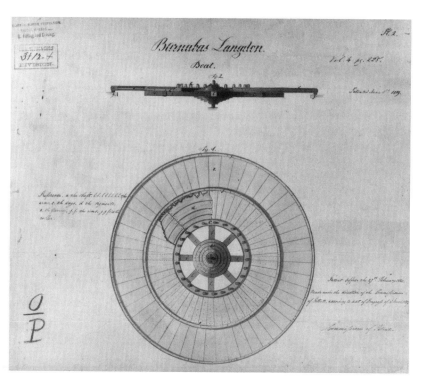

Figure 15. Barnabas Langdon's horizontal treadwheel. Patent drawing number 3112-x. National Archives.

the standard mode of propulsion for North America's horse-powered boats until the middle of the century.

Who was Barnabas Langdon, and what impulses led him to develop his treadwheel mechanism? Like so many of the principal figures in horseboating history, his origins were humble and his motivations obscure. We know that he was born in New York State around 1770 and that as a young man he lived in Stamford, Vermont, not far from the Massachusetts border. In 1800 he and his wife Mary were living on the shores of Lake Champlain in St. Albans, Vermont, and around 1813 they moved to Whitehall, New York, at the southernmost end of the lake. They had four children, three boys and a girl, and tax rolls suggest that they had only a modest income and limited assets.[30]

Barnabas Langdon's line of work during these years is not known, but we can surmise that he was employed as a mechanic, for he was certainly skilled in the design, fabrication, and assembly of complex machinery. He also had a genius for invention and a strong interest in new forms of transportation. In

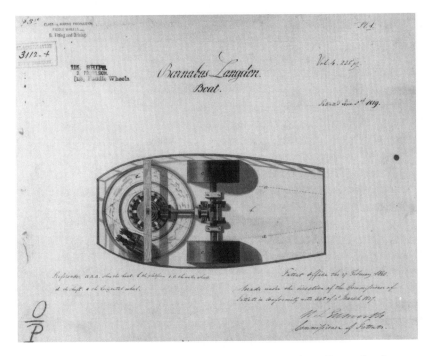

Figure 16. Barnabas Langdon's horizontal-treadwheel horseboat. Patent drawing number 3112-x. National Archives.

1817, two years before the unveiling of the horizontal-treadwheel horse-boat, Langdon patented his "Machine for propelling Carriages &c by Steam, Air or Nitre."[31] This was a three-wheeled, steam-powered tractor fitted with two pistons and steered by a chain-and-crank arrangement; by later standards the device may have seemed crudely designed, but for 1817 it was an advanced concept in steam-powered vehicles.

The steam tractor was impressive, but the horizontal-treadwheel boat was to be Barnabas Langdon's greatest contribution to North American transportation. In 1819, the same year that Langdon patented his invention, he completed a prototype horizontal-treadwheel boat for John G. Vanderhayden, owner of the upper Hudson River crossing at Troy, New York. The *Troy Northern Budget* commented on 1 June:

> The horse boat invented by Mr. Langdon, has now been in operation at Mr. Van Derhayden's Ferry in this city during the last week. The experiment has dissipated all fears of the timorous and confirmed the higher hopes of the inventor and Mr. J. G. Van Derhayden, by whose liberal encouragement and patronage the work progressed to completion. The trial now made of this inven-

tion is an unfavorable though successful one. The machinery is built upon a common scow and by its construction the inventor has been prevented from showing the power and applicability of the machinery to the purposes of propelling a boat in that high degree of perfection it is capable of. But even with a disadvantageously constructed boat and all the little faults always attending the first essays, the boat crosses the river, which is less than a quarter of a mile [400 m] wide at this place, in four minutes and often much less. It is propelled by two horses. Those who have seen this boat in operation have no doubt but it is a highly important invention, and in all places where the distance does not exceed a mile [1.6 km] it will answer a useful purpose. The machinery is not complicated or costly. It is confidently expected that for the purposes of dispatch, and on the grounds of economy, this boat will be in higher repute and general use, throughout the United States.[32]

With this machine and this boat Barnabas Langdon achieved a technological breakthrough: He created a practical, mechanically reliable, and relatively inexpensive horse-propulsion mechanism that could be fitted on a small, single-hulled boat. The cumbersome and expensive twin-hulled ferries were now obsolescent, and their numbers would swiftly dwindle after 1820 as existing catamarans wore out and were retired. North American horseboating had entered its horizontal-treadwheel phase, an era when almost any ferry owner with a modestly profitable ferrying concession could afford to buy and run a teamboat.

The significance of Langdon's boat was not lost upon Yale professor Benjamin Silliman, who crossed the Hudson at Troy during the ferry's first year of operation. In his book, *Remarks made on a Short Tour Between Hartford and Quebec in the Autumn of 1819,* Silliman penned a succinct and informative description of the craft and its novel treadwheel mechanism:

SINGULAR HORSE FERRY-BOAT

The ferry-boat is of a most singular construction. A platform covers a wide flat boat. Underneath the platform, there is a large horizontal solid wheel, which extends to the sides of the boat; and there the platform, or deck, is cut through, and removed, so as to afford sufficient room for two horses to stand on the flat surface of the wheel, one horse on each side, and parallel to the gunwale of the boat. The horses are harnessed, in the usual manner for teams—the whiffle trees being attached to stout iron bars, fixed horizontally, at a proper height, in the posts, which are part of the permanent structure of the boat. The horses look in opposite directions, one to the bow, the other to the stern; their feet take hold of channels, or grooves, cut in the wheels, in the direction of radii; they press forward, and, although they advance not, any more than a squirrel, in a revolving cage, or than a spit dog at his work, their feet cause the horizontal wheel to revolve, in a direction opposite to that of their own apparent motion;

this, by a connection of cogs, moves two vertical wheels, one on each wing of the boat, and these, being constructed like the paddle wheels of steamboats, produce the same effect, and propel the boat forward. The horses are covered by a roof, furnished with curtains, to protect them in bad weather; and they do not appear to labour harder than common draft horses, with a heavy load.

The inventor of this boat, is Mr. LANGDON, of Whitehall, and it claims the important advantages of simplicity, cheapness, and effect. At first view, the labour appears like a hardship upon the horses, but probably this is an illusion, as it seems very immaterial to their comfort, whether they advance with their load, or cause the basis, on which they labour, to recede.[33]

Shortly after he finished and successfully tested his first ferry for Vanderhayden, Langdon was asked to build a boat for Troy's other ferry crossing (the lower crossing); he apparently had this vessel in service by the following year.[34] As word of the new invention spread around the continent, inquiries and orders for new ferryboats began to reach Langdon. The press of business might have been too much for Barnabas had he not joined forces with his mechanically minded son John C. Langdon, who was twenty years old in 1819; at least one other son was involved in their enterprise, but his contributions seem to have been minimal. Together Barnabas and John set about founding a business that sold patent rights for the invention, manufactured and marketed the machinery, and installed treadwheels on ferries throughout the United States and Canada.

In late 1819 or early 1820 the Langdon family moved from Whitehall to Troy to set up their horse-machine factory. Their reasons for selecting Troy were obvious: The city was fast becoming one of North America's leading industrial centers. Its location was ideal, for it lay at the head of sloop and steamer navigation on the Hudson River and would soon be adjacent to the terminus of two of the most successful canals in the United States, the Champlain canal (which opened in 1823) and the famed Erie canal (which opened in 1825). By the early 1820s Troy had become a mecca for wealthy industrialists, small investors, mechanics, and inventive geniuses like the Langdons. New manufactories were built on the banks of the river and alongside mill streams within the town, including blast furnaces for smelting iron, rolling and slitting works for the production of bolts and nails, cotton mills, bleaching mills, tanneries, stoneware and earthenware ceramic factories, soap and candle factories, millstone cutters, a shipyard, and other industries.[35]

Barnabas and John entered into a business association with one of the city's more prominent companies, Starbuck and Gurley's Troy Air Furnace. This firm got its start in 1820 when the brothers Charles and Nathan Starbuck, owners of the patent rights to a superior new type of cast-iron plow, joined in partnership with Ephraim Gurley, part owner of the Troy Air Furnace. At the time the Langdons became associated with the foundry, it was successfully making and selling plows, kettles, stoves, and other iron hardware; its potential as a source for the iron castings necessary to manufacture horse machinery was obvious.[36] The Langdons established their business, Langdon's Machine Shop, adjacent to Starbuck and Gurley's furnace, and it was here that they machined, filed, and assembled the cast-iron gears, wrought-iron drive shafts and axles, coupling boxes, bearings, and other parts that went into each Langdon treadwheel ferry.[37]

The 1820s proved to be a busy, productive, and seemingly profitable decade for Barnabas and John, although the full extent of their business activities and wealth can only be inferred from a sprinkling of primary documents and observations by people outside their company. In the 1824 second edition of his *Tour Between Hartford and Quebec*, Benjamin Silliman remarked that Langdon's boats: "have now become common, and are worked by four horses where the boat is large." Horatio Gates Spafford's *Gazetteer of the State of New York*, published during the same year, was more specific about the number of ferries built under the Langdon patent:

> There are two ferries at Troy, employing Langdon's improved Team Boats, which ought to be more extensively known. The construction is simple and ingenious, and the Inventor, and Sons, have a manufactory in this City, for making these and other machinery. Thirty of his boats are now in successful operation.[38]

If Spafford is correct, Barnabas and John produced five to six horseboats a year between 1819 and 1824, a respectable number, especially if they were traveling around the country to install the machinery on many of these boats. How much money they made from the sale of machinery is not known, but we can get some idea of their profits from the sale of patent rights. A deed granting "exclusive right and liberty of making, constructing, and using" the horizontal treadwheel, dated March 1820, shows that the Langdons received $350 for the sale of rights to just one ferry crossing.[39] This figure, multiplied by thirty boats, would have totaled $10,500 by 1824, a considerable sum of money in early nineteenth-century America. The Langdons may not have realized this much from patent sales, however, for it is likely that some of Spafford's "thirty boats" represented two or more boats working the same crossing, and these presumably would have been covered under a single $350 patent grant.

What do we know about the thirty boats the Langdons had in operation by 1824? Not much at all. Sparse records permit few teamboats built after 1819 to be positively identified as Langdon-patent boats using Langdon-built machinery. But because the majority of horseboats built between 1820 and 1840 were fitted with a horizontal treadwheel, and the Langdons apparently made some efforts to protect their lucrative patent rights, it is likely that most horse-propelled ferries (but certainly not all of them) were using equipment purchased from the Troy machine shop.

One example of an early Langdon contract shows that in May 1821 John Langdon agreed to supply a Canadian named Francis Denault with machinery for a ferry at La Prairie, Quebec. In the contract Langdon promised to prepare a plan of the boat and machinery, to assemble the treadwheel mechanism and supervise its installation, and "to forward the work as fast as lays in his power." Work would begin, it was noted, only after Langdon completed another horseboat that he was building for Mr. Horace Dickinson at Montreal. In return for these services, Denault promised to pay twenty-five dollars for the ferry plans, to pay Langdon three dollars per day and board him while he was actually engaged in the work, and to cover half of his traveling expenses between Troy and La Prairie. No mention is made in the contract of how much Denault was paying for the machinery. Denault, incidentally, may not have been a reliable businessman, since the builder of Denault's earlier teamboat *Edmond* filed a complaint against him in 1819 for nonpayment of wages and expenses.[40]

The Langdons did not put all of their eggs in the horseboat basket, for in 1825 they began to fabricate steam machinery in their shop. In that year they built at least three engines, the first, of ten horsepower, for the Lake Champlain steamboat *General Greene,* and the other two for vessels on the Upper Great Lakes.[41] More engines followed, including one for the Troy ferry in 1826 and one for the Hudson River steamboat *Star* in 1827.[42] The Langdons' manufactory expanded both in its size and in the diversity of its products. Advertisements in the *Troy Sentinel* indicate just how large their enterprise had grown by the end of the decade. The firm offered to build low-pressure engines of any number of horsepower, small high-pressure engines suitable for breweries, tanneries, ropeworks, and sawmills, and boilers for all purposes. Other products included gears for mills and factories, paper mill and oil mill screws, swedging machines for shaping stovepipes, and, of course, "*MACHINERY* for . . . improved Team Ferry Boats."[43]

The newspaper announcements emphasized the shop's convenient location and the flexibility of the owners in responding to all types of orders:

Turning of all kinds, and boreing Cylinders and Pumps of all descriptions—and any other Machinery that may be ordered.

His [John C. Langdon's] Factory stands adjoining Messrs. Starbuck & Gurley's Troy Air Furnace, and within a few rods of Julius Hank's Brass and Bell Foundry; both establishments being well supplied with an extensive assortment of patterns for most kinds of machinery, renders it convenient for procuring any kind of Castings that may be wanted. Applications for Machinery, or for information on any of the above subjects, will meet with prompt and cheerful attention.

Several trends in the Langdons' operations are evident by the late 1820s. All advertisements and references to the business state that it was owned and run by John C. Langdon; for whatever reasons Barnabas was no longer as active in its management as he had been during the earlier years. It is also clear that John's interests now lay primarily in building and installing steam machinery, which is not surprising, since this area of manufacturing was likely more lucrative than horse machinery. One gets the impression that the production of horizontal treadwheel teamboats was by this time more of a sideline than the primary business of the shop. In 1830 the Langdon family seems to have been prospering, for according to that year's *Troy Directory* the "Steam Engine Factory and Machine Shop" employed fifteen men and had an annual disbursement of about fifteen thousand dollars.[44]

Despite its success in the 1820s, the Langdons' enterprise was not destined to last through the next decade: By 1833, for reasons now unknown, the business became financially overextended and unable to meet its debts. An advertisement in the 11 January edition of the *Troy Budget* tells the sad story: John Langdon had made "honorable surrender"of his property to Isaac B. Hart, Ebenezer Prescott, and Joseph H. Shepard, "for the benefit of all his creditors," and everything would be sold at public auction on 15 February. A note at the bottom stated that the company's account books had been turned over to Ebenezer Prescott and requested that all creditors submit their claims without delay.[45]

The auction announcement described the machine shop as a one-and-one-half-story brick building, 29.5 meters (97 ft.) in length by 4.4 meters (14½ ft.) wide, "with good substantial plank floors." The shop contained a variety of equipment, including a four-horsepower steam-engine power plant, lathes and boring machines with all of their tools, drills, anvils and mandrils, swedging machines, and hand tools for every type of metalworking operation. Patterns for shaping engines of all sizes were listed, along with a completed six horsepower engine. Real estate included the lot containing the shop and two adjacent lots. The entire inventory was immense, representing thirteen years of dedication and labor; the loss of the shop and its tools was plainly a terrible blow to John Langdon and his father, and one from which they would never financially recover.

The status of the treadwheel patent at this time is somewhat uncertain. Before 1861 the U.S. government issued fourteen-year patents, with the possibility of a renewal for an additional seven years. Langdon's original patent expired in 1833, at which time income from patent grants would have dried up. The drawings of the Langdon treadwheel patents in the National Archives have the dates 1840 or 1841 written upon them, however, suggesting that Barnabas secured the first seven-year renewal, and he may have applied for a second renewal to cover his patent well into the 1840s. Treadwheel boats began to go out of use by the 1840s, and it is unlikely that Langdon bothered to retain the patent into the 1850s.

Barnabas remained an active inventor in his later years but seemingly met with little success in his endeavors. On 19 July 1837, he was granted a patent for "an improvement in the mode of applying horse or other animal power, to propelling machinery." This was a variant of the whim mechanism that had four horses circle a capstanlike machine. The device got a cold reception from Langdon's fellow inventors. The *Journal of the Franklin Institute of the State of Pennsylvania and American Mechanics' Register* thought Langdon's horse whim was outmoded by the new treadmill horsepowers and prefaced a description of the machine with this mocking observation:

> We have not here a perpetual motion, or anything which actually sins against the laws of mechanics; still we are very apprehensive, that the patentee, who manifestly believes that he has devised an advantageous mode of communicating the motive power of animals to machinery, will eventually discover that he has been treading in a circuitous path, whilst he might, at less expense of time and labour, have gone directly up to his object by one of the more common and direct roads.[46]

Langdon also patented a shingle-cutting machine and a board planing machine in 1838, but like the horse whim, they were apparently not great successes.[47] Barnabas and John seem to gradually fade into obscurity over the course of the next decade. Both are simply listed as "machinists" in the Troy directory, and census data suggest that neither man was wealthy later in life (Barnabas and his wife were living with grandchildren in 1850, and the value of John's personal estate in 1860 was only one thousand dollars).[48]

Although their names are not mentioned in history textbooks, Barnabas and John C. Langdon nevertheless made an enormous contribution to North American transportation in the nineteenth century. They singlehandedly created, manufactured, and marketed a machine that made it possible for ferrying operations large and small to purchase paddle-powered ferries. The decade of greatest activity for the Langdons, the 1820s, was a crucial time for horseboating, for it was during these years that the use of animal-propelled ferries spread far and wide across the North American continent.

VIGNETTES OF THE HORIZONTAL-TREADWHEEL HORSEBOAT

The popularity of the treadwheel design is readily apparent in the decades following Barnabas Langdon's successful trial at Troy in 1819. Accounts of these boats are common in the 1820s and 1830s and continue into the 1840s and 1850s. Journals and narratives of foreign travelers are a particularly good source of information on treadwheel boats, as most Europeans had never seen a horseboat before they journeyed to North America. Like Yale professor Benjamin Silliman, they were intrigued by the engineless sidewheel ferry with a huge wheel spinning underneath the deck, rumbling cast-iron gears, and two or more horses straining at their harnesses but going nowhere.

Englishman Andrew Bell's impressions of the treadwheel ferry he rode at Troy, New York, during his 1835–36 tour of North America stand as a good example of this sort of reference. "The mode of ferrying across the Hudson," Bell wrote, "was a kind of novelty to me." Like most people confronted with a new invention, Bell explained what he saw by comparing it to a device he was familiar with, in this case the human-powered treadmill then used to punish convicts in British prisons:

> At both sides of an immense raft, solid and broad enough to accommodate half a dozen loaded waggons, is placed a horse, each with his head turned diverse ways; they are enclosed in a kind of shed, open at the sides from about mid-height, and when the ferryman gave the word they both commenced walking, but without advancing a single inch, and continued to do so till we had got quite across the river. Every forward movement they made was immediately lost by the retrograde motion of a kind of wheel they were placed on, which all the while kept turning briskly round. Here, then, were two innocent and docile animals put to the treadmill![49]

The American tour of another Englishman, James Stuart, included a trip across the Hudson River in a horseboat in 1828. Stuart, too, felt compelled to describe the appearance and operation of the treadwheel machinery to his readers. He noted:

> The horse-ferry-boat over the river is, I believe, peculiar to America—certainly an American invention—and extremely convenient in situations where the intercourse across a river is considerable, yet not so great as to authorize the expenditure required for a steam-boat.[50]

Two illustrations of treadwheel ferries from the 1820–40 period show what were likely the standard features of two-horse and a six-horse boats. The two-horse treadwheel boat appears in a view of the Connecticut River waterfront of Hartford, Connecticut, in 1841. This ferry was relatively small, with a scow-type hull, paddle boxes for the sidewheels located slightly forward of amidships, and a railing around the deck to keep passengers, livestock, and other deck cargo from falling overboard. Like all horizontal-treadwheel craft for which we have illustrations or detailed descriptions, the wheel was located

Figure 17. A two-horse horizontal-treadwheel ferry on the Connecticut River at Hartford, Connecticut, circa 1840. Courtesy of the Connecticut Historical Society, Hartford, Connecticut.

directly abaft of the paddle wheels. The walkways cut into the deck for the horses each have a simple framework raised around them, with some type of covering overhead to protect the horses from sun and rain.[51]

The second illustration contains the deck plan, interior profile, and section view of a six-horse ferry intended for the Delaware River crossing between Camden, New Jersey, and Philadelphia, Pennsylvania. The plans were prepared by Philadelphia engineer J. C. Trautwine in 1828; it is not clear if he copied existing drawings by the Langdons or some other designer, or if the boat is Trautwine's own concept of a horizontal treadwheel boat. In any event, these are the most detailed contemporary treadwheel ferry plans yet located.[52]

The vessel depicted on the Trautwine plans had a fairly boxy midship with very slight frame deadrise, a hard bilge, and vertical sides. The deck plan shows the locations of the sidewheels and the treadwheel, as well as the semicircular cut-outs in the deck that allowed the horses to stand upon the wheel. Small access hatches in the deck permitted maintenance and lubrication of the drive shaft and gears. Three horses stood on each side of this treadwheel; four large friction wheels were placed beneath the treadwheel to prevent it

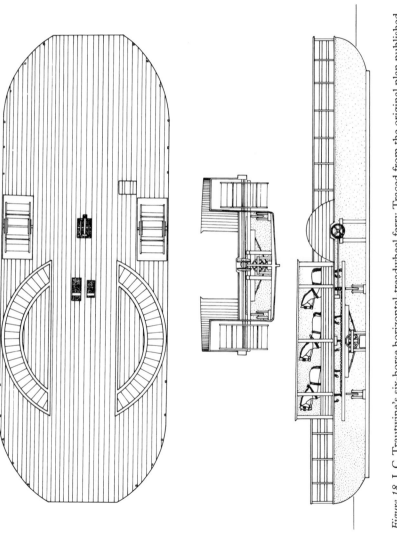

Figure 18. J. C. Trautwine's six-horse horizontal-treadwheel ferry. Traced from the original plan published in Boyer, *Annals of Camden.*

from sagging or collapsing under the weight of the horses. Unlike the horse sheds on the Hartford ferry with their open sides, the sheds on the Trautwine plan were enclosed by planks.

Treadwheel boats saw considerable use on the two bodies of water nearest the Langdons' shop at Troy, the Hudson River and Lake Champlain. The histories of these boats will be examined in the next two chapters. Accounts of ferrying operations in New England between 1820 and 1850 further illustrate the widespread use of treadwheel ferries in the northeastern states. Maine, for example, had a horseboat crossing the Kennebec River between Bath and Woolwich from 1830 until about 1837, and another was in service on the Sheepscot River between Wiscasset and Edgecomb between 1832 and 1847.[53]

At least three major crossings in the Narragansett Bay region of Rhode Island and Massachusetts employed treadwheel horseboats during this era. In Rhode Island, the Portsmouth–Bristol ferry began offering horse-powered crossings in June 1826. The new boat cost its owners eighteen hundred dollars, but it was not especially lucrative. It was reportedly difficult to operate in heavy weather and sank at its wharf in February 1830; although subsequently it was recovered, the craft had an estimated value of only four hundred dollars. A new horseboat was built for the crossing around 1840, but it failed to compete with steamboats and had to be retired in 1845. Treadwheel boats also served the Jamestown–Newport ferry in Rhode Island and Slade's Ferry at Fall River, Massachusetts.[54]

Several crossings on the lower Connecticut River utilized horseboats, including the Rocky Hill–South Glastonbury ferry in Connecticut and the Agawam ferry in Springfield, Massachusetts.[55] The horseboat at Hartford, Connecticut, illustrated in Figure 17, had a brief but tumultuous history, for it was launched in 1836 to compete with a toll bridge. The bridge's owners, the Hartford Bridge Company, had convinced the state legislature to outlaw the city's existing ferry in 1818. The people of East Hartford came to resent the company's monopoly and high tolls, and in 1836 they persuaded the legislature to reverse its decision. The new treadwheel ferry was heavily patronized by a bridge-despising public and generated a storm of political and legal controversy. The bridge company first tried to settle with the town, but their offer to charge East Hartford residents one-half of the standard toll was rejected; then the company convinced the legislature to shut down the ferry in 1841, but that august body changed its mind once again the following year and permitted the horseboat to return to work. State courts finally settled the matter by ruling that the ferry violated the legislature's 1818 contract with the bridge owners. East Hartford's appeal to a higher court was rejected, the ferry was abolished in 1844, and the town was forced to pay the bridge company $12,363.36 for tolls lost to the ferry.[56]

A treadwheel ferry called *Ho Boy* or *Haut Boy* was built around 1829 for use at the Georgeville–Knowlton's Landing crossing on Lake Memphremagog in southern Quebec. This boat was considered a "vast improvement" over the scow that it replaced, and it enjoyed two decades of service. By the 1840s, however, old age began to tell; on 21 October 1843 the ferry began taking on water while crossing the lake during a storm, although the crew managed to bring the ferry in close to shore before it sank. The *Ho Boy* was recovered and put back to work, but the salvaging soon became an annual event:

> After many years' service the hull became decayed and every winter its tired frame used to rest on the bottom of the lake. In the spring a "bee" would be gathered armed with long-handled buckets and the submerged hulk would before night be bailed out, the leaks stopped, and after a thorough oiling the boat was ready for service again. But alas! whiskey would stand in pailfuls all day, free to those who chose to drink, and when the vessel was empty the men were full.[57]

The *Ho Boy* sank for the final time at the Georgetown pier in 1849; the iron-work was removed and the hull was subsequently broken up for firewood.

Treadwheel horseboats also saw extensive use around the Great Lakes. The *Olive Branch,* built at Cleveland, Ohio, entered into service on the Detroit River between Michigan and Canada in August 1825. It was a scow-hulled craft measuring 15.2 meters (50 ft.) in length and 9.8 meters (32 ft.) in breadth. A steam ferry called *Argo* began work at this crossing in 1830, but there was enough business to keep the *Olive Branch* busy, for the horseboat was still on the job in 1831.[58]

The Niagara River, connecting Lakes Erie and Ontario, had two ferry crossings that employed horizontal-treadwheel boats from the late 1820s to the 1840s. The first of these, upriver of Niagara Falls, plied between Black Rock, New York, and Fort Erie, Upper Canada (now the province of Ontario). Service at this crossing began in the 1790s, and for more than three decades relied upon scows that were rowed across the river. When the American ferry charter was due for renewal in 1827, the state of New York insisted that current owners L. Brace and Donald Fraser provide a steam- or horse-powered boat. Brace journeyed to Albany to learn about the latest developments in horse machinery and brought back with him (via the Erie canal) horizontal-treadwheel machinery for a four-horse boat. This machinery was almost certainly purchased from the Langdons. The horseboat built by Brace and Fraser, the *Cossack,* apparently entered service before the end of 1827. At least one other horseboat, belonging to the lessees of the Canadian ferry, operated here in the 1830s.[59]

Tyrone Power Esq. crossed the upper Niagara River on one of these horse-boats in 1833, and like other Englishmen he could not resist the temptation to compare the horses working on this boat with convicts undergoing punishment on the treadmill: "Whether the horses working this were on good behaviour, or not, I could not rightly ascertain, but certainly they were scampish-looking steeds, their physiognomical expression was low and dogged, such as one might expect from the degrading nature of their unvarying task."[60]

Horseboats were slower to make their appearance at the lower Niagara River crossing between Lewiston, New York, and Queenston, Upper Canada. Like the upriver crossing, this spot was served for many years by rowed scows, but when the lease for the Canadian ferry became available in 1829, the province's executive council specified that only bids for horse-powered boats would be accepted. A scow propelled by a two-horse horizontal treadwheel was paddling over and back by 1831. The American ferry concession at Lewiston presumably had one or more teamboats working at this time, but little is known about its operations. A steam ferry named *Oddfellow* replaced the horseboats in 1848.[61]

At least two other horseboats that navigated the margins of the Great Lakes are known from historical records. A horseboat fitted with what was probably a locally made horizontal treadwheel worked on the Sandusky River and Bay in Ohio in the early 1820s. This boat had an unusual hull form reminiscent of the whim-powered catamaran ferries. It consisted of two large pirogues or canoes connected by a platform; the treadwheel sat atop the platform, and cog teeth fitted around the rim of the wheel meshed with cog wheels attached to the axle of the sidewheels. This arrangement may have been similar to the treadwheels shown on the J. B. Robinson and Isaacs–Wilbanks patent drawings (Figure 13). The Sandusky teamboat was clearly a no-frills work vessel, with no covering over the horses and limited cargo capacity in the pirogues. Despite the lack of amenities, the boat was described as "quite useful" and reportedly carried goods up and down the river for several years until it was replaced by a schooner in 1825 or 1826.[62]

In 1844 the Privatt brothers of Toronto, Upper Canada, purchased a two-horse treadwheel boat, 18.3 meters (60 ft.) in length and 7 meters (23 ft.) in breadth, which had been working on the lower Niagara River. Renamed *Peninsular Packet*, the boat became an excursion ferry between the city's waterfront and a small island on the far side of Toronto harbor. The boat's treadwheel must have been worn out, because after two years the owners removed it and installed a horse-whim mechanism. Their willingness to reduce deck space by adding a circular horse walkway indicates that the ferry's chief source of revenue was passengers rather than wagons or livestock. The *Peninsular Packet* remained in service until 1850.[63]

A two-horse, horizontal-treadwheel boat named *Wheeling* operated at Daniel Zane's ferry on the upper Ohio River at Wheeling, West Virginia. In

May 1823 traveler Stephen H. Long took passage on a journey to the west and was favorably impressed by the machinery, noting in his journal that the teamboat "is of a remarkably cheap and convenient construction."[64] In the spring of 1832 a horse ferry at this location, presumably the *Wheeling,* saved Zane and his family from a terrible flood that ravaged the Ohio Valley, an incident that is one of the most dramatic episodes to be recorded in the annals of horseboating.

Daniel Zane lived on an island directly opposite Wheeling, not far from the ferry landing on the Ohio side of the river. On the night of the great flood, the Ohio River's waters quickly rose and covered the island to a depth of 3 meters (10 ft.), trapping the Zanes in their brick house and forcing them to seek refuge on the second story. Logs, trees, and other floating debris began to pound against the north side of the house, bulging the wall and threatening to collapse the entire structure. Had this happened the family would likely have perished, but luckily a large tree lodged across the house and protected the weakened wall from further battering. The house stood through the night.

Zane's two-horse boat, tied to a large walnut tree a short distance below his house, also miraculously survived the night, and at daybreak the ferry's crew, Walker Hunter and John Watkins, resolved to rescue the family from its precarious situation. They managed to maneuver the vessel up against the front of the house, and the Zanes scrambled out a second-story window onto the deck of the ferry. With everyone successfully extricated from the house, the next challenge was to cross the swollen river to the safety of Wheeling:

> The crossing of the angry waters to the town was full of danger as the river was full of heavy driftwood, and the fear that something about the boat might break and usher them all to a watery grave made it an extremely perilous undertaking. It required strong arms and brave hearts to accomplish the passage. A landing was effected in Monroe (now Twelfth) street, midway between Main and Market streets, near a livery stable kept by a person by the name of Fogle. As they landed, the faithful horses, overcome by exhaustion, fell dead in their tracks.[65]

Treadwheel horseboats also appeared on western rivers beyond the Great Lakes and the Ohio River, along what was then the western frontier of the United States. As we noted in the previous chapter, Samuel Wiggins's ferry fleet at St. Louis was equipped with at least one new two-horse craft in 1824. The lower–Missouri River ferry at St. Charles, just north of St. Louis, was equipped with a six-horse treadwheel boat in 1834.[66]

By the 1840s the horizontal treadwheel was being rendered obsolescent by the new horse treadmill, but the turntable departed from the scene only gradually. Several treadwheel boats are known to have operated into the

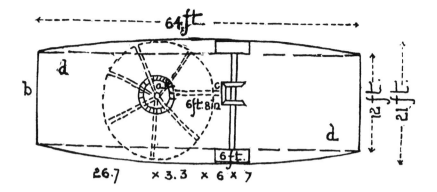

Figure 19. A plan of the two-horse treadwheel ferry at Hallowell, Maine, circa 1850. From Briggs, *History of Shipbuilding.*

1850s, including two at Troy, New York, one at Athens, New York, on the Hudson River, and one at Hallowell, Maine, on the Kennebec River. The existence of the two-horse Hallowell ferry is known from correspondence relating to the proposed construction of a treadwheel horseboat in Massachusetts in 1850. In that year several citizens of modest means who lived along the North River in Plymouth County, Massachusetts, banded together to build a towboat that could haul "sea manure" from the mouth of the river and also serve as a freight carrier between river landings. One of the subscribers to this venture wrote to a friend in Maine, who provided both a detailed description and an unscaled sketch of the horseboat at Hallowell.

According to the Maine correspondent, the Hallowell boat was a scow-hulled craft measuring 19.5 meters (64 ft.) in length and 3.7 meters (12 ft.) in beam, with a deck that extended out from the hull to a maximum breadth of 6.4 meters (21 ft.). A two-horse turntable geared to a pair of 1.8-meter-(6 ft.) diameter sidewheels provided the motive power. The advantages of the gear shift on Langdon-style treadwheel machinery impressed the writer, who noted that "by means of a lever . . . the man readily changes the coupling and backs or goes ahead without stopping the horses"; the ferry was guided by a long steering oar that could be easily unshipped and used at the other end, "for the boat goes as well one way as another." This boat's operator must have been kind to its equine crew, for one of the ferry's two horses was a sea-soned riverboater with ten years of service on the treadwheel. The corre-spondent pointed out the advantages of this mode of propulsion over steam-boats: "You see by the construction you get 64 × 12 clear deck which will hold a great deal—and no danger of a blow up or a melancholy disaster."

The North River group in Massachusetts were favorably impressed by the machinery, as well as by the estimate that the whole cost of building and outfitting would be about $250. This sum was to be raised by the sale of twenty-five shares at $10 each, and by June 1850 twenty and one-half shares in the venture had actually been sold. Further evidence of this boat's existence has not been located, suggesting that the North River horse towboat was never finished.[67]

And so the horizontal-treadwheel boat slowly disappeared from interior waterways, retired by rot, outmoded by other types of horse machinery and by smaller and less-expensive steam engines. For a span of twenty years, however, from 1820 to 1840, this mechanism was the prime mover for most of North America's horseboats; the treadwheel's period of use extended across nearly four decades. In their own humble way, treadwheel horseboats contributed to the nineteenth century's transportation revolution, shrinking the time and effort required to cross inland waters.

6

Hoofbeats across the Hudson

Of all the rivers and lakes in North America, New York's Hudson River had one of the strongest and longest associations with horseboats. As we have seen, the era of the horse-powered ferry began on the waters of the lower Hudson at New York City in 1814; here the earliest catamaran ferries were tested and improved, and their designs and machinery were exported to waterways throughout the eastern half of the continent. Five years after the debut of equine propulsion at New York City, the prototype of the economical, efficient, horizontal-treadwheel ferry first churned its way over the river at Troy. Thanks to the Langdons and their machine shop, Troy would take up where New York City left off, exporting treadwheel machinery to the rest of the United States and Canada.

Ferry owners along the Hudson River greatly benefited from their proximity to the inventors and machine shops that produced horse machinery. From 1814 until the early 1860s, the Hudson's 241 kilometers (150 mi.) of navigable water floated an assortment of horseboats that kept trade and travelers moving briskly between the river's eastern and western banks. The organizations that ran these boats differed greatly in their composition: Some were joint-stock ventures organized and financed by wealthy investors, some consisted of one or two boatmen with limited capital who depended upon ferrying to provide a living for themselves and their families, and other operations were managed as a public service by town or city governments. The monetary returns from Hudson ferry operations were equally diverse; some horseboats seem to have been quite profitable, but others proved to be an expensive headache for their owners.

The history of horse ferries on the Hudson River has two recognizable stages that loosely correspond to the evolution of the horse machine. We have already looked at the first stage, which began on the river in 1814: the era of the whim-powered catamaran ferries operating at the river's busier and more lucrative ferry crossings. These boats saw their greatest use on the lower end of the Hudson at New York City from 1814 until the mid-1820s, and at Newburgh, which was served by the *Moses Rogers* and *Caravan* until the introduction of steam ferries in 1828.[1] The crossings that were profitable enough to justify the purchase of the earliest horseboats usually had enough business to support steam ferries just a few years later. The upper-Hudson ferries at Albany and Athens were an exception, for both had horseboats by 1817, but they continued to use horse power for several decades.

The lesser crossings of the Hudson, especially those located on the upper reaches of the river, could not afford to make the switch from sail or sweep-propelled ferries to horseboats until Barnabas Langdon introduced his economical treadwheel. Once the change in motive power was made, many of the ferries employing horseboats would continue to use them until the 1850s. This chapter will examine the post-1819 years of the river's horseboat era and some of the ferries that operated on the Hudson, starting at the uppermost teamboat crossing (and the first to use treadwheel machinery), John G. Vanderhayden's ferry at Troy.

THE TROY FERRIES

The city of Troy got its start in the late 1780s, when the land around Jacob Vanderhayden's ferry landing on the eastern bank of the Hudson River was divided into streets and businesses and dwellings began to be built.[2] The advantageous location of this site, a few kilometers north of Albany and slightly below the confluence of the Mohawk and Hudson Rivers, promised great things for Troy, and by the second decade of the nineteenth century the city was well on its way to becoming a major industrial center. The ferries that had been operating at this location since the colonial era were simple scows or bateaux, propelled across the river by boatmen equipped with iron-tipped poles. The first crossing, Vanderhayden's ferry, later became known as the "upper ferry" when a second or lower ferry was inaugurated in 1798. A less labor-intensive means of crossing was introduced in the early nineteenth century when current-propelled scows traversed the river on cables stretched between the banks.[3]

The introduction of Barnabas Langdon's revolutionary new horseboat at the upper ferry in 1819 inspired praise from all quarters and placed Troy on

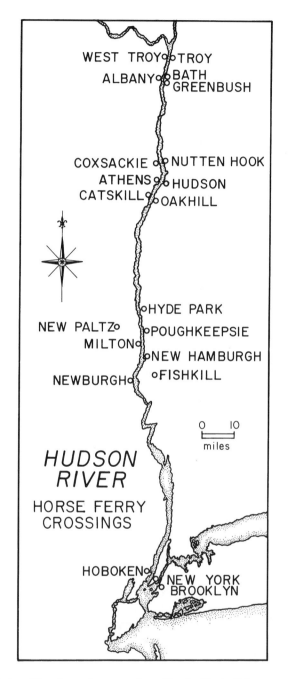

WEST TROY TROY
ALBANY BATH
GREENBUSH

COXSACKIE NUTTEN HOOK
ATHENS HUDSON
CATSKILL OAKHILL

HYDE PARK
NEW PALTZ
MILTON POUGHKEEPSIE

NEW HAMBURGH
NEWBURGH FISHKILL

0   10
miles

*HUDSON
RIVER*

HORSE FERRY
CROSSINGS

HOBOKEN
NEW YORK
BROOKLYN

Figure 20. Hudson River horse ferry crossings. Map by Kevin Crisman.

the cutting edge of transportation developments. The building of a second treadwheel boat for use at the lower ferry sometime around 1820 completed Troy's conversion to this mode of ferrying. Like most ferries, the teamboats at Troy led busy but unremarkable careers. Vanderhayden family business papers have not been found, however, so we can get glimpses of these boats only through other records.[4]

Troy's horseboats figure prominently in several landmark events in the city's history. One of these events occurred on 8 October 1823, when the canal boat *Trojan Trader* prepared to take on the first load of Hudson River merchandise to be shipped westward on the Erie Canal. The canal channel had yet to be excavated as far as the river, and thus it was necessary to transport the *Trader*'s cargo by wagon from the city's waterfront to a completed section of the canal. Vanderhayden, entering into the spirit of the occasion, volunteered the services of both of his boats in transporting the wagons to the opposite bank. By two o'clock that afternoon the *Trojan Trader*, laden to capacity, set off westward "amid the cheers of assembled Trojans."[5]

A Troy horseboat also had the honor of carrying the Revolutionary War hero, the marquis de Lafayette, over the Hudson during the general's triumphant tour of the United States in 1824. On the day of Lafayette's visit to Troy, the ferries spent a busy morning carrying an honor guard of five Albany militia companies over the Hudson. Lafayette himself arrived at the city in a canal packet towed by eight small boats, whereupon he underwent the usual ceremonies that nineteenth-century Americans inflicted upon their heroes: a parade, long speeches, a banquet, and the singing of a song composed in his honor by the headmistress of the local ladies' seminary. At the end of this day, the *Troy Sentinel* tells us, "when he embarked on board the ferry-boat to re-cross the river, his departure was cheered by the presence and the shout of the whole multitude, and by the presence of a long array of our fair country-women, waving their hands and handkerchiefs."[6]

In 1826 John Vanderhayden decided to replace his upper ferry horseboat with a steam ferry and contracted with John C. Langdon & Company for a ten-horsepower engine to drive the vessel. Like the first horseboat at the crossing, the steam ferry had a boxy, scow-built hull; it measured 22.9 meters (75 ft.) in length and 5.5 meters (18 ft.) in width, and it drew only 60 centimeters (2 ft.) of water to enable navigation of the upper river's shallow waters.[7] The new steam ferry went into service in July 1826, but for reasons unknown—probably insufficient revenues—it was not a success and was replaced by another horseboat.

Horse propulsion was to continue at the Troy crossings for another quarter century. A description of the Hudson River valley, published anonymously in 1837, includes a brief and unflattering mention of the two ferries. After describing the elaborate bridge connecting Troy to Green Island in the middle of the river, the narrative went on to note: "A bridge is shortly to be thrown across the Hudson from Green Island to West Troy, and the miserable horse-boats which now convey travelers across the Hudson will eventually fall into disuse."[8] This prediction proved premature, for *Benjamin's New Map of the Hudson River,* published a decade later in 1848, said of West Troy: "This place is connected with the city of Troy by a bridge, and two ferries using horse power."[9]

Written accounts are not the sole source of information on Troy horse-boats, for they appear in at least three printed views of the city that date to the second quarter of the nineteenth century. Two of these prints, "Troy from Mount Ida" (1825), and "View of Troy, N.Y." (1848) show vessels that are clearly horseboats, but the renderings are so small that it is difficult to glean much in the way of details.[10] The third print, a view of the Troy waterfront from the western side of the river in 1845, is more informative.[11] Here, among the busy traffic of steamboats, sloops, and canal boats, a treadwheel horseboat is shown crossing the river. The boat has ramps at either end for loading and unloading its customers, and abaft of the paddle boxes can be seen a pair of plank-sided horse stalls.

All things must come to an end, and so it proved for the horseboats at Troy. In 1854 a decision by the New York Supreme Court annulled the ferry rights belonging to Vanderhayden's heirs and successors, and the operation of the ferries became a state franchise. Not long after this time the last of the horse-boats in service at this crossing, the upper ferry boat, ceased paddling across the river, ending a tradition that had lasted almost forty years. Ferry service was continued by four small, steam-powered passenger boats for several more decades.[12]

A TALE OF TWO FERRIES: THE ALBANY HORSEBOATS

Nine and a half kilometers (6 mi.) downriver of Troy, on the west bank of the Hudson River, lies the city of Albany, the capital of New York State and, since its founding as "Fort Orange" by the Dutch in 1624, the hub of commerce for the upper Hudson valley. Ferrying across the Hudson at this point began in the seventeenth century and continued throughout the eighteenth; the crossing was particularly important for farmers and manufacturers in Rensselaer County, New York, on the eastern bank of the river, as well as for the inhabitants of western Massachusetts and southern Vermont, many of whom looked to Albany as the market or shipping center for their products. Nineteenth-century travelers taking the inland route between New York City and the northern states of New England also depended upon the Albany ferries for getting to and from the steamer docks at Albany. The principal ferry crossing here was between the lower or southern end of Albany's water-

Figure 21. View of Troy, New York, from the west, 1845; detail of horizontal-tread-wheel horse ferry. Courtesy of the Rensselaer County Historical Society, Troy, New York.

front and the town of Greenbush on the eastern shore; a second, less heavily trafficked crossing was situated about 1.6 kilometers (1 mi.) upriver and connected Albany with the east-bank town of Bath.

Horseboating came to Albany in 1817 when boatbuilder Charles Kenyon and mechanic James Rodgers constructed a catamaran-style horseboat for the southern ferry crossing.[13] The vessel was called *Horse's Back* and was evidently capacious, for in 1824 it carried the marquis de Lafayette and his entourage (two four-horse wagons, fifty light horsemen of the escort, and one hundred foot passengers) across in one trip.[14] The operations of this ferry would be plagued by both bad management and bad luck. In 1818, for example, the ferry was caught in a spring flood and washed "about halfway up to Pearl Street."[15] In the 1820s the Greenbush ferry featured poor service, excessive fares, drunken captains, and nefarious business practices.

A new horseboat ferry service was begun in 1821 in response to Albany's vigorous growth, the increasing trade with the region to the east of the river, and the need for more efficient ferries on the upper river. As its name suggests, the "Albany and Bath Ferry Company" was begun to improve the

Hudson crossing between Albany's northern waterfront and Bath (now called Rensselaer). The company, which consisted of local businessmen, elected as its president one of the leading capitalists of the region, iron manufacturer and steamboat investor Isaiah Townsend.[16] The records of this business, meticulously kept by Townsend, are now housed in the New York State Archives at Albany.

The Albany–Bath company wasted no time getting down to business after its formation. During a meeting of the directors on 21 March, the committee to contract and superintend the building of the new boat reported entering into contracts for construction. To meet the costs of building, shareholders were called upon to contribute fifteen dollars for each share of stock they possessed (over and above the cash already paid for each share; unfortunately we do not know how much the original shares cost). Endorsements on the backs of existing stock certificates indicate that most of the fifteen-dollar payments were made within a few weeks of the call.[17]

The team boat company's documents reveal that two contracts were executed for the ferry. The hull was built that spring by the Albany shipbuilding firm of Hand & Kenyon for the sum of $800. This relatively modest price suggests that the ferry was a small, uncomplicated vessel, perhaps a scow. Hand & Kenyon had the boat completed by May, but it ran slightly over budget at $812.65, with additional charges of 62½¢ for a half-gallon of rum (no doubt served as a refreshment during the launching), $5 to build a hatch over the machinery, and $4 to fit four berths. The Albany–Bath company was displeased with some aspect of the construction, for at the bottom of Moses Kenyon's invoice is a notation written by a different hand, stating: "When the pump is put in pay $790."[18]

The manufacture and installation of the machinery for the ferry was handled under a separate contract with mechanic and inventor Henry Burden. One of nineteenth-century Troy's greatest success stories, Burden in 1821 was just embarking on a career in iron manufacturing that would, by mid-century, make him one of the wealthiest and most respected of New York's citizens. Born in rural Scotland in 1791, Henry Burden displayed as a young man a certain genius in working with machinery; in 1819, at the age of twenty-eight, he emigrated to the United States where conditions were favorable for the full employment of his talents. In 1821, at the time he entered into the contract with the Albany and Bath Ferry Company, he was residing in Albany and active in the improvement of agricultural machinery. During the next year he moved to Troy, where he managed Isaiah Townsend's Troy Iron and Nail Factory, a business that he would eventually own and transform into one of the state's largest iron founding operations. Burden was also a prolific inventor, patenting a horseshoe machine in 1835 (within a few years Troy was producing fifty million horseshoes annually) and a railroad spike-making machine. Some of his other inventions were not so successful: Burden's double-hulled "cigar boat" steamer of 1833 was an interesting concept reminiscent of the early catamaran horseboats, but it proved too slow to compete with more conventional steamship designs.[19]

Henry Burden's design for the Albany–Bath ferry's horse machinery has unfortunately never been found, although we know that he prepared detailed plans of the mechanism for potential customers. His correspondence with another ferry owner in 1821–22 suggests that the design employed a two-horse horizontal treadwheel similar to Langdon's; the fact that boats equipped with his machinery were single-hulled craft would tend to support the evidence that he was using a treadwheel. There is no record, however, that Burden was ever charged by the Langdons with patent infringement. The Albany and Bath Ferry Company agreed in 1821 to pay Burden $600 for building and installing the machinery on their new ferry, with $300 advanced in May and the balance to be paid in December. The installation may have been more difficult than anticipated or perhaps was carried out in a particularly exemplary fashion, for Burden was paid an additional $50 in June 1822, "for extra services in building the Horse Boat."[20]

Assorted invoices, receipts, and expense tallies in the Townsend papers detail the final preparations for the debut of the new ferry in 1821. Horses were purchased in April and May for a total of $345 (including $60, $70, and $90 for individual horses and $125 for a pair of horses). One horse was returned to its original owner for unspecified reasons, and the Albany–Bath company was refunded $35.50. A superintendent for the ferry, John Van Valkenburgh, was hired, and a landing on the Bath side of the river was rented from Stephen Van Rensselaer for the annual fee of $300.[21] The teamboat was running by 25 May, for on that date the *Albany Gazette* announced to the public that "A Good and substantial Horse Boat is now in operation at the Ferry between Bath and the City of Albany."[22]

Accounts for 1821 show what were probably typical expenses for most teamboat ferries. Between 17 and 30 May, the first two weeks of the operation, purchases included rope, a bucket, hay and straw, salt, a bell, candles, oats, and corn; money was also expended for crew wages and stabling the horses. Assorted expenses from June through August included oil, oak planks (probably for construction or repair of the landing wharves), a "hames strap" for one of the horse harnesses, whiffletrees, a horse collar, rope, a marlin spike, four "setting poles," and repairs to the ferry's small boat. Oats, corn, hay, and pasturing for the four horses were all predictable monthly expenditures.[23]

The pattern of wage disbursements in the company's accounts suggest that day-to-day operations were managed by the ferry's supervisor John Van Valkenburgh and performed by a crew of four: Adam Frittz and Oliver

Rogers (each of whom were paid $25 a month), Andrew Dunlevee ($20 a month), and E. Gregory ($5 a month). Gregory's low wages hint that he was probably a boy. In addition to these wages for the regular crew, the company also had to meet expenses for part-time labor or maintenance services. A receipt dated 1822, recording the payment of James Van Vorse for "tending the skiff each Sunday" (he was paid 75¢ per day), indicates that the horseboat ran six days a week, with a small skiff being used to carry foot passengers on Sundays.[24]

In the fall of 1821 the ferry was painted by the firm of Smith & Willard for $4.06 (unfortunately the receipt does not indicate the boat's color scheme). In October large oars or sweeps were purchased, presumably to steer the boat or possibly to provide an alternative means of propulsion in the event of a breakdown in the middle of the river. The year's final payment to crewmen Frittz and Dunlevee was made on 14 December, indicating the likely date when the river froze over and ended the 1821 navigation season.

Statements of the Albany–Bath company's credits and debits for 1821 are somewhat confusing. In one document, operational expenses for the first season (17 May to December) added up to $849.49, in addition to $500 paid to John Van Valkenburgh for supervising the ferry and $352.40 in miscellaneous costs, a total of $1,701.89. These expenses were exactly balanced by the $1,687.27 cash received for ferriage and $14.62 cash received for "scow hire." A second document details much the same information as the first, but discusses specific machinery costs, including $14.16 for spur wheels and pinions, $9.29 for gudgeon wheels, and $5.52 for four sheaves.

The third financial summary, titled "General Statement of the Cost and Expenses of the Bath Ferry Boat Establishment," itemized capital investments, including the boat ($1,507.42), horses ($309.50), harnesses and rigging ($34.84), and the wharf and wharf repairs ($244.19). These added up to $2,095.95. Total receipts from Van Valkenburgh for ferriage and use of the scow were listed as $1,725.20, which was offset by $1,674.25 in operational expenses, making a net profit of $50.95. Capital accumulated from stock sales, $40 for each of fifty-seven shares, totaled $2,280. The company declared a dividend of $5 for each share of stock, a total return to investors of $285.[25]

The Albany and Bath Ferry Company continued in routine operation under the financial supervision of Isaiah Townsend until 1825, all the while making a modest profit (in 1824 the net profit, after deduction of expenses, was $257.27, of which $171 was paid out in dividends to the holders of fifty-seven shares, a mere $3 per share). In 1825 new subscribers purchased from the original investors a large proportion of the stock, with the understanding that ferry operations would continue without interruption.[26] The team boat company's financial records do not continue in the Townsend Papers beyond 1825, but everything up to that date suggests that the Albany–Bath horse ferry had served the public well, even if the enterprise did not bring much wealth to its investors.

The same characterization cannot be made for the Hudson River horse ferry that worked between Albany and Greenbush, New York, the operation referred to as the "lower ferry." Documents in the Townsend Papers, travelers' accounts, and municipal records of the Albany–Greenbush ferry all point to a badly managed business that connived to overcharge customers and even demanded payments when ferry services were not rendered. Unfortunately for the traveling public, the Albany–Greenbush crossing served the major stage road between Albany and Boston and was hard to avoid without a lengthy detour.

The city government of Albany was at least partially to blame for the sorry state of affairs at the lower ferry. Every year the corporation of Albany leased the rights to operate the ferry to the highest bidder at a public auction; the lessees, naturally enough, wished to realize a profit from the heavy traffic at the crossing. Neither the city nor the lessees seem to have felt any profound sense of responsibility to serve the public or maintain the boats and wharves. In December 1822, for example, a Mr. Armstrong bid $4,725 for the rights to run the boat for one year, which according to one source was "looked upon as a wild speculation."[27] Armstrong was no fool, however, and he made the ferry—and the public—pay handsomely for his speculation. During the following year the business brought him gross receipts of $7,764; minus his $4,725 rent and $1,668 in operating costs, he made a net profit of $1,371, a hefty amount of money at a time when skilled workmen earned about $1 a day. Two years later, in March 1824, the ferry was leased to a Mr. Wendell for $5,890; with these high rents it is perhaps no wonder that lessees worked so hard to squeeze a profit from their customers.[28]

And squeeze they did. In a petition addressed to the city of Albany and the current lessees of the Albany–Greenbush ferry, and dating to around 1823, Joseph Finch and a group of disgruntled citizens listed their grievances with the lower ferry. The petition did not paint a happy picture. The ferry was charging exorbitant tolls, as well as a "certain novell and insulting imposition in the shape of extra ferriage duties." The lessees of the ferry had also discovered an ingenious means of keeping profits flowing even when ice shut down navigation of the river: They employed a man to break up the ice along the Albany shoreline, except at the ferry landing, and then forced travelers to pass through a toll gate and pay for crossing over the ice by themselves! Finch and his companions viewed this as "dastardly vilanous conduct" and generally condemned the practice of annually subletting the ferry at auctions.

The petition declared "we view with detestation the narrow minded and sordid policy pursued by the corporation of the city of Albany in raising the enormous revenue . . . from such a source."[29]

The petitioners stated their intent to take their business elsewhere: "We much better approve the conducting of the upper ferry to wit, at Bath: where we are not insulted as at the other, and where it is proposed (we understand) we may be carried across for one half the toll exacted at the lower ferry." The petition went on to resolve that the group would henceforth only cross at the Bath ferry and threatened to "desert the Albany Market and carry our produce and procure our goods elsewhere" if the Greenbush ferry operation followed through with its threat to demand tolls even if the petitioners crossed at Bath.

The city and its ferry lessees also gave little thought to maintenance of the ferry. The Albany Common Council cravenly responded to complaints about the dilapidated condition of the scow used for ferrying at night by resolving in December 1823 that it would no longer be responsible for accidents between sunset and sunrise.[30] The council's Ferry Committee examined both the wharves and boats in May 1824 and found them to be in an advanced state of decay. The Greenbush wharf was falling apart because of ice damage to the log cribbing, and the scow used for ferrying at night was described as "rotten & very much worn out," and "very unsafe" for the four to six mail stages that crossed the river between nine o'clock at night at four o'clock in the morning. The committee recommended replacing the scow with a "light two Horse ferry Boat," observing that "such a boat would always accommodate the public much better, *and* with much less danger attending it." The estimated cost of a light horseboat was only six hundred dollars more than it would have cost simply to build a new scow.[31] The committee's suggestion seems to have been accepted, for a two-horse horizontal- treadwheel ferry was in operation at the crossing by 1828.[32]

The petitions and complaints of an unhappy public do not appear to have had much of an effect on the management of the Albany–Greenbush crossing. The travel journal of Captain Basil Hall of the Royal Navy includes a description of a ferry passage between Albany and Greenbush and confirms that in 1827 the lower ferry was still suffering under the direction of incompetents:

> At starting from Albany we had to cross the Hudson, and in this troublesome operation lost much time; for it happens in America, as in other parts of the world, that things are not always best managed at those places where it is expected they will be found in the highest order. The ferry-boats in general, it is true, in this part of America, are admirably contrived for both foot passengers and carriages; being made so wide that half a dozen stages and carts, besides

twice that number of horses, may easily find room on their decks. The moving power is almost invariably that of horses; generally six or eight in number, whose strength is applied to paddles similar to those of a steam-vessel.

On reaching the water's side, we had the mortification of seeing the boat just entering the dock at the opposite shore; so that if we had been five or ten minutes sooner, we might have saved more than an hour's delay. Owing to something having gone wrong at the ferry, a long time was spent in disembarking the cargo of horses, sheep, carts, waggons, and people; while we had nothing to do but sit on the bank, looking at the retreating multitude streaming out of the boat, and wending their way up the hill, like the flight into Egypt in the old pictures.

At length the boat put off, and slowly recrossed the water to our side; where, however, we were kept in the most provoking manner some twenty minutes after everything was ready for moving, by the obstinacy of the ferryman, who would not stir a foot. What his reasons were we could not make out; though probably he was nettled at the unmeasured abuse of the stage-driver, who indulged his spleen in a tirade of oaths and scurrility such as I had not heard before in America.

I fancy our surly skipper had taken an extra glass of whiskey; for, by dint of a more ingenious piece of nautical mismanagement than any sober man would have thought of, we bungled our entry into the docks on the eastern side of the river, and, in spite of many an oath, and many a thump bestowed on a worn-out horse—Charlie by name—we fairly stuck fast, with the bow of the vessel jammed between two pier-heads, while her stern was held tight down the stream by the ebbing tide. I was rather amused than otherwise by the dilemma, and for some time refrained from interfering, as I have generally seen professional persons make matters rather worse than better by their spluttering on these occasions. At last the ferryman, after urging his poor beasts to turn the paddles to no purpose, threw down his whip in despair, gave the horse nearest him a sound box on the chops, and roared out, to the horror of the good company, "D——n your soul, Charlie, why don't you get up!"

I now thought it high time to make a move, and jumping from the carriage, rigged out a spar over the starboard quarter, and reaching to the bow of a sloop lying at the wharf, by which means we boomed-off the ferry-boat's stern, till she came exactly in a line with the entrance of the dock. Poor Charlie, knowing instinctively that his services could now be of some use, ran round quite merrily, and we slipped into our birth.[33]

In 1828 the common council purchased the steamer *Chancellor Lansing* for the Albany–Greenbush ferry (the *Horse's Back* was presumably retired at the same time).[34] The two- horse treadwheel ferry remained in service, and the entire operation was able to maintain its record of dissatisfied customers well into the 1830s (British tourist Harriet Martineau's crossing on this ferry in 1834 led her to conclude that the horse-powered boat was "a device so cruel, as well as clumsy, that the sooner it is superseded the better . . . I was told that the strongest horses, however well kept up with corn, rarely survive a year of this work").[35] One of the crossing's horseboats met an ending appropriate to the ferry's history on 29 October 1850, when it sank at five o'clock in the morning with eight horses and milk wagons aboard, four of which were lost overboard.[36]

CATSKILL HORSEBOATS: THE FERRIES OF GREENE COUNTY

Greene County, New York, on the west bank of the Hudson River, lies roughly 48 kilometers (30 mi.) south of Albany and 208 kilometers (130 mi.) north of New York City. Although this region is best known for its lofty and spectacular Catskill Mountains, it also holds a special place in the history of the team ferry: During the first half of the nineteenth century, the county was home to a veritable flotilla of horseboats. The long and generally fruitful association with the horse-propelled boat occurred at the county's three principal river ports: Coxsackie, Athens, and Catskill. The three towns occupied a 16-kilometer (10 mi.) stretch of riverbank, with Coxsackie at the northern end, Catskill at the southern end, and Athens in the middle.

Unlike the Albany–Troy region to the north, which was rapidly expanding into a major center of trade, industry, and transportation, Greene County's development in the first half of the century was more limited. The riverside towns participated in the busy commerce on the Hudson by serving as markets for the mountainous back country's farms and forests ("the whole county affords a larger proportion of arable land than could have been supposed" said Spafford's *Gazetteer of the State of New York* in 1824). By the standards of the time, Coxsackie, Athens, and Catskill were not particularly large towns: the first two had slightly more than two thousand residents each in 1824, and Catskill was home to thirty-five hundred.[37] All three, however, were large enough to require regular ferry service to the towns and villages of Columbia County on the opposite bank of the river. Although modest in their size and revenue, the ferry operations at all three towns contributed much to local transportation and trade; at the same time these ferries managed to have interesting and diverse histories.

Coxsackie, the uppermost of Greene County's three ports, was an old Dutch farming community that had remained relatively undeveloped until 1800, when increasing population and trade led to an expansion in the size of the village. By 1824 there were about a hundred dwellings and fifteen stores clustered near the side of the river.[38] Coxsackie at this time had three points along its waterfront where boats could tie up to wharves for loading or unloading— the upper, middle, and lower landings. Ferry services across the river to Nutten Hook (or Newton Hook) in Columbia County had worked on an informal basis since the colonial era, but this changed in 1800 when the state legislature responded favorably to a petition by Ephraim Bogardus for a monopoly on ferrying at Coxsackie's upper landing. Like most ferry grants, this one required that Bogardus keep a sufficient number of safe boats and ready crews to accommodate the public and that he strictly adhere to the toll rates and hours of operation established by the courts of Greene County. He was also required to post a bond to ensure compliance with the legislature's directives.[39] From 1800 to 1819 the Coxsackie crossing was served by an oar-propelled scow that shuttled back and forth on a regular basis when weather and wind conditions permitted.

The latest advances in nineteenth-century technology caught up with Coxsackie ferrying in 1820, when William Judson, Andrew Witbeck, and John L. Sharp received a twelve-year grant from the legislature to operate a ferry between the town's middle landing and Nutten Hook. A horseboat was built for the new ferry at the Coxsackie shipyard of Samuel Goodrich in 1819–20; not much is known about the dimensions or appearance of the boat, although it was equipped with a horizontal treadwheel that was probably provided by Barnabas and John C. Langdon. When the boat began service in 1820, its daily running was placed under the direction of William Judson, who apparently captained the vessel himself with the assistance of one or sometimes two crewmen (the ferry was obviously not a large one). For the next fourteen years the Coxsackie horseboat seems to have had an uneventful and fairly unprofitable career, during which time ownership passed into the hands of two heirs to the original owners, Edward B. Judson and Henry L. Sharp.

In 1834 Judson and Sharp decided to sublet the venture to George Fuller of Coxsackie for the paltry sum of $312 per annum (this amount certainly hints that the ferry was not a moneymaker for the owners). The original ferryboat was approaching an advanced state of decay by this time, and Judson and Sharp therefore promised to provide Fuller with a new horseboat and a new rowboat for the opening of the navigation season. The treadwheel machinery must have been rather worn by 1834, but nevertheless it was recycled into the new boat. The terms of the Judson–Sharp lease required Fuller to replace the hardwood planks that lined the treadwheel's horse walkway on a regular basis, to ensure that the horses did not break through and mortally injure themselves. Fuller also had to promise that he would adequately crew the ferry both with men and with sound, sturdy horses. William Judson, incidentally, laid claim to all the manure generated by the ferry's horses, stipulating that each day's equine deposits were to be gathered and left by the side of the ferry barn for him to collect.[40]

The crossing's second teamboat operated through the 1830s and early 1840s, again with seemingly little in the way of triumphs, calamities, or profits. The ownership of the operation continued to change hands until 1844, when all shares of the ferry were in the hands of three men: George Reed, Silas Holbrook, and attorney Peter Silvester. In that year the three successfully petitioned the legislature for a twelve-year extension of the ferry monopoly and stated their intention to construct another horseboat to replace the existing ferry. Their new vessel, called *W. V. B. Hermance,* was reportedly built as a horseboat and later converted to a steamboat.[41] A photographic image of the steamboat *Hermance* shows a vessel that looks like a horizontal-treadwheel horseboat, so the report of its conversion seems credible.[42] The *W. V. B. Hermance* had a lengthy career, continuing as a ferry until 1878, when it was replaced by the steamer *Coxsackie.*

The history of horseferrying at Athens, 8 kilometers (5 mi.) downriver from Coxsackie, also involved three horse-powered craft. The town and village of Athens were created from the southern part of Coxsackie and the northern part of Catskill and incorporated in 1815; by 1824 the riverfront village of Athens had grown to about 150 houses and a population of one thousand. The place had a few minor industries, including a ropewalk, a distillery, and a stoneware pottery, but like Coxsackie and Catskill, it served primarily as a center for marketing and shipping Greene County's timber and agricultural surpluses. The city of Hudson, New York, directly across the river from Athens, was the county seat for Columbia County and was a much larger community, with a population of thirty-six hundred and extensive commerce and manufacturing; in 1824 Hudson was considered to rank fourth among the state's cities in terms of its annual trade.[43] Obviously, a reliable ferry link between Athens and Hudson was of some importance, especially for the people of Athens.

Ferrying at this location was formalized in 1778 when Conradt Flaack was authorized by the city of Hudson to begin service between the opposite shores. One of Flaack's earliest ferries consisted of two canoelike craft connected by a deck or platform; this catamaran toted passengers, cargo, wagons and carts across the river, although horses or other large livestock had to swim alongside. Later ferries included a leeboard-equipped sailing boat and a scow. In 1790 the operation was taken out of private hands and controlled by Hudson; after the incorporation of Athens in 1815, the ferry was administered as a joint venture between the two towns. Expenses incurred by the building and maintenance of the ferry and any profits generated by the business were equally shared.[44] A direct governmental role in the operation of a ferry was rather unusual for this period, for as we have seen most were privately owned and managed.

The first Athens–Hudson team ferry appeared on the scene during the earliest years of the horseboating era, around 1816. The boat seems to have been typical of the early catamaran-type ferries with a centrally mounted paddle wheel powered by nine horses walking around a circular track, and a circular deckhouse to shelter the horses. The ferry was constructed by a boat-builder named William Johnson and probably built to Moses Rogers's design; it cost six thousand dollars, about the standard price for an early catamaran horseboat.[45] The greater financial resources of the two towns may explain why the Athens–Hudson ferry was able to purchase an expensive catamaran horseboat several years before most of the privately operated crossings on the upper Hudson River, for traffic there does not seem to have been substantially busier or more lucrative than at any of the other ferries on the upper river in 1816.

The inaugural passage of the Athens–Hudson teamboat ferry was memorable. Local dignitaries, including Hudson's mayor and town council, rode along on deck to experience the difference their new ferry would make on the river. They got more than they bargained for when the pilot, unfamiliar with steering this new and somewhat cumbersome craft, rammed another vessel "so forcibly, as to bring the official party to a level with the deck."[46]

Ferrying between Athens and Hudson was hindered by the "Middle Ground," a large, partially exposed bank of sand and mud that extended down the middle of the river. For decades ferries had been forced to pass around the southern end of this flat, and during its first two years of service the new Athens–Hudson horseboat made the same detour. In 1818, however, the two towns agreed to sponsor jointly the digging of a canal 18.3 meters (60 ft.) wide by 1.5 meters (5 ft.) deep through the bank. The sides of the canal were supported by a structure of heavy timbers covered with planks and extensively reinforced with stone fill. The ferry canal stayed in use for many years, but it did not always work: When the tide was slack horseboats could pass through with little difficulty, but when the tide was running it was necessary to detour around the bank, as the ferries could not get up enough speed to paddle through the cut.[47]

In 1824 the catamaran teamboat was sold by the ferry corporation and replaced by a single-hulled sidewheel boat powered by a six-horse horizontal treadwheel. This boat was built and outfitted by Alexander Coffin for three thousand dollars, half the cost of the first ferry. Royal Navy Captain Basil Hall crossed from Athens to Hudson on the ferry in 1827 but had little to say other than that the boat was "commodious."[48]

A report on the finances of the operation in 1826 makes it clear that the ferry was not a moneymaker for Athens and Hudson and in fact was probably a regular drain on the municipal budgets. The annual expenses do not appear exorbitant, but rather were typical for this business. The boat's captain, Samuel Waring, was paid $30 a month during the ferrying season (nine and one-half months in 1826), deckhand Simeon Bartley received $20 per month, and the horses needed stabling, feed, shoeing, and occasional replacements. Tree bark left over from tanning operations was purchased for

12½¢ a cartload and scattered on the treadmill walkway to provide the horses with better footing. The boat hull and treadmill mechanism needed periodic maintenance and repair, and the entire craft required a major overhaul during the winter. And finally, like most of the other ferry operations on the river, a small scow equipped with oars and sails was kept by the ferry corporation to provide service when the horseboat was laid up for the night or needed repairs; the captain of the scow, Henry Signer, was also paid $30 per month.

During the 1826 navigation season, from 11 April to 23 December, the horseboat brought in revenues of $1,505 plus $35.50 for "commutation tickets"; the scow ferry, operating during the same time, brought in $353.75. In all, the Athens and Hudson jointly collected $1,894.25 during the entire year. Expenses exceeded this amount by $961.60, however, a difference that was made up by equal contributions from the two towns.[49] When the fares collected by this ferry in 1826 are compared with the gross receipts of the Albany–Greenbush ferry in 1822—$7,764—it is clear that the Athens–Hudson crossing drew only a modest amount of business. The ferry did provide an important public service, however, and the citizens of Athens and Hudson may not have minded the infusion of cash required from each town in 1826 ($480.80) to balance the books and keep the boat running.

In the early 1830s the Athens–Hudson crossing retired its second horseboat and made the switch to steam propulsion with its new ferry; this boat ran for about five years, but it proved unsuitable (like the first steam ferry at Troy, it was probably just too expensive to run at this location), and so the ferry reverted to horsepower. The third horseboat, a six-horse treadwheel craft called *Horse Boat*, was purchased sometime in the second half of the 1830s. Illustrations of this boat have been found in the form of a painting and a print.[50]

The painting is a broadside view, from a perspective slightly abaft the port beam, and it provides an excellent idea of what a later-period treadwheel boat looked like. The hull appears to be boxy and scowlike, with a pair of sidewheels located slightly forward of amidships and the six-horse treadwheel situated slightly aft of amidships. The horse wheel extends out beyond the sides of the boat; on deck, inboard of the walkways, a pair of upright posts probably represent a truss that supported the deck over the wheel. The horses have only a rudimentary shelter—a canvas awning—over their heads, unlike the plank stalls seen on many other treadwheel ferries. Forward of the paddle boxes, and situated on opposite sides of the deck, are two small, planked cabins for passengers; stovepipes indicate that both shelters could be warmed with a cast-iron stove on cold days. A bell mounted on the top of a tall pole was probably used to announce the departure of the ferry prior to each crossing of the river and may also have been rung continuously on foggy days to

Figure 22. The third Athens–Hudson six-horse treadwheel ferry, *Horse Boat.* Painting from the collection of the New-York Historical Society.

alert river steamers and sloops of the ferry's presence. A second view of this ferry (or a boat very much like it) can be found as a print in the 5 January 1889 issue of *Harper's Weekly;* the print's perspective of the boat differs from the painting, but all the details are the same.

The third horseboat at the Athens–Hudson crossing had a career of about two decades and was among the last horse-powered ferries on the Hudson River. Its retirement came in 1858, when the steam ferry *John T. Waterman* was built in an Athens shipyard to ply between the two towns.[51] The *Waterman* also ended slightly more than four decades of nearly continuous teamboat service at this crossing, a record that must be one of the longest (if not the longest) in North America.

Eight kilometers (5 mi.) downriver of Athens lies Catskill, the third and largest of Greene County's river ports and the seat of county government. The village in 1824 boasted fifteen hundred residents, 250 houses and stores, county government buildings, two banks, and an academy; it was also the crossroads of three major turnpikes. The mouth of nearby Catskill Creek served as a safe anchorage for river sloops and other small craft.[52] Catskill experienced much traffic and trade by land and water, and obviously it needed a good ferry connection to the eastern shore of the river.

Like most of the major riverside towns on the upper Hudson, Catskill had ferries since the colonial era, but it was not until 1804 and the passage of the Catskill Ferry Act by the New York legislature that the ownership and structure of the business were fixed. A monopoly on ferrying was granted for twenty years to Henry Van Gorden and Garret Abeel, giving them exclusive rights to all business along a 3.2-kilometer (2 mi.) stretch of the river. The boats built for the crossing consisted of sailing scows with a mast on one side, a steering oar hung off the stern, and a pair of oars for use when the winds were unfavorable. Van Gorden and Abeel's boat captain, "Black Ben" Hallenbeck, ran an efficient ferry, for it was reported that one of their boats "in the short space of two hours . . . conveyed from the west to the eastern shore . . . one hundred fat cattle, three wagons, eleven horses, with their drivers and riders and sundry footmen; and this at a time when there was much ice a-floating the river, and the wind and tide by no means as favorable as at many other times."[53]

In 1814 Van Gorden and Abeel advertised in the *Catskill Recorder* that they were willing to lease the ferry to a responsible party; "none other need apply."[54] The following year saw a wealthy Catskill native, Thomas T. Thomson, acquire six of the ferry's eight shares for the sum of $7,125 (Van Gorden sold two of his four shares, and Abeel sold out entirely). Thomas Thomson, his brother John Alexander Thomson, and Henry Van Gorden continued to operate the ferry with sailing scows for several years after 1815, although as we noted in Chapter 3, in the spring of 1817 they considered Moses Rogers's offer to sell them a catamaran horseboat for $5,000. At the same time, they examined the horseboats being built by James Rodgers and Charles Kenyon of Albany and obtained a statement of expenditures for the first year of the Albany–Greenbush horseboat.[55] The $9,486 spent in the first year of the Albany team-ferry operation was for that time an enormous amount of money (it equaled the value of all eight Catskill Ferry shares), leading the Thomsons to conclude that their business could not possibly bear the expense of a whim-powered catamaran boat.

Langdon's invention of the economical treadwheel ferry in 1819 offered the Thomsons and Van Gorden the opportunity to convert their operation to horseferrying. Before they could act by purchasing a patent license from the Langdons, however, two Troy businessmen, Isaac Lovejoy and Amos Allen, beat them to it, buying on 9 March 1820 the "exclusive right and liberty of making, constructing and using" Langdon machinery at the Catskill crossing. Lovejoy and Allen certainly did not intend to go into the ferrying business themselves at Catskill, nor could they have done so had they wanted to: The ferry monopoly belonged solely to the Thomsons and Van Gorden. Lovejoy and Allen were obviously profiteers who intended to sell the $350 patent license to the ferry owners with a fat markup in the price; there are hints that they planned to make the Thomsons and Van Gorden buy the actual horseboat from them as well, no doubt for a substantial amount of money.[56]

The nefarious dealings of Lovejoy and Allen were among several crises confronting the owners of the Catskill Ferry in 1820–21. Thomas Thomson died in 1821, leaving to his brother John the majority of his estate, including the ferry interests. Henry Van Gorden also experienced severe legal and pecuniary difficulties that year and was forced to mortgage his two ferry shares to John Thomson for three years (Van Gorden was evidently unable to pay the mortgage, for by 1825 Thomson owned the shares). Around 1821 a businessman from Hudson, New York, John R. Hallenbeck, became an active partner in the ferry operation, although the full extent of his financial involvement is not clear.[57]

Thomson and Hallenbeck may have been dismayed by the speculations of Lovejoy and Allen, but they resourcefully found a way around the dilemma. In 1821 they approached Henry Burden, who was just completing his first horseboat for the Albany and Bath Ferry Company, and discussed the possibility of his building a vessel for the Catskill Ferry. Burden, as previously noted, had prepared a horseboat design of his own, apparently employing a treadwheel, that was not controlled by the Langdon patent. The negotiations with Burden neatly outflanked the position of Lovejoy and Allen and left them with a $350 patent license that was essentially worthless.

John Thomson and Henry Burden began discussing the particulars of the new teamboat and its machinery in the fall of 1821. In response to questions about patent infringement raised by the Catskill ferry owners, Burden responded: "I have sent . . . a sketch of my newly invented horse boat with references annexed to it as also the sketch of the horse boat [Langdon's design?] which will serve to explain to your partners the difference." Burden went on to say: "Respecting the horse boat lately built at Albany of which you speak his patent (if he has obtained one) *is good for nothing* for altho I did not apply for a patent I had it equally well secured long before his pretended right."[58] It is unfortunately not clear exactly which man Burden is referring to here—Barnabas Langdon, Lovejoy, Allen, or some other party.

On 3 January 1822 Burden pressed Thomson to make the final arrangements to build Catskill's first horseboat:

> I have now got satisfied respecting the usefulness of my new plan of horse boat machinery. It exceeds my expectations and I have no hesitation to building upon my own responsibility, for no machinery can be applied to horse boats to more advantage than this. I have been making information [*sic*] respecting getting the boat built at Albany and I think I can get it done to more advantage here than at Catskill. I wish you now to come to Albany as soon as possible as the season is far advanced and I have pressing applications for boats to go to the Connecticut river but have postponed giving them a definite answer as to the time I will be able to execute them until I see you as I have always calculated to finish yours first.[59]

A contract was finally signed with Burden to build the Catskill boat, and in March Burden concluded a construction agreement with Albany shipwright Moses Kenyon. The price for the hull was to be $850, which according to

Burden was "as low as can be done in the way agreed on." Thomson and Hallenbeck were particularly desirous that their new vessel should be strong and long lasting. Hallenbeck specified that Kenyon was to use the best pine timber on the sides and that the bottom should be tar papered to prevent leaks. Burden ensured that the first specification was met, but after conferring with Kenyon he did not recommend papering: "It is superfluous and . . . is never done unless on vessels going to warm climates as a preventative for worms destroying the plank, or on leaky vessels where it is necessary to do so in order to make them tight." Building the bottom with two layers of plank tightly caulked and payed with tar, Burden reassured Hallenbeck, would be more than adequate for a freshwater ferryboat.[60]

Kenyon began work on the ferry in late March or early April, and it is clear from Burden's correspondence that he closely supervised all aspects of the work and was continually making small improvements. In April he came up with the idea of sheathing the horse treads with iron to keep the planking from wearing out and to protect the horses from accidentally breaking through the walkway. The directors of the Albany–Bath ferry gave him permission to try the iron sheathing on their boat, but the results of this experiment are not known.[61]

Once Kenyon had the hull near completion, Burden went to work installing the ferry's propulsion machinery, a task that seems to have taken several weeks. The boat was finally launched on 15 June 1822. Burden wrote Thomson on the same day and requested that the horses be sent up to Albany to train for two days on the Albany–Bath teamboat, after which time they would propel the new ferry down the river to Catskill. He added: "I am sorry you was not here to see the bottom of the boat upon the stocks previous to her being launched[;] it is pronounced by competent judges to be the best bottom they ever saw, I have no hesitation in saying so myself."[62] Henry Burden delivered the boat on 22 June and received partial payment of $1,000 and a promissory note for the balance of the ferry's price. The finished boat cost $1,757, of which John A. Thomson paid $1,098.12 and John Hallenbeck paid $658.88.[63] This was a substantial savings over the $5,000 that Moses Rogers had proposed for his catamaran ferry five years earlier, proving the old adage that good things can come to those who wait.

Less than two weeks after the launch at Kenyon's yard, Catskill had entered into the age of horse-propelled ferrying, the last of Greene County's ports to do so. Burden wrote on 29 June:

> I am glad to hear you succeed so well in managing the boat and that she still maintains her reputation, but from the information I have received, together with my own private opinion am somewhat sorry that Jacobs does not find the new horses better up to their work, for you may depend on it that if they are

learned to creep along slow at first you will never be able to break them from it, as it is all important to train the horses to go at a good open step at the beginning and should they refuse flog them until they obey.[64]

The new ferry was not universally welcomed: Ben Hallenbeck, captain of the scow ferry at Catskill, greatly regretted the end of his sailing career, and it reportedly "almost broke his heart when he had to give way to the horse-propelled ferry."[65]

Thomson, Hallenbeck, and Van Gorden still had not heard the last of Isaac Lovejoy and Amos Allen of Troy, holders of the Langdon patent license for Catskill. We do not know exactly what was said or written between these two parties, but two surviving legal documents provide a good indication of what transpired. Lovejoy and Allen, no doubt galled to find their money-making scheme gone awry and themselves out $350, must have threatened the ferry owners with a patent infringement suit, a legal nuisance that promised to cost much in the way of legal fees and possibly hinder the operation of the ferry. Thomson, Hallenbeck, and Van Gorden therefore agreed to a settlement: They would pay $225 for the Langdon license if Lovejoy and Allen would agree to drop all of their claims. The appropriate documents were drawn up in early March 1822 and were signed by everyone.[66] Thomson and his colleagues were out $225, and Lovejoy and Allen had thrown away $125 on their scheme; everyone lost in this transaction.

A list of supplies and labor for the Catskill horseboat's first six years of operation is made up mostly of predictable expenses, including hay, oats, and "cut shorts" for the horses, and nails, plank, and tools for repairing the boat and docks. Other items purchased for the ferry give us clues to the boat's appearance and to the daily life of the horses and crew. The first purchase was a "persuader": a cowhide whip that cost 43¢. In August 1822 a "large sweep to steer the boat" was obtained for $4 (the use of a steering oar rather than a rudder suggests that the horseboat must have had a shallow draft). In 1826 $55.50 was expended on "planks for the horse boat," presumably to replace a deck that had become worn and leaky after four years of service. Elements of the horse mechanism wore out and had to be replaced from time to time, including oak planks for the walkway, small bevel gears, spur gears, cast- iron rollers, wrought-iron pins, and "friction wheels" (these appear to have been large-diameter wheels placed under the treadwheel to support the weight of the horses and extend the life of the wheel). The record of repairs to the machinery certainly hints that Burden's design had some minor flaws that needed correction. The Catskill operation kept a rowboat and scow for use when the horseboat was not in service.[67]

A statement of ferry receipts for 1828 shows not only the gross profits from the enterprise, but also seasonal traffic patterns. The winter of 1828 must have been a mild one, with only minor icing of the river, for the ferry brought in money steadily from 4 January until the end of the year. The statement shows a moderate amount of business until 1 June, with $30 to $50 in receipts every two weeks; after 1 June traffic picked up somewhat, until the second half of August through October, when profits made a big jump (this was harvest season, when farmers were bringing grain, produce, and livestock to market). The single most profitable period was 16–30 September, when the ferry made $169.95. The gross profits for the year were $1,450.70 (Thomson's statement actually reads $1,510.76, but a check of the numbers shows an error in adding them up). After operational expenses were subtracted from these receipts, Thomson and Hallenbeck could not have made much of a profit.[68]

By the early 1830s John Thomson was evidently sole owner of the ferry, but his financial affairs were otherwise in poor shape because of some bad business deals and legal problems with the estate of his deceased brother Thomas. In an effort to meet interest payments on his debts, Thomson offered shares of the ferry in 1831 to Herman Livingston of Oak Hill. Livingston's family owned the ferry landing on the eastern shore of the river and was also active in Hudson River shipping. Livingston was not interested in buying into Thomson's operation, but he did provide financial backing for Thomas Newbury's lease of the Catskill ferry from Thomson in 1831.

By 1831 the Burden-built teamboat was worn out and due for retirement, and so the new proprietors of the ferry arranged to have a replacement built. Not much is known about the dimensions or appearance of the second horseboat, although we can be relatively certain that it was propelled by a horizontal treadwheel. It was a capacious craft, for according to an advertisement in the 8 October edition of the *Catskill Messenger,* the decks were capable of carrying at one time eight two-horse wagons, fifty oxen, or six hundred sheep. The transportation of livestock was a major part of the ferry's business, and measures were taken to encourage continued patronage: "The local situation is such as to give it decided advantages over any other Ferry on the river, particularly to Drovers, they have erected a yard on the east side of the river to secure cattle and sheep as they land."[69]

The second Catskill horseboat served throughout the 1830s and 1840s; Thomson's business records suggest that the business was operating under a lease for most of this time. A five-year lease agreement dated 30 April 1845 between Thomson and Livingston provides a glimpse of the operation at this time. In it Livingston agreed to "make use of all proper & Reasonable Exertions to advance the Reputation of said ferry," to keep a four-horse ferry running at all times, and to maintain the long dock, horse stables, roads, and other fixtures of the ferry; profits from the business were to be divided in half between Livingston and Thomson.[70]

John Alexander Thomson died the following year, apparently leaving an estate still encumbered by debt. Ownership of the ferry passed to Thomson's four nieces. The ferry subsequently came under pressure from the state of New York to upgrade its boats, but Thomson's nieces did not have the resources to build a new ferry or make other substantial changes. This state of affairs continued until 1853, when the steam ferry *Knickerbocker* was purchased for twenty-three hundred dollars and placed in service at the crossing, ending thirty-one years of horseboating at Catskill. The Thomson connection with the ferry also ended at this time, when John Thomson's four nieces sold the *Knickerbocker* and the ferry's facilities to Catskill resident Charles L. Beach.[71]

In this chapter we have examined the histories of six horseboat operations located on the upper Hudson River; the 180.8 kilometers (113 mi.) of river between Catskill and New York City floated many other horse-propelled ferries with equally diverse careers. Lower-river crossings included Hyde Park, Poughkeepsie, Milton, New Hamburgh, and Newburgh.[72] A four-mule treadmill ferry established at a minor crossing in Milton, New York, in 1849 may have been the last of these craft on the Hudson. According to a local historian, the Milton ferry "ran regularly and was a great convenience to the entire neighborhood," a statement that neatly summarizes the Hudson valley's experience with horseboating.[73] The Milton mule ferry was retired in 1862, nearly five decades after animal propulsion first appeared on the river.

7

Mountain Teamboats

The Horse Ferries of Lake Champlain

Lake Champlain, the focus of this chapter, lies a short distance to the north of the Hudson River. Extending approximately 193 kilometers (120 mi.) on a north–south axis, the lake is situated between the Adirondack Mountains of upstate New York and the Green Mountains of Vermont, and it drains northward into Quebec. Lake Champlain's orientation and overall length are similar to the Hudson River's, but its central reaches are considerably wider, expanding to a maximum breadth of 19.3 kilometers (12 mi.) between the western (New York) shore and eastern (Vermont) shore. The lake has no strong currents and unlike the river is not affected by tidal flow, but it is occasionally swept by fierce wind squalls and short, high waves that can be fatal to unwary mariners and their ships. In many respects Lake Champlain offered horseboats a more challenging set of navigational conditions than those encountered on the Hudson River.

Before the advent of railroads and highways Lake Champlain was a strategic military and trade route through the northeastern part of the North American continent. The first European to see its waters was French explorer Samuel de Champlain in 1609; for the next 174 years ownership of the lake and its surrounding valley was contested by competing European powers, principally France and Britain. The conclusion of the American Revolutionary War in 1783 brought a measure of stability to the

112

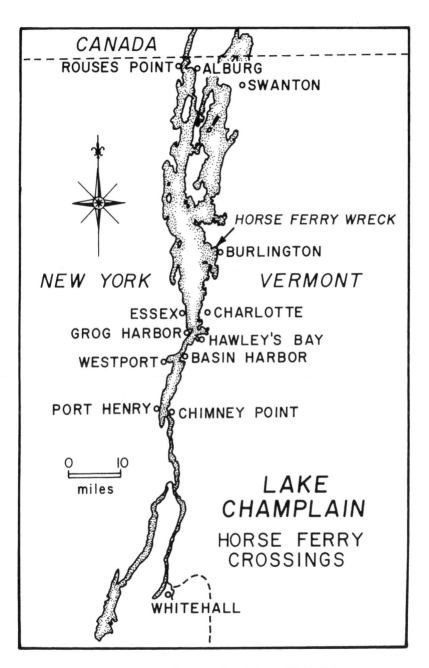

Figure 23. Lake Champlain horse ferry crossings. Map by Kevin Crisman.

Lake Champlain frontier, and settlers from New York and the New England states poured into the Champlain valley to establish farms, industries, and communities.

During the last two decades of the eighteenth century, numerous ferrying operations appeared on the shores of the lake, some of them known for their efficiency and fair rates and others for their dangerous, leaky boats and scandalously high tolls. By 1797 the state of the ferry services on the lake had become a matter of some concern to the Vermont legislature, prompting the passage of three regulations. Prefaced by the comment "great advantage has been taken by ferrymen, demanding unreasonable prices for their service," these regulations established penalties for charging tolls in excess of those fixed by town selectmen, for operating without a license, and for unreasonably refusing to carry persons or property. Failure to keep ferryboats in an adequate state of repair could result in revocation of a ferry license.[1]

The boats and modes of propulsion used for ferrying on the lake at this time were typical of those employed throughout the continent: small craft propelled by oars and poles at narrow, shallow crossings, and sail-equipped vessels at wider crossings. The lake's island-studded northern end and sheltered, riverlike southern end were suitable for ferries of modest dimensions and simple construction (scow-hulled craft were frequently used at these locations). The open waters of central Lake Champlain are wide and sometimes rough, requiring very different sorts of ferries—stout sloops and schooners, and (after 1809) steamboats. Human and animal-propelled ferries were neither practical nor safe on the "broad lake."

Despite the suitability of Lake Champlain's northern and southern ends for horse-powered ferries, they did not become popular there until the late 1820s and early 1830s, surprisingly late in North America's horseboat era. This delayed start is all the more perplexing in light of the large numbers of teamboats in use on the nearby Hudson River by the early 1820s and the proximity of the Langdon machine shop at Troy. Certainly most of the ferry owners on the lake must have been aware of the treadwheel soon after its invention. It is possible that until the late 1820s there was not enough cross-lake traffic to warrant the expense and effort of replacing sailing scows and small sloops with horseboats.

The earliest known horse ferry on the lake was the aptly named *Experiment,* which was operating between Port Henry, New York, and Chimney Point, Vermont, by 1826.[2] The success of the *Experiment* seems to have inspired other ferry owners, and half a dozen new horseboats were launched over the next few years. For the next three and one-half decades the drumming of hooves on treadmill planks and the splashing of horse-propelled paddle wheels would be familiar sounds on the waters of Lake Champlain.

THE *ECLIPSE*

The horseboat *Eclipse* was not the first of its type to traverse the waters of Lake Champlain, but this ferry would hold three of the lake's other teamboat records: the largest vessel, possibly the longest career for a single boat, and certainly the most famous horseboat of its time. It therefore seems fitting that we should begin with a look at this boat and its many productive years of carrying people and their possessions between Charlotte, Vermont, and Essex, New York.

Ferrying at this location was closely associated for many years with the McNeil family, who first settled in Charlotte, Vermont, in 1784 when John McNeil of Litchfield, Connecticut, purchased from Ethan Allen a parcel of land that fronted the lake. John and his family lived the hardscrabble existence of frontier farmers for several years, but by 1790 the growth of population and commerce in the area was sufficient to support his establishment of a sailing ferry between Charlotte and Essex.[3] The business would continue to use sailing craft for many decades, first under the direction of John McNeil, and later under the management of his son Charles.

In 1820 Charles McNeil entered into a ferrying partnership with Essex lawyer and capitalist Henry H. Ross, and the following year they submitted a petition to the Vermont legislature for the right to operate a horse-powered boat at the ferry crossing. The request was approved on 21 October 1821, but there is no evidence to show that they actually got around to launching such a vessel at this time; it is possible that they just could not afford to build a horseboat, or that they determined to delay until they could build a steamboat.[4] In any event, records suggest that a sail ferry remained on the job through 1827.

By 1827 McNeil and Ross were able to finance the building of a steam ferry and contracted with Captain William P. Phillips to run up the vessel at a shipyard in Essex. The new 134-ton steamer, named *Washington*, measured 27.4 meters (92 ft.) long on deck, 6.3 meters (20 ft., 6 in.) wide, with a depth of hold of 2.4 meters (7 ft., 9 in.); power was provided by a thirty-five-horsepower low-pressure engine built by John C. Langdon. The vessel, reportedly built "in a superior style," was launched in November 1827 at a cost of fourteen thousand dollars.[5]

McNeil and Ross intended to have the *Washington* ready for service by the spring of 1828, but by the time of the launching they had changed their minds about using the vessel as a ferry at their crossing and put it to work as a "passage boat" instead, towing canal boats and carrying passengers and freight up and down the length of the lake. Steamboat historian Ogden J. Ross speculated that McNeil and Ross found the vessel too expensive to run as a ferry, which seems as likely an explanation as any for their choosing to employ the *Washington* as a general-purpose lake steamer.

At the time of the *Washington*'s launch McNeil and Ross announced their plans to begin construction immediately of a horseboat for the Charlotte–Essex ferry, and a contract was signed to assemble the vessel at the shipyard on Shelburne Point in Shelburne, Vermont. The new ferry was launched in the spring of 1828 and called *Eclipse*, after a famous American race horse of the 1820s. The horseboat, described as "superior" by the owners, measured 20.7 meters (68 ft.) long and about 7.6 meters (25 ft.) wide on deck. The *Eclipse* was fitted with a six-horse horizontal treadwheel, probably purchased from the machine shop of John C. Langdon, and no doubt looked much like the Delaware River six-horse treadwheel ferry depicted by Philadelphia engineer J. C. Trautwine (Figure 18). An advertisement for the vessel in 1833 claimed that it had "every convenience for the shelter and comfort of the traveler," which suggests that it had heated deckhouses similar to those shown on the third Athens–Hudson horse ferry (Figure 22).[6]

The *Eclipse* began service in the summer of 1828 under the command of Captain Harvey Hinckley. Advertisements for the horseboat, dated 1833 and 1844, show precisely the same schedule of three round trips per day, with departures from one side of the lake at 7 A.M., 11 A.M., and 4 P.M., and departures from the opposite shore at 8 A.M., noon, and 5 P.M. An additional round trip per day was added during the late summer and fall to accommodate the extra traffic generated by farmers bringing their harvest to market.[7] The owners took turns stabling and feeding the horses and housing Captain Hinckley, with McNeil housing and boarding the crew for one season at Charlotte and Ross doing the same the next season at Essex.[8]

The distance between McNeil's Cove in Charlotte and the waterfront of Essex Village was 4.8 kilometers (3 mi.), a long haul even for a six-horse boat. The crossing time between the two shores, in good weather, averaged about thirty minutes, meaning that the six horses were able to get the *Eclipse* up to the respectable speed of 5.2 knots (9.6 km or 6 mi. per hour).[9] The lake here is open and exposed to strong winds, especially in the spring and fall, and in those seasons when Champlain's waters are grey, cold, and choppy, the lengthy crossing here must have pushed the endurance of the horses and the practical limits of horseboating. Charlotte historian William Wallace Higbee recalled:

The captain, Harvey Hinckley, was engineer-in-chief, and the fuel was a whip and an increased demand for speed meant more energetic application of rawhide.

It was hard on horses at best, but in rough weather, with heavy seas and head winds, the engineer had to crowd on lots of steam, so the horses thought, with that merciless whip of his.[10]

There was another danger for the horses, one faced by all horses working on treadwheel ferryboats: breaking through the plank surface of the walkway. Higbee noted of the *Eclipse*: "The horses had to be sharp shod [to keep their footing], and the planking renewed every few days. Occasionally a plank would break and then it was a broken-legged horse."[11] The results of these accidents must have been horrible to witness, and one can only hope they were a rare occurrence on the *Eclipse*. The expense of replacing a mortally injured horse no doubt provided a strong incentive for Hinckley and his crewmen to pay attention to the condition of the hardwood tread planks.

The horseboat may have been difficult and dangerous for the horses, but the entire venture reportedly made "large money" for McNeil and Ross. By the second quarter of the nineteenth century the Charlotte–Essex ferry was one of the key crossing points on the lake and drew business from a wide hinterland on both sides of the Champlain valley. Vermont historian Zadock Thompson remarked in 1842: "McNeil's ferry is generally known throughout the state as one of the most important, safe and well conducted ferries on the lake." The fact that this part of the lake was often free of ice earlier in the spring and later in the fall than other ferry crossings to the south must have also contributed to the profits of McNeil and Ross.[12]

In addition to carrying the everyday traffic of local citizens and their goods and livestock, the *Eclipse* occasionally participated in more exotic events. A notice in the 1 August 1832 edition of the *Burlington Free Press* informed citizens of Vermont that a three-day religious revival or camp meeting was to be held on the lakeshore 1.6 kilometers (1 mi.) south of Essex between 17 and 21 September. The announcement added: "There is a comfortable and safe conveyance from Charlotte in a Horse Boat, the proprietors of which, have kindly proposed to ferry all the ministers free, and all others for half price, coming to and returning from the meeting." The *Eclipse* also conveyed members of the Society of Friends from Vermont to their annual meetings on the New York side of the lake.[13]

The transportation of livestock across the lake was another task that kept the *Eclipse* busy, particularly in the fall. W. W. Higbee said of the horseboat: "Her capacity was by no means inconsiderable, and she needed it all to accommodate the cattle traffic between Essex and McNeils."

In those days Jack Simonds did an immense business butchering cattle in Shoreham, Addison county [40 km (25 mi.) south of Charlotte], and great droves of beeves were picked up in northern New York, largely in St. Lawrence county, driven to the vicinity of Essex and there held on adjoining farms until ferried across, seventy-five to one hundred at a time. On this side, bunches were held until the entire drove was over when the drive would be resumed to Simond's slaughter yards. It was no uncommon thing to see McNeil's pastures and meadows crowded with cattle after haying and harvesting when the handling was liveliest.[14]

In addition to ferrying revivalists, Quakers, and droves of cattle, the *Eclipse* assisted the flood of migrants pouring westward from New England to new land and new opportunities in western New York and in frontier states like Ohio, Michigan, and Indiana. Many of these people were farmers from mountain communities, and it is a safe bet that most had never been on the water in anything larger than a canoe or a rowboat; to them the horseboat must have seemed a strange and wonderful craft. For many of these people, too, the westward crossing of the lake, over the water and out of New England, truly signaled their departure for a new life. W. W. Higbee observed: "Many a longing eye looked back over the three miles [4.8 km] of blue water to catch a last glimpse of its rocky shore, for over there were the migrants' parents and friends, old homes and tender memories."[15]

Narratives of horseboat crossings on Lake Champlain are rare, and we are fortunate to have the reminiscences of Oscar H. Leland, whose family crossed on the *Eclipse* in 1834 to visit relatives in Essex County, New York. Only eight years old at the time, Leland had never been on a boat before, and thus his memories of the event appear to have been especially vivid. Describing the voyage to a cousin many decades later, he recalled:

> At Charlotte we stayed overnight and the next morning we took passage from Charlotte on a ferry boat of six horse power, bound for Essex. It was said to be three miles across the lake, the raging Lake Champlain, at that place and there we were upon that vast watery waste, with no compass to guide us, nothing to depend upon except the rudder to our boat, and the horse power which propelled us and what we could see on the other side of the lake. The six propelling horse power of the boat was applied in this way. There were three horses on each side of the boat, one working right behind the other. These horses stood upon a horizontal wheel which was made to revolve under the deck of the boat when the horses were made to pull while standing upon this wheel. I remember that on the Charlotte side of the lake the beach had a very gradual descent and was sandy. On the Essex side we drove off on a platform. This was 58 years ago this coming September, and I remember Essex at that time seemed to be quite a place, and that the wharves and all about them were covered with lumber piled up as high as I could see.[16]

Champlain valley commerce at this time relied heavily upon the sailing ships, canal boats, and steamships that plied the lake, and for this reason the ferry dock at Charlotte developed into an important destination in its own right. Merchant craft on the lake regularly stopped to pick up produce from Vermont farms that was being shipped south via the Champlain canal to markets in the Hudson River valley and New York City. Vessels sailing back from the southern end of the lake likewise stopped to drop off salt, sugar, molasses, cases of Old Holland gin, dry goods, notions, and other merchandise required by Vermont shopkeepers. Facilities around Charles McNeil's ferry landing expanded to include an inn, a storehouse, and a retail store. The store was managed by Sylvester I. Lovely, a son-in-law of McNeil, and he did "a rushing business," according to W. W. Higbee, "as goods could be sold cheaply on account of no expense in hauling after leaving the boats."[17]

The ferry landing at Essex was but one element in a bustling waterfront that also included warehouses, wharves, and yards for building and repairing ships. Charlotte may have served as a focal point for the trade of the surrounding Vermont countryside, but Essex served the commerce of the entire lake. The New York town had been settled before the Revolutionary War, but it was not incorporated and did not really start to grow until the beginning of the nineteenth century. The vast timber resources contained in nearby forests and the arrival of several shipwrights combined early in the century to turn Essex into a center for lake shipbuilding. The opening of the Champlain canal between the lake and the upper Hudson River in 1823 greatly boosted the demand for merchant craft, and for the next half century the town's yards launched enormous numbers of canal boats and sailing vessels. In addition to producing much of the lake's tonnage, Essex carried on a thriving trade in timber, potash, iron, and cut stone.[18] The daily arrivals and departures of the *Eclipse* provided a dependable commercial and social link between the village and communities on the Vermont shore.

The *Eclipse* ran throughout the 1830s and well into the 1840s, but as with all wooden boats, the ferry's hull began to weaken with age and steady use. Records indicate that the horseboat underwent extensive rebuilding in the spring of 1840, enabling McNeil and Ross to keep it in service for a few more years.[19] The *Eclipse* eventually fell victim to a weighty cargo that had been carried for years—fattened cattle on their way to the slaughter house. The end, when it came in 1847, was sudden and final:

> The horse boat continued for many years to cover herself with glory and also proved a wealth producer to her owners, but . . . one day, when loaded with cattle from the Essex side, she gave such unmistakable evidences of a collapse before reaching shore, that the horses were taken out of their merry-go-rounds, the deck sides knocked off, and horses and cattle unceremoniously plunged into the lake. The old horse boat was floated over the bay where for many moons the mermaids sported in the water-logged cabin.[20]

Another, more succinct version of this episode, went thus:

> Nearing this side one day, with a heavy load of cattle, it collapsed, like the parson's one-horse chaise. Cattle and horses had to swim for it, and the worn-out old boat was towed to the south side of the bay and beached on the sand.[21]

Figure 24. Broadside advertising the horseboat *Eclipse*. The printer of this broadside has cleverly turned a steamboat woodcut into a vessel resembling a treadwheel ferry by trimming off the bowsprit, smokestack, and engine. Courtesy of the Shelburne Museum, Shelburne, Vermont. Photograph by Ken Burris.

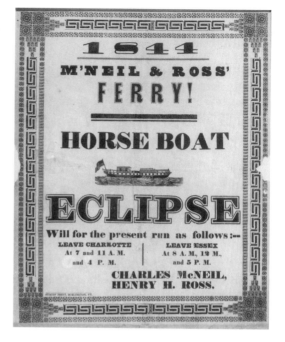

McNeil and Ross, anxious not to lose business at their crossing, asked ship-wright Orson Spear, of Burlington, Vermont, to replace the *Eclipse* with a similar, but slightly longer and sharper-hulled team boat.[22] Before Spear carried out these instructions, however, McNeil and Ross reconsidered power sources and decided to give steam another try. The new ferry, a 25-meter (82-ft.) long, 80-ton steamer called *Boquette,* was built in Essex in 1848 and ran at the crossing for a number of years.[23] The *Boquette* eventually proved uneconomical as a ferry and was sold off to the Northern Transportation Company for use as a towboat.[24] The ferry company came full circle after the *Boquette,* for the next vessel placed in service was a sail ferry, which did not work on a schedule but instead crossed over when signaled by a flag on the opposite shore.[25]

Clearly the Essex–Charlotte ferry of McNeil and Ross entered into a decline in the years following the retirement of the *Eclipse,* but this decline cannot be attributed to bad management by the proprietors. It was, rather, one symptom of a significant change taking place in the transportation system of the Champlain valley, a change that was occurring throughout the United States. Charlotte historian W. W. Higbee, writing several decades after the fact, recognized exactly what had happened:

During all those years other agencies had been at work, other avenues of trade and commerce had come into competition. The whistle of the first locomotive of the Rutland and Burlington railroad, about 1849, signaled the end of certain kinds of lake traffic. The competition of the Vermont Central, about 1854, opened still another way into Boston, and quantities of business that had formerly gone to Troy, Albany and New York went elsewhere. Gradually, but surely, the business of the "ferry" grew less and less. Human ingenuity or enterprise were powerless to prevent it. Railroad transportation acted like a tonic on humanity and everybody was all at once in a hurry. Merchants could hardly stand the delays in the old ways of obtaining goods, for customers pushed them to expedition and the public is inclined to be inexorable.[26]

The decline of lake shipping that followed the introduction of railroads hit Essex hard in the later decades of the nineteenth century, and as shipbuilding and trade dried up and people moved away the once-busy port metamorphosed into a quiet little village perched on the shores of Lake Champlain. Oscar Leland, who crossed on the *Eclipse* in 1834, saw Essex again in 1891 and remarked: "There did not seem to be near as much town there now as there was then." Charlotte was less affected by the railroad revolution and remained what it always had been, a bucolic farming community. The two towns are still there, and every year when the ice leaves the lake two diesel-powered, steel-hulled ferryboats ply the *Eclipse*'s old route, back and forth over the waters that separate Charlotte and Essex.

THE "SUPERIOR HORSEBOAT *EAGLE*"

The *Eclipse* may have been one of Champlain's busier ferries in the 1830s and 1840s, but it was not the only (nor the first) horseboating operation in this part of the lake. A ferry crossing 6.4 kilometers (4 mi.) to the south, between Hawley's Bay (now Kingsland Bay), Vermont, and Grog Harbor, New York, had been serving the public since the 1790s. By 1826 the owners of the ferry, Samuel Strong of Vergennes, Vermont, and Judge James S. Whallon of Essex, had a horseboat in service here, "in good order and prepared to accommodate the public." The ferry was not located along a heavily traveled thoroughfare but was supposedly cheaper than the nearby *Eclipse*, and cattle and sheep drovers preferred it for its economy.[27] There was also a tavern at either end of the crossing, which probably attracted some business as well. The Strong and Whallon horseboat was still running in 1829, but its history after this time has not been traced, and the lack of records suggests that it may have gone out of business by the early 1830s.[28]

A second and seemingly more prosperous horse ferrying venture was begun in 1832 between Basin Harbor, Vermont, and Westport, New York, a crossing 12.9 kilometers (8 mi.) to the south of the Charlotte–Essex ferry. Like many of the other horseboat crossings on the lake, this one appears to have operated for several decades with sailing craft before the switch to horsepower. The owners in 1832 were Charles and C. B. Hatch of Westport, and the boat's captain was the "careful and obliging" Asahel Havens of the same town. There are indications that Havens later bought into the ferry and thus became a part owner of the business. The Basin Harbor–Westport horseboat, the *Eagle,* was described in November 1832 as "new, well built, safe and commodious."[29] The *Eagle* was a horizontal-treadwheel boat and seems to have been a modest craft of two horsepower.

The Basin Harbor–Westport run holds the record as the longest horseboat crossing on Lake Champlain—5.6 kilometers (3½ mi.). Like the horses that powered the *Eclipse,* those on the *Eagle* probably worked up a lather on each trip, and crossings made into a strong headwind must have left the horses shaking with exhaustion. In their later advertisements the proprietors did point out an advantage that their operation had over the McNeil–Ross ferry: "The peculiar situation of this Ferry, protected as it is by mountains, renders crossing safe and certain, even in the most boisterous times."[30]

The *Eagle* made three round trips per day during the height of the summer, although only one round trip was made on Sundays. Two round trips per day was the standard schedule during the spring and fall. The owners also offered to make extra trips for "urgent cases." The ferriage rates for the *Eagle* in 1835 were $1 for every wagon or sleigh drawn by two horses, 75¢ for each one-horse vehicle, 37¢ for a horse and rider, and 18¢ for an individual passenger.[31] By 1841 the fare had risen to 37½¢ for a horse and rider and 25¢ for passengers. Rates for ferrying herds of horses, cattle, sheep, and hogs were described as "low in proportion."[32]

In the late autumn of 1841 Captain Havens proved that he and his horseboat were capable of meeting challenges beyond the routine business of ferrying people and goods. On the morning of 16 November the citizens of Westport awoke to the sight of a steamship lying stationary and in apparent distress opposite the town, near Button Bay on the Vermont shore. Conditions on the lake were typical for November—strong, cold winds were blasting the surface of the lake, and the waves were high and rough. Heedless of the gale, Havens hitched his team to the boat and, accompanied by twenty townspeople, set out to render assistance to the hapless vessel.

The *Eagle* made the trip across safely, although the horses no doubt had a hard pull all the way. The rescuers found the 137-ton *Macdonough,* a 27.1-meter (89-ft.) long steam towboat owned by the Champlain Transportation Company, holed by a rock and being thrashed to pieces by the storm. Nearby lay the cause of the *Macdonough*'s demise, the canal boat *Citizen,* which had broken loose from its tow in the high winds. The *Citizen* was also aground and going to pieces. Captain Havens managed to extricate the crews of the two vessels without any serious injuries or loss of life, but the steamer and the canal boat were completely wrecked.[33] This is the only instance we have encountered of a horseboat coming to the rescue of a steamship.

The competition of the nearby Charlotte–Essex ferry and the need to make the business turn a good profit induced Havens to extend the ferrying season for as long as possible. The shelter provided by the New York mountains no doubt aided Havens in making his wintertime runs. On 5 January 1842, for example, the *Essex County Times and Westport Herald* reported: "The Ferry between this village and Basin Harbor is suspended for the season. The Horse-Boat attempted to cross to day, but was prevented by ice." This was extending the season very late indeed. Two and one-half months later, on 23 March, the paper reported that even though the lake was not completely free of ice Captain Havens had already made one crossing and was about to commence regular service for the season. By 6 April, the *Eagle* was running on its usual schedule.

Ten years seems to have been about the average length of time that a team-boat could operate before rebuilding was required. During the winter of 1842–43 the *Eagle* was pulled up on land and overhauled and was ready to continue in service between Basin Harbor and Westport by that spring.[34] The last mention of the *Eagle* in the local paper comes in the 17 April 1844 edition of the *Essex County Times*, when Havens (described, as always, as "polite and obliging") and the *Eagle* ("eminently sea-worthy") commenced the new navigation season. The horseboat was now making a shorter, 3.2-kilometer (2 mi.) crossing south of Westport, between Adams' Landing (now Arnold's Bay) in Vermont and Barber's Point, New York. For unknown reasons, perhaps economic, perhaps structural, the old boat was no longer able to work between Westport and Basin Harbor.

After April 1844 the *Eagle* disappears from the historic record, at least from the obvious records.[35] What happened to this horseboat? We can only speculate that it succumbed to advanced age, competition from other ferries, or changing patterns of local trade and transportation. The *Eagle*'s final resting place also remains a mystery.

OTHER LAKE CHAMPLAIN HORSEBOATS

The *Eclipse* and *Eagle* enjoyed long careers and left a clear record of their existence in newspapers, local histories, and various reminiscences. The same cannot be said, unfortunately, of the horseboats that operated in the northern waters of the lake. At least three horseboat ferries worked around the islands near the Canadian border in the late 1820s, but information about them is sparse. On 19 October 1828 the Vermont legislature approved Alburgh, Vermont, resident Elijah Loomis's petition to run a horse ferry line on the narrow passage between Alburgh and Hog Island in Swanton, Vermont. On the same date the legislature granted permission to a second

Grand Isle entrepreneur, William Mott, to operate a horseboat between the west shore of Alburgh and Rouses Point, New York. Mott clearly considered the official stamp of approval a certain thing, for according to the petition his two-horse boat ("procured at considerable expense") had already been in service for three months when the legislature convened.[36] Yet another grant for a horse ferry in the Alburgh area was made in 1829, this time to Nathan and John Niles. Their boat was reportedly unprofitable and did not stay in service long.[37]

The crossing between Port Henry, New York, and Chimney Point, Vermont, 16 kilometers (10 mi.) south of the Westport–Basin Harbor ferry, probably holds the record as the crossing with the longest employment of horse ferries on Lake Champlain. As previously mentioned, Port Henry–Chimney Point was home to the lake's first documented horseboat, the *Experiment* of 1826. The crossing had a long history before the *Experiment*, with regular sail ferry service commencing in 1785. A ferry dynasty of sorts began in 1823 when Asahel Barnes Sr. took up residence at Chimney Point and acquired the ferry the following year from James Lewis.[38] It was Barnes who modernized the crossing by purchasing the horseboat *Experiment* around 1826.

An advertisement for Barnes's horse ferry in 1828 described the ferry as a vessel "of suitable capacity to accommodate six waggons with horses" and assured the public that it was strong and safe, capable of functioning in any weather, "which will insure to the traveler certainty in his conveyance."[39] The boat passed directly between Port Henry and Chimney Point, a distance of 2.8 kilometers (1¾ mi.), but if necessary it could make a slight detour to pick up or drop off customers from nearby Crown Point, New York. Barnes and his business partner William H. Meacham promised ferry patrons: "no exertions . . . will be wanting to accommodate the public in the best possible manner."

Like many of the horse ferry proprietors on the Hudson River, Barnes and Meachum ensured uninterrupted service by keeping two sail ferries on hand for times when the *Experiment* was not available. The two existing sailing boats were deemed unworthy of repair in 1832 and replaced the following winter by two entirely new vessels. An advertisement for these boats, typical of public ferry notices of the day, sought to reassure travelers about the quality of the sailing craft and their crews: "They are very staunch built, well constructed boats, perfectly safe in almost any weather, and will be sailed by skillful, careful, and attentive men."[40]

The day-to-day operations of the *Experiment*, or any other horseboats, at the Chimney Point–Port Henry crossing in the 1830s and early 1840s are not well known. A new horse-powered ferry called *P.T. Davis* entered service here around 1847 (the boat was advertised as "new" in 1847, but the same claim was being made two years later, so we cannot be certain that the *Davis* was launched in 1847). The ferry was propelled by four horses and probably equipped with a horizontal treadwheel, but as a new form of horse machinery, the treadmill, was coming into general use at this time, it is possible that the *P. T. Davis* had one of these devices. By 1847 Asahel Barnes was apparently no longer directly involved in ferrying operations, for the *P. T. Davis* was owned by G. B. Pease and captained by G. A. Hammond.[41]

In April 1847 the *P. T. Davis* was making four round trips per day, starting at 7 A.M. and completing the last trip about 6 P.M. Only two round trips were made on Sundays. Fares were seventy-five cents for two horses and a carriage and thirty-one cents for a horse and rider. Business must have fallen off slightly by 1849, for only three round trips were being made per day, even at the height of the harvest season. The *P. T. Davis* apparently worked through most of the 1850s, and probably it is the Chimney Point–Port Henry horseboat that was reported to have been completely wrecked on 26 October 1857. According to a news account of the sinking, the ferry came adrift from its moorings during a gale and was blown onto the rocks at Port Henry, where the hull was irreparably damaged. The loss left the crossing with nothing more than a small boat for ferrying.[42]

Asahel Barnes's son Asahel Jr. provided the crossing with a new boat in the spring of 1858 when he launched and outfitted the four-horse, treadmill-equipped *Gipsey.* This vessel was advertised as a "good staunch boat" guaranteed to run "promptly and regularly."[43] During the ferry's inaugural season Barnes certainly seems to have impressed his patrons, for a newspaper commented during the following year: "The promptness and reliability of his ferry during the last season is a pretty safe guarantee that Mr. Barnes understands his business and the wants of the public, and will promptly fulfill all engagements."[44]

The *Gipsey*'s mechanism differed from the earlier treadwheel boats by having each sidewheel hooked up to its own treadmill. This arrangement worked adequately when the horses on the two treadmills walked at the same speed, but if they walked at different speeds the boat had a tendency to turn in a circle. According to one historian, "The magic ingredient for a straight true course was the long whip of the 'engineer' who sat usually in one of the passenger's buggies and applied encouragement to one team or another, depending on which was lagging."[45] Barnes was said to have solved the problem eventually by purchasing even-gaited Canadian ponies.

To the best of our knowledge the *Gipsey* was the lake's last team ferry, but we still do not know exactly when Asahel Barnes Jr. retired his boat from service. Some sources have suggested that the *Gipsey* passed from the scene before the Civil War, which, if correct, would indicate the boat was either a mechanical or a financial failure.[46] Records are not clear whether a sailboat or a steamboat immediately followed the *Gipsey,* but by the later years of the century a small steam ferry was chugging across the lake between Chimney Point and Port Henry.[47]

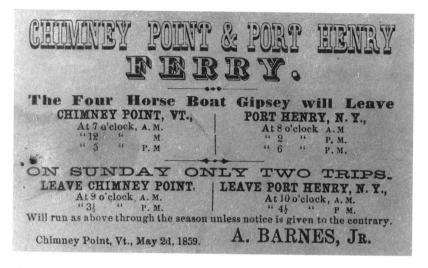

CHIMNEY POINT & PORT HENRY FERRY.

The Four Horse Boat Gipsey will Leave

CHIMNEY POINT, VT.,	PORT HENRY, N. Y.,
At 7 o'clock, A. M.	At 8 o'clock A. M.
"12 " M.	" 2 " P. M.
" 5 " P. M	" 6 " P. M.

ON SUNDAY ONLY TWO TRIPS.

LEAVE CHIMNEY POINT,	LEAVE PORT HENRY, N. Y.,
At 9 o'clock, A. M.	At 10 o'clock, A. M.
"3½ " P. M.	" 4½ " P M.

Will run as above through the season unless notice is given to the contrary.

Chimney Point, Vt., May 2d, 1859. A. BARNES, Jr.

Figure 25. Business card for the horseboat *Gipsey.* Courtesy of the Chimney Point State Historic Site, Vermont Division for Historic Preservation.

Horseboats were an important element in the transportation network of the Champlain valley in the 1830s and 1840s, providing a means of propulsion that was cheaper than steam and considerably more reliable than sail. Nine horse ferry operations working at seven crossings have been identified, but the actual number of horseboats built may have been slightly less than this number, since it is likely that boats from financially unsuccessful ventures were sold to other ferry owners and reused. Three horseboat crossings in particular— Charlotte–Essex, Westport–Basin Harbor, and Chimney Point–Port Henry—seem to have contributed much to the economic well-being of the regions they served.

Champlain's horseboat era also witnessed the glory days of sail and steam navigation on the lake. The introduction of railroads into the Champlain valley in the 1840s led to a reorientation of trade from lakeside wharves to rail depots. Horse-powered ferries were only the first casualties of the new form of transportation: Steamboats and commercial sailing craft would also decline in numbers over the next few decades, until they became nearly extinct by the beginning of the twentieth century. In 1903 W. W. Higbee reflected on the changes that were ending a way of life enjoyed for more than a century by lake sailors and merchants. He philosophically concluded:

The departure of the old has not lessened the beauties of the new. The same eternal hills mirror themselves in the waters of this magnificent lake. Sunrise and sunset paint the same glorious tints on sky and cloud.[48]

8

"Portable Horsepower"

The Treadmill Mechanism

Langdon's horizontal treadwheel was a clear advance over the earlier whim-type machines and was the favored means of propelling horseboats for three decades, but the system had some drawbacks of its own. The wheel was a cumbersome piece of equipment, subjected to considerable strain from the weight of horses walking on its outer rim. Constant maintenance of the treadwheel's wooden structure and regular replacement of bearings and gear wheels would have been required of every ferry owner, especially after the boat had been in service for several years. The treadwheel worked adequately on boats, but its size and weight did not make it a good general-purpose power source for farmers, sawyers, or others who wished to substitute horse power for the more expensive and limited human labor. Agriculture and industry needed a horse machine that was portable, easily adapted to many uses, and capable of being inexpensively manufactured and maintained. Throughout the 1820s and 1830s inventors tinkered with a variety of devices that seemed likely to meet these criteria.

Some products of this mechanical experimentation were, like the treadwheel, nineteenth-century versions of machines that would have been familiar to the Greeks and Romans or medieval Asians and Europeans. A good example of this sort of recycled technology was William Whitman's plan for a "rotary horse-power," a vertical internal treadwheel that was essentially an enlarged squirrel wheel for horses. The Patent Office found it sufficiently novel and granted Whitman a patent in 1836.[1] No working examples of

127

Whitman's vertical equine wheel are known, but people-powered squirrel wheels were occasionally employed in the United States in the early nineteenth century.[2]

The internal vertical horse wheel proved a technological dead end, but another device under development in the second quarter of the nineteenth century would eventually answer the labor-saving needs of the farmer and the small-scale entrepreneur. This machine was to prove of great value to ferry owners as well and lead to a new type of horse-powered boat.

A "NEW APPLICATION OF HORSE POWER"

The third and final major development in animal-powered mechanisms, the treadmill or "horse power," arrived on the scene in the early 1830s. The equine treadmill requires little explanation, for human-powered versions are common today in fitness centers and medical offices; the device consists of a revolving platform or "endless floor," upon which one or more horses, contained in a rectangular stall, walk in place.

Just who deserves the credit for building the first working endless-floor treadmill is not clear, for several inventors brought out their own versions in the late 1820s. According to one source a horse-powered railroad locomotive working on the treadmill principle was invented by C. E. Detmold of New York around 1829.[3] The engine, called *Flying Dutchman,* won Detmold a five-hundred-dollar prize from the South Carolina Railroad and was employed on the company's 9.6-kilometer (6 mi.) track in 1829 and 1830. The *Flying Dutchman* seems to have performed adequately, carrying twelve persons at the respectable pace of 19.2 kilometers (12 mi.) per hour.

Another source has credited Hiram and John Pitts of Winthrop, Maine, with the creation of the first portable horse-powered treadmill in 1830.[4] The August 1831 edition of the *New England Magazine* recognized yet another inventor, George Page of Keene, New Hampshire, as the inventor of a "New Application of Horsepower." The magazine described Page's machine as a band of leather fitted with narrow tread planks, which passed around two cylinders or drums; smaller wheels helped to support the leather tread between the cylinders. The *Magazine* concluded by noting that thus far the device had only been used for sawing wood ("this it performs with great expedition"), but it would probably find its greatest use propelling boats on rivers.[5]

The true inventor of the treadmill may never be identified, but this much is certain: American inventors regarded the horse treadmill as a promising technology, and many of them spent the decade between 1830 and 1840 perfecting designs and components. Their results are evident in the patent applications filed at this time and in the treadmill descriptions published in tech-

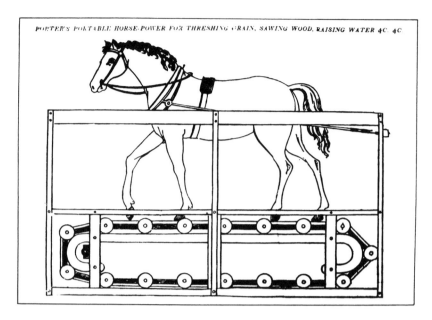

Figure 26. Porter's Portable Horse-Power. From the *New York Mechanic*, 6 February 1841.

nical journals. In 1833, for instance, Messrs J. and L. Hale patented their "Animal Power," a metallic chain-link tread extending around two cylinders and supported (beneath the horse) by a series of large wheels.[6] M. Davenport's "Horse Power," patented in 1835, employed an interlocking-joint tread to partially support the weight of the horses and provide for a more even walking surface.[7] Lane's "Portable Horse Power," also introduced in the 1830s, used a durable iron grate for the tread; Rufus Porter's "Portable Horse-Power" relied upon a series of roller wheels, attached to the outside of the tread and running around a track, to support the weight of both tread and horse.[8] There were many other inventors and mechanics who contributed innovations or improvements to treadmill machinery.[9]

The drawings and descriptions of the earliest treadmills reveal a minor controversy over the question of whether or not the device should be fixed in an inclined or horizontal position. Inclining the treadmill forced the animal to walk uphill and was thought by many to increase the amount of power generated by the machine; the learned members of the Franklin Institute's Committee on Science and the Arts believed otherwise, remarking in 1835: "No advantage is perceived . . . to arise from the inclination of the platform."[10] There were, however, other advantages to be derived from sloping the walkway. For example, the animal working the tread had little choice but to keep moving as the platform revolved under its weight. Also, unlike horizontal treadmills, which required a harness to resist the animal's forward motion, inclined treadmills did not always require a harness or whiffletree (this is evident from numerous photographs of these machines in action). In time all treadmills would be inclined.

The horses' reaction to this new contraption was mixed. The hardwood or iron treads of the mill may have been hard on the horses' feet, and the rumbling and clattering of the floor linkages and gearing was no doubt unnerving to skittish animals. One eyewitness to a treadmill-operated threshing machine in 1843 considered the horse to be reluctant participant:

> A large bony horse was brought to the foot of the power; his eyes showed he did not like to go up there, but with threats and loud words he was got up—a strong man checking him from going over the power. The tugs hooked so he could not go out forward, the bale-strap fastened to prevent backing out, a chain under his belly so he could not lie down—and the horse was ready. The captain loosened the brake and the horse started. It seemed wonderful. . . . All at once the old horse began to pull back and tried to lie down—then you should have heard the captain![11]

An entirely different viewpoint on treadmill work was offered by a Michigan farmer in 1891:

> The objection that the tread is hard on horses is more sentiment than fact. I do not hesitate at all to put my horses or colts in this machine. They seem not to mind it at all, and in winter are as well, if not better, for doing this work. It does not seem hard, and affords excellent exercise.[12]

Whether they liked it or not, walking the treadmill was to become part of the daily routine for generations of North American horses. The 1830s witnessed the treadmill's development by inventors, and in the 1840s manufacturers began to produce them in large numbers and entrepreneurs aggressively marketed the machines to potential customers. Treadmill advertisements first show up in agricultural journals in the late 1830s, and by the 1840s lengthy, illustrated descriptions (often including testimonials from satisfied farmers and small businesses) were commonplace.[13] Some of the firms producing this equipment in the nineteenth century included the J. I. Case Company, the Cherry Company of Chicago, Horace L. Emery & Sons of Albany, New York, the Appleton Manufacturing Company of Appleton, Wisconsin, and A. W. Gray's Sons of Middleton Springs, Vermont.[14]

Treadmills were built in one-, two-, or three-horse models, the choice of which depended upon the purchaser's anticipated needs and ability to pay. Not surprisingly, as production of treadmills increased in the 1840s and manufacturers began to compete for business, the prices of the machines dropped. In 1837 "Gleason's Portable Horse-power" cost $135 for the single-horse treadmill without any attachments; ten years later, the "Wheeler's Horse-power" package deal included a single-horse mill, a threshing machine, and a grain "shaker," all for only $110 (the treadmill alone cost just $75).[15] Treadmill manufacturers also produced a full inventory of spare parts that permitted fast replacement of broken or worn out components.

For thousands of Americans and Canadians, the compact, portable, inexpensive horse treadmill was a harbinger of the new age of mechanization that was sweeping North America. Farmers were undoubtedly the greatest single market for treadmills, for when combined with various attachments the machines could thresh and clean grain, cut silage, churn butter, pump water, and fill silos. The lightweight machines could be moved easily around the farmyard or field to wherever the mill was required. Itinerant mechanical threshing businesses moved from farm to farm in the harvest season, finishing in a few hours a task that had previously taken many days to complete. Woodcutters could set up temporary milling operations in the midst of the forest by purchasing treadmills with attachments for circular and drag sawing. Although most treadmills were built for horses, smaller versions propelled by cattle, goats, sheep, dogs, and even children were produced for use around the farmyard and home.[16]

The treadmill's compact size and minimal weight opened up new possibilities for transportation on land and water. Some of the applications suggested for the new device, such as Rufus Porter's "Car for Removing Houses

Figure 27. Emery's Patent Horsepower. What the modern horse is doing: this talented animal can pump water, churn butter, and saw wood, all at the same time. From the *Cultivator*, June 1852.

Figure 28. Rufus Porter's Car for Removing Houses. From the *American Mechanic,* 28 May 1842.

or Other Ponderous Bodies," appear to have grossly overestimated the capabilities of both horse and treadmill. The secret of the car, Porter confided to readers of the 28 May 1842 edition of *American Mechanic,* was all in gear ratios that transformed the motion of one horse on the treadmill into the equivalent energy of one hundred horses pulling directly on the house carriage. The car was slow: A horse walking at the pace of 4.8 kilometers (3 mi.) per hour would advance the house only 39 meters (128 ft.) in one hour. The inventor was not concerned about steep hills: "This horse will be able to exert the power of 100 horses in holding back the car from too rapid a movement in descending."[17] One can only hope that Porter's faith in the strength of a wooden framework, cast-iron gears, and the determination of one horse was never put to the test on a precipitous slope.

An eminently more practical form of horse-treadmill-powered transportation, the railway locomotive, saw considerable experimentation and limited use in the second quarter of the nineteenth century. We have already noted C. E. Detmold's *Flying Dutchman* on the South Carolina Railroad in 1829–30, which was replaced by the steam locomotive *Best Friend* in 1830 (and, we might add, the little engine violently exploded in 1831). A horse-power device called the *Clycloped* was tested briefly in 1829 on England's Liverpool–Manchester Railway, but it failed to compete with steam.[18]

The Baltimore and Ohio Railroad also ran a horse-treadmill locomotive on its track in the early 1830s. The machine worked "indifferently well" but was retired after an embarrassing bovine-induced derailment: "When drawing a car filled with editors and other representatives of the press, it ran into a cow, and the passengers, having been tilted out and rolled down an embankment, were naturally enough unanimous in condemning the contrivance."[19] Another of these machines was tested in England in March 1838 as a substitute for steam engines on short or branch sections of tracks that did not have enough business to support steam. By this time some of the kinks in the treadmill mechanism seem to have been worked out, and the trials proved highly successful, with the 3.6-metric-ton (4 ton) locomotive reaching speeds of up to 25.6 kilometers (16 mi.) per hour.[20]

In the propulsion of railway cars, however, just as in the propulsion of vessels, there was never any real question about which form of power ruled the rails. An early report on the building of the South Carolina railroad, dating to around 1829, spoke prophetically: "The [steam] locomotive shall alone be used. The perfection of this power in its application to railroads is fast maturing, and will certainly reach, within the period of constructing our road, a degree of excellence which will render the application of animal power a gross abuse of the gifts of genius and science."[21]

TREADMILL HORSEBOATS

The date when a treadmill was first installed on a boat is still open to question. The *New England Magazine* predicted in 1831 that treadmills would find employment on the water, but the adoption of treadmill propulsion clearly did not happen overnight. The treadwheel's relatively inexpensive and proven technology may have delayed the acceptance of treadmills on ferries, and early versions of the mill may have been unreliable. The first proposal for such a craft that we have found dates to 1835, when inventor William Burk submitted to the Franklin Institute's Committee on Science and the Arts his concept for a treadmill-and-spiral-propeller device for canal boats. The committee examined Burk's plans and rejected them as impracticable, citing both an inefficient propeller design and a flawed placement of the entire unit on a vessel's bow.[22]

Rufus Porter's "Horse Power Boat," published in the *American Mechanic* in 1842, is our earliest example of a vessel powered by a horse treadmill. Like its inventor, the boat was somewhat unusual. Designed for use in the shallow rivers of the southern and western states, it was a simple, flat-bottomed craft 9.1 meters (30 ft.) in length by 1.8 meters (6 ft.) in breadth. The hull drew no more than 22.9 centimeters (9 in.) of water when fully laden with ten passengers, horse, and treadmill. The horse and machinery occupied the middle third of the boat and were managed by the elevated steersman, who also controlled the rudder by an arrangement of lines and a rudder yoke. A painted awning and curtains completed the comfortable accommodations for the passengers. Porter's prototype cost two hundred dollars complete and ran at an average speed of 9.6 kilometers (6 mi.) per hour. "They will come into use," Porter assured the public, "and we may expect to see farmers har-

Figure 29. Rufus Porter's Horse Power Boat. From the *American Mechanic,*
24 September 1842.

ness their horses in a boat, to take a ride up or down a river, as familiarly as
they now do in a buggy or gig."[23]

The two decades between 1840 and 1860 witnessed the shift from the horizontal treadwheel to the new treadmill; most teamboats built after 1850
appear to have been treadmill-powered craft. By this time the advantages
for horse ferry owners were many—thanks to mass production and competition among manufacturers, treadmills were remarkably inexpensive when
compared to earlier types of machines; they were simple and cheap to maintain, took up little deck space, and did not weigh very much. Unlike treadwheels, which had to be built inside a hull and required specialized and
somewhat complicated hull construction, treadmills could be installed on a
ferry's deck and worked well on low-cost hull forms such as scows.

Photographs and prints show that the most common configuration for a
treadmill ferry had two one-horse machines placed on opposite sides of the
hull, with a passage up the middle for deck traffic. The Lake Champlain
horseboat *Gipsey* illustrated the drawback of having treadmills operate each
sidewheel independently: Horses walking at different paces made the boat
turn in a circle. This veering could be avoided or minimized, however, by
using horses of a similar size and gait. There were at least two variations in
treadmill-horseboat designs: a sidewheel boat with a single, centrally
mounted treadmill (this eliminated the steering problems caused by independently propelled sidewheels), and a sternwheeler propelled by a pair of
two-horse mills placed amidships.[24]

Two trends in North American horseboating become apparent in the second half of the nineteenth century. First, although scores of these craft would
be built and used after 1850, written descriptions and discussions of them
become increasingly scarce. Later references to horseboats by travelers are
often so generic—"crossed the river on a ferry worked by horses"—that it is
impossible to learn anything useful about the appearance or operation of

Figure 30. Sidewheel horseboat propelled by two one-horse treadmills, Chillicothe, Ohio, circa 1900. From the collection of the Public Library of Cincinnati and Hamilton County.

these ferries. The reason for this brevity is obvious: the novelty had worn off. By midcentury treadmills and teamboats were familiar to most people and thus did not inspire lengthy explanation. Fortunately, the paucity of written records is offset by the invention of photography, and it is through photographs that we are able to learn much of what we know about horse ferries of the late nineteenth and early twentieth centuries.

The disdainful or humorous tone of later nineteenth-century horseboat descriptions also suggests that the public perception was changing, that these craft were increasingly viewed as rustic, antiquated relics of a bygone era. The comment of a traveler to Omaha, Nebraska, in 1862 is typical: "We crossed the Platte at Oreapolis on a little rickety horse-power ferry boat. It looked to us as if we might have rolled up our pants, waded, and saved the ferryman's fee, but we didn't."[25]

The second trend in later nineteenth-century horse ferry use was their ongoing replacement at heavily trafficked water crossings by railroads, bridges, and steam ferries. The trend was particularly apparent in the industrialized northeastern region of the United States, where transportation developments eliminated horsepower at most ferries by the 1860s. Pictorial and written evidence after 1850 strongly hints that horse-powered craft were being relegated to the economic margins of North America, to rural regions with low population density and a lack of sufficient capital to develop railroads or build bridges. The majority of treadmill ferries seem to have been employed in the American midwest and far west and on remote stretches of Canadian lakes and rivers.

Samuel Wiggins retired his St. Louis horseboat ferries in the late 1820s, but equine-powered craft remained in common use on the Mississippi River—particularly on the upper reaches of the river—until the beginning of the twentieth century. Photographs of upper-Mississippi ferries show what were probably typical late nineteenth-century horseboats at the minor ferry crossings on this river. For example, there is the picture of the two-horse, two-treadmill boat that worked the crossing between Cassville, Wisconsin, and the Turkey River in Iowa.[26] The ferry had a shallow-draft scow hull about 13.7 meters (45 ft.) in length, covered by a broad, overhanging deck. The paddle boxes and guards are supported by two transverse trusses (upright wooden posts with wrought-iron rods tightened by turnbuckles). In the view, taken from off the boat's starboard bow, the ferry has just pulled into shore; the horses stand in their inclined stalls, and two wagons and teams (clearly representing the ferry's maximum capacity for wheeled vehicles) wait to roll off the deck and onto the riverbank. The steering oar has been taken out of its socket on the ramp and placed on the starboard guard.

The Cassville ferry was converted to gasoline power sometime before 1915. A second photo of the ferry, taken around the time of the conversion, shows the treadmills removed or covered. Two horses stand in the center of the deck, and it would appear that the photographer and the ferry's two crewmen are making a statement: Horses now ride on this boat as passengers, not as part of the crew.[27]

Another example of an upper–Mississippi River treadmill ferry, photographed around 1890, operated between Gordon's Ferry in Jackson County, Iowa, and Simond's Ferry west of Galena, Illinois. The ferry's owner, Miles Simond, lived on the Illinois side of the river, but Iowans wishing to cross the river could raise a flag, and he would load up his horses and go pick them up. The photo indicates that Simond made extra money by using his ferry as a floating billboard, for the slogan "Use YEAST FOAM" is painted in bold letters on the paddle box. The ferry was said to be a great convenience for Iowans transporting cattle to the Galena market and returning home with foodstuffs, hardware, and barrels of beer.[28]

Photographs and brief historical accounts indicate that horse ferries were a familiar sight on the lower Missouri River. A six-horse horizontal-treadwheel boat was operating in 1834 at St. Charles, but the greater number of

Figure 31. Horseboat ferry at Cassville, Wisconsin, circa 1900. Courtesy of the State Historical Society of Wisconsin. Negative number (F4)320.

Missouri River teamboats were built in the 1840s and later. Crossings known to employ these craft included Washington, New Haven, Jefferson City, Rocheport, Booneville, and Waverly in Missouri, and farther upriver Kansas City, Leavenworth, Port Lamb, and Atchison in Kansas all had horseboats working along their river fronts.[29] Undoubtedly there were many others, but records relating to these boats have proved elusive. We do know, however, that William M. Chick's mid-nineteenth-century horse ferry at Kansas City once hauled a traveling circus over the river, including a reluctant elephant that had to be coaxed on board. Jumbo completed the trip in excellent shape, but the same could not be said for the elephant-trodden boat, and Chick was forced to sue the circus owner for ten dollars to cover the costs of deck repairs.[30]

The sternwheel horseboats that operated along the Missouri River during the second half of the nineteenth century differed from all other known types of treadmill ferries in their hull designs and machinery layout. Photographs of the Missouri sternwheelers show vessels resembling western river steamboats.[31] These ferries had molded bows, quite unlike the flat-ended, scow-hulled treadmill boats we have seen elsewhere. Loading and unloading were accomplished by ramps that lowered from the sides rather than the ends, and carriages, wagons, and livestock all rode on the open foredeck. The amidships portion of the deck was sheltered by a roof, and a fully enclosed deckhouse

Figure 32. Sternwheel treadmill horseboat *Tilda-Clara,* New Haven, Missouri, circa 1880s. This photograph was taken early in the ferry's career. Note the "powerplant" amidships (two two-horse treadmills) and the long drive chain that extends aft along the stern cabin to the sternwheel. From the collection of the Public Library of Cincinnati and Hamilton County.

in the stern protected passengers from the elements. In the grand tradition of Mississippi and Missouri River steamers, a pilothouse, complete with a huge wheel, was placed atop the superstructure.

Power for the sternwheel was provided by a pair of aft-facing two-horse treadmills mounted amidships, where their weight would place the least amount of strain on the hull and have little effect on the ferry's fore-and-aft trim. The motion of the horses on the treadmills was transmitted to the stern-wheel by a dual chain-and-sprocket-wheel arrangement that extended along the port and starboard sides of the stern cabin. When the ferry was ready to start for the opposite shore, the pilot released a brake on the treadmills and the horses would start walking, slowly at first and then with greater speed as the ferry picked up momentum; at the end of the passage the brake would be reapplied, but gradually, so that the horses and paddlewheel were not jerked abruptly to a stop.[32]

Figure 33. Sternwheel treadmill horseboat *Tilda-Clara,* New Haven, Missouri, circa 1880s. The ferry has aged and is now reinforced by a pair of longitudinal hogging trusses (the man in the upper left is leaning against one of the trusses' support posts). The name painted on the front of the pilot house has faded and is partially obscured by a board posting the *Tilda-Clara*'s ferriage rates. Courtesy of Ellen Zobrist, New Haven, Missouri.

The New Haven ferry *Tilda-Clara* operated in the 1880s and was named for Tilda Strutman and Clara Blaske, daughters of the boat's owner-captains, Henry Strutman and Frank L. Blaske. According to one account, Strutman and Blaske once asked an old steamboat captain named William Heckman for help in obtaining a license to operate their ferry. Heckman replied tersely: "You don't need a license to shovel horse shit."[33]

The *Tilda-Clara* was the stage for an amateur production of "Mutiny on the Horseboat" when one of the equine crew opted to violently jump ship. The mutineer in question belonged to the Blaske family (Blaske's son Hugh described the horse as a "family pet") and was apparently aboard as a temporary replacement for a disabled horse. Several weeks of unaccustomed labor on the treadmill brought simmering resentment to the boiling point, and one day, as the *Tilda-Clara* was picking up a load of cattle from Boeuf

Island, the animal began to kick its way out of the treadmill. The ferry's human crew made a valiant effort to quell the riot, but the wooden sides of the stall proved unequal to the spirit they contained, and the mutineer successfully broke free and escaped over the side. A shore party apprehended the horse that night when it sought shelter in a Boeuf Island barn.[34]

Like the western river steamboats that the *Tilda-Clara* resembled, the lightly built hull eventually began to droop (or "hog") at the ends. Blaske and Strutman temporarily remedied the problem by installing a pair of hogging trusses consisting of two canted posts supporting a heavy iron rod that extended in an arc from amidships to the stern. A steam ferry called *Vienna* replaced the *Tilda-Clara* at New Haven ferry in 1888, and the horseboat was sold to the ferry keeper at Glasgow, Missouri.[35]

Around the turn of the century, a treadmill-equipped ferry crossed the Columbia River at Wallula Landing, Walla Walla County, Washington. This vessel belonged to ferry man E. A. Linn, who operated it in a highly unorthodox manner. Because of the strong currents at Wallula, Linn had the ferry's single horse, Old Jim, walk along the riverbank and tow the boat upstream for about 800 meters (half a mile); the horse would then board the craft, take his place on the treadmill, and the ferry would push off from the bank. The pilot controlled the angle of the boat in the current with a long steering oar as Old Jim churned away on the mill, and between them they would bring the ferry into the landing opposite their starting point. Here the horse would disembark and start the process over again. The job apparently affected Old Jim after a while, for a later owner described him as "cockeyed."[36]

During the second half of the nineteenth century some of the horse-treadmill craft in North America found employment as general-purpose workboats. At least three vessels of this description could be found on Lake Winnipesaukee, New Hampshire, in the 1870s and 1880s, hauling passengers and freight to communities not served by Winnipesaukee's steamboats, transporting building materials such as lumber, bricks, and stone, ferrying sheep and cattle out to summer pastures on the lake's islands, and supplying steamers and lakeside towns with firewood. Two of the boats, belonging to Frank Wentworth of Meredith and Frank Smith of Long Island, stayed in service until the late 1870s, and the third, built by Stephen Wentworth of Center Harbor and commanded by Captain Leander Levallee, operated on the lake between 1878 and 1890. Photographs of Levallee's boat show an arrangement of machinery and hull like no other we have seen; obviously, this vessel was created specifically for Winnepesaukee's navigational conditions and local economy and was the product of local talent working with limited resources.[37]

Levallee's horseboat and others like it on Winnepesaukee were humble working craft and were not well documented in their day. Fortunately for us

Figure 34. Leander Levallee's Lake Winnepesaukee horseboat. Courtesy of the Wolfeboro Historical Society, Wolfeboro Falls, New Hampshire.

a maker of wooden model ships, Gordon A. Meader, took an interest in the lake's horseboats, and around 1930 he began collecting information from photographs and from lake boatmen, including Leander Levallee. Meader published his reconstructed plans and description of a typical late nineteenth-century horseboat in 1932, and his wooden model may still be seen at the Wolfeboro Historical Society, Wolfeboro Falls, New Hampshire.[38]

According to Meader's best estimates (based principally upon the recollections of old lakemen), the scow-hulled Winnepesaukee boats measured about 18.3 meters (60 ft.) in overall length and 12.2 meters (40 ft.) in length on the bottom, giving the ends an overhang of 3 meters (10 ft.). The hulls had a maximum beam amidships of 3.4 meters (11 ft.), and the sides were about 1 meter (3 ft.) high. These dimensions made for long, narrow, shallow-draft boats, perfectly suited for the nature of the work on the lake. According to Meader the minimal draft and long overhang at the bow permitted Levallee and other horseboat captains to pull their boats close in to just about any shore when loading and unloading cargoes. The forward two-thirds of the vessels was simply an open hold; the after third was occupied by the propulsion system and crew quarters.

Propulsion was provided by a standard two-horse treadmill mounted with the tread at gunwale level. The power-transmission arrangement was elementary: two spur gears, one on the treadmill and one on the sidewheel axle. The treadmill gear was half the size of the axle gear, a ratio that allowed the tread to turn faster than the paddles and generate a greater amount of power. The weight of the cargo could greatly alter the draft of these boats, so the paddle wheels and their axle were placed between upright posts where they could be adjusted easily up or down by means of levers and secured with wooden pegs. Construction costs were kept to a minimum— there were no paddle boxes over the sidewheels, nor was there any type of covering to protect the horses from the weather.

Winnepesaukee is a large lake, and the call of business could take a horseboat far from its home port, so the vessels were fitted with two small deckhouses that overhung the sides abaft of the treadmill, allowing the crew to live aboard for extended periods of time. The houses were painted white and sometimes fitted with a small window facing aft; one house was used for cooking and the other for sleeping. The space between the two houses was decked at treadmill level to allow the horses to be loaded on and off from the stern. In contrast to the imposing pilothouses on the Missouri horse ferries *General Harrison* and *Tilda Clara*, the "pilothouse" on Winnepesaukee horseboats consisted of a heavy plank resting on the roofs of the two deckhouses; from atop this vantage point the pilot could see ahead, over the heads of the horses, and control the boat by means of an 5.5-meter (18 ft.) sweep that hung off the stern on an iron swivel. Some of the more talented captains learned to control the sweep with one foot, presumably to free their hands for important tasks like whittling or smoking a pipe. The pilot's assistant, the "engineer," attended the horses with a whip or a shovel, depending upon the needs of the moment. A third crewman was sometimes hired to assist with maneuvering the boat and transferring cargoes.

Cargo-hauling horseboats were reportedly numerous on the lake between 1850 and 1875, and though the earlier versions varied in their design and dimensions, the later boats were more uniform in appearance. One old lakesailor recalled:

> In a calm or light breeze a horse-boat could make 5 to 7 miles [8–11 km] an hour depending on the load, but in a high wind they were helpless and usually sought shelter in the lee of some island until the wind went down. On a still day the clatter of the treadmill could be heard for miles. When the horses became tired oats were sometimes held in front of them to speed them up. Although there were many builders and owners, all [horseboats] were built near the place of their origin. They were built bottom-up on the shore of the lake during the winter. Of course there were never any plans.[39]

Leander Levallee retired the last Winnepesaukee horseboat in 1890 or 1891 and went on to become a celebrated lake steamboat captain.

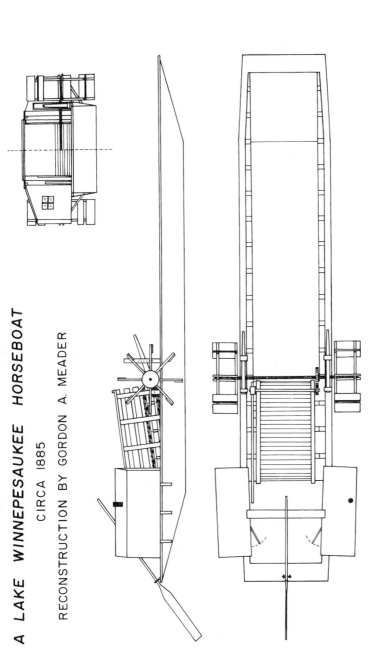

A LAKE WINNEPESAUKEE HORSEBOAT

CIRCA 1885

RECONSTRUCTION BY GORDON A. MEADER

Figure 35. Reconstruction of a Lake Winnepesaukee horseboat by Gorden A. Meader. Traced from Meader's plan in the *Mariner* (1932).

Treadmill horseboats worked on many other lakes and rivers in lumbering operations, quarrying businesses, hauling livestock between farms and pastures, and in just about any sort of task that required a low-cost, self-propelled freight carrier. Vessels on this sort of career track are, unfortunately, even more obscure in the historical record than teamboat ferries, and it is difficult to learn much about them.

SWEEP POWER: THE RETURN OF THE HORSE WHIM

Another slightly earlier use of a horse-powered craft as a workboat deserves special mention here. This was a late-1840s revival of the "horse boat as a long-distance cargo carrier" concept that proved so unsuccessful for John Brookhart's *Horse Boat* in 1807–8 and William Bird's *Genius of Georgia* in 1820. The later effort, the brainchild of Captain Ben Wilson of Coalsmouth (now St. Albans), West Virginia, was called *Adventurer*. The vessel was built on the banks of the Kanawha River, a tributary of the Ohio. Wilson's "boat" was one of the largest horse-powered craft ever built, measuring 36.6 meters (120 ft.) in length by 5.5 meters (18 ft.) in beam; it should perhaps be referred to as a "horseship." The motive power for the *Adventurer* was four horses, who walked in a circle on the deck to rotate a horse-whim mechanism attached to a pair of sidewheels. The vessel's pilot navigated from a pilot-house placed on the bow.

Ben Wilson's plan was simple: take on a cargo of West Virginia salt and head for New Orleans via the Kanawha, Ohio, and Mississippi Rivers, then return with a cargo of molasses and sugar. With a crew of five men and four horses, the *Adventurer* set off in early April 1848 and seemingly met with an extraordinary degree of good luck all the way down and back. The vessel paddled back up the Kanawha to Coalsmouth only seven months later, on 21 October. It is difficult to believe that four horses could have made any headway propelling so large a craft against the current of the lower Mississippi, and it seems likely that Wilson was towed by a steamer at least part of the way back home. The molasses and sugar sold well in West Virginia, and the voyage was reportedly a profitable one for Ben Wilson. Half a year of continuous work at the horse whim had a predictable effect upon the horses: "They were observed walking in a circle when turned out to pasture."[40] We will never know if another voyage would have been attempted, for during the winter of 1848–49 river ice sank the *Adventurer*. Wilson's dizzy horses could not have mourned the loss.

The *Adventurer* highlights an interesting phenomenon in North American horseboating, that is, the reemergence of the horse-whim mechanism on teamboats. Although eclipsed by the turntable, horse-whim boats may not have entirely disappeared between 1820 and 1840. Paintings of the

St. Lawrence River waterfront between Quebec City and Point Levi, Quebec, dating from the late 1820s and early 1830s, show a horse-whim-propelled ferry in operation.[41] Unlike the earlier whim ferries used in North America, this one was built upon a single hull. The space taken up in the center of the deck by the horse walkway is considerable, and there appears to be room on this boat only for passengers, baggage, livestock, and possibly one or two small carriages. For a short-distance ferry crossing with a limited amount of business, which seems to have been the case with the Quebec–Point Levi operation, a boat with this sort of machinery was no doubt sufficient.

Barnabas Langdon's patent of 1837 and other whim-machinery patents of the 1830s and 1840s show that this type of power equipment was being improved at the same time that the treadmill was being developed and mass produced.[42] For land-based applications the horse whim did have certain advantages: The largest treadmills had a capacity of just three horses, whereas whim mechanisms could harness many more horses and thus generate more power. Indeed, some of the larger versions were rotated by as many as six teams (twelve horses). By the second half of the nineteenth century farm-equipment manufacturers were turning out portable whims with folding or detachable arms; known as "sweep powers" or "lever powers," the devices were used to run large-capacity threshing machines, saws, churns, feed mills, pumps, and corn shellers.[43]

The J. I. Case Company advertised its sweep power under the heading "A merciful man is merciful to his beast," but there is no evidence to suggest that the horses plodding in circles around these later machines found the work less oppressive than on earlier versions. Nevertheless, whims had the advantage of being mechanically simple, a fact that may account for their reappearance on later horse-powered boats. This was a machine that could be purchased or fabricated by boatmen who could not afford treadmills; the whim may also have provided a slightly greater margin of power for boats operating against a stiff current.

Besides Captain Ben Wilson's 1848 *Adventurer,* at least seven examples of later horse-whim boats have been identified (and there were undoubtedly many others that we do not know about). Illustrations and descriptions suggest that most sweep-power boats were locally designed and built on an extremely tight budget. Captain Henry Strutman's first horseboat is a perfect example of the low-budget concept: a catamaran floating on two hollowed-out cottonwood logs and powered by one horse turning in a circle.[44] It should be noted that although the whim returned to horseboating in the late nineteenth century, catamarans like Strutman's seem to have been a rarity.

A four-horse sweep-power boat is featured in photographs belonging to the Georgeville, Quebec, Historical Society. The boat, known locally as the *Hayeater,* navigated Lake Memphremegog in the 1880s and 1890s.

Propulsion was provided by a pair of crude, narrow-bladed sidewheels located amidships and powered by four horses or mules walking in an extremely tight circle between the paddle boxes. The hull of this craft was unusual for a late nineteenth-century horseboat, for instead of the typical scow form it had the long, narrow, streamlined shape and high freeboard typical of contemporary lake steamships. One eyewitness to the boat's trips across the lake recalled the yells of the boy driver: "Far away on moonlit evenings or in the calm of a summer afternoon one could hear the nasal exhortation, 'G'lang naow! What y'abaout!' as a wagon was being taken across." A former passenger on this boat remembered: "many pleasant moonlight excursions . . . with the patient horses walking round and round to operate the paddles."[45]

At least three horse-whim ferries navigated the Columbia River in Oregon and Washington at the turn of the century. The first of these boats was built by Jehu Switzler sometime after he took over ferrying operations in 1896 at Umatilla, Oregon.[46] The most striking feature of Switzler's scow-hulled craft was its overhead radial bar, an element reminiscent of the 1732 horseboat design of Maurice, comte de Saxe. A pair of horses harnessed beneath oppo-

Figure 36. Whim-powered sidewheel horseboat on Lake Memphremegog. This boat was known to its patrons as the *Hayeater.* Courtesy of the Georgeville Historical Society, Georgeville, Quebec.

Figure 37. Jehu Switzler's Columbia River horseboat, Umatilla, Oregon, circa 1900. Traced from a faded photograph in the collection of the Umatilla County Historical Society.

site ends of the bar orbited the outside of the boat, turning the bar and revolving a central axle fitted at either end with gear-and-chain drives that spun the sidewheels. The early catamaran horseboats built at New York in 1814 concentrated the machinery and walkway in the center of the vessel and left the surrounding deck for passengers and cargo. Switzler, limited to a small, shallow-draft scow, took the opposite approach and constructed a pen to contain horses, cattle, and pedestrians within the walkway. The ferry had a peculiar appearance but was a masterpiece of creative engineering.

A slightly different form of whim-powered ferry shows up in the photographic collections of the Umatilla County Historical Society; the boat is identified as Switzler's, but information on its career is lacking. It probably succeeded the craft described above. On this ferry the whim crossbar was lowered to waist level, and the circular horse track was moved to one end of the boat, leaving the other end free for horses, cattle, and people.[47]

The third example of a sweep-powered horseboat on the Columbia River was a scow-hulled vessel built in 1901 and put to work at the Beverly, Washington, ferry crossing. This boat was built for ferry man George Borden, and though similar in general layout and design to the overhead-crossbar Umatilla boat, it was even smaller and flimsier in appearance. Because of this ferry's diminutive size (about 9 m or 30 ft. long), the horse walkway extended proportionately much farther out from the sides; seen from above, the vessel would have looked like a floating circle with a pair of protruding ramps. The central cargo stall had a capacity limited to perhaps ten cattle, and when a larger cargo required passage the ferry towed it across on a barge. The

Switzler and Borden boats were all replaced by steam- or gasoline-engine boats sometime before World War One.[48]

A pictorial record of another whim-powered ferry was preserved for posterity when W. M. Collins of New York submitted his photograph of a horseboat to *Leslie's Weekly* in 1907. The photo won the magazine's five-dollar first prize and inclusion in the 13 June edition of the paper. The caption under the picture reads like an epitaph, both for this boat and for the age of horseboats in general: "Curious craft of the olden time—last of the horsepower ferry-boats on the Mississippi River at St. Mary's, Mo., now replaced by modern vessels."

The boat in Collins's photo had the most elementary of hulls and machinery arrangements. The vessel's broad form and low freeboard indicate that it was nearly square in length and breadth and consisted of a decked-over scow hull surrounded above by a crude, open railing. The sweep power was located in the middle of the deck and rotated by four horses and mules walking in a tight circle. The machinery spun a pair of small, side-by-side sternwheels. The boat was steered by a long oar fixed on a support slightly to starboard of the paddle wheels. The homemade look of the entire craft, its hull, propulsion system, and steering apparatus, does not inspire confidence; this was obviously a low-budget ferry that brought its owner a few hardearned coins with each day's service on the river.[49]

FINALE

The equine-powered boat survived into the twentieth century at various obscure ferry crossings around North America, but the writing was on the wall: Floating horsepower was an anachronism and could not last much longer. The last horseboat to pass from service may have been a small, treadmill ferry propelled by a single blind horse; this boat, run by Ike Napier and Morgan Bolton, operated until the late 1920s at the Rome crossing on the Cumberland River in Tennessee.[50]

The end of the horse ferry era cannot be blamed on that perennial rival, the steam engine, for by the beginning of the twentieth century, steam had also passed through its glory days on lakes and rivers and was on its way to becoming an obsolete technology. Rather, a number of agents and circumstances, some old, some new, were combining to finally nudge the horseboat out of existence. By the beginning of the twentieth century the railroad had consolidated its hold over the countryside, and little in the way of freight or passenger traffic moved any distance unless it was over the rails. Bridge technology and bridge construction, too, continued apace, and every year new spans over the water drove a few more sail, horse, or steam ferries out of existence.

Figure 38. Sternwheel horseboat operating at St. Mary's, Missouri, circa 1900. From the collection of the Public Library of Cincinnati and Hamilton County.

Perhaps most importantly, a new source of power was taking hold in the early years of the twentieth century, one that would eventually supplant both horses and steam: the internal combustion engine. With its extremely compact size, simple and relatively safe operation, and enormous power-generating potential, this device would do for the twentieth century what the steam engine had done for the nineteenth, and even more. All facets of life and work in North America, transportation, agriculture, industry, indeed, society itself, were to be transformed in some way by the internal combustion engine.

The new machine had profound implications for draft horses everywhere, whether they worked on farms, in the fields and forests, on the streets and roads, or aboard boats paddling over the water. Within a few decades most horse-powered transportation would become purely recreational, a form of relaxation or entertainment, rather than an essential element in the working world. Farm horses would only occasionally contribute their labor, treadmills were tossed on the junk pile, and wagons and horse-drawn plows were left at the edge of fields to rot and rust. After centuries of hard work, the majority of North America's horses were going on a vacation of indefinite length.

Before we close the book on horseboat history and proceed to horseboat archaeology, let us take one last look at a ferrying business that operated in the twilight years of the teamboat era.

Figure 39. Louisville, New York–Aultsville, Ontario, ferry, St. Lawrence River, circa 1898. From Croil, *Steam Navigation.*

If you were in the little town of Louisville, New York, around 1910 and needed to cross the St. Lawrence River to the Ontario shore, then you likely would have taken passage on Robert Donnelly's horseboat.[51] The ferry ran the 1.6-kilometer (1 mi.) distance between Louisville Landing on the New York side to Empy's Landing at the foot of Max Island (from the landing it was only 1.6 kilometers or 1 mile to Aultsville, Ontario). Donnelly had a farm on the Canadian side of the river and made the crossing on an as-needed basis only. Customers on the American shore raised a white flag when they needed the ferry; Donnelly would send out a couple of boys to round up the boat's power plants from where they were grazing along the roadsides, and the boat would push off.

The Louisville–Aultsville horseboat was a small, economical affair, with a shallow hull, a narrow deck, a pair of sidewheels, and a railing around the sides. The power mechanism, a single two-horse treadmill, was mounted in the middle of the deck just abaft the sidewheels; vehicles and most livestock had to ride on the short length of deck forward of the treadmill. The foredeck could accommodate two horse-drawn wagons or buggy rigs, or two cars (although cars were rare in this part of the state in 1910). Donnelly made extra money by freighting local cattle out to the river's islands in the springtime to graze through the summer months and then took them home in the fall. He also took Sunday-school picnickers out to the islands for a day's outing.

Donnelly's boat had been operating since the 1890s (if not earlier) and charged 50¢ to cross the river; he later had to raise the fare to 75¢ to make any profit at all. Despite this reasonable rate the horseboat had competition, for some riverfront dwellers made extra money rowing people across the St. Lawrence for only 25¢. By 1910 the horseboat had made a good many revolutions on its sidewheels and much water had passed under the keel, but Robert Donnelly kept up with the maintenance and squeezed several more years of ferrying out of his boat before competition from motor boats became too strong to stay in business.

PART TWO

The Archaeology of the Burlington Bay Horse Ferry Wreck

9

The Wreck in
Eight Fathoms

Our introduction to the wreck of the horseboat in Burlington Bay took place in June 1984. At that time we were engaged in an intensive side-scanning sonar survey—sponsored by the Champlain Maritime Society and the Vermont Division for Historic Preservation—to locate and inventory shipwrecks in Lake Champlain. One of the areas chosen for inspection was Burlington Bay, Vermont, the focus of much commercial activity in the nineteenth century and the scene of numerous vessel losses. Wrecks sunk in the bay included sloop- and schooner-rigged sailing craft and an assortment of canal boats; some of these wrecks had already been located, and others had yet to be found and were known to us only through contemporary newspaper accounts.

There was one wreck in Burlington Bay we particularly wanted to see. During the previous year, a privately initiated sonar survey directed by James Kennard and Scott Hill of Rochester, New York, had located an unusual vessel off the Burlington shore. According to their report to state archaeologist Giovanna Peebles, the wreck had a pair of sidewheels, but no evidence of a boiler or steam engine; they suspected that their find was a horse-powered ferry. Like most historians of Lake Champlain, we had seen references to horse ferries in books and old newspapers, but in the absence of good illustrations or descriptions of these craft we had absolutely no idea what a typical horse ferry looked like or how it operated. The prospect of actually seeing such a vessel was tantalizing.

We did not have to wait long once our survey began. The sonar operator, Alan Bieber of Ocean Survey, Inc., picked up a likely looking target in a depth of about 15.2 meters (50 ft.) of water at the northern end of the bay. On subsequent dives we confirmed that it was the site reported by Kennard and Hill. The wreck lay upright, with a slight list to starboard; the lower hull was half-buried in the lake bottom and its interior was partially filled with soft, oozy sediments. The bow of the wreck (which could be identified by its curved stem—the stern had a straight post) pointed to the north. Two features were particularly prominent: the deck, which covered the after two-thirds of the hull, and the sidewheels with their eroded spokes that extended out like the splayed fingers of skeletal hands. The machinery that turned the sidewheels appeared complete, but there was nothing to suggest that the vessel ever carried a steam engine, only an arrangement of iron gears and a shaft that extended aft from the sidewheel axle to an enormous, horizontally oriented spoked wheel under the deck.

The absence of any signs of steam equipment certainly hinted that the 19.2-meter (63-ft.) long vessel had been powered by horses, but how did it work? How did the horses turn the wheel? And what was the wreck doing here in Burlington Bay? To the best of our knowledge horseboats had never worked on this part of the lake. As we hovered in the cold, hazy, yellow-green water around the wreck, it was clear that in 1984 our knowledge of horse-propelled watercraft was hopelessly inadequate to make sense of this find.

The archaeological significance of the ferry wreck was, for us, beyond question: It was the only horse-powered boat ever found in Lake Champlain. Indeed, to the best of our knowledge it was the only known example of an intact horseboat in the world. The wreck was wonderfully preserved, and we were certain that archaeological study could answer questions about this particular craft and illuminate a nearly forgotten form of maritime technology. Little did we know that the quest for knowledge about this wreck and North America's age of horseboats would involve four years of diving beneath the lake, countless hours in libraries and archives, and more than twelve years of research and analysis. The horse ferry has perfectly illustrated the simple but underappreciated reality of nautical archaeology: Finding a shipwreck is the easy part; ensuring that it is properly studied and preserved is an altogether different matter.

During the last one hundred years Lake Champlain, like most bodies of water around the world, has witnessed a wide variety of strategies in the study and preservation of shipwrecks, each with varying degrees of success or failure. These episodes offer a series of case studies to guide our present-day treatment of submerged archaeological sites. In the past century many significant wrecks have been found under the lake, often by people with a sincere interest in the warfare and commerce that were central to the region's

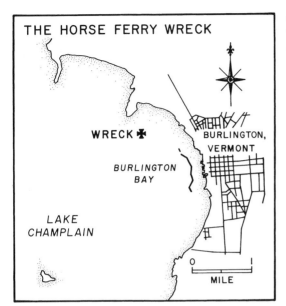

Figure 40. The horse ferry wreck in Burlington Bay. Map by Kevin Crisman.

early history. Some wrecks were found in shallow water, where they could be seen from the surface. More recently, searchers were able to find deeper wrecks by dragging wires across the bottom of the lake.

Many of the vessels thus located were raised to the surface to satisfy the curiosity of the finders and to provide souvenirs of a distant battle or trading activity. Unfortunately, the recovery of these wrecks in nearly all instances destroyed them, either immediately by dismemberment or more slowly by weathering and decay. The list of vessels lost to the practice of indiscriminate recovery includes the first large English warship on Lake Champlain, the brig *Duke of Cumberland* (1759), gunboats from Benedict Arnold's ill-fated Revolutionary War flotilla (1776), and the lake's first steamboat, *Vermont* (1809). A few recovered wrecks have survived, because of the foresight of their salvagers in shielding them from souvenir hunters and the elements. These include the Revolutionary War gunboat *Philadelphia,* now displayed at the Smithsonian Institution in Washington, D.C., and the War of 1812 schooner *Ticonderoga* at the Skenesboro Museum in Whitehall, New York.

The raising of shipwrecks has all but ceased in recent decades, but the number of underwater discoveries has greatly increased due to the development of a new and effective array of electronic underwater survey technologies. Side-scanning sonars, magnetometers, subbottom profilers, remotely operated vehicles (ROVs), and navigational control systems have allowed us to find shipwrecks, no matter where or how deep they may lie. The issue at hand is not how to locate underwater archaeological sites, because we have the capability to find nearly all of them, but rather what to do with ship-wrecks after they are found. The way we answer this question, and the deci-sions we make at this time, will directly determine what we preserve for the knowledge and enjoyment of future generations.

The horse ferry in Burlington Bay presented Vermont's Division for Historic Preservation with some difficult choices. As the official custodian of the state's submerged archaeological sites, the division is charged with pro-tecting wrecks on the Vermont side of Lake Champlain from accidental dam-age or intentional vandalism, overseeing archaeological study, and manag-ing the site in the public interest. Elements of the ferry's deteriorated hull were potentially vulnerable to injury, particularly the eroded oaken spokes of the sidewheels and the fragile softwood planks of the deck. Large numbers of divers visiting the wreck could greatly accelerate the deterioration of the wooden structure. On the other hand, the wreck was a fascinating relic of the lake's past, was certain to attract curious divers who wanted to know more about the vessel, and contained information that could be of great value to archaeologists and maritime historians.

The original finders of the wreck, Scott Hill and James Kennard, prepared a research plan that called for the creation of a photomosaic of the site; their plan ensured that no matter what happened to the site, there would be a visual record of the wreck's appearance at the time of its discovery. Hill and Kennard's plan was approved by the Division for Historic Preservation, and the systematic photographing of the wreck was success-fully carried out in 1984 with assistance from the division and the Champlain Maritime Society. After more than three months of cutting and fitting, Hill and associates Dennis Floss and Milton Shares completed a stem-to-stern mosaic of the ferry.

One side effect of the photographic work on the site was a series of arti-cles in local and regional newspapers, leading to a strong interest among area divers in seeing the wreck for themselves. Some of the local divers who par-ticipated in the photomosaic project occasionally revisited the site with selected friends, and over time the wreck's location became general knowl-edge. The increased diving activity raised concerns that eventually the hull would be inadvertently damaged, by anchors dropped from dive boats or by divers colliding with the fragile timbers.

During the winter of 1988 a research team sponsored by the National Geographic Society came to Lake Champlain to seek one of Benedict Arnold's missing gunboats from the 1776 battle of Valcour Island. While on the lake they were approached by members of the horse ferry project crew, and when the gunboat could not be located the decision was made to bring in ROVs to examine the ferry wreck through a hole cut in the ice. Maritime historian Donald Shomette of Maryland subsequently proposed to write an

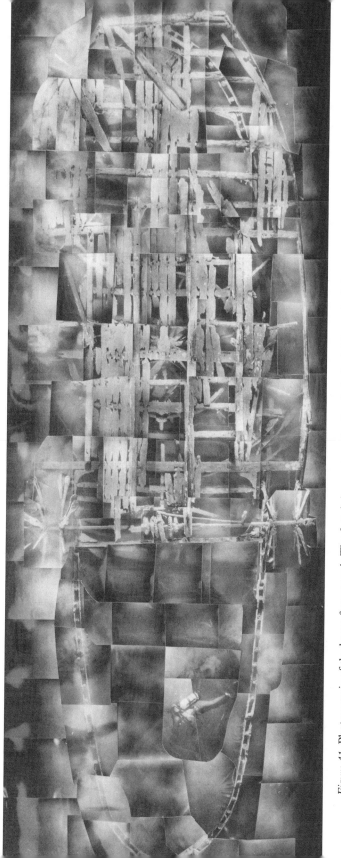

Figure 41. Photomosaic of the horse ferry wreck. The ferry's bow, minus the foredeck, is visible on the left; the sidewheels can be seen amidships, at the break of the deck; and the deteriorated horizontal treadwheel can be seen beneath the afterdeck. Courtesy of the Vermont Division for Historic Preservation. Mosaic developed by Scott Hill, Dennis Floss, and Milton Shares for the state of Vermont.

article about the ferry for *National Geographic* magazine. A lengthy series of negotiations took place between the Vermont Division for Historic Preservation and the National Geographic Society concerning publication and simultaneous protection of the site. The result of these discussions was an article on the ferry wreck (including a foldout of Hill's superb photomosaic) in the October 1989 issue of *National Geographic* and the donation of funds from the society to Vermont to assist in the management and study of the wreck.

A spirited but friendly debate arose among the preservation officials, archaeologists, historians, and divers about how the ferry wreck should be managed in the wake of the magazine article. Since its discovery the wreck had been considered too fragile to be opened to the public as one of the state's underwater historic sites (or "underwater preserves"), but the increased attention generated by the *National Geographic* article called for a reexamination of this approach. The consensus that emerged from the meetings and discussions was that the greatest threat to the wreck was likely to be divers dragging boat anchors in an attempt to locate the site.

The Division for Historic Preservation decided that the threat could best be minimized by including the wreck in the state's preserve system and establishing two heavy-duty mooring systems to facilitate visitation. Increased diver activity around the hull was likely to cause deterioration of hull timbers, but this was considered the lesser of the dangers. In light of this decision, the division also decided to begin a full-scale archaeological study to ensure that the information contained in the ferry's structure would be preserved no matter what happened to the wreck.

Preparation of the site for public visitation occurred in the summer and early fall of 1989. Signs indicating "fragile elements" were placed on the paddle wheels to encourage divers to avoid contact with the spokes, and strongly worded recommendations for "no impact" buoyancy control were written into preserve pamphlets and literature. Since its opening in 1989 the site has been monitored to identify problems related to diver visitation, and at the time of this writing the wreck has received only fairly minor damage, principally to the spokes and deck planking. Thus far, the inclusion of the horse ferry into the state's historic preserve program appears to have worked well in sharing this remarkable site with hundreds of interested divers, while minimizing deterioration of the site.

THE 1989 SURVEY OF THE WRECK

Turning the horse ferry into a preserve provided a way for divers to visit the wreck but did little to share this unique craft with archaeologists, maritime historians, and the nondiving public. The Division for Historic Preservation therefore initiated a multiyear program of archaeological study, the objective of the work being to complement Hill's photomosaic with detailed measurements, written descriptions, scale plans, photographs, and video footage of the vessel and its construction. This information would constitute a permanent archival record of the ferry and could be used to analyze the hull and its horizontal-treadwheel mechanism. The archaeological data would allow the preparation of scale plans showing the ferry's design, assembly, and original appearance. Finally, intensive study of the wreck had the potential to yield clues to the ferry's identity, date of construction, operational career, and the date and circumstances of its sinking.

The first phase of the archaeological study was a two-week effort, conducted by Kevin Crisman and a team of three divers in September 1989. The objectives of this preliminary study were simple: to document parts of the hull protruding above the lake bottom (particularly fragile timbers such as the softwood deck planking that might be easily damaged by visiting divers), and to study the mysterious treadwheel–sidewheel propulsion mechanism.

Project logistics and dive scheduling for the 1989 project were simplified by the small size of the crew, the proximity of the wreck to the Burlington waterfront, and the moderate depth of water over the wreck. Dive operations were staged out of the Waterfront Diving Center, and mooring over the site was facilitated by the installation of concrete pads in preparation for opening the site as a preserve. The crew was divided into two-person teams and all dives were conducted as no-decompression dives. As diver safety is always the highest priority, a set of procedures regarding minimum air, backup air systems, thermal comfort (in other words, chilling), and maintaining contact with one's diving "buddy" were adopted to maximize the safety and efficiency of the operation.

Each diver was assigned one or more measuring tasks for each dive. Our approach was low-tech: Measurements were taken with rulers, yardsticks, and tapes calibrated in feet and inches. We chose to use the imperial rather than the metric standard for recording because the ferry was probably built by shipwrights working in that system. All measurements, sketches, and observations were recorded with mechanical pencils on sheets of plastic drafting film attached to conventional clipboards. The data recorded underwater were recopied onto graph or notebook paper at the end of each day and entered into a project notebook.

The hull specifications collected during the initial survey in 1989 were used to prepare a plan view of the horse ferry and a preliminary report on its design and construction.[1] The survey also provided the information necessary to organize the subsequent phases of the horse ferry archaeological study. We had been collecting documents relating to horse ferries ever since our first look at the hull in 1984, but the process of archival research greatly accelerated in 1989. An effort was begun to systematically locate and copy historical records pertaining to horse ferry design, construction, and use on Lake Champlain and other waterways throughout North America.

DIGGING FOR ANSWERS, PART ONE: THE 1990 EXCAVATION

The first phase of the horse ferry project in 1989 focused entirely on the wreck's exposed topsides, but the goals for the 1990 season of work were somewhat more ambitious and involved partial excavation of the sediments filling the interior of the ferry's bow. Our reasons for selecting the bow were twofold. First, the ends of a wooden hull generally say a great deal about how a vessel was designed and built, and we wanted to see how the forward end of the hull was assembled. Second, the deckless bow was highly accessible, and divers would not have to squeeze between deck beams while they were digging and measuring. The two-week 1990 project was sponsored jointly by the Vermont Division for Historic Preservation and the Lake Champlain Maritime Museum. The dive team consisted of project directors Crisman and Arthur Cohn, five divers, and an artifact cataloger.

Efficient organization of the land and water aspects of the project was necessary to accomplish the season's objectives effectively. The shoreside base for the 1990 project was a nearly empty storage shed on the Burlington waterfront that belonged to the U.S. Naval Reserve. For the onwater part of the work, a good primary dive boat was all-important, and we were fortunate to have at our disposal the RV (Research Vessel) *Neptune*, a 12.2-meter (40 ft.) steel-hulled boat with a nearly perfect mix of protected interior space and open deck area. Captained by veteran lake mariner Fred Fayette, the *Neptune* was equipped with marine radios, a galley, a head, and ample space for diving equipment, artifact storage, and water pumps that powered our excavation dredges. A 5.2-meter (17 ft.) inflatable boat served as a tender for launching and retrieving divers.

The removal of sediments from inside of the ferry's bow was accomplished by means of a water dredge system powered by a 5-centimeter (2 in.) water pump. Materials vacuumed up by the dredge were moved off the site through a long discharge pipe and then sifted through a fine-mesh net bag to ensure that small artifacts overlooked during excavation were not lost. At the completion of each excavation level the net bags were changed, brought to the surface, and carefully checked by support personnel.

A grid measuring 4.6 meters in length by 1.5 meters in width (15 ft. × 5 ft.) was placed over the port side in 1990 to define the extent of our excavations and to serve as a reference point for mapping artifacts and hull timbers. The grid was subdivided into three 1.5-meter (5-ft.) square excavation units numbered, from fore to aft, 201, 202, and 203. Smaller, irregularly shaped

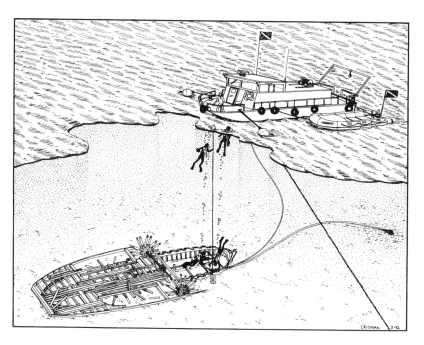

Figure 42. Perspective of the ferry wreck and the RV *Neptune*. Drawing by Kevin Crisman.

excavation units were created by extending grid material outboard from the main grid to the interior of the port side; these smaller units were numbered, from fore to aft, 101, 102, and 103. Vertical control of the excavation was maintained by establishing a datum point on the inside of the stem's apron timber; the vertical control of the excavation and the location of artifacts were determined by measurements with a plumb bob and a line level.

Excavation of each unit was assigned to a team of two divers, who worked through the day on a rotational system with one dive in the morning and one in the afternoon. Most teams alternated tasks on each dive, with one person handling the actual digging and the other taking notes and measurements, tagging and bagging artifacts, and keeping track of bottom time and air consumption.

In order to control the pace of digging and ensure that artifacts were properly recorded, divers were instructed to remove sediments in 10-centimeter (4 in.) levels. The locations of artifacts found during the digging were carefully recorded with measurements and sketches, and significant finds were left in place until they could also be recorded with photographs and video footage. Once artifacts had been tagged, bagged, and brought to the surface, they were turned over to an artifact cataloger who assigned each item a permanent number and entered all relevant data into a master artifact log-book. The artifact inventory was divided into six categories, with prefix numbers that indicated material type: 01 for wood, 02 for stone, 03 for metal, 04 for leather, 05 for glass or ceramic, and 06 for bones or other organic materials.

After each excavation unit had been cleared of sediment down to the interior of the hull, the exposed frames, planking, and other structural timbers were photographed, drawn, and measured. Our measurements of the hull included two levels of recording: the location, relative to the excavation grid, of all exposed hull timbers beneath an individual unit, and the location of all exposed portside timbers relative to one another. This dual approach to hull recording yielded redundant measurements of the structure, thereby allowing greater accuracy in vessel construction drawings.

Because of the ferry's list to starboard, the accumulations of sediments inside the hull were deepest on the starboard side and progressively decreased toward the port side; the three outboard units excavated in 1990, units 101–3, had only a thin covering of silt over the frames and ceiling. The three centerline units, 201–3, had a similar stratigraphic sequence with 7.6–12.7 centimeters (3–5 in.) of loose, almost soupy, grey-brown silt mixed with bits of lake weed. The dredge sucked this material up with little effort, but great care had to be taken not to stir it up when the dredge was not running, because the suspended silt could reduce visibility to a few centimeters. Beneath the layer of unconsolidated silt was a denser, light grey silt that became increasingly firm with depth. This material continued down to the frames and planking of the hull. The differing density of the silts appears to have resulted from the lower deposits becoming compacted over time.

The horse ferry wreck lies in fairly deep water, in an area little affected by strong currents or by the outflow of nearby rivers. Thus the sedimentary material that we removed from inside the hull during the project did not represent the workings of a dynamic environment—merely the slow, steady accumulation of fine debris settling out of the lake over a period of about 150 years. It is possible, however, that the interior of the wreck accumulated sediments at a faster rate than the surrounding lake bottom, as the sides of the hull might act as a trap for materials being transported by the slight bottom currents that we noted from time to time.

All of the excavation units yielded a curious stratigraphic feature at the juncture of the loose upper sediments and the compacted lower layer. This was a mass of unburned coal and fused chunks of coal clinkers or slag. The fact that the coal was suspended in the sediments indicated that it was not related to the horse ferry but rather was dropped into the wreck after its sinking. The source of the coal and slag was obvious: steamboats cleaning their fireboxes and dumping the contents overboard. During the slightly more

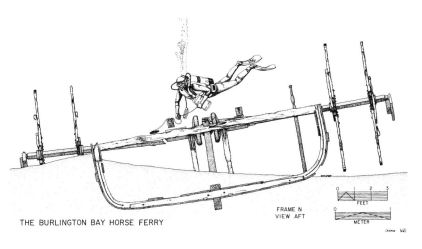

THE BURLINGTON BAY HORSE FERRY

FRAME N
VIEW AFT

Figure 43. Hull section of the horse ferry at the sidewheel axle, view aft. The ferry settled on the bottom with 9° list to the starboard side. Drawing by Kevin Crisman.

than one century between the sinking of the ferry and the retirement in 1950 of the lake's last sidewheeler, the horse ferry wreck lay directly beneath the path of coal-fired steamships entering and exiting Burlington harbor and inadvertently collected their waste.

Before we started digging we had no idea of the quantity or types of artifacts we would find within the ferry. That there would be at least a few items was a near certainty; we had never examined a wreck that did not have some refuse in the bilges. Two objects were visible before we even started digging: a heavily corroded iron gear wheel (03-011) lying on the port cant frames (the forward-angling frames in the bow) forward of unit 201, and two eroded planks protruding from the silt in the forward corner of unit 201 (see Chapter 10 and Appendix B for descriptions and illustrations of artifacts recovered from the horse ferry).

With the exception of the coal slag and a few heavily eroded scraps wood, most of the silt inside the bow's port side was devoid of natural or cultural debris. It was only when the excavation approached the wooden hull structure that artifacts associated with the ferry appeared. One of the first hull-related timbers to be uncovered was the ferry's keelson, the principal "backbone" timber bolted down the centerline of the hull's interior. As our intent in 1990 was to excavate only one side of the bow, we stopped digging on the starboard side of the keelson. The artifacts we uncovered began to bring the vessel's career and crew (both human and equine) into focus. There was no question we were dealing with a horse ferry: Several broken horseshoes were found in the bilges, along with fragments from a horse collar and leather

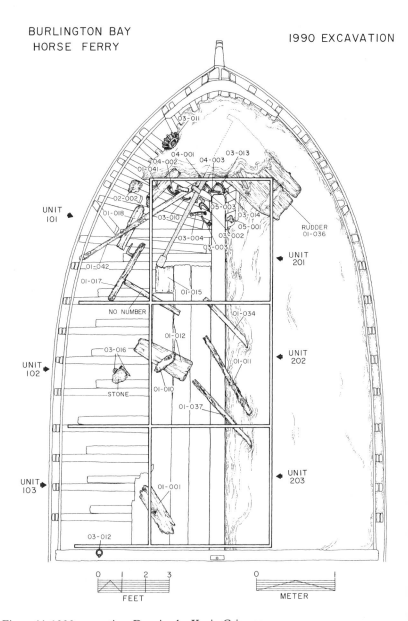

Figure 44. 1990 excavation. Drawing by Kevin Crisman.

harness-strap fragments. One of the more curious finds from the 1990 season was the base, spout, and body fragments from a brown-glazed, red earthenware teapot. What was a teapot doing on this vessel? We could only speculate.

The work in 1990 turned up not only a small but intriguing array of artifacts, but also well-preserved timbers that had previously been hidden from our view. At the forward end of the keelson, the base of a curved timber that reinforced the stem—the apron—appeared, as well as a series of cant frames. Divers cleared away the sediment down to 2.5-centimeter (1-in.) thick interior planks or "ceiling," recorded their dimensions and appearance, then gently removed them to expose the spaces between the frames, which were also dredged clean of silt. This permitted us to record frame construction patterns and record the curvature of the frames using an angle-measuring device called a goniometer.

During the two weeks of the 1990 project, 110 dives were staged on the wreck of the horse ferry.[2] The entire port side of the bow was exposed, measured, photographed, and recorded on video tape. The last task of the season was to backfill the exposed areas with sandbags to return the wreck to a condition and appearance similar to the way we found it at the beginning of the excavation.

DIGGING FOR ANSWERS, PART TWO: THE 1991 EXCAVATION

The principal objective of the third field season on the Burlington Bay horse ferry wreck was straightforward: to complete the study of the vessel's bow by excavating the starboard side of the hull and the semicircular area directly abaft the stem and apron. Secondary objectives for the project included excavation of the lower ends of the stem and sternpost, outside the hull, to record the dimensions of these timbers and to see how they were fastened to the ends of the keel.

Captain Fred Fayette's RV *Neptune* again served as the primary work platform over the wreck site, and two inflatable boats were available to serve as auxiliaries. The U.S. Coast Guard station at Burlington Bay graciously agreed to let us stage our operations out of their facility. A large trailer was rented and moved to the station to serve as our shore base for the duration of the project.

There was one major difference between the 1990 and 1991 projects, and that was in the nature of the project personnel and sponsoring institutions. The study of the horse ferry in 1991 was organized as a five-week nautical archaeology field school, jointly sponsored by the University of Vermont and Texas A&M University. Logistical support and funding were again provided by the Lake Champlain Maritime Museum and the Vermont Division for Historic Preservation, with additional support from the Institute of

Nautical Archaeology, a nonprofit research organization based at Texas A&M University.

Unlike the 1990 project, which had the single purpose of archaeologically investigating the ferry wreck, the 1991 field school combined both archaeological and educational objectives. This necessarily resulted in a different kind of field season, one that was longer and more measured in its pace. Project staff consisted of codirectors Crisman and Cohn, divemaster and photographer John Butler, Captain Fayette, five nautical archaeology graduate students from Texas A&M University, and six undergraduates from the University of Vermont.

The diving and archaeological procedures and the equipment employed during the 1990 excavation proved satisfactory, and, with one exception, no major changes were made in our 1991 project. The single exception was a change in our system of switching net bags at the end of the dredge spoil pipe; in 1990 we had used a cumbersome system of rubber connectors, hose clamps, and a nut driver, but in 1991, at the suggestion of team member Joe Cozzi, we adopted the quick-disconnect couplings used on fire hoses. The new couplings allowed us to switch dredge bags in less than thirty seconds, a major savings in time and frustration over the old procedure.

Excavation control and a reference for recording were again provided by a 4.6-by-1.5-meter (15 × 5 ft.) grid subdivided into three 1.5-meter (5-ft.) square units. The grid was placed within the starboard side of the bow, although the narrow breadth of the hull meant that the grid overlapped slightly into the area excavated in 1990. The three units were numbered, from fore to aft, 301, 302, and 303. A semicircular excavation unit, designated unit 200, was created inside the forwardmost part of the hull by adding a length of grid material to the forward edge of the main grid. Three smaller excavation units were created later in the excavation outboard of the main grid's starboard side; they were numbered, from fore to aft, 401, 402, and 403. These excavation units defined the extent of our digging within the hull in 1991.

The excavation, outside the hull, of the stem and the sternpost was not defined by a grid, nor did we attempt to remove the silt in 10-centimeter (4 in.) levels. The decision to dispense with controlled excavation outside the hull was based on two considerations: the limited amount of time we had for digging and the likelihood that the sediments outside the hull would contain little or no artifactual material. We did, however, retain the nylon net catch bag on the end of the dredge spoil pipe to retain any small objects overlooked by excavators.

The first week of the project was spent formally instructing the field school students on various aspects of lake history, archaeological excavation and

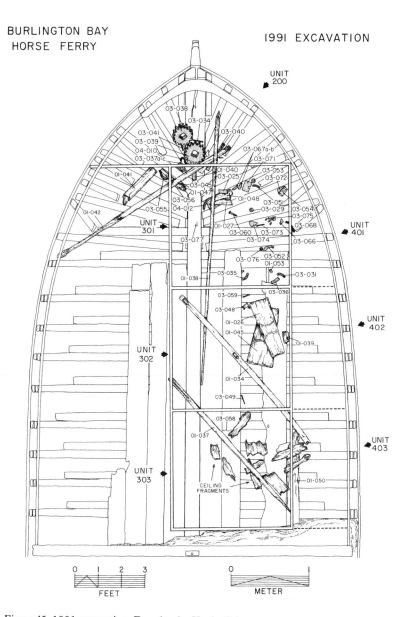

Figure 45. 1991 excavation. Drawing by Kevin Crisman.

recording, and diving and safety procedures. Our shore base and equipment were prepared for field work, and students were given orientations to the wreck. The second week saw the team begin work in units 301 to 303 and in bow unit 200. The removal of sediments proceeded at a slower pace than in 1990, because the students needed time to become familiar with dredging operations and recording procedures. The ferry's list to starboard also meant that we had a deeper accumulation of sediment to dredge before we reached the interior of the hull.

The uppermost 25.4 to 50.8 centimeters (10–20 in.) of sediments in starboard side units 301, 302, and 303 were composed of a soft, grey-brown silt containing a great quantity of decayed lake weed that resembled blades of grass clipped to 6.3-millimeter (¼ in.) lengths. The layer of dead weeds was not observed in the port side hull sediments in 1990, suggesting that this material had a tendency to settle in the lower part of the hull. Chunks of coal and slag were found near the bottom of the weed layer, and small fragments of highly eroded wood were mixed throughout the sediments. The upper layer of loose silt and organic material rested on a densely packed, light grey silt that extended down to the wooden hull structure.

The vertical location of artifacts within the hull followed the same pattern that we noted in 1990: Nearly every artifact lay at the bottom of the hold, either on the ceiling planking or between the frames. The greatest concentration of objects lay in units 200 and 301, in the forwardmost part of the bow. One particularly unexpected discovery was the ferry's complete rudder, which consisted of an iron post and two edge-fastened planks that made up the rudder blade (the ends of the planks had first been noted protruding from the sediments in 1989). The fact that the rudder was lying in the bow, rather than hanging off the sternpost, hinted that the ferry was probably not in working order when it sank. We completed the excavation of the rudder and then raised it to the surface where it could be recorded with measurements, drawings, and photographs. When the documentation was completed we reburied the rudder on the lake bottom.

Beneath the rudder lay an assortment of artifacts, the most impressive being two cast-iron spur gears (03-038 and 03-039) wedged directly on top of the apron timber. Adjacent to the gears were iron spikes, a leather harness fragment, and a well-used caulking iron (03-040). Also located in this area, within the unit designated 301, was a wooden-backed bristle brush (01-040) and horseshoe fragments. Further aft in unit 301 we found a complete horseshoe (03-035) as well as four horseshoe halves. Various fasteners such as iron nails, spikes, washers, bolts, and a brass tack were also found in 1991. The density and nature of the artifacts in the forward end of the vessel indicated that this part of the ferry's hold was used to store spare equipment and odds and ends of metal, leather, and wood that were being saved for repairs or scrap.

Units 302 and 303 and outboard units 401, 402, and 403 did not yield the same density of artifacts as units 200 and 301, but significant objects nevertheless turned up. These included an extremely worn brass bushing (03-048), two worn, hardwood tread planks from the horse walkway (01-026 and 01-045), and a length of wooden railing (01-034). We will take a closer look at the artifacts and what they can tell us in the next chapter. As in the previous season, once the artifacts and sediments were removed down to the ceiling planking and frames, the pine planks were lifted off the frames and the spaces between the frames were cleared of silt. Divers then concentrated on recording timber dimensions, construction techniques, and the shapes of selected frames.

At the conclusion of the field school, the artifacts located in 1990 and 1991 (with the exception of the hull timbers and the rudder) were packed and transported to Dr. D. L. Hamilton's conservation research laboratory at Texas A&M University. Here wood, metal, leather, and ceramic items were treated by nautical archaeology graduate student Tina Erwin, then rendered as ink drawings for inclusion in the artifact catalog (see Appendix B).[3] During the five weeks of the 1991 field school, 289 dives were staged on the wreck of the horse ferry; completion of hull measuring in the two weeks following the field school required an additional 34 dives.

DIGGING FOR ANSWERS, PART THREE: THE 1992 EXCAVATION

The last chapter in our horse ferry fieldwork came in 1992, with the fourth season of diving on the wreck. Having completed our study of the bow during the previous two years, attention was now turned to the interior of the stern, specifically the port side of the stern just abaft the treadwheel. Information on the hull form and the frame construction of this part of the wreck was essential for completing our goal of rebuilding the hull on paper. Other goals for 1992 included further excavation and recording of the stem and the recovery of wood samples for identification purposes from various hull timbers. We allocated three weeks for the project, which seemed reasonable given the time and resources at our disposal.

By this time the diving and excavation techniques employed on the wreck had been tested by two years' experience. We had to dispense with our standard 1.5-meter (5-ft.) square grids (for reasons discussed below), but otherwise no substantive changes were made in any of our procedures. The RV *Neptune* and a one-inflatable-boat consort again provided surface support for the diving operations. The Coast Guard station was undergoing major reno-

Figure 46. Diver recording frame sections with a torpedo-level goniometer. This simple device permitted us to record detailed frame sections in the bow and stern of the horse ferry. Photograph by John Butler.

vations, so our land base returned to the U.S. Naval Reserve station on the Burlington waterfront. We used a trailer once more to house our onshore operation. The 1992 project was again organized as a field school, with the same institutional players and staff as the previous season.

Our work in the stern was complicated by the presence of deck structure overlying the hull. This called for a careful, deliberate approach, for we did not want to damage the deck in any way, nor did we want any member of the diving team to get wedged under the deck beams. While preparing for the project we checked the gaps between the deck beams and determined that there was ample room for a diver to fit between them, provided that the diver moved slowly into position and kept gear tucked close to his or her body. To ensure safety in this confined space, every diver was equipped with a small, redundant scuba system known as a "pony bottle," and a full-sized spare tank and regulator were positioned under the deck near the working diver. A second diver monitored the below-deck diver, kept track of time and air, and stood by to render assistance in whatever way necessary.

We could not use our usual metal grid units for excavation and recording, because there was scant room under the deck to install them. A below-deck grid would also have constituted an entrapment hazard for divers working in the confined space. In place of the metal grid we used the deck beams located just above the divers to define the limits of our digging. The spaces between the beams were each given a numerical designation for recording purposes. The inboard limits of our excavation were determined by measuring the beam of the hull and selecting a point slightly starboard of the ferry's centerline; this ensured that we exposed the entire keelson within the trench. Digging proceeded quickly this year, and we were able to expose a substantial area of keelson, frames, and planking in just a few days' time.

Our stern trench revealed stratigraphy similar to what we had seen in the port side of the bow: soupy, grey-brown silt for the first 10 to 15.2 centimeters (4–6 in.) that transitioned into light grey, claylike material that stayed consistent in its color and texture down to the interior of the hull. The sediments in the stern held only minor amounts of coal and coal slag—not surprisingly, as the deck over the stern had been nearly intact when the ferry was found in 1983. The planking no doubt deflected sinking coal and clinkers and kept this material from accumulating inside the hull. The stern contained few artifacts: wood chips, a handful of iron spikes, and two leather harness fragments (04-014 and 04-015). There was no evidence on deck of a hatch that would have permitted access to the below-deck space in the stern, and the lack of artifacts confirmed that this part of the hull was not used for storage of equipment or refuse.

After we exposed and recorded the ceiling planks, they were removed and the spaces between frames were excavated to facilitate study of frame construction and curvature. Documentation of the exposed timbers included measuring, sketching, video and still photography, and the use of our angle-measuring goniometer to record the sweep of three frames and the stern knee. During this time we also employed a team of divers to recover wood samples from key hull timbers. The shipwright's choice of woods for a hull is a good indicator of expectations for strength and longevity; it was essential, therefore, that we knew what woods were selected for the various hull components. Samples were taken by chiseling 2.5-centimeter (1-in.) square pieces from individual timbers for identification by Dr. Roy Whitmore, professor emeritus of the University of Vermont Forestry Department (see Appendix C).

As in the previous seasons of study, the digging, recording, and backfilling kept us fully occupied right up to the end of our allotted time on the wreck. Over the course of the 1992 project the field crew made 160 dives on the horse ferry. In all, between 1989 and 1992, more than 700 dives had been staged to investigate the wreck and slightly less than half of the sediments filling the interior of the ferry were removed by our dredges (to be replaced by bottom sediments and bags of sand to protect the wood for the future). There is still much more to be learned from the ferry wreck, but by

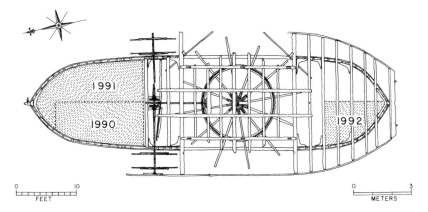

Figure 47. Horse ferry excavations, 1990–92. The shaded areas indicate the extent of our excavations within the hull over three field seasons. Drawing by Kevin Crisman.

1992 it was time to hang up our dredges, clipboards, and measuring tapes and start making sense of the data that we had already acquired.

The intensive four-year study of the horse ferry resulted in an enormous amount of information on the ferry's design, assembly, and career, information that was literally bulging out of our project notebooks. The next phase of the archaeological project was the part that the public rarely sees: hundreds of hours of analysis in laboratories, in libraries, at computers, and at a drafting table, the process whereby the minutiae collected under the water and in archives are transformed into written descriptions, ship plans, artifact catalogs, and museum exhibits. The ultimate product of archaeology is knowledge about the people who have gone before us, in this case about the North Americans who designed, built, and operated horse-powered boats.

The conserved horse ferry artifacts have returned to Vermont, where they are displayed at the Lake Champlain Maritime Museum as part of an exhibit about the lake's horse-powered vessels. Besides telling the story of horse ferries on Lake Champlain, the exhibit explains to the public how the discovery of the wreck and its archaeological study have led us to a greater understanding of the contribution of horse machinery to the mechanization of North America in the nineteenth century. In the fall of 1996 the exhibit added a half-scale horseboat treadwheel mechanism, designed for operation by children, so that young visitors can experience directly the effort required to propel a ferry by muscle power.

The horse ferry has now been a site in the Vermont Underwater Historic Preserve system for nearly a decade. It quickly gained a reputation for being one of North America's most interesting dive sites and has been visited each year by hundreds of divers. Since public visitation began, no vandalism or intentional damage has occurred, and indeed, most visitors seem to have gone out of their way to ensure that the site remains in its present condition for future generations. Unfortunately, as this chapter is being written, a new biological phenomenon accidentally introduced to North American lakes and rivers from Europe, the zebra mussel, threatens to cover all exposed portions of the hull and treadwheel machinery. We predict these tiny, prolific molluscs will quickly obscure all details of the horse ferry, making our archaeological study all the more timely and important.

Pieces of the Horseboat Puzzle

The Artifacts

We humans are a creative but inherently messy species. As we travel through life we continually shape and use objects, wear them out or break them, and then dispose of the remnants in the nearest convenient location. We are careless and accident prone, too, and manage to lose still-useful possessions on a regular basis, items as small and insignificant as a straight pin or a button, or as large and valuable as a fully laden ship. The debris intentionally or unintentionally left by our ancestors has a certain value, a value that should be measured as knowledge: It is an informal but intimate record of how they lived their lives. The business of the archaeologist is to locate the debris of the past, determine the manner in which it was created, used, and then discarded, and from it learn about the people who preceded us.

Nowhere is the human propensity for generating refuse more apparent than in the bilges of a wooden vessel. During a ship's lifetime the hull acts as a trash bin, collecting the debris produced by the builders and crew: wood chips, food remains, broken containers of wood, glass, and ceramic, remnants of various cargoes, lost tools and fittings. These bits of trash and lost equipment contain a wealth of information about a vessel's construction, career, and sinking, but the clues they hold can be deciphered only by careful archaeological work. Each artifact's location within the wreck must be recorded during excavation, and each must be properly preserved, cataloged, and analyzed after excavation if we are to realize its full potential for telling us about the past.

From the start of the horse ferry archaeological project in 1989, we fervently hoped that this vessel would be like any other wreck that we had previously studied and that its bilges would yield a rich collection of informative refuse. We began excavation with a long list of questions about the ferry, some of them specific and others quite general. Heading the list of specific questions were names, places, and dates: Whose horseboat was this, when was it built and who built it, where did it operate, and when did it sink? A name would allow us to connect the people, places, and events of nineteenth-century Lake Champlain with this particular wreck, and thereby reconstruct its unique story.

We were realistic, however, about the likelihood of learning the name of the vessel solely through excavation. Objects bearing a ship's name, or perhaps the name of a crewman, are occasionally found on wrecks, but just as often there is only circumstantial archaeological evidence for dating and identifying a vessel. In these instances, if archaeologists hope to find a name, they must combine evidence from a wreck site (the hull's size, location, or cargo, for example) with clues from archival sources. Clearly, the best way to identify this wreck would be to discover a written account of its loss.

Some of our questions about the ferry were more general and thus more likely to be answered by archaeological study of the hull and artifacts. We wanted to know more about the construction, operation, and maintenance of the vessel and its mysterious treadmill machinery, and there was little doubt that excavation would shed light on these aspects. We also hoped to learn as much as we could about the human and equine crew. How many people and horses were employed on board the ferry, and what tasks were part of their daily operation and maintenance of the vessel? And what about the "engines": was the boat propelled by massive Clydesdales, tiny Shetland ponies, or an intermediate size of horse?

Finally, we hoped to answer questions about the length of the ferry's service and the causes of its sinking. Was this a brand-new ferry at the time of the sinking, or was it a rotted-out old hulk, kept afloat only by constant caulking and pumping? And what sent the boat to the bottom—a storm, a collision, leaky seams, or intentional scuttling? Did everybody get off the boat in time, or were lives and property lost?

Although the horse ferry was hardly laden to the gunwales with artifacts, the bow and stern excavations nevertheless yielded a fine selection of objects. Over three seasons of digging we cataloged 278 artifacts of all shapes, sizes, materials, and functions. Three broad categories of finds were apparent to us, categories based on function: (1) hull elements (iron bolts, spikes, nails, plank and rail timbers, and the rudder), (2) propulsion machinery (cast-iron gears and an axle coupling, a copper-alloy axle bushing, and treadwheel planks), and (3) horse equipment (whole and broken horseshoes and iron, wood, and leather harness fragments). A fourth category was created to encompass everything else: miscellaneous finds (a glazed earthenware teapot, a caulking iron and other tools, organic debris, and an assortment of metal, wood, glass, and ceramic bits and pieces).

From the first artifact discovery in 1989 (a gearwheel lodged between two frames near the bow), patterns began to emerge in the variety, condition, and location of the artifacts. With each season of digging and each new find, our understanding of the vessel was revised; earlier ideas and explanations were confirmed or discarded, some of our longstanding questions were answered, and a whole range of new inquiries appeared before us. Much of the pleasure to be found in archaeological work lies in its dynamic nature: Every new bit of information adds to what was previously known, but the direction of the inquiry can zig and zag in unexpected directions.

The following is an overview of the artifacts that we found within the wreck of the horse ferry and a summary of what we learned from them. Artifact reference numbers are included in the text to aid readers in locating the objects in artifact illustrations, artifact distribution plans, and in the catalog (Appendix B).

HULL-RELATED FINDS

It has been our experience in a decade and a half of archaeological field-work that hull-related artifacts are the most commonly encountered finds on a shipwreck. This is hardly surprising. The timbers, planks, bolts, and spikes that a wooden hull comprises can total several dozen pieces in even the smallest of rowboats; a fairly large wooden hull, like that of the horse ferry, is assembled from thousands of individual components. During a vessel's construction and working lifetime, pieces of the hull are continually lost or discarded, and a substantial number of the castoffs fetch up in the bilges. The process of sinking generally breaks up a ship's hull, and even after the wreck settles into the bottom, more timbers and fasteners work loose from the surviving structure.

The amazing preservative properties of Lake Champlain's freshwater were instantly apparent when we first examined the horse ferry. If this vessel had sunk in saltwater, it would have been quickly attacked by wood-boring organisms like teredo worms, and within a few years all hull timbers not covered by mud, sand, or cargo would have been utterly consumed. The lake, by contrast, has no ship-eating worms and provides a relatively cool, dark, and stable environment. Under these circumstances wooden elements are preserved quite well, though not perfectly. Iron, too, fares relatively well in freshwater, compared to iron that has been submerged in saltwater.

The upper levels of silt inside the hull contained small and heavily eroded bits of hull timber, but the greatest concentration of well-preserved, hull-related artifacts lay deep within the wreck, on or just above the intact hull structure. These timbers or fasteners were already detached from the hull when it sank, or dropped in the bilges just after the sinking, and were therefore the first pieces to be covered by the preserving silts that gradually filled the wreck.

Lying in the forward part of the bow, the ship's rudder (01-036) was instantly identifiable when it was uncovered in 1991, as were the two lengths of railing (01-034 and 01-042) we brought to the surface in the same year. These were easy to recognize; identifying the purpose of the many pine plank fragments and shaped pieces of wood was usually more challenging. Most of the wooden fragments were probably from the planking (called "ceiling") that partially covered the insides of the frames or from the deck planks; the function of most other wooden artifacts could only be conjectured.

One of the many intriguing but unidentifiable pieces was found on the port side of the hull, atop the two forwardmost floor timbers. It consisted of a decayed softwood post with an L-shaped iron bracket protruding from one end (01-017). The post was wedge shaped in section and had six small nails protruding from it. The bracket was certainly intriguing. It suggested that the post had been a stanchion at one end of the deck or perhaps was located in one of the horse stalls where the bracket held a removable barrier such as a plank, rope, or chain.

The two sections of wooden rail (01-034 and 01-042) that once extended around the deck were easily identified by their general size and shape, the slight curvature over their lengths, and especially by the rectangular mortises cut into their undersides to fit the tops of the rail stanchions. About one-third of rail 01-042 was badly deteriorated (it protruded above the sediments inside the wreck), but the two rails otherwise appeared to be in good shape. Their location within the hull was curious, for if they had still been in place around the topsides of the ferry when it sank they would have logically fallen outside the hull or would have floated away as the upperworks deteriorated. The rudder also overlay rail 01-042. All of this strongly suggested that the rails were deposited within the hull before it sank.

The provenience of the rudder was likewise curious. It lay in the forward-most part of the hull, atop the apron timber and forward end of the keelson. The blade of the rudder, composed of two thick planks, was partially sticking out of the silt when the ferry wreck was first discovered and had suffered from some natural deterioration. When we recovered the rudder in 1991 for a closer look, signs of wear that occurred during the ferry's working life were

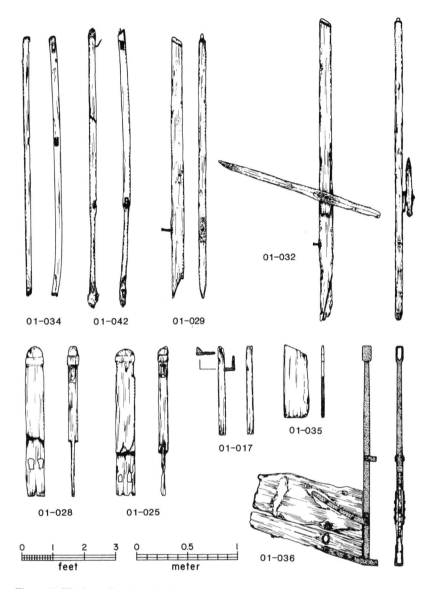

01-032

01-034   01-042   01-029

01-028   01-025

01-017

01-035

01-036

0 1 2 3   0   0.5   1
┗┻┻┻┻┻┻┻┻┛   ┗┻┻┻┻┻┻┻┻┻┻┛
    feet   meter

Figure 48. Timbers. Drawings by Kevin Crisman and Tina Erwin.

also evident. A section of the upper blade plank had cracked off and was fastened back in place with five small iron nails. The metal straps that once held the upper part of the rudder blade to the iron rudder post had broken and were reattached to the post with a rivet.

The location of the rudder was a none-too-subtle clue about the circumstances of the ferry's sinking. The rudder was heavy (this we knew for a fact, since the efforts of several people were required to lift it out of the water in 1991). It is difficult to believe that the rudder could have slipped off its substantial pintles during the sinking and then settled inside the opposite end of the boat, a distance of 18.3 meters (60 ft.) forward of the sternpost. The rudder, like the two sections of rail, was probably already inside the bow when the ferry sank.

The excavation of the sternpost, outside the hull, turned up a length of tongue-and-groove plank (01-035), the only one of its type found on the wreck. The unique nature and location of this plank raised the possibility that it was not from the ferry. The chances of the plank being from some other source seemed remote, however, for there are no other wrecks in this vicinity, and the ferry is located more than one and a half kilometers (1 mi.) from the Burlington waterfront. Since we encountered no evidence of tongue-and-groove planking on the lower hull or deck, we presume it was part of an above-deck structure, perhaps the semicircular boxes that covered the sidewheels or the sheds that were built over the horse walkways.

In addition to the detached hull pieces we excavated and recovered from inside the wreck, four loose structural timbers found around the wreck were brought temporarily to the surface for study. These timbers were all part of the truss structure that supported the ferry's deck over the turntable, a feature that is described in greater detail in the next chapter. The timbers consisted of two upright "king posts" (01-025 and 01-028) and a pair of diagonal supports (01-029 and 01-032) that once locked the king posts in place. Bolted to support 01-032 was a long, square-sectioned post that was obviously once part of the shed structure over one of the horse walkways; the post was bolted to the support through one corner, rather than through one side, suggesting that the horse sheds were semicircular and closely fit the semicircular openings in the deck for the treadwheel walkway.

By the late 1820s and early 1830s, the era when the horse ferry in Burlington Bay was probably built, iron production was fairly advanced, and iron for building ships was abundant and cheap. Studies of shipwrecks in North American lakes and rivers have shown that shipwrights building vessels for inland waters relied almost exclusively on iron nails, spikes, and bolts to fasten timbers and planking together. We expected that the ferry would be iron fastened throughout, and this was exactly what we found.

The bilges of the horse ferry yielded about fifty-five whole or broken nails and spikes. Nails were used to fasten ceiling planks to frames and deck planks to deck beams, and they were no doubt used in the construction of the paddle boxes and horse sheds. Spikes were used for heavier jobs, such as securing the outside planking to the frames. The nails' shanks measured about 3.2 millimeters (⅛ in.) square, and the spikes' shanks were about 6 millimeters (¼ in.) square. Round iron drift bolts fastened the ferry's largest timbers together, although no detached bolts were found during our excavations.

The ferry's hull also contained a scattering of other fasteners, of no readily apparent function: two brass tacks, two threaded iron bolts (one with an attached iron nut), and six iron washers. A deteriorated iron ring bolt (03-012) was found attached to the forwardmost deck beam and was recovered for conservation and study after it came loose. Two similar bolts were noted on the after deck but left in situ; all were plainly used to tie down wagons, livestock, and other deck cargo during rough-weather crossings.

Two shaped pieces of oak (01-014A–B) resembling wooden fasteners called "treenails" were found in the bow, and other treenaillike lengths of wood, which functioned as plugs, were noted between the frames in the bow and stern, protruding from the outside planking. When planking the ferry, the shipwrights were careful to remove from the wood any knots, which could eventually work loose and cause a major leak. Oaken dowels were then driven into the knot holes to fill them and make them watertight.

A short length of iron chain with eight links (03-068) and three individual iron chain links (03-033, 03-050, 03-069B), all found in the bow, were likely used in the operation of the ferry, perhaps to anchor the harnesses of the treadwheel horses or to cordon off the open ends of the boat while it was underway. It is also possible that they were part of an anchor chain.

PROPULSION MACHINERY

The wreck retained the complete propulsion mechanism, including the horizontal treadwheel, the power-transmission gears and axles, and the sidewheels. The mechanism was hardly in perfect condition (the wooden components of the treadwheel and sidewheels were heavily eroded, and the iron gears were covered by an amorphous layer of corrosion), but nevertheless it showed exactly how the ferry operated. During the fours years of underwater fieldwork, we spent many hours recording the propulsion mechanism but could not risk damaging the wreck by removing attached parts and bringing them to the surface for more intensive study. Nor could we in good conscience chip off the iron crust that obscured some iron components, because this would have accelerated the deterioration of the remaining metal.

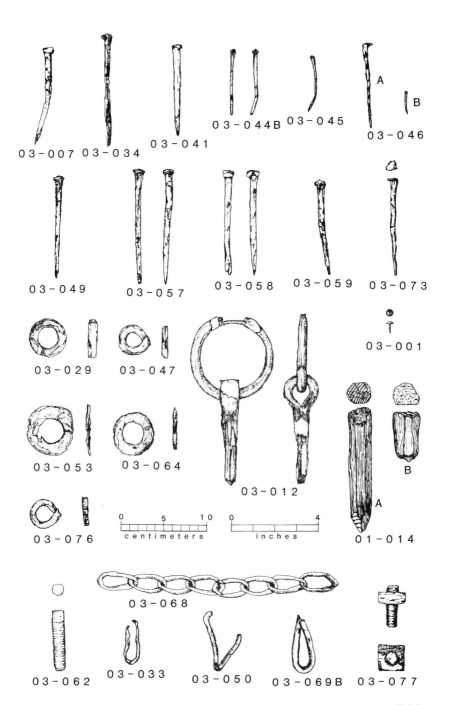

Figure 49. Hull fasteners: bolts, spikes, nails, tacks, and treenails. Drawings by Erick Tichonuk, Tina Erwin, and Erika Washburn.

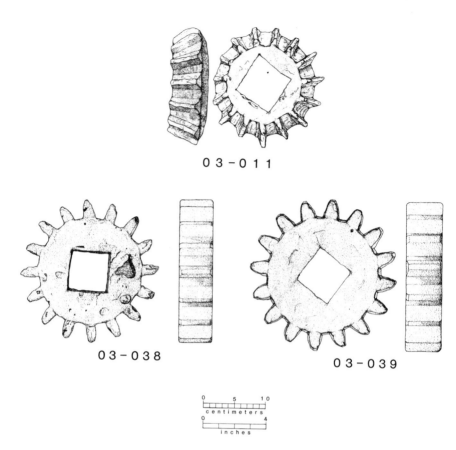

Figure 50. Propulsion machinery: gears. Drawings by Erick Tichonuk, Tina Erwin, and Erika Washburn.

We were therefore pleased to discover several loose pieces of machinery in the bow, for these artifacts could be recovered for further study without damaging the intact structure of the ferry. The loose machinery elements included three cast-iron gears, a copper-alloy axle bushing, fragments of a shattered iron axle coupling, and three hardwood tread planks. Several other objects that may have been part of the machinery were also recovered. The machinery-related finds were not particularly numerous, but after cleaning and conservation they yielded many clues to ferry's operation and the length of its career.

The three cast-iron gears found in the forwardmost part of the bow were among the most interesting finds. The first of these to be found, a straight bevel gear (03-011), lay upon two portside cant frames, above the sediments inside the hull; the gear was coated heavily with the products of iron corro-

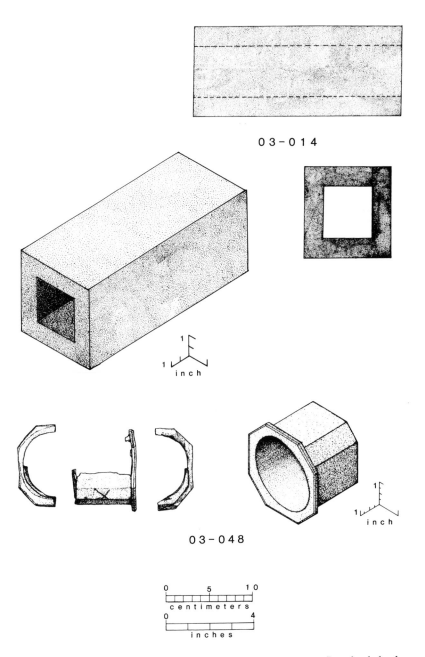

03-014

03-048

Figure 51. Propulsion machinery: axle coupling (top, reconstructed) and axle bushing (bottom; as-found, left; reconstructed, right). Drawings by Kevin Crisman.

sion because of its unburied state. This gear clearly fit on the forward end of the iron shaft that transmitted the motion of the treadwheel to the sidewheel axle. An identical gear, also heavily crusted over, was still attached to the transmission shaft.

The other two loose gears (03-038, 03-039), of a type known as "spur gears," were found in the forwardmost part of the bow, atop the apron, where they were buried and therefore not nearly as corroded as the bevel gear. These gears were designed to fit on the after end of the transmission shaft and rolled on the ring of gear teeth fixed atop the treadwheel. Another spur gear, this one heavily encrusted, was still in place at the after end of the power shaft.

We initially thought the gears were spares, carried to replace broken or worn-out gears, but close examination of their surfaces after cleaning and conservation showed that the opposite was true. All had seen long use and were deposited in the hull when they were replaced by new gears. The two spur gears, though worn about the teeth, looked as if they could have been reused at least temporarily. The straight bevel gear, however, was beyond redemption: The teeth were badly worn from extended use, and nearly half of them were broken or ground down to nubs. It could not have been reused even in a pinch.

All three gears were closely examined after treatment for evidence of manufacturing techniques, maker's marks, and letters, numbers, or symbols. They were obviously cast in an open mold, for one side of each gear showed the irregularities that often occur on the upper (exposed) surface of an open cast. There were no obvious maker's marks to tell us who manufactured and supplied these gears, but the likeliest candidates would of course be Barnabas and John C. Langdon, with the casting performed by Starbuck and Gurley's Troy Air Furnace.

A copper-alloy axle bushing (03-048) found on the starboard side of the bow during the 1991 excavations provided some insights into how the machinery's designers dealt with friction generated by the rotation of the sidewheel axle. The ferry's wrought-iron axle extended across the breadth of the boat, supported in the center by a pair of iron pillow blocks; the outboard end of each axle fit into an iron block attached inside the guard timbers. At all four support points, some type of nonferrous bushing was needed to prevent the serious friction problems that would quickly develop with direct, iron-on-iron contact.

We could not see any evidence of nonferrous bushings on the intact propulsion machinery, perhaps because they were obscured by the thick layer of rust on the bearing blocks, or possibly because they were no longer on the machinery. The bushing found in the hull was our only tangible evidence of how the ferry's designer reduced friction on the axle. The bronze or brass bushing certainly saw hard use before being discarded: Less than half of the original metal remained, the rest having been worn away by the rotation of the axle.

When it was new the bushing resembled a broad-lipped cup with an octagonal exterior and a round interior; it fit into one of the iron blocks inside the guard timbers and in turn contained one end of the axle. Like the gears we recovered from the wreck, the bushing had no obvious maker's marks on its surviving surfaces, but it was likely cast for the Langdons at Julius Hank's Brass and Bell Foundry in Troy, New York. All of the ferry's copper-alloy axle bushings would have been subject to considerable wear with each season's crossings, and they must have needed replacement even more frequently than the cast-iron gears. The Langdons probably provided the owner of each new ferry with a supply of extra bushings and sold replacements regularly during the ferry's lifetime.

During the excavation of the bow, ten chunks of cast iron were found around the forward end of the keelson. After all of the pieces had undergone conservation treatments they were reassembled into their original form, a hollow rectangular box or sleeve. Examination of the surviving propulsion mechanism showed similar boxes, of two different sizes, near the center of the axle. The boxes were couplings that joined the three separate lengths of the axle and permitted the ferry crew to disassemble the axle in sections and replace worn bushings or make other needed repairs. We could not determine if the axle coupling broke during use, when it was being installed or removed, or while it was being carried as a spare. A series of deep file grooves around the interior of the coupling showed that it had been shaped for better fit around the axles.

At least some of the unidentified pieces of wood and metal found in the hold were probably used in the treadmill machinery, but as they were no longer in context this could not be verified. Examples include five thin iron plates found on the starboard side of the bow (03-025, 03-054, 03-067b, 03-071, 03-072). One of the plates (03-054) was clearly the catch for a door latch, but it seems doubtful that the ferry had doors requiring this plate; the other four plates appear to have been cut from scrap metal. The best explanation for these plates is that they were shims for the treadwheel mechanism, perhaps to tighten the fit between the axle and its couplings. A hardened spatter of lead found in the bow (03-030) may likewise indicate that molten lead was sometimes poured into the seams between metal pieces to provide a tighter fit. The two threaded iron bolts and iron washers that we classified as "hull fastenings" might well have been part of the machinery (similar threaded bolts were used on the sidewheels to attach the spokes to wheel hubs).

Three identical planks found in the bow showed how the treadwheel walkway was prepared for the use of the horses. The tread planks (01-012,

01-026, 01-045) were all of hardwood, possibly elm or maple, of about the same length, 73.6 centimeters (29 in.), and thickness, 3.8 centimeters (1½ in.), and all were wider at one end than the other. These planks and others like them were placed side by side in the walkway, with the narrow end of the plank nearest the center of the treadwheel, until the entire circumference of the wheel was planked. Two of the three tread planks we recovered had seen use (they were worn in the center by the horses' hooves), but none of them had any fastener holes, indicating that the planks were not spiked or nailed in position.

These planks were probably the most frequently replaced elements in the treadwheel mechanism, since the sharp-shod hooves of the horses must have worn through their surfaces in just a few weeks' time. Historian W. W. Higbee's observations concerning the Lake Champlain treadwheel boat *Eclipse* make it abundantly clear that a broken plank could have dire, indeed fatal, consequences for the horse that stepped through it. One hopes that the owners of this boat were attentive and never had to deal with the results of a plank failure.

We were naturally curious to know how the hardwood tread planks were supported, and we searched the fragile remains of the treadwheel for clues. Most of the "subtread" planks had fallen away from the wheel, but one timber was found in situ, and we temporarily recovered it for inspection. The plank (01-046) was fashioned from softwood, probably white pine, and each of its ends was nailed in position between the arms of the treadwheel.

HORSE EQUIPMENT

A considerable amount of horse-related material was found in the ferry's bilges, which is surprising when we consider that the horses themselves never ventured below deck. The finds consisted of one whole and nine broken iron horseshoes, fourteen leather harness fragments, and two fragments from a horse collar. Twenty-three of the twenty-six horse-related artifacts were found in the bow, primarily in the forwardmost part, and the remaining three were recovered during the stern excavation. All of these finds were examined by Dr. Gary Potter of the Animal Science Department at Texas A&M University, who offered insights into the size, care, and outfitting of the equine crew.

The horseshoes were all discovered in the forward part of the hull, near the forward end of the keelson. Not one of the nine broken shoes could be matched with another to form a whole shoe. According to Potter three of the shoe halves were originally attached to the right hoof of a horse, five were from a left hoof, and one could not be matched either way; three of the shoe halves were further identified, with two from a left front hoof and the other from a left rear hoof. None of the half shoes showed signs of extensive wear, indicating that weaknesses in their construction or extremely hard use caused them to break.

Horseshoe 03-013 had an indentation under the toe clip, a feature that may have been intentional or may simply have been the result of poor workmanship or deterioration of the metal after the shoe was discarded. Potter thought that the indentation, if intentional, could have been made for a horse suffering from "seedy toe," a condition in which the hoof wall separates from the toe. In this circumstance the indentation in the shoe would have relieved some of the pressure on the horse's toe and made the animal more comfortable.

The one complete horseshoe (03-035) was originally attached to the front left hoof of a horse. Two of the shoe's nails were present when the shoe was recovered. The shoe is approximately size zero, indicating that the horse was fairly small, probably weighing less than 453.6 kilograms (1,000 lbs.). The other shoes, of varying sizes, were also relatively small, suggesting that the horses were definitely modest in size, though not exactly ponies.

We found fourteen leather pieces inside the wreck, of which nine were positively identified as part of a harnessing system. Two of the harness fragments (04-004 and 04-014) had buckles used to tighten harness assemblies; fragment 04-004 consisted of straps, two leather keepers, an iron buckle, and a snaffle ring; and fragment 04-014 had two straps, two leather keepers, and an iron buckle. The typical horse harness can have half a dozen adjustment points, and therefore the original placement of these buckles could not be determined.

It was possible to identify the basic function of six other harness fragments. Strap 04-002 was a brow band for a bridle and would have been placed over a horse's head, in front of the ears. A small loop of leather (04-005) was clearly a keeper for the strap on a harness buckle, straps 04-001, 04-003, and 04-010 each had four buckle adjustment holes and one or two holes for a stud, and strap 04-013 had a hole for a harness stud; none of the five could be precisely placed within a harness system. All of the remaining leather pieces were probably remnants of horse harnesses, but were too fragmentary to determine either position or function.

The two remaining identifiable horse-related artifacts were fragments from a light hame or collar that secured the traces to the horse. A small, curved piece of iron with a loop on either end, found with an iron ring fixed in one of the loops, was a hame fastener (03-003), the fitting used as a flexible joint between the two rigid halves of the collar. The other find was one end of a hame (03-004), composed of wood and an iron reinforcing band. The iron band was fastened to the wood with small screws, but the screws no longer exist.

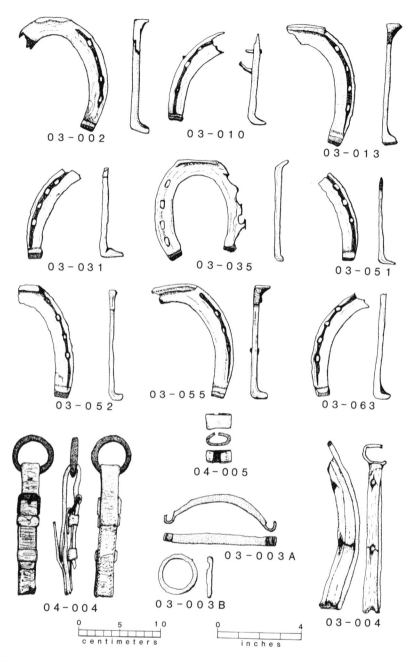

03 – 002

03 – 010

03 – 013

03 – 031

03 – 035

03 – 051

03 – 052

03 – 055

03 – 063

04 – 005

03 – 003 A

04 – 004

03 – 003 B

03 – 004

```
0        5        1 0
|--|--|--|--|--|--|--|--|--|--|
    c e n t i m e t e r s
```

```
0                              4
|--------|--------|--------|--------|
          i n c h e s
```

Figure 52. Horseshoes and harness fragments. Drawings by Erick Tichonuk, Tina Erwin, and Erika Washburn.

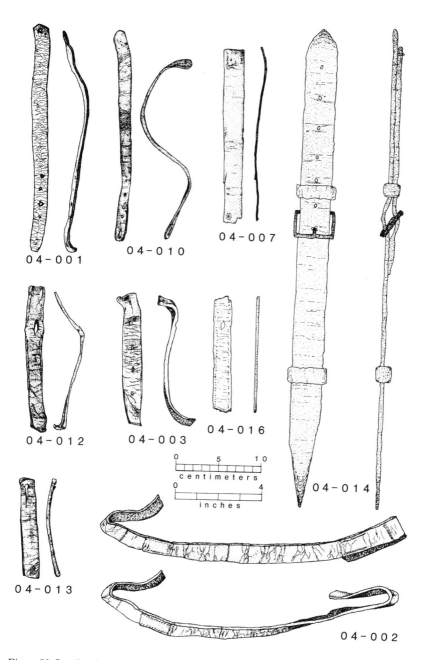

04-001
04-010
04-007
04-012
04-003
04-016
04-014
04-013
04-002

0   5   10
c e n t i m e t e r s
0   4
i n c h e s

Figure 53. Leather harness fragments. Drawings by Erick Tichonuk, Tina Erwin, and Erika Washburn.

MISCELLANEOUS FINDS

As we noted earlier, this category is a catchall for the many odds and ends we retrieved from the wreck: four tools, a teapot, glass and ceramic fragments, organics (that is, nonwood or nonleather organic finds), as well as unidentified bits of wood, metal, and stone. Some of these artifacts have yielded insights into the operation and maintenance of the ferry, but the purpose of other objects continues to be a mystery.

The four tools found within the hull of the horse ferry represent at least three different maintenance activities that the crew performed during the lifetime of the vessel. One tool that was instantly identifiable upon excavation was a wooden-backed bristle brush (01-040). This was found in the forwardmost part of the bow, atop the apron. When it was first recovered the brush contained the intact though worn remains of the bristles, but these proved so fragile that they did not survive the trip to the conservation lab. The brush could have been used to groom the horses, although it seems more likely that grooming would have taken place each evening after the horses were stabled on shore. The most obvious use for a brush such as this one would be periodic cleaning of the ferry's machinery and upperworks.

The second tool, a caulking iron (03-040), was discovered only a few inches from the brush, between two frames on the starboard side of the apron. Caulking irons are used on wooden ships to drive hemp-fiber caulking—called "oakum"—into planking seams to render them watertight. This iron was of an unusual style, with a narrow driving edge and a long, angled shaft; known as a "crooked spike iron," it was used to caulk short, hard-to-reach seams that were not accessible to standard, shorter irons.[1] The head of the iron was severely mushroomed, indicating that it was repeatedly struck by a metal hammer rather than by the wooden mallet traditionally used by caulkers.

The presence of this well-used caulking iron hints at the state of the ferry at the time of its sinking. Every wooden ship gets caulked when it is built, and then undergoes the process again regularly when the old caulking wears out. As the planking on a ship gets older the seams need more attention, until chronic leaking forces the owner either to replace the planking or abandon the vessel. The presence of this tool suggests that the crew caulked the ferry's hull frequently and kept the iron handy for this purpose.

The remaining two tools from the wreck consisted of a truncated iron spike (03-060) and an iron wedge (03-016A); both had been heavily hammered at their broad ends (they were somewhat mushroomed by repeated impacts), and slightly deformed at their pointed ends. They resembled, and may have been, "nail sets," tools used to drive the head of a nail or spike below wooden surfaces. They could have been used, however, for any task that required concentrating the force of a hammer blow on a small area or object.

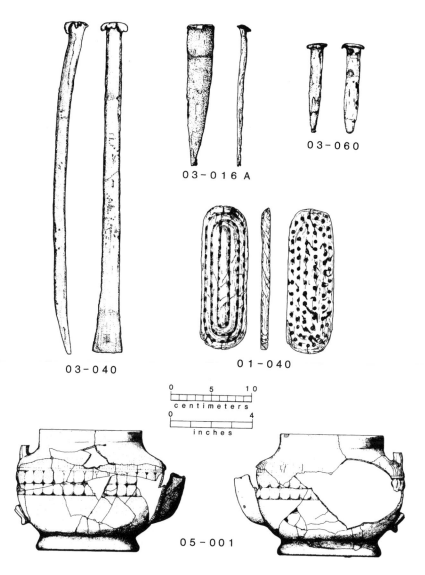

03-040

03-016 A

03-060

01-040

0 5 10
centimeters
0 4
inches

05-001

Figure 54. Miscellaneous artifacts: tools, brush, and teapot. Drawings by Erick Tichonuk, Tina Erwin, Robert Barros, and Erika Washburn.

The excavated portions of the ferry wreck yielded few objects that related directly to the daily lives of the crew and passengers. The personal objects we found that did fall into this category consisted of ceramics and glass, but even here, with one exception, the finds were sparse. The exception was a brown-glazed, red earthenware teapot (05-001 et al.) found shattered around the forward end of the keelson. Forty-three pieces of this pot were recovered, and when pieced together they composed the greater part of the vessel's body; the end of the spout, the handle, and the removable lid were missing.

The teapot had a thin body of red earthenware, covered by a glaze that was dark brown outside and lighter brown within (the color variation probably reflects slightly different exposure to heat during firing). The pot's oval body had a band of molded decoration just below the shoulder; the decoration consisted of two rows of raised circles, with a series of impressed vertical lines above them. The glaze was spread unevenly over the vessel and had flaked off in some places. Inside and out, the teapot had a cheap, utilitarian look about it and could not have been an expensive purchase.

What was this pot doing in the ferry's hold, when there were almost no other objects that related to the crew's diet, dress, or entertainment? We can only speculate. Perhaps it was carried down to the ferry on a cold day in the fall or early spring, filled with hot coffee or tea to warm the chilled crew. The pot must have been more or less intact when it was deposited in the hold, for if it had broken on deck, the crew would presumably have swept the pieces over the side.

The one other ceramic find from the ferry was a tiny fragment of whiteware; the chip was nondescript and too small to determine if it was from a plate, bowl, or cup. Six small pieces of broken glass were also encountered in the bilges; five of clear glass and the sixth tinted green. One of the glass fragments (05-004) had an oval pattern etched into its surface and looked as if it might have come from a drinking glass.

The fine-mesh net bags placed on the end of our dredge discharge pipe during excavation allowed us to recover botanical remains from the bilges of the ferry. The small collection of pits, nutshells, and seeds, identified by Texas A&M University graduate student John Bratten, indicated that the ferry's crew or passengers snacked on a variety of fruits and nuts. These included black cherries, wild plums, nuts from hickory, butternut, beech, and black walnut trees, and possibly some type of melon.[2]

The remaining artifacts in the miscellaneous category, of metal, wood, and stone, may have had a role in the building or operation of the ferry, but we do not have sufficient knowledge of horseboats to recognize their purpose. Other unidentified objects may have had nothing to do with the running of the ferry and may represent materials left behind by wagons or passengers, by recreational activities on the part of the crew, or simply by the random collection of potentially useful or interesting objects.

The carefully trimmed, 3.4-meter (11 ft.) sapling that lay along the starboard side of the keelson (01-038) looked like a crude fishing pole, and it is quite plausible that one of the crew may have entertained himself (and caught dinner) by angling for perch in the intervals between crossings. A second pole found nearby (01-037) was shorter and thicker and seems too heavy for fishing; perhaps it was used like a boat hook to maneuver the ferry around a dock or catch onto a distant object. A neatly carved wooden stake or wedge that had been pounded on one end many times (01-047) also left us scratching our heads: Was it of use in the operation of the ferry, or did it have some other, totally unrelated function? We cannot really be sure what purpose any of these items served without asking the crew, and that, of course, is no longer possible.

CONCLUSIONS

The ferry's original crew undoubtedly would have been perplexed, and probably amused, if they could have seen us carefully measuring, cataloging, conserving, photographing, and studying the artifacts we found in the bilges. Most of the objects we found were worn or damaged and must have been of little use or value when they were deposited in the hold; in fact, we can safely assume that they were regarded by the owner and crew as worthless junk, or at best as spare parts. We did not find anything in the hold that would have been of significant monetary value to anyone.

The nature and quality of the artifacts we found in the ferry's hold served to illustrate the boat's "economic context": Despite its innovative machinery, this was still a humble working craft. The ferry provided the owner and crew with a living, but it probably did not make them wealthy (especially as winter ice shut down business for three or four months in most years). The objects found in the hold were utilitarian and well used, seeming to indicate that every effort was made to keep operational expenses to a minimum.

The collection of broken horseshoes and harness fragments in the hold is particularly telling about the attitudes of the people who worked on the ferry. At least one member of the crew had learned well the habits of frugality and, instead of tossing broken horse equipment over the side, took the time to gather up the pieces and deposit them in the bow, to be retrieved and reused later. The pieces of leather harness might have been grafted onto another harness with a few minutes of cutting and stitching, but the iron shoe halves would have been difficult if not impossible to repair and had little value except as scrap.

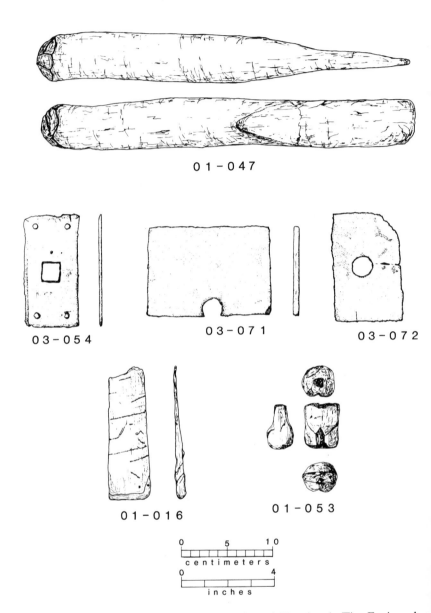

01-047

03-054   03-071   03-072

01-016   01-053

0   5   10
centimeters
0   4
inches

Figure 55. Miscellaneous artifacts of wood and metal. Drawings by Tina Erwin and Erika Washburn.

The dearth of crew-related artifacts, such as buttons, buckles, shoes, coins, eating utensils, food containers (except the teapot), and other easily broken or lost items, is a good indicator that there were no living quarters for the crew on board the ferry. Certainly there would have been no reason to accommodate the crew in the dark, damp, and extremely confined space below deck when they could tie the boat to a dock each evening and eat and sleep ashore in their own houses. The lack of personal items further indicates that most of the daily activities took place on the deck and that crew members ventured below only to retrieve spare equipment, stow odds and ends, and inspect and maintain the hull and propulsion machinery.

The broken horseshoes found in the bow showed that the ferry's horizontal treadwheel was powered by small or medium-sized horses. In general the iron shoes did not hold up well under steady use and broke before they wore out. The treadwheel walkway upon which the animals paced was covered with hardwood planks to resist wear from their shoes; the tread planks were not fastened in place and could simply be lifted out for quick replacement.

The tread planks were not the only element in the treadwheel mechanism that required periodic replacement. Copper-alloy bushings were used to reduce friction at the four bearing blocks that supported the middle and ends of the sidewheel axle. These would have worn through relatively quickly and could be replaced only by partially dismantling the axle assembly. The iron gears on the ends of the power transmission shaft also had to be replaced during the ferry's working life (at least three spur gears were used at the after end of the shaft). The owner of this boat must have periodically ordered spare bushings, gears, cast-iron axle couplings, and other parts from the original manufacturer, most likely Langdon's machine shop in Troy.

The excavation and recovery of loose timbers revealed information about the hull that would otherwise not have been evident. The hull, as expected, was fastened throughout with iron bolts, spikes, and nails; treenaillike oaken pegs were noted, but they appear to have been used only to plug knot holes in the outer planking. The concentration of artifacts immediately abaft the stem was a sure indicator that the now-missing forward deck had a hatch for access to the hold, a hatch that was probably located immediately above the keelson's forward end.

Other archaeological finds located during the excavation and recording of the wreck shed light on the configuration of the ferry above the level of the main deck. The two lengths of cap rail recovered from the bow showed that the ferry's deck was surrounded by a railing to keep passengers and their belongings from accidently going over the sides. The stanchion that supported the horse shed, found bolted by one corner to a truss timber, indicated that the horse sheds were semicircular, the same shape as the openings cut into the deck for the treadwheel walkways. The railings and semicircular sheds suggest a deck arrangement similar to the six-horse tread-wheel ferry plan prepared by J. C. Trautwine in 1827. Finally, a thin tongue-and-groove board found next to the sternpost, outside the hull, hinted that the paddle boxes and horse sheds may have been sheathed with this style of planking.

There can be no doubt that this ferry successfully completed thousands of round-trip crossings of Lake Champlain during the course of its career. The accumulation of broken horseshoes and harnesses in the bow, the worn-out gear wheels and axle bushing, the repairs to the rudder, the wear evident in ceiling planking and frames, all spoke of steady use over many years. In 1991, during the excavation of the starboard side of the bow, a hole in the bottom of the hull enabled us to reach under the vessel and touch the outside of the planking in a place that had been buried (and thus protected) by the mud ever since the day the ferry sank. We found the surface of the hull to be rough, eroded, and much thinner than expected, a sure sign of advanced age.

The archaeological evidence does not permit us to determine the exact age of the ferry with any degree of certainty. Construction materials and methods, navigational conditions, and maintenance can all greatly affect how quickly a vessel ages. The existing hull and the artifacts found in it suggest that the horseboat was at least ten years old when it sank, and possibly as much as twenty years old.

So the ferry was worn out, and at a minimum it would have required a complete replanking if it were to continue in service. How did it end up at the bottom of Burlington Bay, when there is absolutely no historical evidence that horse ferries ever operated in this vicinity? Obviously, after many years of service at another location, the worn-out vessel was brought to Burlington, perhaps under its own power, or more likely under tow by a steamer. It was probably taken there for one of the following reasons: to completely rebuild the hull and machinery (possibly at the yard of Burlington shipwright Orson Spear), to salvage the mechanism and parts of the hull, or to show it to prospective used-ferry buyers.

The horse boat could have sunk accidentally in Burlington Bay while it was being towed there or to another destination, but we suspect that the sinking was entirely intentional. The ferry was clearly under tow on its final voyage, since the rudder had been removed and stored inside the hull. With the possible exception of the caulking iron, the hold was cleared of all useful equipment. And the location of the wreck, in relatively deep water just outside the main harbor, hints that an effort was made to sink the hull in a place where it would not obstruct navigation.

One other clue suggests deliberate scuttling. It was apparent from the ferry's attitude on the bottom (bow-down with a slight list to starboard) that

Figure 56. The cause of the horse ferry's sinking? The hole in the planking between frames on the starboard side of the bow. Photograph by Kevin Crisman.

water most likely flooded into the ferry from the starboard bow. When we excavated this area in 1991 we encountered a place between two frames where a section of plank was missing. Although it is possible that the piece cracked free when the hull hit the bottom, the absence of any damage to surrounding planks and frames seems to indicate that the plank was removed intentionally; in other words, someone knocked a hole in the bottom of the ferry to sink it. The wood was so decayed that one solid kick might have been sufficient to do the job.

One question that we have not yet answered concerns the now-missing foredeck: Did it separate from the hull before, during, or after the sinking? The foredeck was probably not in any better shape than the rest of the hull at the time of the sinking, and it is hard to imagine that the timbers would have been worth salvaging before scuttling the ferry. Because of the wreck's evident bow-down, starboard-list impact with the bottom, the foredeck may have taken the brunt of the impact and torn free of the hull; if it floated off immediately after the hull hit the bottom, however, the loose timbers we found in the bow should have floated away as well. They didn't. Perhaps the foredeck was loosened by the impact but stayed in place for a time, holding loose pieces of wood in place until they became waterlogged and sank to the bottom. Then, some outside disturbance such as a dragged anchor pulled the deck off the wreck.

The identity of the ferry is still a mystery, for the excavation did not produce definitive clues to the vessel's name or ownership nor did a search of local newspapers and other records turn up any mention of a horse ferry sinking in Burlington Bay. Historical records eliminate some possibilities: The six-horse *Eclipse* was abandoned in McNeil's Cove at Charlotte, Vermont; the *P. T. Davis* was wrecked at Port Henry, New York, in 1857; and the *Gipsey* was powered by a treadmill, not a horizontal treadwheel. A half-dozen likely candidates remain, including the three boats that commenced ferry service around Alburgh, Vermont, at the northern end of the lake, in 1828 and 1829. How long the Alburgh boats remained in service, and what happened to them afterward, has not been determined.

There are two strong candidates from the crossings south of Burlington— the Westport–Basin Harbor *Eagle* and the Port Henry–Chimney Point *Experiment*. The *Eagle* seems to have been about the size of the ferry in Burlington Bay, went into service in the late 1820s or early 1830s, and worked until 1844 or slightly thereafter, a career of at least twelve years. The *Experiment* could accommodate six wagons with horses on its deck (about the capacity of the Burlington Bay wreck), entered service around 1826, and was apparently replaced by the *P. T. Davis* in 1847. The horse ferry wreck's frames were constructed in an unusual manner (to be discussed in the next chapter), and it is tempting to think that the name *Experiment* might have referred to both the horse machinery and the mode of framing. This is all speculation, however.

If the ferry was towed out on the lake and deliberately scuttled, then its passing may have gone unrecorded. References to lake shipping in contemporary newspapers mostly concern the building of new vessels, fatal accidents, and the volume of trade, with a strong emphasis on the lake's steamboats. The disposal of a small and elderly horseboat equipped with obsolete machinery might not have been considered a newsworthy event. But with or without a name, the horse ferry wreck in Burlington Bay still qualifies as an archaeological treasure, a rare find that has shed light on a nearly forgotten aspect of North American maritime history.

11

How It All Works

The Hull and Machinery of the Horse Ferry

In the preceding chapter we examined the small finds, the bits and pieces of loose debris excavated from the horse ferry's bilges, and discovered some of what they had to tell us about the ferry's history and day-to-day operations. Now it is time to take a closer look at the largest artifact of all: the hull and its propulsion machinery. The recording and reconstruction of the ferry's hull structure and machinery was, from the start of the archaeological project, one of our primary objectives, for the simple reason that detailed plans or descriptions of early treadwheel craft have never been found. This was the perfect opportunity to learn about horseboat technology, for here we had a tried-and-proven machine that operated on the lake for many years.

During the four-year underwater study, thousands of measurements and sketches were taken of nearly every accessible part of the hull and machinery, and samples were collected from many of the timbers to permit identification of the wood types preferred by (or available to) the ferry's builders. Photographs and videotape footage were also taken of the wreck, inside and out, to create a visual record of the vessel in its "as found" condition. This data became the raw material for a rebuilding of the horseboat, a reconstruction that took place not in a shipyard but at a drafting table.

The process of rebuilding a ship on paper requires patience and many weeks of time; the work is comparable to assembling a jigsaw puzzle with many missing, deformed, or damaged pieces. In the case of the horse ferry,

201

it was possible to recreate many missing or heavily eroded structural elements from clues remaining in the hull. The forward deck, for example, was entirely missing, but the dimensions and spacing of its beams could be determined by the notches cut into the top of the deck-supporting clamp timbers. We were fortunate that so much of the horse ferry's original structure was present and well preserved, and that preparation of hull plans involved minimal guesswork.

The results of the structural study are presented on the following pages. In keeping with the usual practice of wooden-ship builders, we will start with the keel and work up, more or less following the original sequence of construction. Readers may wish to refer to the plans of the hull, and a summary of hull scantlings and the wood species used in the vessel's construction may be found in Appendix C.

THE KEEL, STEM, AND STERNPOST

Like many wooden watercraft the horse ferry had a backbone composed of four elements: the keel, stem, sternpost, and keelson. The first three were the first to be laid down on the stocks, and they were crucial, for they defined the overall length of the vessel, provided much of its longitudinal strength, and served as the foundation upon which the rest of the vessel was built. How the shipwright went about selecting, shaping, and fastening the timbers for the hull's spine can be a good indication of the construction materials that were available, the skills of the builder, and the navigational conditions under which the ferry would operate.

The keel was, unfortunately, the least-accessible timber in the wreck, because of the ferry's upright orientation and semiburied condition. The extreme forward and after ends of the keel were exposed and examined during the excavation of the stem and sternpost, and the top of the keel could be felt, but not easily seen, after we completed our excavations inside the hull. The keel was composed of one or more likely two pieces of red elm, a strong and fairly rot-resistant wood, although not easy to work because it is tough and splintery. According to our best estimates the keel was 16.7 meters (54 ft., 10 in.) in length, which seems a little long for a single timber; most likely the keel was fashioned from two timbers joined end to end amidships with an overlapping scarf. The dimensions of the keel in section, 20.3 centimeters (8 in.) high (or molded) and 12.7 centimeters (5 in.) wide (or sided) were modest but about what could be expected for a vessel this size.

The shipwright and his assistants cut horizontal V-shaped grooves or rabbets into the top of the keel's two sides; at a slightly later stage in the construction process, the innermost strakes of outside planking, or "garboards," were shaped to fit into the rabbets to provide a tight fit that could easily be caulked and made watertight. The attachment of the keel to the stem was fairly conventional, consisting of a 1.2-meter (3 ft., 11 in.) flat scarf. The joining of the keel to the sternpost was rather peculiar, for instead of mortising the post into the top of the keel (the usual practice of nineteenth-century North American shipbuilders), the ferry's builder extended the sternpost to the bottom of the hull and scarfed its forward end to the keel. The scarf was formed by lapping the keel over the bottom of the post.

The construction of the stem was intricate, considering its relatively small size, and there are hints that its timbers may have been damaged and repaired during the ferry's career. Four white oak timbers composed the stem: the forefoot, the upper and lower main posts, and the apron. The first three stem components were located outside the hull and parted the waters as the ferry advanced through the lake; the apron, situated inside the hull, reinforced the entire structure and provided a surface for nailing down the ends of the outside planking. The seam between the main posts and the apron followed the planking rabbet, and its exact location was obscured by the ends of the planks. The two main posts were unusually narrow pieces of timber, flat butted to one another rather than scarfed together. A hole was drilled across this join, and a wooden dowel called a "stopwater" was driven through and wedged in place; as its name suggests, the stopwater prevented water from seeping between the timber seams and into the hull. A second stopwater was inserted into the seam between the lower stem and forefoot.

The narrow dimensions of two main posts and the unusual butt joint between them strongly suggest that at some time in the ferry's history the lower part of the stem was severely damaged in a grounding or a collision. The damage was apparently repaired by trimming back the injured parts of the upper and lower stem and replacing them with the large forefoot. A 2.5-centimeter (1-in.) thick strip of iron was added to the front of the stem assembly to protect it from further damage.

The ferry's stern assembly consisted of two white oak timbers, the sternpost, and a stern knee (the latter closely resembled the apron). The sternpost had a straight after edge to accommodate the rudder, but the planking rabbets cut into its forward corners were curved to match the hull's rounded stern, and the seam between the post and the stern knee also appears to have been curved. The most unusual feature of the stern, as we have already noted, was that the post did not sit atop the keel but extended all the way to the bottom of the hull.

THE FRAMES

The keel, stem, and stern defined the ferry's length and the shape of its ends, but it was the frames that defined the breadth and form of the hull from stem

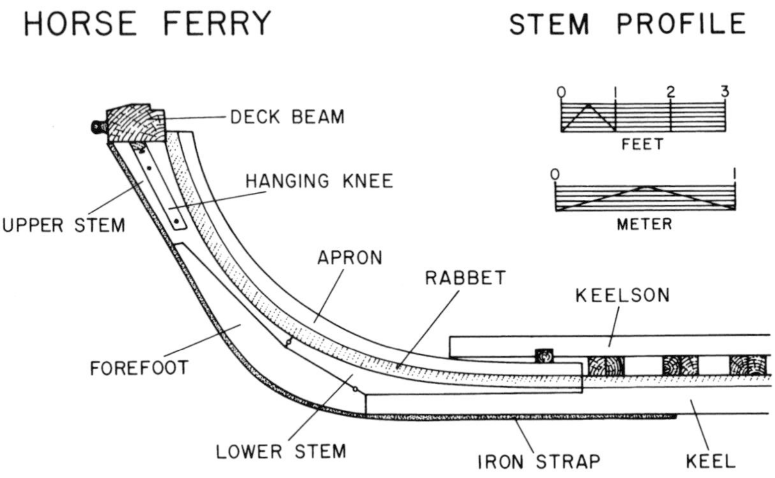

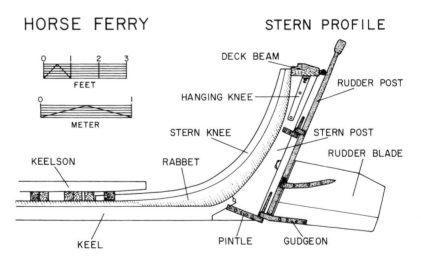

HORSE FERRY

STEM PROFILE

DECK BEAM

HANGING KNEE

UPPER STEM

APRON

RABBET

KEELSON

FOREFOOT

LOWER STEM

IRON STRAP

KEEL

FEET

0 1 2 3

METER

0 1

Figure 57. Profile of the horse ferry's keel, stem, and apron. Drawing by Kevin Crisman.

HORSE FERRY

STERN PROFILE

FEET

0 1 2 3

METER

0 1

DECK BEAM

HANGING KNEE

RUDDER POST

STERN KNEE

STERN POST

RUDDER BLADE

KEELSON

RABBET

KEEL

PINTLE

GUDGEON

Figure 58. Profile of the horse ferry's keel, sternpost, stern knee, and rudder. Drawing by Kevin Crisman.

to stern. The horse ferry contained thirty-eight square frames (frames composed of a floor timber and two futtocks that crossed the keel at a right angle), two floor timbers without attached futtocks (one at each end of the hull), twelve pairs of cant timbers at the bow and thirteen at the stern, and a pair of hawse pieces alongside the stem apron and stern knee.

The thirty-eight square frames that made up the central portion of the hull were bolted to the top of the keel at intervals of approximately 38.1 centimeters (15 in.) from center to center. Fashioned from white and red oak, the individual frame timbers were remarkably uniform in their dimensions, with both the floors and futtocks averaging 10.2 centimeters (4 in.) molded and sided. The floors were nearly straight pieces of timber about 3.2 meters (10 ft., 6 in.) in length; the futtock timbers were laterally fastened to the floors by a pair of iron bolts, and the heels of each frame's futtocks butted over the centerline of the keel. The forwardmost twenty-two square frames had the futtocks fastened to the after side of the floors, and the aftermost sixteen had the futtocks fastened to the forward side of each floor.

The ferry's builder prevented bilge water from collecting and stagnating between the frames by cutting a pair of drains, known as "water courses" or "limber holes," into the base of each square frame. The holes were fairly small, 7.6 centimeters wide by 2.5 centimeters high (3×1 in.) and were located about 7.6 to 10.2 centimeters (3–4 in.) out from each side of the keel. We did not find any evidence of a pump well in the excavated portions of the hull, but presumably there was some location where the daily accumulation of bilge water was collected and removed from the vessel.

The method used to shape and assemble the square frame futtocks was unlike anything we had ever encountered on a nineteenth-century wooden hull, and it deserves special notice here. When the eroded portside futtocks in the bow were first examined in 1989 and 1990, we noticed that most appeared to be split up the middle, a perplexing feature that we thought could have been caused by the hull's impact with the bottom during the sinking. During the excavation of the bow's starboard side in 1991, Texas A&M graduate student Tommy Hailey observed the same lengthwise splits in the upper end of each starboard futtock, and he realized that they were too consistent to be impact damage. The splits were, in fact, deliberate saw cuts from the top of each futtock down to the turn of the bilge.

Once the cuts were identified it was easy to determine their purpose: They allowed the shipwright to bend the futtocks easily to the desired shape. The technique began with the selection of a straight, 3-meter (10 ft.) length of 10.2-centimeter (4-in.) square red or white oak (the choice of red oak for some futtocks was surprising, as it is inferior to white oak in its resistance to rot). The shipwright and his assistants sawed one end of the timber across its width for a distance of about 1.4 meters (4½ ft.), creating two parallel

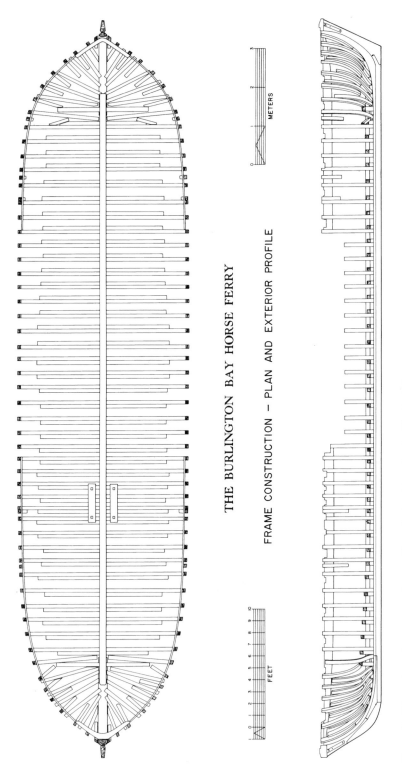

THE BURLINGTON BAY HORSE FERRY

FRAME CONSTRUCTION – PLAN AND EXTERIOR PROFILE

METERS

FEET

Figure 59. Horse ferry frames: exterior profile and plan. Drawing by Kevin Crisman.

pieces measuring 5 by 10.2 centimeters (2 × 4 in.). To prevent the lower portion of the timber from splitting during the bending process, a 1.3-centimeter (½-in.) diameter iron bolt was driven into a hole drilled across the base of the saw cut.

The futtock was undoubtedly steamed to make the wood pliable (the shipyard probably had a steam box that enclosed the timber, concentrating the hot vapor and speeding the softening of the wood fibers). When the timber reached the desired state of flexibility, it was removed from the steam, placed on a mold, and bent using some type of windlass or large clamps. After bending the wood, the shipwright probably drove a few nails or spikes through the saw cut to prevent the futtock from returning to its former shape.

The use of this novel technique for shaping frames suggests that naturally curved timber ("compass timber") may have been scarce in the Champlain valley by the late 1820s and early 1830s. Sawing, steaming, and bending futtocks had advantages and disadvantages. It must have saved a great deal of time and money, for straight lengths of milled oak would have cost much less than compass timber, and the process of sawing, steaming, and bending almost certainly required less labor and time than was needed for locating good pieces of compass timber and cutting them to the correct shape with an adze. Bent timber could also be made to fit the hull design precisely; finding timber crooks that precisely matched the necessary length and curve of the futtocks would have been a challenge. Molded futtocks may have been slightly weaker than futtocks fashioned from good compass timber, and because more of the wood surface was exposed to moisture they were probably more prone to rot. They also would have been more flexible and have shown an inclination to straighten out over time, altering the form of the hull; the hull is definitely asymmetrical today, but whether or not this was a problem during the ferry's working life has not been determined.

The horse ferry is the only nineteenth-century wreck known to us with this method of frame assembly, and its appearance raises many questions. Was the horse ferry merely an isolated experiment, or were other nineteenth-century lake vessels built in this manner? And was the practice of sawing, steaming, and bending employed elsewhere in North America during the first half of the nineteenth century?

One question, at least, has been satisfactorily answered, and that concerns the origins of this building method. The 1816 edition of a British technical journal, the *Repertory of Arts, Manufactures, and Agriculture,* contains a description of the technique by its inventor, shipwright William Hookey of the Royal Navy yard at Woolwich, England. Hookey began the article by describing the timber problem facing the nation's shipwrights and the advantages to be found in his new method for shaping timbers:

The constant want of compass timber, and the difficulty of obtaining it, is apparent, and seems to increase every year. The consequence is manifest to all persons who have knowledge of shipbuilding; and the high importance of whatever relates to the British navy, requires no comment.

The method adopted by me has not only the effect of lessening the consumption of timber, but of adding strength to that which is used, as the timber can be worked much longer without being cut across the grain, which is more frequently the case, and indeed unavoidable in the usual mode of moulding ship timber.

My plan has been tried, and found to answer every end intended, and is likely to become a general benefit to the United Kingdom.[1]

Hookey modestly added to this: "Many persons have thought [it] impossible to be done, till by my perseverence they saw it accomplished." Significantly for the horse ferry, the patent drawings of Hookey's device showed that it could also be used to bend frames for smaller craft.

Hookey certainly worked on a massive scale. In 1813 he bent a 1.4-meter (4 ft., 8 in.) curve into an oaken floor timber for the seventy-four–gun ship *Black Prince;* the timber measured 9.1 meters (30 ft.) in length and was 40.6 centimeters (16 in.) square. The time necessary to bend this timber with a windlass on his adjustable form was a mere eight minutes.

How did William Hookey's idea migrate across the Atlantic to Lake Champlain? Any progressive North American shipwright who subscribed to the *Repertory of Arts, Manufactures, and Agriculture* could have read Hookey's article and used the information to set up a frame-bending apparatus of his own. One man, however, stands out as a strong candidate: William Annesley of Albany, New York. Annesley was one of those inventors who appears in every age, a man who, like steamboater John Fitch, was slightly ahead of his time with a good idea. In 1818 he patented a revolutionary method for building boats and ships without frames by laminating planks over a mold.[2] The result was a vessel that required little or no compass timber to build, was strong and seaworthy, and maximized cargo capacity.

Annesley worked energetically to sell his idea and his boats to ship builders and owners around North America, and he managed to persuade Lake Champlain ship owners to build frameless canal boats and sailing ships for his merchant fleet. These prototypes were apparently quite successful, but laminate boat building did not catch on at this time, perhaps because it departed so radically from the centuries-old tradition of plank-on-frame construction. Only in the twentieth century would laminate construction become common for some types of wooden vessels.

Annesley lived in Great Britain between 1817 and 1820, and during this time he met government and private shipbuilders, built laminated-hull boats,

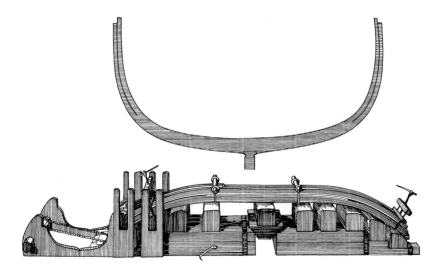

Figure 60. William Hookey's "Improved Method of bending Timber." Drawn from a print in *The Repertory of Arts*, volume 28.

published pamphlets, and otherwise promoted his invention; it seems highly likely that while there he would have seen or heard of Hookey's apparatus for bending frames and learned of its advantages.[3] Annesley subsequently settled in Albany, New York, and was listed in the city's directory as a "patent boatbuilder." Did Annesley promote Hookey's framing technique in North America and did he persuade Barnabus and John C. Langdon in nearby Troy to build horseboats using bent frames? He and the Langdons shared a common interest in new forms of watercraft, and we know that the Langdons built and installed the engine on Annesley's laminate-hulled steamboat *Star* in 1827.[4] The *Star*, incidentally, was built at a shipyard in Troy. Although we have not yet found a definitive connection between the bent-frame horseboat in Burlington Bay and William Annesley, the possibility of a connection appears very strong.

The horse ferry's double-ended hull had a similar framing pattern at the bow and stern. The square frames that composed the central part of the hull terminated at either end with a single futtockless floor timber that was notched underneath to fit into the top of the apron or stern knee. The remaining frames, the cants, consisted of individual pieces that angled forward in the bow and aft in the stern. It is clear that the cants were added during a slightly later stage of construction, when the hull was at least partially planked, for they are spiked to the outside planking only (and in some cases to the apron or stern knee).

At each end of the hull seven pairs of long cant frames extended from the side of the apron or stern knee part way up the side of the hull. In the bow five pairs of shorter cants, placed higher in the hull, filled the spaces between the longer cants; six pairs of shorter cants did the same thing in the stern. The forwardmost and aftermost pairs of framing timbers, known as "hawse pieces," paralleled the apron and stern knee. In the stern, the forwardmost pair of cants were sawn, steamed, and bent to achieve the correct shape, but all other cant frames in the hull were fashioned from compass timber.

After the cant frames were fastened in place, the stem and stern were each reinforced by bolting a large, curved white oak timber to the interior faces of three forward and three after pairs of cants (this timber was known as a "breasthook" in the bow and a "cheek piece" in the stern).

THE KEELSON AND PLANKING

After the ferry's square frames were bolted to the keel, the builder added a second longitudinal reinforcing timber that sat atop the frame floors and paralleled the keel. This was the keelson. Sawn from white ash, the horse ferry's keelson measured 15.2 meters (50 ft.) in length and averaged 11.4 centimeters (4½ in.) molded and 19 centimeters (7½ in.) sided. It was probably composed of two or three lengths of timber scarfed end to end, but this could not be determined because we did not uncover the central portion of the keelson. The corners of the keelson's forward end were beveled, and the top corners appeared to have been chamfered over its full length. Iron drift bolts fastened the keelson to the frame floors and keel every two or three frames.

A pair of 96.5-centimeter (3 ft., 2 in.) timbers were bolted to the frames beneath the sidewheel axle, 12.7 centimeters (5 in.) from either side of the keelson. These pieces served as the foundation for the two pairs of stanchion posts that supported the axle and crown-gear bearings.

The keelson was probably reinforced with parallel lengths of timber or "sister keelsons" beneath the treadwheel, for this machinery and the horses walking upon it would have placed a tremendous strain on the central part of the hull. The severely limited space under the treadwheel did not allow us to excavate there and see exactly how the hull was reinforced.

The ferry's hull was planked outside with 2.5-centimeter (1-in.) thick planks, fastened in place with an average of two iron spikes per plank per frame. The planks were heavily eroded on their outer surfaces; some of this erosion occurred during the ferry's career, for as we noted in the last chapter the bottom planks, protected by mud since the sinking, were found to be only 1.3 centimeters (½ in.) thick and extremely worn outside. The uppermost planking strake on each side of the hull, the sheer strake, was notched at regular intervals to fit the deck beams that protruded out from the side of the hull.

The third strake from the sheer differed from the rest of the outside planking, for it was much thicker (about 7.6 cm or 3 in.) and the planks were flat scarfed together (the rest of the outside planks were simply butt jointed). This extra-thick band of planking, known as a wale, is common on larger wooden vessels and is designed to strengthen and support the sides of the hull above the waterline. The ends of the horse ferry's wales were let into 2.5-centimeter (1 in.) deep mortises cut into the sides of the stem and sternpost. The wales were 16.5 centimeters (6½ in.) wide; the rest of the outside planking ranged between 20.3 and 35.6 centimeters (8–14 in.) in width.

In the bow and stern of the ferry, four or five strakes of white pine ceiling were fastened to the frames on either side of the keelson; above the turn of the bilge the frames were exposed up to the clamps. Planking that lines the inside of a hull is known as "ceiling." The ceiling planks were 1.3 centimeters (½ in.) thick and 22.9 to 33 centimeters (9–13 in.) wide, and fastened in place with small iron nails. Amidships, between the sidewheel axle and the after end of the treadwheel, strakes of ceiling covered the frames from the keelson to the underside of the deck-supporting clamp timber.

The ferry's clamps consisted of planks, 2.5-centimeter (1-in.) thick by 26.7-centimeter (10½-in.) wide, spiked to the insides of the frames 10.2 centimeters (4 in.) below the tops of the frames and the sheer strakes. They served as shelves to support the deck beams and were notched at regular intervals to fit the beams. At the ends of the hull the clamps tapered to a point and terminated below the breasthook and cheek piece. The clamps were secured in place by two iron spikes per futtock or cant frame. A second strake of planking, 2.5 centimeters (1 in.) thick by 17.8 centimeters (7 in.) wide, was spiked to the frame tops directly below each clamp; they extended from the aftermost bow cant frames and the forwardmost stern cant frames to the treadwheel openings amidships.

The openings for the treadwheel were an interesting feature, necessitated by the treadwheel's diameter extending beyond the breadth of the hull. The treadwheel openings began at the paddle beam abaft the sidewheels and extended aft a distance of 5.5 meters (17 ft., 11 in.). The sides of the hull dropped 47 centimeters (19½ in.) here and were defined by the top of the wale. A cap plank covered the wale, frame tops, and ceiling of the port and starboard treadwheel openings. These openings significantly lowered the ferry's freeboard and seemingly would have allowed water to wash into the hull in any kind of rough weather. The ferry's owner may have attached covers around the openings to keep water out, but if he did we found no evidence of their existence.

THE TREADWHEEL MECHANISM

The treadwheel mechanism was perhaps the most interesting feature of the horse ferry, for until the wreck was discovered the details of this clever and widely used machine had been shrouded in mystery. We spent many hours underwater recording the propulsion system, and after four field seasons we had a clear idea of how the treadwheel worked, although one element of the mechanism, the bearing that supported the treadwheel axle, proved inaccessible and was never examined. For purposes of description we have divided the propulsion system into its three major components: the treadwheel, the power transmission and axle, and the paddle wheels.

The treadwheel harnessed the energy generated by the horses walking on the wheel's surface and converted it into power that could be used to propel the ferry. The device consisted of a horizontal, twelve-spoked wooden wheel 6.7 meters (21 ft., 11 in.) in diameter; its top surface was 33 centimeters (13 in.) below the top of the planked deck and 89 centimeters (2 ft., 11 in.) above the top of the keelson. The axis of the treadwheel was an upright iron axle, 12.7 centimeters (5 in.) in diameter, that revolved in some type of bearing attached to the top of the keelson. We were disappointed to find the bearing inaccessible, as it would have been instructive to see how this component was designed to withstand the steady wear it would have received. The upper end of the treadwheel axle was held in place by a block of wood fixed between two deck beams and reinforced by a pair of L-shaped iron brackets.

The hub of the treadwheel consisted of two iron plates, each 3.8 centimeters (1½ in.) thick and 1.2 meters (3 ft., 10½ in.) in diameter. The plates were fitted on the axle one above the other, and the outer portion of each was divided into twelve arms; the wheel's twelve white pine spokes were sandwiched between the plates, and each was fixed in place by three threaded bolts. The spokes of the wheel were each about 3.2 meters (10½ ft.) in length and tapered in height, but not in width, toward the outside of the wheel.

Unlike the treadwheels shown in the Langdon and Trautwine diagrams, the outside of this wheel was not supported underneath by a series of roller wheels. Instead, each spoke was reinforced by a supporting arm that extended up from the base of the axle.

The walkway for the horses occupied the outermost 90.2 centimeters (2 ft., 11½ in.) of the treadwheel. The sides of the walkway were defined by raised wooden rings that contained the planks upon which the horses walked. The walkway, as we discussed in the last chapter, had to be strong enough to bear the considerable weight of the horses, yet light enough not to put too much strain on the spokes of the wheel. The builder sought a middle ground by constructing the walkway of two layers of planks.

HORSE FERRY PROPULSION MACHINERY

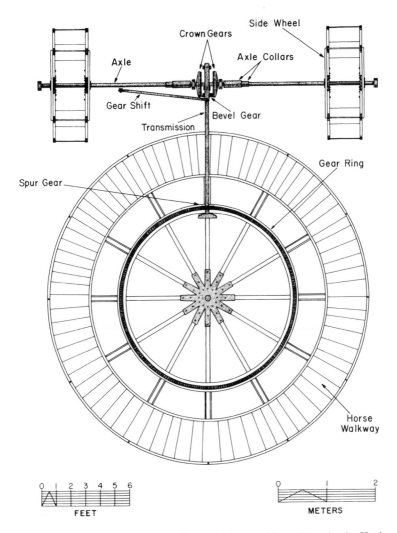

Figure 61. Plan view of the horse ferry's propulsion machinery. Drawing by Kevin Crisman.

The lower (subtread) planks were thin pieces of softwood that extended between the spokes and were nailed at either end to thin, shelflike strips of wood fixed to the sides of the spokes. The tops of the subtread planks were even with the top surfaces of the spokes. Thicker hardwood tread planks were placed atop the subtreads and spokes, between the walkway's inner and outer wooden rings. The tread planks were placed in a radial fashion, at a right angle to the orientation of the subtreads.

A smaller and much narrower wooden ring, measuring 3.8 meters (12 ft., 4 in.) in outside diameter, was let into the tops of the spokes inside the horse walkway. Attached to the top of this inner ring were articulating sections of cast-iron gear teeth that together formed a complete circle around the top of the treadwheel. The sections of gear teeth were extremely corroded, and the length of the individual sections could not be determined.

In contrast with the treadwheel, which was built of a combination of wood and iron, the power transmission and axle were assembled entirely from cast- and wrought-iron components. The 2.6-meter (8-ft., 6-in.) long wrought-iron power transmission shaft carried the power generated by the revolving treadwheel forward to the sidewheel axle. The shaft was nearly square in section, but it was rounded at either end to permit it to turn freely in the support bearings. A cast-iron spur gear at the shaft's after end sat atop the treadwheel's gear rack and spun the shaft with each revolution of the treadwheel; at the forward end of the transmission shaft a cast-iron straight bevel gear meshed with one of the two crown gears on the sidewheel axle.

A rudimentary shifting mechanism built into the power transmission enabled the ferry to change directions without having to turn the horses around on the treadwheel. The bearing that supported the forward end of the transmission was at the top of a pivoting iron post. A shift lever fitted to this post allowed the shaft and its bevel gear to be moved sideways between the two crown gears; meshing the bevel gear with one crown gear made the side-wheels turn in one direction, and vice versa. Although it was not necessary to turn the horses around when changing directions, it was probably standard practice to slow them down a little before shifting: Abruptly shifting between forward and reverse while the ferry was advancing at cruising speed would have jolted the entire mechanism and run the risk of breaking gear teeth.

Wear patterns on the worn-out bevel gear recovered from the wreck indicated that the treadwheel customarily turned counterclockwise (the port horse faced forward and the starboard horse faced aft); the power shaft, therefore, when viewed from behind, turned clockwise. The bevel gear at the forward end of the transmission shaft normally meshed with the crown wheel on the port side of the axle to advance the ferry over the water.

The axle for the ferry's sidewheels was 6.9 meters (22 ft., 9 in.) in overall length. The core of the axle appeared to be composed of three sections of

HORSE FERRY SIDEWHEEL

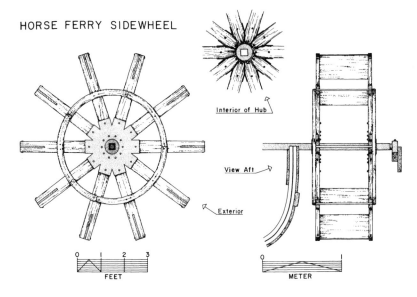

Figure 62. Horse ferry sidewheel assembly. Drawing by Kevin Crisman.

8.9-centimeter (3½-in.) square wrought-iron rod, with one shorter section in the middle with the crown gears and the two longer sections on either side. Cast-iron axle collars on each side of the crown wheels joined the three axle sections and allowed the ferry owner to disassemble the entire axle to replace worn components.

Just outboard of each crown wheel, the axle was supported by iron pillow blocks that presumably had some type of copper-alloy bearing to reduce friction. The outboard ends of the axle turned in copper-alloy bushings inside iron bearing blocks; the bearing blocks were bolted inside the guard planks that extended around the outside of the deck beam ends. We noted that slightly outboard of its starboard collars, the axle was broken in two, a break that probably occurred during the sinking when the starboard sidewheel hit the bottom.

The horse ferry's two sidewheels each consisted of a pair of ten-spoked wheels measuring 2.4 meters (7 ft., 11 in.) in diameter, separated by a distance of 63.5 centimeters (25 in.). At the center of each wheel was an iron hub; the outside of each hub was divided into ten open sockets that fit the ten spokes. The spokes, fashioned from oak, were secured to the hub by two bolts each and notched at their outer end to fit the softwood paddle blades or "buckets." A single bolt on each spoke held the buckets in place. The buckets had disintegrated on the wreck, with the exception of small fragments preserved by their contact with the iron bolts at the spoke ends. A narrow wooden ring, 1.4 meters (4 ft., 9 in.) in outside diameter, was fitted to the side of each individual wheel to reinforce the spokes. Overall, the sidewheels were simple yet functional in design, and seemingly quite sturdy.

THE DECK AND RUDDER

The deck was undoubtedly the horse ferry's most prominent feature, for it overhung the sides of the hull by several feet and covered most of the propulsion mechanism. It was the deck that made the profit for the ferry's owners, too, by carrying the wagons, livestock, goods, and people from one side of the lake to the other. When complete the deck measured 19 meters (62 ft., 5 in.) in length and 7.2 meters (23 ft., 8 in.) in breadth. Its primary structure was made up of twenty-eight beams of varying dimensions; the forwardmost nine beams were missing when the wreck was discovered, but notches in the sheer strake and clamp clearly defined the location and sided dimensions of these missing pieces. The remaining beams were in a degraded condition but were for the most part complete; all were cut from white pine but the aftermost beam, which was of white oak. Much of the deck planking was missing, and the rest was in very poor shape.

The deck beams were laid down unevenly, but their spacing forward and aft of the paddle wheel housings averaged 76.2 centimeters (2 ft., 6 in.) from center to center. The beams were fit into notches cut 15.2 centimeters (6 in.) into the top of the sheer strake and 5 centimeters (2 in.) into the top of the clamp. Each beam was fastened in place on the hull by a single iron drift bolt driven into the sheer strake. The sheer strakes were thin planks and did not make very secure attachment points, a potential weakness that was remedied by bolting horizontal lodging knees between the frame tops and the sides of beams. The knees were added at strategic locations and must have greatly lessened the likelihood of the deck tearing free of the hull in a collision or when the vessel was tossed about in extremely rough weather. Five pairs of short timbers were spiked between the frame tops to provide attachment points for the lodging knees.

The deck beams averaged 12.7 centimeters (5 in.) square, although three beams in the center of the hull proved substantially larger. The first two over-sized beams were the "paddle beams," which supported the paddle boxes over the sidewheels. The second paddle beam sat above the forward end of the treadwheel opening in the hull, and the third oversized beam was situated over the after end of the treadwheel opening.

Between the large beams that defined the ends of the treadwheel opening were seven smaller deck beams attached in an unusual manner. Because the treadwheel extended beyond the sides of the hull in this location, the seven beams could not be fastened to the sheer strakes and clamps, and the deck

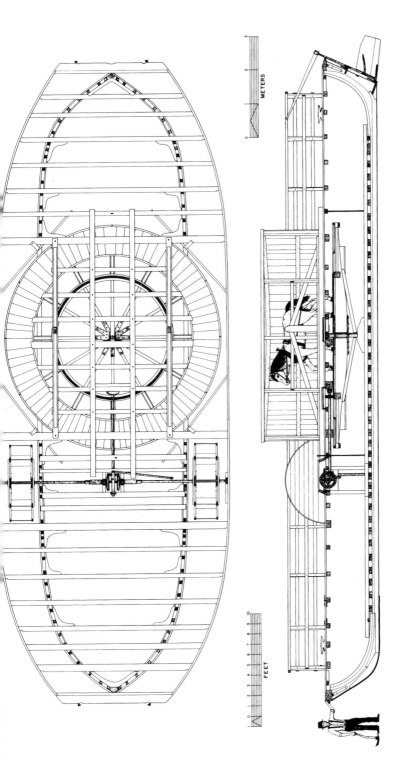

THE BURLINGTON BAY HORSE FERRY

DECK CONSTRUCTION AND INBOARD PROFILE

FEET

METERS

Figure 63. Horse ferry interior profile and deck construction. Drawing by Kevin Crisman.

could not be supported from below. The designer of the ferry cleverly solved the problem by suspending the deck over the treadwheel with a bridgelike structure. The seven deck beams were bolted beneath two pairs of longitudinally oriented timbers or deck stringers. The two inner stringers were 7.9 meters (26 ft.) in length and 12.7 meters (5 in.) square; they may have been added later, as additional reinforcement, for they were bolted down over the existing deck planking. The outboard pair of stringers, located just inside the horse walkways, were shorter and larger in section, being 20.3 centimeters (8 in.) molded, 16.5 centimeters (6½ in.) sided, and 5.8 centimeters (19 ft.) in length.

The two outer stringers were each fitted with a king-post truss to prevent the suspended deck from sagging or collapsing. The center of each stringer had a mortise cut through it, and into these mortises were fit upright posts. The base of each post extended below the stringer and had two square mortises cut through it, a feature that carpentry expert John Butler identified as a double-mortise "tusk tenon." Wedged tenons could be driven into the square mortises to lock the king post in place against the underside of the stringer; the tenons could be tightened if the truss loosened up and easily removed if it became necessary to disassemble the entire structure. Tusk tenons are sometimes encountered in the post-and-beam construction of Dutch-derived barns in the Hudson River valley.[5]

The final and essential addition to the king-post truss system was a pair of wooden braces that extended diagonally between mortises cut in the ends of each stringer and the sides of the king post. The braces locked the post in place, and the post in turn supported the center of the stringer and the deck. Clearly, the builder wanted the deck suspended over the treadwheel to be strong enough to bear the concentrated weight of heavily loaded wagons, teams of horses, or herds of cattle.

Other modifications were made to the deck structure to accommodate the propulsion machinery. The iron transmission that connected the treadwheel with the axle extended several centimeters above the treadwheel, and the builder found it necessary to alter the four deck beams that extended over the shaft. The three smaller beams were notched underneath to fit over the transmission; the fourth beam, the large after paddle beam, had a hole drilled through its center to fit the transmission. The central portion of the beam that supported the after transmission bearing was thickened to bear the weight of the iron shaft.

The forward- and aftermost beams on the vessel's deck supported the boarding ramps used to load and unload the ferry. The forwardmost beam was missing, but it was likely identical in construction and material to its counterpart at the stern. Both were fastened atop the end posts with iron drift bolts and reinforced by a pair of hanging knees. The after beam was

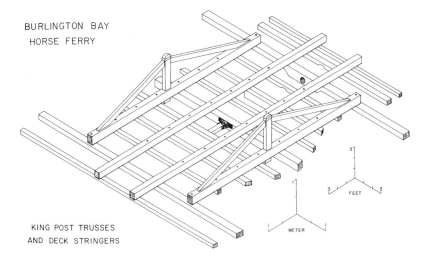

BURLINGTON BAY
HORSE FERRY

KING POST TRUSSES
AND DECK STRINGERS

Figure 64. The king-post trusses and deck stringers supporting the deck amidships. Drawing by Kevin Crisman.

notched along its forward edge to fit the ends of the deck planks and beveled along its after edge for easy passage between the deck and boarding ramp. Two iron pintles attached to the after edge of the beam showed that the stern ramp was hinged for raising and lowering. A semicircular cut in this deck beam's after edge permitted the ferry's iron rudder post to extend above deck level.

A strake of heavy oaken planks, the "guard," was attached to the outside ends of the beams on each side of the deck. The guards were an important addition, for they stiffened the deck structure both longitudinally and laterally and provided a measure of protection for the deck in the event of a collision. The two planks that made up each guard strake were flat scarfed together amidships and edge fastened with three iron drift bolts. The guards were fastened to each beam end with two iron spikes.

The deck was covered with pine planks measuring 17.8 to 22.9 centimeters (7–9 in.) wide and 2.5 centimeters (1 in.) thick. The planks were attached to the deck beams with iron nails, with an average of two nails per plank per beam. Ring bolts were fixed to the deck at various locations to be used as tie-downs for wagons or livestock. Notches in the ends of every other deck beam abaft the treadwheel showed where the stanchions for the rail were placed. The one possible stanchion we found on the wreck was eroded and broken, but two sections of oaken top rail found in the bow had mortises in their undersides that indicated the approximate size of the stanchions.

The ferry assuredly would have had paddle boxes over its sidewheels to protect the deck and passengers from spray, but no trace of the boxes was found. The stalls that covered the horse walkways were almost as mysterious, but the discovery of a stanchion for the starboard stall, bolted at an odd angle to the forward king-post truss brace, provided strong evidence that the stalls were semicircular, like those seen on the 1827 Trautwine plan. It is likely that the stalls were sheathed with thin planks (perhaps tongue-and-groove planks), as they would have been more durable and probably cheaper than canvas awnings in the long run. We know that some of the other horse-boats built around North America had small deck cabins, sometimes outfitted with wood stoves, to shelter passengers from inclement weather. There were no signs of these structures on the horse ferry wreck, and it seems unlikely that they ever existed. The vessel did not have much room on its deck to begin with, and the addition of such a shelter would have left scant room for wagons and livestock.

The rudder was probably one of the final pieces of equipment to be added to the horse ferry before it entered service. The rudder's wooden blade consisted of two planks (the lower one of oak, the upper of pine) edge fastened together with a single iron bolt and secured to the iron rudder post by two pairs of iron straps. A rectangular iron socket at the top of the rudder post once held the ferry's tiller, and two gudgeon loops welded to the front of the post hinged on a pair of pintles bolted to the ferry's sternpost. The gudgeon-pintle arrangement is reversed from that typically seen on contemporary vessels, which had the pintles attached to the rudder and the gudgeons to the stern; the horse ferry's unusual mode of hanging the rudder may have been designed to protect the rudder during grounding, for it could have ridden up on the pintles a considerable distance without falling off or suffering serious damage.

CONCLUDING OBSERVATIONS

What has the archaeological study told us about the hull and machinery of the horse ferry? We can start with the basic dimensions and characteristics. The hull measured 18.4 meters (60 ft., 4 in.) long between perpendiculars and had a maximum breadth of 4.6 meters (15 ft.), giving the ferry a moderately lean length-to-beam ratio of four to one. The overall length of the deck was 19 meters (62 ft., 5 in.), not including the ramps that extended from the bow and the stern; the deck extended beyond the sides of the hull to a maximum breadth of 7.2 meters (23 ft., 8 in.). The ferry had a shallow hull, with a rabbet-to-sheer height amidships of 1.4 meters (4 ft., 8 in.) and a depth of hold (from the top of the frame floors to the undersides of the deck beams) of only 1.2 meters (3 ft., 10 in.).

The hull was double ended, with a moderately raked curved stem and straight sternpost, a fairly short entrance and run, and a lengthy, full midsection that featured nearly flat floors, a hard bilge, and vertical sides. The construction of this vessel was light throughout: The principal scantlings, the keel, endposts, frames, and keelson were all of modest dimensions, and the planking inside and out was fairly thin. The iron bolts, spikes, and nails that fastened the timbers together were sufficient for the job in terms of their size and numbers, but this was not a heavily fastened craft.

Ships directly reflect the society and circumstances that create them. The Burlington Bay horse ferry was built in the late 1820s or early 1830s in response to increasing commerce in the Champlain valley and a rising demand for faster and more reliable transportation across the lake. The owners of this horseboat, like most ship owners, wanted a vessel that was economical to build and operate, durable, profitable, and seaworthy; they also sought the most up-to-date technology that they could afford to make their boat efficient and to attract customers.

Steam engines were the most powerful form of marine propulsion available at this time, but the people who purchased this ferry must have weighed the expenses of buying and maintaining a steam engine against the potential income their ferry crossing would yield, and they opted for a cheaper source of power. The mode of propulsion they chose, the horse-powered horizontal treadwheel, was also a new technology and one that offered the same reliability as steam over short distances. By the time the Burlington Bay horse ferry was built, the horizontal treadwheel was in service on dozens of ferries throughout eastern North America and could be counted on to work well on Lake Champlain.

The supplier of the machinery and hull plans for the ferry has not been identified by documents or archaeological evidence, but circumstances strongly suggest that this boat was fitted with a propulsion system manufactured by Barnabus and John C. Langdon of Troy, New York. The Langdon design had proven its reliability in the early 1820s; the Langdons appear to have been alert to the threat of patent infringement; the Langdon machine shop was in full production during the boom in horseboat building on Lake Champlain in the late 1820s and early 1830s; and the opening in 1823 of the Champlain canal between Troy and Whitehall, New York, meant that horseboat machinery and spare parts could be shipped quickly and inexpensively to the lake. A non-Langdon source for the machinery cannot be ruled out, but the possibility seems remote.

The size of the boat and the dimensions of the horse-walkway openings indicate that the ferry was propelled by two horses working on opposite sides of the deck. The treadwheel–sidewheel gear ratio for this vessel was determined by David Andrews, one of the participants in the archaeological

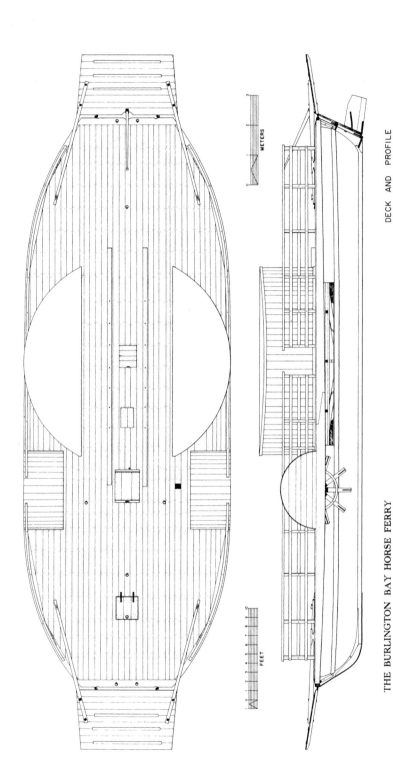

THE BURLINGTON BAY HORSE FERRY

DECK AND PROFILE

Figure 65. Horse ferry exterior profile and deck plan. Drawing by Kevin Crisman.

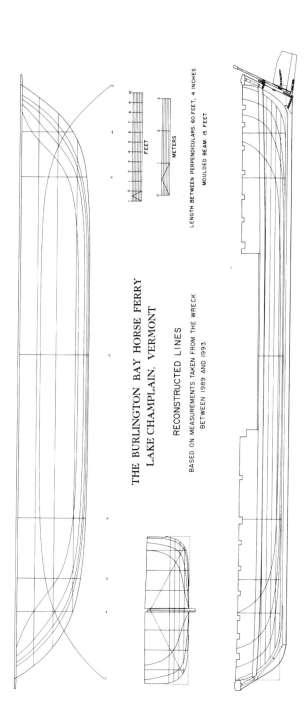

THE BURLINGTON BAY HORSE FERRY
LAKE CHAMPLAIN, VERMONT

RECONSTRUCTED LINES

BASED ON MEASUREMENTS TAKEN FROM THE WRECK
BETWEEN 1989 AND 1993

FEET

METERS

LENGTH BETWEEN PERPENDICULARS: 60 FEET, 4 INCHES

MOULDED BEAM: 15 FEET

Figure 66. The reconstructed lines of the horse ferry. Drawing by Kevin Crisman.

fieldwork. Andrews measured the diameter of the horse walkway, the tread-wheel gear rack, and the sidewheels, and counted the number of teeth on the gear ring and the various gears on the transmission shaft and axles. From these figures he calculated that two horses moving 1.6 kilometers (1 mi.) per hour (a pace of 26.8 m or 88 ft. per minute) spun the treadwheel at the rate of 1.47 revolutions per minute and the sidewheels at the rate of 9.7 revolutions per minute.

So how fast did this boat go? The customary pace of the horses and the speed at which the ferry moved over the water are both difficult to estimate, for there are many variables that would affect performance, such as the friction in the machinery, the efficiency of the hull form in moving through the water, the strength and endurance of the horses, the weight of the deck cargo, and the strength and direction of winds and waves. Some idea of the speed of these craft may be deduced from the report that the six-horse *Eclipse* regularly made the 4.8-kilometer (3 mi.) crossing between Essex, New York, and Charlotte, Vermont, in thirty minutes, an average speed of 5.2 knots (9.7 km or 6 mi. per hour). The Burlington Bay ferry was slightly smaller than the *Eclipse* but had just one-third of its horsepower and likely moved a little slower.

The limitations imposed by the horse-powered mechanism were evident in the design and construction of the hull. The ferry had to be relatively light in construction and shallow in draft for the horses to be able to make any sort of headway, particularly against strong winds and high waves. The draft of the ferry would have varied slightly on each passage across the lake, depending upon the weight on deck, but the vessel probably drew no more than about half a meter (2 ft.) of water. The minimal draft no doubt made the horses' job easier, but the ferry must have been difficult to steer in moderate or strong crosswinds (and north or south crosswinds are frequent for boats that traverse the breadth of Lake Champlain). Under these conditions the craft would have shown a tendency to slide over the water surface to leeward. The molded hull and double-ended form of the Burlington Bay vessel would have cut efficiently through the water, however, much more so than the flat-ended, scow-type hulls that were common among river-going horseboats. The ferry's design must have been fairly stable, for we found no evidence of ballast in the hold.

In its construction the ferry incorporated a recent invention, the sawn, steamed, and bent frames developed by Royal Navy shipwright William Hookey. This framing technique allowed the builder to substitute straight lengths of oak for compass timber, a probably scarce and certainly more expensive material. Hookey's frames may have also required less labor to prepare than compass timber futtocks and thus could have kept building costs down.

We have conjectured that the ferry's frames may be the work of William Annesley, a "patent boatbuilder" living in Albany, New York, around the time this ferry was built. Annesley, we know for a fact, lived in England when Hookey was active and later worked with the Langdons and built ships in Troy. The frames could have been manufactured in Troy and sent by canal boat up to a lakeside shipyard for assembly (it is unlikely that the horseboat was built in Troy, since it was too wide to fit through the locks of the Champlain canal). Like the Langdon connection to the ferry's machinery, evidence for an Annesley connection to the hull is merely circumstantial.

Despite the advantages of using bent frames, the technique does not appear to have caught on in the nineteenth century, perhaps because it made the futtocks more prone to rot or because hulls built in this manner were too flexible and leaky. There is also the possibility that most North American shipwrights were just not interested in adopting a radically new system of building, despite its merits. Like Annesley's laminate building method, the widespread use of bent timbers would have to wait until the twentieth century.

Two potential problems with the ferry's design were identified during the recording and analysis of the hull. The first concerned the openings that permitted the treadwheel to extend beyond the sides of the hull. These substantially lowered the ferry's freeboard amidships, leaving a distance of less than 45.7 centimeters (1½ ft.) between the waterline and the top of the hull. The craft would have been highly vulnerable to being struck broadside by large waves, unless canvas hoods or some other type of covering were placed over the treadwheel openings.

The second weakness in the vessel was the deck suspended over the treadwheel. The longitudinally oriented deck stringers and the pair of king-post trusses would have provided adequate support, but only if the deck were not repeatedly overloaded with wagons or livestock. The collapse that ended the career of the Lake Champlain ferry *Eclipse* in 1847 undoubtedly happened when the suspended central deck gave way under the load of cattle it was supporting and dropped onto the revolving treadwheel.

In general, the quality of the workmanship and materials seen in the hull was adequate but not exceptional. This was a no frills hull. The shipwright who directed the construction was not a stickler for precise measuring and fitting. Much of the shaping and assembling was obviously measured by eye; the slightly irregular spacing of the frames and deck beams attest to this practice. The use of rot-prone red oak for frame timbers, and red elm and white ash instead of white oak for the keel and keelson, suggests that either the builder was indiscriminate in his selection of woods or that good shipbuilding timber was increasingly hard to come by in the second quarter of the nineteenth century. We suspect the latter to be the case.

In the foregoing analysis we have pointed out some possible shortcomings in the design, construction, and materials of the horse ferry, but there is no indication that any of these ever seriously troubled the ferry's crew during what was obviously a long career on Lake Champlain. The fact that the vessel remained in service for so long also suggests that it served its customers well and was at least modestly profitable for its owners. In its own time and way, the horse ferry contributed to the worldwide transportation revolution that was just getting underway in the early nineteenth century.

The Burlington Bay horseboat has had two ferrying careers. The first lasted ten or perhaps as long as twenty years, involved frequent paddling back and forth over the lake, and ended when the vessel sank beneath the waves. The second began with the discovery of the wreck. Although the waterlogged old timbers of the vessel still lie half-buried in the lake bottom, they have become a transport for our imaginations and an inspiration for archaeological research, ferrying us back through time to an era when horses walked on water.

Appendix A

*A
Langdon
Patent
Concession*

Whereas the full and exclusive right and liberty of making, constructing, using and vending to others, to be used, "a new and useful improvement in the Horse Boat," hath been granted to Barnabas Langdon and John C. Langdon, of the city of Troy, in the state of New-York, by Letters Patent under the great seal of the United States, bearing date the fifth day of June, in the year of our Lord one thousand eight hundred and nineteen, as by the said Letters Patent, reference being thereunto had, will more fully and at large appear. And whereas the said John C. Langdon, by deed, under his hand and seal, bearing date the fifth day of February, in the year of our Lord one thousand eight hundred and twenty, hath released to the said Barnabas Langdon, his executors, administrators and assigns, all the rights, title and interest of him, the said John C. Langdon, in and to the said Patent Rights, in and over the state of New-York, and all the states, territories and waters within the United States, east of the said state of New York.

Now Know all Men by these presents,
That I, Barnabas Langdon, one of the patentees aforesaid, for and in consideration of the sum of Three Hundred & fifty Dollars to me in hand paid by Isaac Lovejoy and Amos Allen of the City of Troy the receipt whereof is hereby ackowledged, have, and by these presents do, bargain, sell, grant and convey unto the said Isaac & Amos their executors, administrators and assigns, the full and exclusive right and liberty of making, constructing and using the said New Boat across the Hudson River, at the Village of Catskill, at or near the present Catskill ferry extending one mile on each side of the present ferry up and down said River, and for no other ferries & at no other place whatsoever.

227

And I, the said Barnabas Langdon, do hereby covenant and agree to and with the said Isaac Lovejoy & Amos Allen to defend him during the continuance of the said Patent Rights, in the peaceable and uninterrupted enjoyment of the grant hereby made, against all persons whomsoever, claiming by, through, or under me.

In Witness whereof I have hereunto set my hand and seal this twenty ninth day of March 1820

B^n Langdon
SEALED AND DELIVERED
IN THE PRESENCE OF
Archit Bull

Source: Catskill Ferry Papers, Rensselaer County Historical Society, Troy, New York.

Appendix B

A Catalog
of
Artifacts Found
on the
Horse Ferry Wreck

HULL TIMBERS

01-001. Pine deck plank. Unit 203, level A. It has a maximum length of 71.1 centimeters (28 in.), a maximum width of 20.3 centimeters (8 in.) and a maximum thickness of 2.5 centimeters (1 in.). See Figure 44.

01-010. Softwood plank fragment. Unit 202, level unknown. It has a maximum length of 35.6 centimeters (14 in.), a maximum width of 10.2 centimeters (4 in.), and a maximum thickness of 1.3 centimeters (½ in.). See Figure 44.

01-012. Tread plank. Unit 202, level unknown. It is rectangular and narrows from one end to the other. This was one in a series of planks on which the horse would walk while propelling the boat. It has a maximum length of 74.9 centimeters (29½ in.), a maximum width of 26.7 centimeters (10½ in.) tapering to 19 centimeters (7½ in.), and a maximum thickness of 3.8 centimeters (1½ in.). This was a replacement plank and is similar to artifacts 01-026 and 01-045. See Figure 44.

01-015. Ceiling plank. Unit 201, on frame. It has five nail holes, three along one edge and two along the other. It has a maximum length of 34.3 centimeters (13¼ in.), a maximum width of 23.2 centimeters (9⅛ in.), and a maximum thickness of 1.3 centimeters (½ in.). See Figure 44.

01-017. Softwood post. Unit 101, on ceiling. This post has a pintle and six nails protruding from it. The post has a maximum length of 83.8 centimeters (33 in.), a maximum width of 7 centimeters (2¾ in.), and a maximum thickness of 2.2 centimeters (⅞ in.). The pintle is attached to the post 20.3 centimeters (8 in.) from the top. See Figures 44 and 48.

01-018. Plank fragment. Unit 101, level A. This softwood plank has a maximum length of 61 centimeters (24 in.), a maximum width of 12.7 centimeters (5 in.), and a maximum thickness of 1.3 centimeters (½ in.). It has a nail hole in one corner. See Figure 44.

01-025. King post. This oaken post was originally located on the port outboard deck stringer. The top has a decorative finish above the mortise. The mortise has a maximum depth of 8.9 centimeters (3½ in.) on one side and 8.7 centimeters (3⅜ in.) on the other. Also, both mortises show tool marks from an auger. The post has a maximum length of 137.2 centimeters (54 in.), a maximum width of 18.4 centimeters (7¼ in.), and a maximum thickness of 10.2 centimeters (4 in.). See Figure 48.

01-026. Tread plank. Unit 302, level D. This timber, of elm or maple, is similar to artifact 01-012 except for wear in the middle, indicating use. It has a maximum length of 73.7 centimeters (29 in.), a maximum width of 25.4 centimeters (10 in.) tapering to 19 centimeters (7½ in.), and a maximum thickness of 4.4 centimeters (1¾ in.). See Figure 45.

01-027. Wood fragment. Unit 301, level C. This fragment is semicircular, and one side is notched with a nail in it. It has a maximum length of 30.5 centimeters (12 in.), a maximum width of 7.6 centimeters (3 in.), and a maximum thickness of 2.9 centimeters (1⅛ in.). See Figure 45.

01-028. King post. This oaken post was mortised into a deck stringer on the starboard side. It is similar to artifact 01-025 in design and dimensions. It has a maximum length of 137.2 centimeters (54 in.), a maximum width of 19 centimeters (7½ in.), and a maximum thickness of 10.2 centimeters (4 in.). See Figure 48.

01-029. Truss support. This timber was located on the starboard side. It has a bolt 63.5 centimeters (25 in.) from the bottom of the post protruding from the post 8.7 centimeters (3⅜ in.). The support has a maximum length of 248.9 centimeters (98 in.), a maximum width of 13.3 centimeters (5¼ in.), and a maximum thickness of 9.5 centimeters (3¾ in.). See Figure 48.

01-032. Truss support. This timber was located on the port side and has a horse shed post bolted to it with one bolt. This truss support has a maximum length of 288.3 centimeters (113½ in.), a maximum width of 14 centimeters (5½ in.), and a maximum thickness of 7 centimeters (2¾ in.). The shed post has a maximum length of 167.6 centimeters (66 in.), a maximum width of 7 centimeters (2¾ in.), and a maximum thickness of 7 centimeters (2¾ in.). See Figure 48.

01-034. Rail timber. Unit 402/302, level unknown. This curved timber, probably of oak, has two and one-half rectangular mortises on its underside; the rail is broken at one of the mortises. The top surface shows evidence of weathering. There are also two nail holes, one in each of the complete mortises. The timber has a maximum length of 246.4 centimeters (97 in.), a maximum width of 6.4 centimeters (2½ in.), and a maximum thickness of 5.7 centimeters (2¼ in.). See Figures 44, 45, and 48.

01-035. Tongue-and-groove plank. This plank, fashioned from pine, was recovered behind the sternpost. The plank has tongue-and-grooved edges and three nail holes with two nails remaining. The plank has a maximum length of 68.6 centimeters (27 in.), a maximum width of 24.1 centimeters (9½ in.), and a maximum thickness of 2.5 centimeters (1 in.). See Figure 48.

01-036. Rudder. Unit 200, on top of apron. This is a composite item made of wood (oak and pine) with the post made of wrought iron. The rudder has an overall length of 106.7 centimeters (42 in.), a maximum width of 71.1 centimeters (28 in.) and a maximum thickness of 6.4 centimeters (2½ in.). The post has a maximum length of 207.6 centimeters (81¾ in.), a maximum width of 6 centimeters (2⅜ in.), and a maximum thickness of 5.7 centimeters (2¼ in.). The two gudgeons have an outside diameter of 8.3 centimeters (3¼ in.) and an internal diameter of 5 centimeters (2 in.). They are spaced 40.6 centimeters (16 in.) apart. Their arms have a 6.4-centimeter (2½ in.) maximum width, and their maximum length along one face of the rudder is 66 centimeters (26 in.). See Figures 44 and 48.

01-039. Plank fragment. Unit 302, level F. This softwood piece has a maximum length of 15.2 centimeters (6 in.), a maximum width of 8.3 centimeters (3¼ in.), and a maximum thickness of 1.9 centimeters (¾ in.). See Figure 45.

01-041. Plank fragment. Units 200 and 201, level unknown. It has a maximum length of 59.7 centimeters (23½ in.), a maximum width of 10.8 centimeters (4¼ in.), and a maximum thickness of 2.5 centimeters (1 in.). See Figures 44 and 45.

01-042. Rail timber. Unit 200, level D. This curved timber, probably of oak, has three rectangular mortises on its underside. One end was cut with a bevel and has two nails attached to the top and one spike protruding from the mortise. The other end was exposed above the sediments within the hull and is heavily eroded. The rail has a maximum length of 282.9 centimeters (103½ in.), a maximum width of 7 centimeters (2¾ in.), and a maximum thickness of 6.4 centimeters (2½ in.). See Figures 44, 45, and 48.

01-043. Timber fragment. Unit 200, level E. The fragment resembles an eroded section of rail. It has a maximum length of 24.8 centimeters (9¾ in.), a maximum width of 5.4 centimeters (2⅛ in.), and a maximum thickness of 1.9 centimeters (¾ in.). There are possible adze marks on one edge.

01-044. Plank. Unit 302. This is an eroded softwood plank fragment with a maximum length of 34.6 centimeters (13⅝ in.), a maximum width of 9.5 centimeters (3¾ in.), and a maximum thickness of 1.6 centimeters (⅝ in.).

01-045. Tread plank. Unit 302, level unknown. This plank, of elm or maple, would be used the same way as artifacts 01-012 and 01-026. It has a maximum length of 74.9 centimeters (29½ in.), a maximum width of 35.6 centimeters (14 in.), tapering to 24.1 centimeters (9½ in.), and a maximum thickness of 3.8 centimeters (1½ in.). See Figure 45.

01-046. Subtread plank. Port side of treadwheel. This was one of the softwood planks that supported the hardwood tread planks of the horse walkway. There are six nail holes; three on one end, two on one side, and one at the other end. It has a maximum length of 125.7 centimeters (49½ in.), a maximum width of 20.3 centimeters (8 in.), and a maximum thickness of 4.4 centimeters (1¾ in.).

01-048. Plank fragment. Unit 301, between frames. One surface of this softwood plank is severely eroded. It has a maximum length of 35.6 centimeters (14 in.), a maximum width of 14.6 centimeters (5¾ in.), and a maximum thickness of 1.9 centimeters (¾ in.). See Figure 45.

01-049. Plank fragment. Unit 302, level G. Fashioned from softwood, the plank has a maximum length of 25.4 centimeters (10 in.), a maximum width of 15.9 centimeters (6¼ in.), and a maximum thickness of 1.3 centimeters (½ in.).

01-050. Ceiling plank. Unit 303/403, level D. This softwood plank was still fastened to the frames when uncovered, but it was cut and removed to permit the study of the frames. It was heavily eroded and had a maximum length of 72.4 centimeters (28½ in.), a maximum width of 17.8 centimeters (7 in.), and a maximum thickness of 2.5 centimeters (1 in.). See Figure 45.

FASTENERS

01-014 A–B. Treenail fragments. Unit 201, level A. These are probably from plugs inserted in knotholes in the outer planking. Treenail A measures 14 centimeters (5½ in.) in length and 2.5 centimeters (1 in.) in diameter; the tapered point is 2.5 centimeters (1 in.) long. Treenail B is 5.4 centimeters (2⅛ in.) long and 3 centimeters (1³⁄₁₆ in.) in diameter. See Figure 49.

03-001. Brass tack. Unit 203, level B. The tack is 1.3 centimeters (½ in.) long, the shaft is 1.5 millimeters (¹⁄₁₆ in.) square, and the head is 7.9 millimeters (⁵⁄₁₆ in.) in diameter. See Figure 49.

03-005. Iron spike fragment. Unit 103, level A. The fragment is 4.8 centimeters (1⅞ in.) long, the shaft is 7.9 millimeters (⁵⁄₁₆ in.) square, and the head is 9.5 millimeters (⅜ in.) in diameter.

03-006 A–B. Iron nail, two pieces. Unit 201, between frames. Both pieces are severely corroded. Piece A is 6.3 millimeters (¼ in.) long and has a 4.7-millimeter (³⁄₁₆ in.) maximum width; piece B is 2.2 centimeters (⅞ in.) long and has a maximum width of 3.1 millimeters (⅛ in.).

03-007. Iron spike. Unit 201, between frames. The spike is corroded and slightly bent. It measures 11.1 centimeters (4⅜ in.) long, the shaft is 9.5 millimeters (⅜ in.) square, and the head is 1.3 centimeters (½ in.) across. See Figure 49.

03-008 A–B. Iron nail, two pieces. Unit 103, level A. This extremely corroded nail broke into two pieces before conservation. Piece A is 2.5 centimeters (1 in.) long, with a 6.3-millimeter (¼ in.) maximum width, and the shaft is 4.7 millimeters (³⁄₁₆ in.) square. Piece B is 7.9 millimeters (⁵⁄₁₆ in.) long with a maximum width of 1.3 millimeters (⅛ in.).

03-009 A–C. Iron nail fragments. Unit 201, between frames. All are extremely deteriorated and crumbled partially before the conservation process. Piece A is 5.7 centimeters (2¼ in.) long with a 4.8-millimeter (³⁄₁₆ in.) square width. Pieces B and C articulate and together measure 5.9 centimeters (2⁵⁄₁₆ in.) in length, with a shank 6.3 by 3.1 millimeters (¼ × ⅛ in.) in section.

03-012. Iron ring and bolt. Unit 103, level A. The ring's outside diameter is 9.5 centimeters (3¾ in.) and its maximum thickness is 1.3 centimeters (½ in.). The length of the bolt is 11.9 centimeters (4¹¹⁄₁₆ in.); it has a 2.5-centimeter (1 in.) maximum thickness. The hole in the bolt through which the ring passes is 2.2 centimeters (⅞ in.) in diameter; the outer diameter of the bolt loop is 4 centimeters (1⁹⁄₁₆ in.).

03-015. Iron spike fragment. Unit 201/101, between frames. The 7.6-centimeter (3-in.) long spike is heavily corroded. The head is 1.4 centimeters ($\frac{9}{16}$ in.) wide and the shaft is 6.3 millimeters ($\frac{1}{4}$ in.) wide.

03-016 B. Iron washer. Unit 102, between frames. The washer has an outer diameter of 5.7 centimeters ($2\frac{1}{4}$ in.), an inner diameter of 2.5 centimeters (1 in.), and a thickness of 6.3 millimeters ($\frac{1}{4}$ in.). See Figure 44.

03-026. Iron spike concretion. Unit 402, level B or C. The metal of the spike has entirely disappeared, leaving only a concretion mold. It measures 3.2 centimeters ($1\frac{1}{4}$ in.) long and 6.3 millimeters ($\frac{1}{4}$ in.) square.

03-028. Iron nail fragment. Unit 200, level A. The nail is severely corroded. It is 4.6 centimeters ($1\frac{7}{8}$ in.) long and 3.1 millimeters ($\frac{1}{8}$ in.) square in section.

03-029. Iron washer. Unit 301, level F. The washer is severely corroded. It has a 4.1-centimeter ($1\frac{5}{8}$ in.) outer diameter, a maximum thickness of 7.9 millimeters ($\frac{5}{16}$ in.), and an inner diameter of 2.4 centimeters ($\frac{15}{16}$ in.). See Figures 45 and 49.

03-032. Iron nail. Unit 301, between frames. The nail is in good condition and is 3.2 centimeters ($1\frac{1}{4}$ in.) long. The shaft is 4.7 millimeters ($\frac{3}{16}$ in.) square and the head is 6.3 millimeters ($\frac{1}{4}$ in.) wide.

03-033. Iron chain link. Unit 301, between frames. The link is broken but otherwise in good condition. The link is 5 centimeters (2 in.) long, 1.9 centimeters ($\frac{3}{4}$ in.) wide, and 4.7 millimeters ($\frac{3}{16}$ in.) thick. See Figure 49.

03-034. Iron spike. Unit 200, level D. This corroded spike is 11.6 centimeters ($4\frac{9}{16}$ in.) long. The shaft is 6.3 millimeters ($\frac{1}{4}$ in.) square and the head is 1.4 centimeters ($\frac{9}{16}$ in.) wide. See Figures 45 and 49.

03-041. Iron spike. Unit 200, level E. The spike is 10.3 centimeters ($4\frac{1}{16}$ in.) long, the shaft tapering from 7.9 to 3.1 millimeters ($\frac{5}{16}$–$\frac{1}{8}$ in.) wide. The head is 9.5 millimeters ($\frac{3}{8}$ in.) square. See Figures 45 and 49.

03-044 B. Iron nail. Unit 200, level E. The nail is 7.6 centimeters (3 in.) long and has a shank 3.1 millimeters ($\frac{1}{8}$) square. See Figure 49.

03-045. Iron nail. Unit 200, level E. The nail has a slight bend and is 6.4 centimeters ($2\frac{1}{2}$) long. The shaft tapers from 3.1 to 1.5 millimeters ($\frac{1}{8}$–$\frac{1}{16}$ in.) wide, and the head is 4.8 millimeters ($\frac{3}{16}$ in.) square. See Figure 49.

03-046 A–B. Iron nails. Unit 401/301, level F. The nails are in poor condition. Nail A is 5 centimeters (2 in.) long, with a 4.7-millimeter ($\frac{3}{16}$-in.) wide shaft and a 1.3-centimeter ($\frac{1}{2}$-in.) wide head. Nail B is 2.5 centimeters (1 in.) long and 1.5 millimeters ($\frac{1}{16}$ in.) wide. See Figure 49.

03-047. Iron washer. Unit 401/301, level F. The washer was crudely fashioned by looping a flat piece of iron; the metal is now deteriorated. The outside diameter is 3.5 centimeters ($1\frac{3}{8}$ in.), the thickness is 7.9 millimeters ($\frac{5}{16}$ in.), and the inner diameter is 1.7 centimeters ($\frac{11}{16}$ in.). See Figure 49.

03-049. Iron nail. Unit 302, level F. The nail is 11.4 centimeters ($4\frac{1}{2}$ in.) long. The shaft tapers from 9.5 to 3.1 millimeters ($\frac{3}{8}$–$\frac{1}{8}$ in.) square, and the head is 1.3 centimeters ($\frac{1}{2}$ in.) square. See Figures 45 and 49.

03-050. Iron chain link. Unit 302, level F. The link is open and bent. It is 6.6 centimeters ($2\frac{5}{8}$ in.) in length and 6.3 millimeters ($\frac{1}{4}$ in.) thick. See Figure 49.

03-053. Iron washer. Unit 301, level F. The washer is corroded and broken. Its outside diameter is 5.9 centimeters ($2^5/_{16}$ in.), its maximum thickness is 1.6 centimeters ($5/_8$ in.), and its inner diameter is 2.5 centimeters (1 in.). See Figures 45 and 49.

03-057. Iron spike. Unit 301, between frames. The spike is 13 centimeters ($5^1/_8$ in.) long. The shaft tapers from 1.1 centimeters to 1.5 millimeters ($7/_{16}$–$1/_{16}$ in.) wide, and the head is 1.3 centimeters ($1/_2$ in.) square. See Figure 49.

03-058. Iron nail. Unit 303, between frames. The nail is 12 centimeters ($4^3/_4$ in.) long and in good condition. The shaft tapers from 9.5 to 1.5 millimeters ($3/_8$–$1/_{16}$ in.) wide, and the head is 1.3 centimeters ($1/_2$ in.) square. See Figure 49.

03-059. Iron nail. Unit 302, level G. The nail's length is 10.8 centimeters ($4^1/_4$ in.). The shaft tapers from 1.1 centimeters to 1.5 millimeters ($7/_{16}$–$1/_{16}$ in.) wide, and the head is 1.3 centimeters ($1/_2$ in.) wide. See Figures 45 and 49.

03-061. Iron nail. Unit 301, between frames. The nail is in two pieces and in poor condition. It is 6.3 by 6.3 millimeters ($1/_4 \times 1/_4$ in.) square and 1.9 centimeters ($3/_4$ in.) long.

03-062. Threaded bolt shaft. Unit 301, between frames. The shaft is in good condition, 7 centimeters ($2^3/_4$ in.) long, and 1.3 centimeters ($1/_2$ in.) in diameter. The threaded portion of the shaft is 5.4 centimeters ($2^1/_8$ in.) long. See Figure 49.

03-064. Iron washer. Unit 301, between frames. The washer is in good condition. Its outside diameter is 5 centimeters (2 in.), its inner diameter is 2.5 centimeters (1 in.), and it is 6.3 millimeters ($1/_4$ in.) thick. See Figure 49.

03-068. Iron chain links. Unit 301, between frames. The eight attached links are all in good condition; the chain is 28 centimeters ($11^1/_8$ in.) long. Each link is 4.8 centimeters ($1^7/_8$ in.) long, approximately 2.2 centimeters ($7/_8$ in.) wide, and 6.3 millimeters ($1/_4$ in.) thick. See Figures 45 and 49.

03-069 B. Iron chain link. Unit 301, between frames. The link is in good condition, 6.6 centimeters ($2^5/_8$ in.) long, and 6.3 millimeters ($1/_4$ in.) thick. Its maximum width is 2.5 centimeters (1 in.). See Figure 49.

03-070. Brass tack. Unit 301, hull cleaning. The tack has the same measurements as 03-001: 1.3 centimeters ($1/_2$ in.) long, a shaft 1.5 millimeters ($1/_{16}$ in.) in diameter, and a head 7.9 millimeters ($5/_{16}$ in) in diameter.

03-073. Iron spike. Unit 301, between frames. The spike is 11.1 centimeters ($4^3/_8$ in.) long. The shaft tapers from 9.5 to 3.1 millimeters ($3/_8$–$1/_8$ in.) wide, and the head is 1.3 centimeters by 9.5 millimeters ($1/_2 \times 3/_8$ in.) wide. See Figures 45 and 49.

03-076. Iron washer. Unit 301, between frames. The 6.3-millimeter ($1/_4$ in.) thick washer has a 3.8-centimeter ($1^1/_2$ in.) outside diameter and an inner diameter of 1.9 centimeters ($3/_4$ in). See Figures 45 and 49.

03-077. Iron bolt and nut. Unit 301, on hull. The bolt and nut are fused together by corrosion. The bolt, which is missing its head, is 4.8 centimeters ($1^7/_8$ in.) long and 1.3 centimeters ($1/_2$ in.) in diameter. The nut is 3.2 centimeters ($1^1/_4$ in.) square and 1.3 centimeters ($1/_2$ in.) thick. See Figures 45 and 49.

03-078. Iron nail. Unit 301, on hull. The nail is in poor condition and is 5.4 centimeters ($2^1/_8$ in.) long. The head is 9.5 millimeters ($3/_8$ in.) wide, and the shaft tapers from 4.7 to 1.5 millimeters ($3/_{16}$–$1/_{16}$ in.) wide.

03-079 A–B. Iron spike fragments. Stern trench 1, level A. Both fragments are corroded. Fragment A is 3.5 centimeters (1³⁄₈ in.) long and 6.3 millimeters (¼ in.) square. Fragment B is 5 centimeters (2 in.) long.

03-080 A–C. Iron spike fragments. Stern trench 3, level A. Fragment A is 6.4 centimeters (2½ in.) long, the shaft is 7.9 by 4.7 millimeters (⁵⁄₁₆ × ³⁄₁₆ in.), and the head is 1.6 centimeters by 9.5 millimeters (⁵⁄₈ × ³⁄₈ in.). Fragment B, a piece of wood with a heavily corroded spike hole, is 6.4 centimeters (2½ in.) long, with a maximum thickness of 2.5 centimeters (1 in.); the spike hole measures 6.3 by 1.3 centimeters (¼ × ½ in.). Fragment C is 5.4 centimeters (2⅛ in.) long and has a maximum width of 2.2 centimeters (⅞ in.).

03-081 A–B. Two iron spike fragments. Stern trench 3, level B. The two fragments have substantial core corrosion. Fragment A is 4 centimeters (1⁹⁄₁₆ in.) long with a 2.7- centimeter (1¹⁄₁₆ in.) maximum width and a 1.3-centimeter (½ in.) maximum thickness. Fragment B is 2.4 centimeters (¹⁵⁄₁₆ in.) long, with a maximum width and maximum thickness of 7.9 millimeters (⁵⁄₁₆ in.).

03-084. Iron spike fragment. Stern trench 2, level unknown. The spike is 5.7 centimeters (2¼ in.) long. Its maximum width is 3.2 centimeters (1¼ in.), and the head is 1.9 centimeters (¾ in.) wide.

03-085 A–C. Iron spike fragments. Stern trench 2, level unknown. The condition of the fragments is poor. Fragment A is 3.3 centimeters (1⁵⁄₁₆ in.) long, with a maximum width of 1.3 centimeters (½ in.). Fragment B is 3 centimeters (1³⁄₁₆ in.) long with a maximum width of 4.7 millimeters (³⁄₁₆ in.). Fragment C is 1.1 centimeters (⁷⁄₁₆ in.) long and has a maximum width of 7.9 millimeters (⁵⁄₁₆ in.).

03-089 A–B. Iron spike fragments. Stern trenches 1 and 3, level unknown. The spikes are highly corroded. Fragment A is 2.8 centimeters (1⅛ in.) long and 9.5 millimeters (⅜ in.) square. Fragment B is a nail concretion 4.4 centimeters (1¾ in.) long and 1.3 centimeters (½ in.) thick, with a 2.5-centimeter (1 in.) maximum width.

03-090 A–B. Iron spike fragments. Stern trench 3, level unknown. The spikes are both corroded. Fragment A is 4.4 centimeters (1¾ in.) long and 3 centimeters (1³⁄₁₆ in.) wide. Fragment B is 4 centimeters (1⁹⁄₁₆ in.) long, 1.9 centimeters (¾ in.) wide, and 6.3 millimeters (¼ in.) square in section.

03-091. Iron spike. Stern trench 2, level unknown. The spike is 10 centimeters (3¹⁵⁄₁₆ in.) long, the head is 1.3 centimeters (½ in.) wide, and the shaft tapers from 1.1 centimeters to 3.1 millimeters (⁷⁄₁₆–⅛ in.).

03-093. Iron nail. Stern trench 1, on ceiling planks. The nail is 5.4 centimeters (2¹⁄₁₆ in.) long. The head is 6.3 by 4.7 millimeters (¼ × ³⁄₁₆ in.), and the shaft tapers from 7.9 to 3.1 millimeters (⁵⁄₁₆–⅛ in.).

03-094 A–C. Iron spike fragments. Stern trench 2, on ceiling. The fragments are heavily corroded. Fragment A is 7 centimeters (2¾ in.) long, the encased spike is 7.9 millimeters (⁵⁄₁₆ in.) in diameter, and the wood attached is 6.6 centimeters (2⅝ in.) wide. Fragment B is 6.2 centimeters (2⁷⁄₁₆ in.) long, the encased spike has a 7.9-millimeter (⁵⁄₁₆ in.) diameter, and the wood attached is 2.2 centimeters (⅞ in.) wide. Fragment C is 4 centimeters (1⁹⁄₁₆ in.) long, the encased spike has a diameter of 7.9 millimeters (⁵⁄₁₆ in.), and the wood attached is 1.6 centimeters (⅝ in.) wide.

03-095. Iron nail. Stern trench 4, level unknown. The ends are broken off the nail. It is 5.7 centimeters (2¼ in.) long and tapers from 7.9 to 4.7 millimeters (⁵⁄₁₆–³⁄₁₆ in.).

03-096. Iron spike fragment. Portside, just aft of deck beam 16. The corroded fragment is 7 centimeters (2¾ in.) long and 7.9 millimeters (⁵⁄₁₆ in.) square.

03-082, 03-086, 03-087. Iron spike fragments. 03-082 is from stern trench 3, and 03-086 and 03-087 are from stern trench 2; all were from a dredge bag. The fragments are so degraded that they were not cataloged or measured.

MACHINERY-RELATED EQUIPMENT

03-011. Cast-iron straight bevel gear. Unit 200 (recovered in 1989), on frames. This gear has considerable surface corrosion, and the teeth are extremely worn and broken. It is 8.3 centimeters (3¼ in.) thick and has an outside diameter of 24.1 centimeters (9½ in.) and a center hole 8.3 centimeters (3¼ in.) square. The fifteen teeth are, on average, 2.2 centimeters (⅞ in.) in length, 2.5 centimeters (1 in.) wide at their bases, and spaced from top to top about 3.8 centimeters (1½ in.) apart. See Figures 44 and 50.

03-038. Cast-iron spur gear. Unit 200, on apron. The gear shows evidence of moderate wear on the teeth and minor surface corrosion. It is 7 centimeters (2¾ in.) thick, with a maximum outside diameter of 28.9 centimeters (11⅜ in.) and a center hole 8.3 centimeters (3¼ in.) square. The sixteen teeth are 3.8 centimeters (1½ in.) in length and 2.5 centimeters (1 in.) thick at the base. See Figures 45 and 50.

03-039. Cast-iron spur gear. Unit 200, on apron. The gear shows moderate wear on the teeth and minor surface corrosion. It has a maximum outside diameter of 30.5 centimeters (12 in.), a maximum thickness of 7.6 centimeters (3 in.), and a center hole 8.1 centimeters (3³⁄₁₆ in.) square. The sixteen teeth are 3.8 centimeters (1½ in.) in length and 3.2 centimeters (1¼ in.) thick at the base. See Figures 45 and 50.

03-048. Cast-copper alloy axle bushing. Unit 302, between frames. The bushing is worn from excessive wear, and less than half of the original metal remains. It has a maximum length of 7.3 centimeters (2⅞ in.), and the diameter of the axle hole is 7.6 centimeters (3 in.). The lip is 9.2 centimeters (3⅝ in.) across, with a maximum thickness of 6.3 millimeters (¼ in.) at the lip. There is evidence of filing marks on some of the remaining outside surfaces, and a raised mark resembling an X was cast into one of the faceted outside surfaces. See Figures 45 and 51.

03-014: 03-037 A–C, 03-042 A–B, 03-043, 03-044, 03-056, and 03-069 A. Cast-iron axle coupling. The coupling has been reconstructed from ten fragments found in units 200, 201, and 301, on the hull. When whole, the coupling was 24.1 centimeters (9½ in.) long, 10.2 centimeters (4 in.) wide, and 2.2 centimeters (⅞ in.) thick. It was used (or was intended to be used) to connect two lengths of the ferry's axle. The inside surfaces of many of the fragments indicate that the collar had been filed. See Figures 44, 45, and 51.

HORSE-RELATED EQUIPMENT

03-002. Iron horseshoe. Unit 201, level C. One branch of the shoe is broken off and missing below the reinforcing bar, but it is otherwise in fair condition. It is 13.3 centimeters (5¼ in.) in length and 2.5 centimeters (1 in.) in maximum width. The maximum thickness of the reinforcing bar is 1.9 centimeters (¾ in.); of the heel, 2.5 centimeters (1 in.); and of the branch, 9.5 millimeters (⅜ in.). The shoe half has four nail holes; two nails were found in the holes. See Figures 44 and 52.

03-003 A–B. Iron hame fastener and iron ring. Unit 201, level C. Both are corroded, and the loops that held the rings to the end of the bar are broken. The fastener is 13.7 centimeters (5⅜ in.) in length, with a maximum thickness of 1.1 centimeters (⁷⁄₁₆ in.), and the two ring loops have 1.3-centimeter (½ in.) external diameters. The iron ring has a 4.8-centimeter (1⅞ in.) maximum external diameter and a maximum thickness of 6.3 millimeters (¼ in.). See Figures 44 and 52.

03-004. Iron and wood harness (hame) fragment. Unit 201, level C. The metal fragment is corroded, and the loop on the end is broken. The wood shrank during conservation treatment. The piece is 19.7 centimeters (7¾ in.) long, with a 2.2-centimeter (⅞ in.) maximum width and two holes for fastening the metal to the wood (both 6.4 mm [¼ in.] in diameter). The iron loop, which is broken, is 3 centimeters (1³⁄₁₆ in.) long and 3.1 millimeters (⅛ in.) thick, with a maximum width of 2 centimeters (¹³⁄₁₆ in.). See Figures 44 and 52.

03-010. Iron horseshoe. Unit 201, between frames. The shoe consists of one branch without the reinforcing bar. It has three nail holes, with two bent nails still in place. It is 10.7 centimeters (4³⁄₁₆ in.) in length and 2.2 centimeters (⅞ in.) in maximum width. The heel is 2.2 centimeters (⅞ in.) thick, and the maximum thickness of the branch is 7.9 millimeters (⁵⁄₁₆ in.). See Figures 44 and 52.

03-013. Iron horseshoe. Unit 201, level B. One branch of the shoe is missing below the reinforcing bar. It is 1.7 centimeters (5¹¹⁄₁₆ in.) in length, with a maximum width of 2.5 centimeters (1 in.) and a maximum thickness of 6.3 millimeters (¼ in.) in the branch. It is 1.3 centimeters (½ in.) thick at the reinforcing bar and 1.9 centimeters (¾ in.) thick on the heel. The fragment has four nail holes. See Figures 44 and 52.

03-031. Iron horseshoe. Unit 301, level F, between frames. The shoe consists of one branch without the reinforcing bar. It is 10.6 centimeters (4³⁄₁₆ in.) in length, with a maximum width of 2.2 centimeters (⅞ in.). The maximum thickness of the branch is 9.6 millimeters (⅜ in.), and the heel is 2.9 centimeters (1⅛ in.) thick. The fragment has four nail holes. See Figures 45 and 52.

03-035. Iron horseshoe. Unit 301, between frames. This is a whole horseshoe with considerable corrosion on one side. It was found with two nails. The shoe is 12 centimeters (4¾ in.) long and 10.5 centimeters (4⅛ in.) wide. Each branch is 2.4 centimeters (¹⁵⁄₁₆ in.) wide and 9.5 millimeters (⅜ in.) thick, the heel is 1.3 centimeters (½ in.) thick, and the reinforcing bar is 1.6 centimeters (⅝ in.) thick. The shoe has eight nail holes. See Figures 45 and 52.

03-051. Iron horseshoe. Unit 301, level F. The shoe consists of one branch without the reinforcing bar. There is one nail (2.5 cm [1 in.] long) and three nail holes. The shoe is 10.3 centimeters (4¹⁄₁₆ in.) in length, with a maximum width of 2.2 centimeters (⅞ in.). The branch is 6.3 millimeters (¼ in.) thick, and the heel is 2.4 centimeters (¹⁵⁄₁₆ in.) thick. See Figures 45 and 52.

03-052. Iron horseshoe. Unit 301, level F. The shoe is broken in half at the reinforcing bar. The shoe is 13 centimeters (5⅛ in.) in length. The branch has a maximum width of 2.5 centimeters (1 in.) and a maximum thickness of 9.5 millimeters (⅜ in.).

The reinforcing bar is 1.1 centimeter ($^7/_{16}$ in.) thick, and the heel is 1.9 centimeters ($^3/_4$ in.) thick. The fragment has four nail holes. See Figures 45 and 52.

03-055. Iron horseshoe. Unit 301, between frames. The shoe is broken in half at the reinforcing bar. The piece is 13.7 centimeters ($5^3/_8$ in.) in length, with a maximum width of 2.54 centimeters (1 in.). The branch is 9.5 millimeters ($^3/_8$ in.) thick, the reinforcing bar is 1.9 centimeters ($^3/_4$ in.) thick, and the heel is 2.2 centimeters ($^7/_8$ in.) thick. The fragment has four nail holes. See Figures 45 and 52.

03-063. Iron horseshoe. Unit 301, between frames. The shoe consists of one branch without the reinforcing bar. It has a 12.4-centimeter ($4^7/_8$ in.) maximum length and a 2.2-centimeter ($^7/_8$ in.) maximum width. The maximum thickness of the branch is 6.3 millimeters ($^1/_4$ in.), and of the heel, 1.6 centimeters ($^5/_8$ in.). The fragment has four nail holes. See Figure 52.

04-001. Leather strap. Unit 201, level C. The strap is worn, with many superficial cracks, but appears to be in one piece. It is 25.9 centimeters ($10^3/_{16}$ in.) long and 3.1 millimeters ($^1/_8$ in.) thick, with a maximum width of 1.7 centimeters ($^{11}/_{16}$ in.). It has five buckle holes. See Figures 44 and 53.

04-002. Leather strap (harness brow band). Unit 201, between frames. The worn strap has three lines of stitching holes, forming a U shape, visible near each end. The ends fold back on the strap and it appears as if another object (possibly a leather strap) was attached through the stitching holes. The total length of the strap is 35.6 centimeters (14 in.); it has a maximum width of 2.5 centimeters (1 in.) and 3.1 millimeters ($^1/_8$ in.) thick. See Figures 44 and 53.

04-003. Leather harness strap. Unit 201, level B. The strap is worn and broken on one end (possibly where a buckle would be), with five buckle holes punched 2.5 centimeters (1 in.) apart, with one torn, perhaps from use. The strap is 14.9 centimeters ($5^7/_8$ in.) long and 4.8 millimeters ($^3/_{16}$ in.) thick, with a maximum width of 2.2 centimeters ($^{14}/_{16}$ in.). See Figures 44 and 53.

04-004. Leather straps, buckle, and ring (bridle or harness straps). Unit 201, level B. The leather is cracked and worn, but the iron is in good condition. The three leather straps appear to be buckled together, with the iron ring attached at one end and the other end broken. The straps are 15.2 centimeters (6 in.) in length, with maximum widths of 2.2 centimeters ($^7/_8$ in.); the three straps together are 1.6 centimeters ($^5/_8$ in.) thick. The ring has a 4.9-centimeter ($1^{15}/_{16}$ in.) outside diameter, and the metal ring is 6.3 millimeters ($^1/_4$ in.) thick. The buckle is 2.2 centimeters ($^7/_8$ in.) long, 2.9 centimeters ($1^1/_8$ in.) wide, and 3.1 millimeters ($^1/_8$ in.) thick. Two buckle holes are visible. See Figure 52.

04-005. Leather harness fragment (keeper). Unit 201, level A. The fragment is worn but otherwise in good condition. It is a small, leather strap ring for a bridle or harness. The strap is 3.2 centimeters ($1^1/_4$ in.) long, with the ends folding inward, 3.2 millimeters ($^1/_8$ in.) thick, and 1.9 centimeters ($^3/_4$ in.) wide. See Figure 52.

04-006. Leather fragment. Unit 202/102, between frames. The fragment is broken, worn, and deteriorated. It is 4.4 centimeters ($1^3/_4$ in.) long, 1.5 millimeters ($^1/_{16}$ in.) thick, and has a maximum width of 2.2 centimeters ($^7/_8$ in.).

04-007. Leather strap fragment. Unit 201/101, between frames. The strap is worn, broken at one end (with one possible buckle hole), and has eight stitching holes at the other end. The piece is 19.7 centimeters (7¾ in.) long and 1.5 millimeters (¹⁄₁₆ in.) thick, with a maximum width of 2.4 centimeters (¹⁵⁄₁₆ in.). See Figure 53.

04-010. Leather strap. Unit 200, level D. The strap is fragile, with superficial cracks and wear. It measures 23.7 centimeters (9⁵⁄₁₆ in.) long, 1.4 centimeters (⁹⁄₁₆ in.) wide, and 3.1 millimeters (⅛ in.) thick. It has five buckle holes. See Figure 45 and 53.

04-011. Leather fragment. Unit 200, level D. The fragment has three holes 1.6 centimeters (⅝ in.) apart at one end and is 9.4 centimeters (3¹¹⁄₁₆ in.) long. It has a maximum width of 2.9 centimeters (1⅛ in.) and a maximum thickness of 3.1 millimeters (⅛ in.).

04-012. Leather harness strap. Unit 301, between frames. The strap is slightly worn and has a bend in it at one end, with a hole at the bend shaped like an elongated diamond, and stitching 3.1 millimeters (⅛ in.) from the sides. The strap has an overall length of 16.5 centimeters (6½ in.), a maximum width of 2.5 centimeters (1 in.), and a maximum thickness of 4.7 millimeters (³⁄₁₆ in.). See Figures 45 and 53.

04-013. Leather strap fragment. Unit 301, on hull. The strap measures 11.4 centimeters (4½ in.) long and 6.3 millimeters (¼ in.) thick, with a 2-centimeter (¹³⁄₁₆ in.) maximum width. It has one hole with a 2.2-centimeter (⅞ in.) cut at one end. See Figure 53.

04-014. Leather harness, strap, and buckle. Stern trench 1, between cant frames. The leather is in good condition, but there is some corrosion on the iron buckle. The buckle holds two leather pieces together. There are two keepers on either side of the buckle to secure strap ends. The straps are a total of 55.3 centimeters (21¾ in.) long, 3.6 centimeters (1⁷⁄₁₆ in.) wide, and 6.3 millimeters (¼ in.) thick. The keepers are 4.4 centimeters (1¾ in.) long, 1.6 centimeters (⅝ in.) wide, and 1.6 centimeters (⅝ in.) thick. There are seven buckle holes, all about 2.9 centimeters (1⅛ in.) apart. The buckle is 3.2 centimeters (1¼ in.) long, 4.7 millimeters (³⁄₁₆ in.) thick, and 1.6 centimeters (⅝ in.) wide. See Figure 53.

04-015. Leather strap fragment. Stern trench 2, between frames. The ends of the strap are worn and broken. It measures 11.7 centimeters (4⅝ in.) long, 1.9 centimeters (¾ in.) wide, and 1.5 millimeters (¹⁄₁₆ in.) thick.

04-016. Leather strap fragment. Stern trenches, between frames. The strap has cracks on its surfaces and is broken at the ends. It measures 13.3 centimeters (5¼ in.) long and 3.1 millimeters (⅛ in.) thick, with a 2-centimeter (¹³⁄₁₆ in.) maximum width. It has one hole through it and stitching along both sides. See Figure 53.

MISCELLANEOUS—TOOLS

01-040. Wooden scrub brush. Unit 200, level D. The brush was in good condition when found, with fragile remnants of the bristles still attached to the wooden back. The bristles separated from the brush when the brush was being transported to Texas A&M University for conservation. The wooden handle of the brush is 17.5 centimeters (6⅞ in.) long, 5.7 centimeters (2¼ in.) wide, and 1.1 centimeters (⁷⁄₁₆ in.) thick. There are eighty-three bristle holes located in the grooves carved out of the underside of the handle. The brush may have been used to groom horses or to clean the ferry's upperworks. See Figures 45 and 54.

03-040. Caulking iron. Unit 200, between starboard side cant frames. This tool, called a "crooked spike iron," was fashioned from iron. The metal is in excellent condition. The iron measures 39.7 centimeters (15⅝ in.) in length, with a shaft 2.2 by 1.6 centimeters (⅞ × ⅝ in.) in section, and a driving edge 3.8 centimeters (1½ in.) in width. Caulking irons are used to drive oakum into the seams between planks, thereby making the seams watertight. This iron's unusually long shaft and crooked form indicate that it was used to drive oakum into short, hard-to-reach plank seams. The mushroomed condition of the head indicates considerable use. See Figures 45 and 54.

03-016A. Iron wedge. This wedge of iron resembles a nail set and measures 7.1 centimeters (6¾ in.) long, with a maximum width of 3.3 centimeters (1⁵⁄₁₆ in.) and a maximum thickness of 7.9 millimeters (⁵⁄₁₆ in.). The broad end of the wedge has been heavily pounded and the item appears to have been used as a nail set or similar tool. See Figures 44 and 54.

03-060. Iron nail set. Unit 301, between frames. This item resembles a nail set and measures 10.8 centimeters (4¼ in.) in length. The shaft is 1.3 by 1.6 centimeters (½ × ⅝ in.) in section and the head is 2.4 by 1.7 centimeters (¹⁵⁄₁₆ × ¹¹⁄₁₆ in.). A set is used to sink nails or spikes below wood surfaces. See Figures 45 and 54.

MISCELLANEOUS—CERAMIC AND GLASS

05-001: 05-003 A–V, 05-005, 05-006, 05-010 A–C, 05-011 A–B, 05-012, 05-013 A–C, 05-014, 05-015, 05-017 A–F, and 05-018. Brown-glazed red-earthenware teapot. Forty-three sherds of a dark-brown glazed, red-earthenware teapot were recovered from units 101, 200, 201, and 301 in the bow of the horse ferry. The lid, handle, end of the spout, and a few body fragments were missing, but most of the pot could be reconstructed. The oval pot has a dark brown (almost black) glaze on the outside and is lighter brown on the inside; it has a band of molded decorations around the shoulder. The base is 12.7 centimeters (5 in.) long and 11.3 centimeters (4⁷⁄₁₆ in.) wide. The top of the teapot has the same dimensions as the base. The body's maximum length is 18.4 centimeters (7¼ in.). The pot is 14.6 centimeters (5¾ in.) high. The broken spout is 7 centimeters (2¾ in.) long and has a 2.5-centimeter (1 in.) maximum width. The body has an average thickness of 3.1 millimeters (⅛ in.). The materials and workmanship are somewhat crude, suggesting that this was an inexpensive teapot. See Figures 44 and 54.

05-002. Clear glass fragment. Unit 201. It has a maximum length of 1.1 centimeters (⁷⁄₁₆ in.), a maximum width of 4.7 millimeters (³⁄₁₆ in.), and a maximum thickness of 3.1 millimeters (⅛ in.).

05-004. Decorated glass fragment. Unit 101, level A. The fragment is clear and has an oval pattern etched into one surface. It has a 1.4-centimeter (⁹⁄₁₆ in.) maximum length, a 9.5-millimeter (⅜ in.) maximum width, and a 1.5-millimeter (¹⁄₁₆ in.) maximum thickness.

05-007 A–D. Four glass fragments. Unit 201/101, between frames. Fragments A–C are of clear glass, and fragment D is a greenish color and possibly burned. Fragment A has a 2.4-centimeter (¹⁵⁄₁₆ in.) maximum length, a 9.5-millimeter (⅜ in.) maximum width, and a 1.5-millimeter (¹⁄₁₆ in.) maximum thickness. Fragment B has a maximum length of 1.4 centimeters (⁹⁄₁₆ in.), a maximum width of 1.6 centimeters (⁵⁄₈ in.), and a maximum thickness of 1.5-millimeters (¹⁄₁₆ in.). Fragment C has a maximum length of 2.4 centimeters (¹⁵⁄₁₆ in.), a maximum width of 2 centimeters (¹³⁄₁₆ in.), and a maximum thickness of 3.1 millimeters (¹⁄₈ in.). Fragment D has maximum length of 2.4 centimeters (¹⁵⁄₁₆ in.), a maximum width of 1.4 centimeters (¹⁄₁₆ in.), and a maximum thickness of 1.5 millimeters (¹⁄₁₆ in.).

05-013 D. Blue-glazed ceramic rim sherd. Unit 200, level E. Fragment D has a 1.1-centimeter (⁷⁄₁₆ in.) maximum length, a 7.9-millimeter (⁵⁄₁₆ in.) maximum width, and a 3.1-millimeter (¹⁄₈ in.) thickness.

05-016. White pottery sherd. Unit 301. Measurements and condition unavailable.

MISCELLANEOUS—WOOD

01-002 A–B. Shaped wood fragments. Unit 203, level unknown. These two eroded pieces fit together to form a rectangular stick, but their function is unknown. Fragment A has a maximum length of 8.3 centimeters (3¹⁄₄ in.), a maximum width of 1.6 centimeters (⁵⁄₈ in.), and a maximum thickness of 6.3 millimeters (¹⁄₄ in.). Fragment B has a maximum length of 9.8 centimeters (3⁷⁄₈ in.), a maximum width of 1.1 centimeters (⁷⁄₁₆ in.), and a maximum thickness of 6.3 millimeters (¹⁄₄ in).

01-003. Shaped wood fragment. Unit 103, level A. This wood is broken and eroded, with saw marks on it at one end. It has a maximum length of 10.2 centimeters (4 in.), a maximum width of 3.8 centimeters (1¹⁄₂ in.), and a maximum thickness of 1.4 centimeters (⁹⁄₁₆ in.).

01-004. Wood slat. Unit 201. This wood is eroded and broken. It has a maximum length of 7.9 centimeters (3¹⁄₈ in.), a maximum width of 2 centimeters (¹³⁄₁₆ in.), and a maximum thickness of 4.7 millimeters (³⁄₁₆ in.).

01-005 A–B. Shaped wood fragments. Unit 201, level unknown. This wood is broken and eroded. Fragment A has a maximum length of 12.7 centimeters (5 in.), a maximum width of 3.8 centimeters (1¹⁄₂ in.), and a maximum thickness of 7.9 millimeters (⁵⁄₁₆ in.). Fragment B has a maximum length of 15.9 centimeters (6¹⁄₄ in.), a maximum width of 1.3 centimeters (¹⁄₂ in.), and a maximum thickness of 6.3 millimeters (¹⁄₄ in.).

01-006. Shaped wood fragment. Unit 103, between frames. Condition and measurements not recorded.

01-007 A–H. Wood fragments. Unit 103, between frames. All fragments are broken and eroded and resemble construction debris or dunnage. Fragment A has a maximum length of 10.2 centimeters (4 in.), a maximum width of 7.6 centimeters (3 in.), and a maximum thickness of 9.5 millimeters (³⁄₈ in.). Fragment B has a maximum length of 6.6 centimeters (2⁵⁄₈ in.), a maximum width of 4.1 centimeters (1⁵⁄₈ in.), and a maximum thickness of 2.9 centimeters (1¹⁄₈ in.). Fragment C has a maximum length of 7 centimeters (2³⁄₄ in.), a maximum width of 4.4 centimeters (1³⁄₄ in.), and a maximum thickness of 1.3 centimeters (¹⁄₂ in.). Fragment D has a maximum length of 13.7 centimeters (5³⁄₈ in.), a maximum width of 1.4 centimeters (⁹⁄₁₆ in.), and a maximum thickness of 1.3 centimeters (¹⁄₂ in.). Fragment E has a maximum length of 9.5 centimeters (3¾ in.), a maximum width of 1.6 centimeters (⅝ in.), and a maximum thickness of 6.3 millimeters (¼ in.). Fragment F has a maximum length of 6.6 centimeters (2⅝ in.), a maximum width of 1.1 centimeters (⁷⁄₁₆ in.), and a maximum thickness of 3.1 millimeters (⅛ in.). Fragment G has a maximum length of 4.8 centimeters (1⅞ in.), a maximum width of 2.2 centimeters (⅞ in.), and a maximum thickness of 6.3 millimeters (¼ in.). Fragment H has a maximum length of 2.9 centimeters (1⅛ in.), a maximum width of 9.5 millimeters (⅜ in.), and a maximum thickness of 7.9 centimeters (⁵⁄₁₆ in.).

01-008. Shaped wood fragment. Unit 103, below level A, between frames. This wood is broken at one end and eroded; the other end is rounded. It has a maximum length of 17.8 centimeters (7 in.), a maximum width of 7.6 centimeters (3 in.), and a maximum thickness of 7.9 millimeters (⁵⁄₁₆ in.).

01-009 A–C. Wood fragments and piece of charcoal. Unit 201, between frames. The wood is eroded and broken. Fragment A has a maximum length of 14.9 centimeters (5⅞ in.), a maximum width of 4.8 centimeters (1⅞ in.), and a maximum thickness of 9.5 millimeters (⅜ in.). Fragment B has a maximum length of 3.2 centimeters (1¼ in.), a maximum width of 2.2 centimeters (⅞ in.), and a maximum thickness of 1.2 centimeters (⅝ in.). Fragment C is a small lump of charcoal.

01-011. Branch (possible dunnage). Unit 202, level unknown. The branch has its original rounded surface, but the ends were cut flat. It has a maximum length of 111.8 centimeters (44 in.), a maximum width of 6.4 centimeters (2½ in.), and a maximum thickness of 4.4 centimeters (1¾ in.). See Figure 44..

01-013. Shaped wood fragment. Unit and level unknown. The wedge-shaped piece is broken and shows signs of erosion. It has a maximum length of 19 centimeters (7½ in.), a maximum width of 4.8 centimeters (1⅞ in.) and a maximum thickness of 3.5 centimeters (1⅜ in.), tapering to 1.9 centimeters (¾ in.).

01-016. Wooden wedge. Unit 202/102, between frames. It has a maximum length of 14 centimeters (5½ in.), a maximum width of 4.4 centimeters (1¾ in.), and a maximum thickness of 1.1 centimeters (⁷⁄₁₆ in.), tapering to 3.1 millimeters (⅛ in.). See Figure 55.

01-033. Wood fragment. Unit 403, level E. The fragment is broken and eroded. It has a maximum length of 4 centimeters (1⁹⁄₁₆ in.), a maximum width of 1.3 centimeters (½ in.), and a maximum thickness of 3.1 millimeters (⅛ in.).

01-037. Wooden pole. 303/403, on hull. The first 30.5 centimeters (1 ft.) of the pole's length is split. It has a maximum length of 229.9 centimeters (90½ in.) and a maximum diameter of 6 centimeters (2⅜ in.). See Figure 45.

01-038. Wooden pole. Unit 302, level E. This resembles a crude fishing pole. It has a maximum length of 341.6 centimeters (34½ in.), a maximum width of 5 centimeters (2 in.), and a maximum thickness of 3.2 centimeters (1¼ in.). See Figure 45.

01-047. Wedge-shaped stake. Unit 200, level unknown. This stake has bark attached to it and appears to have been pounded many times on the top; the bottom was cut to form a wedge shape. It has a maximum length of 41 centimeters (16⅛ in.) and a maximum width of 5 centimeters (2 in.), tapering from a thickness of 4.8 centimeters (1⅞ in.) down to a 3.1-millimeter (⅛ in.) point. See Figures 45 and 55.

01-051. Tapered wooden pole. Unit 301, between frames. Condition and measurements not recorded.

01-052 A–B. Wooden fragments. Unit 301, between frames. Condition and measurements not recorded.

01-053. Wooden plug or stopper. Unit 301, between frames. This item resembles a wooden plug with one end tapered to provide a grip for fingers. It has a maximum length of 4.8 centimeters (1⁷⁄₈ in.) and a maximum diameter of 3.8 centimeters (1½ in.). See Figures 45 and 55.

01-054 A–B. Wood fragments. Unit 200, level D. These are two sticks with knots, resembling dunnage. Fragment A is 14 centimeters (5½ in.) long and 3.5 centimeters (1³⁄₈ in.) in diameter. Fragment B is 22.2 centimeters (8¾ in.) long and 10.2 centimeters (4 in.) in diameter.

01-055. Wood fragment. Unit 200, level D. A stick with a knot, resembling dunnage, it is 10.5 centimeters (4⅛ in.) long and 2.2 centimeters (⅞ in.) in diameter.

01-056 A–B. Two wood fragments. Unit 200, level D. Fragment A resembles a large chip of wood, with a maximum length of 8.9 centimeters (3½ in.), a maximum width of 7.6 centimeters (3 in.), and a maximum thickness of 1.3 centimeters (½ in.). Fragment B is a stick with a maximum length of 25.4 centimeters (10 in.) and a maximum diameter of 1.9 centimeters (¾ in.).

01-057. Bark fragment. Stern trenches 1 and 3, level unknown. This appears to be birch bark. The fragment has a maximum length and width of 4.1 centimeters (1⁵⁄₈ in.).

MISCELLANEOUS—STONE

02-001. Stone chunk. Unit 201, level B. This is a hard, grey stone, probably granite. It has a maximum length of 5.7 centimeters (2¼ in.), a maximum width of 5.4 centimeters (2⅛ in.), and a maximum thickness of 1.1 centimeters (⁷⁄₁₆ in).

02-002. Stone chunk. Unit 101, level A. This stone resembles 02-001. It has a maximum length of 14 centimeters (5½ in.) and a maximum width of 12.7 centimeters (5 in.). See Figure 44.

02-006 A–C. Piece of coal and two stones. Stern trenches 2 and 3, between frames. Fragment A is a small chunk of coal. Fragment B, a small, water-rounded stone, has a maximum length of 4.4 centimeters (1¾ in.), a maximum width of 2.8 centimeters (1⅛ in.), and a maximum thickness of 1.6 centimeters (⅝ in.). Fragment C, a rough chunk of granitelike rock, has a maximum length of 9.5 centimeters (3¾ in.), a maximum width of 5.7 centimeters (2¼ in.), and a maximum thickness of 3.8 centimeters (1½ in.).

MISCELLANEOUS—METAL

03-025. Iron fragment. Unit 301, level C. The fragment is deteriorated. It has a maximum length of 12 centimeters (4¾ in.), a maximum width of 6.4 centimeters (2½ in.), and a maximum thickness of 9.5 millimeters (⅜ in.). See Figure 45.

03-027 A–B. Iron concretions. Unit and level unknown. Fragment A has a maximum length of 3.2 centimeters (1¼ in.) and a maximum width of 2.5 centimeters (1 in.). Fragment B has a maximum length of 5 centimeters (2 in.) and a maximum width of 1.9 centimeters (¾ in.).

03-030. Lead fragment. Unit 301, level F. The fragment has a maximum length of 6.4 centimeters (2½ in.), a maximum width of 4.4 centimeters (1¾ in.), and a maximum thickness of 1.5 millimeters (¹⁄₁₆ in.).

03-036. Iron fragment. Unit 301, level F. The fragment has a maximum length of 11.4 centimeters (4½ in.), a maximum width of 3.8 centimeters (1½ in.), and a maximum thickness of 6.3 millimeters (¼ in.). See Figure 45.

03-054. Iron plate. Unit 301, between frames. This was a rectangular plate for a door latch. It is 6 centimeters (2⅜ in.) wide and 3.1 millimeters (⅛ in.) thick, with a maximum length of 11.9 centimeters (4¹¹⁄₁₆ in.). The edges of the plate are beveled. It has six screw holes with 6.3-millimeter (¼ in.) diameters and one center hole for a bolt that is 1.9 centimeter (¾ in.) square. See Figures 45 and 55.

03-065 A–B. Two iron fragments. Unit 301, between frames. Condition and measurements not recorded.

03-066. Iron fragment. Unit 301, between frames. Condition and measurements not recorded.

03-067 A–B. Iron fragments. Unit 301, between frames. Fragment A has a maximum length of 9.5 centimeters (3¾ in.), a maximum width of 3.2 centimeters (1¼ in.), and a maximum thickness of 6.3 millimeters (¼ in.). Fragment B has a maximum length of 9.7 centimeters (3³⁄₁₆ in.) and a maximum width of 2.7 centimeters (1¹⁄₁₆ in.). See Figure 45.

03-071. Iron plate. Unit 301, between frames. The plate has a circular hole through one edge. It has a maximum length of 13.7 centimeters (5⅜ in.), a maximum width of 9.5 centimeters (3¾ in.), and a maximum thickness of 6.3 millimeters (¼ in.). The hole has a diameter of 1.9 centimeters (¾ in.). See Figures 45 and 55.

03-072. Iron plate. Unit 301, between frames. It has a maximum length of 11.4 centimeters (4½ in.), a maximum width of 7.3 centimeters (2⅞ in.), and a maximum thickness of 4.7 millimeters (³⁄₁₆ in.). There is a hole in the center 2 centimeters (¹³⁄₁₆ in.) in diameter. See Figures 45 and 55.

03-074. Iron fragment. Unit 301, on hull. Condition and measurements not recorded.

03-075. Lead fragments. Unit 301, on hull. Condition and measurements not recorded.

03-083 A–C. Iron fragments. Stern trench 3, level D. These fragments are severely corroded and are mostly iron corrosion product. Fragment A is 6 centimeters (2⅜ in.) long and has a maximum width of 7.8 centimeters (1⅞ in.). Fragments B and C are each 2.9 centimeters (1⅛ in.) long and 7.9 millimeters (⁵⁄₁₆ in.) square in section.

03-088 A–D. Iron fragments. Stern trench 3, level unknown. Fragments A–D are iron spike holes in wood. The iron has corroded and preserved adjacent portions of wood. Fragment A is 8.3 centimeters (3¼ in.) in maximum length and 2.2 centimeters (⅞ in.) thick; the hole in the center has a 9.5-millimeter (⅜ in.) diameter and a maximum width of 4.8 centimeters (1⅞ in.). Fragment B is 4.1 centimeters (1⅝ in.) long, with a maximum width of 1.6 centimeters (⅝ in.) and a center hole 6.3 millimeters (¼ in.) square. Fragment C is 4.6 centimeters (1¹³⁄₁₆ in.) long, with a maximum width of 1.6 centimeters (⅝ in.) and a center hole 6.3 millimeters (¼ in.) square. Fragment D measures 2.5 by 2.2 centimeters (1 × ⅞ in.).

03-092. Iron fragment. Stern trench 2, level unknown. The fragment is severely corroded. It is 2.5 centimeters (1 in.) long with a maximum width of 1.3 centimeters (½ in.).

MISCELLANEOUS—ORGANIC REMAINS

06-001 A–C. Nutshell fragments and pine cone. Unit 202/102, between frames. There is (A) one whole butternut 1.9 centimeters (¾ in.) long, (B) one walnut shell fragment 2.9 centimeters (1⅛ in.) long, and (C) one pine cone 1.9 centimeters (¾ in.) long.

06-002. Nutshell fragment. Unit 101, level A. It is a broken and unidentified, 1.9 centimeters (¾ in.) long.

06-003 A–B. Nutshell fragments. Unit 201/101, between frames. They are probably butternut. Fragment A is 1.9 centimeters (¾ in.) long, and fragment B is 9.5 millimeters (⅜ in.) long.

06-006 A–B. Burrs. Unit 403, level E. One is 1.9 centimeters (¾ in.) long, the other is 2.5 centimeters (1 in.) long, and both are 9.5 millimeters (⅜ in.) wide.

06-007. Walnut shell. Unit 403, level unknown. It is 4.4 centimeters (1¾ in.) long.

06-008. Seed. Unit 403, level unknown. It is 1.1 centimeters (⁷⁄₁₆ in.) long and perhaps belongs to the squash family.

06-009. Nutshell fragment. Unit 303/403, level unknown. It is 1.3 centimeters (½ in). long.

06-010. Seeds or pits. Unit 200, level D. Measurements not recorded.

06-011 A–C. Pine cone and seeds. Unit 301, levels F and G, between frames. The pine cone is 1.9 centimeters (¾ in.) long. Two seeds are each 6.3 millimeters (¼ in.) long.

06-012. Seeds. Unit 303, level E. Measurements not recorded.

06-013. Nutshell. Unit 302, between frames 6 and 7. Measurements not recorded.

06-014. Nutshell fragments and seeds. Unit 301, on hull. Measurements not recorded.

06-015. Nutshell fragments. Unit 301, dredge bag. Measurements not recorded.

06-016 A–B. Tar pieces. Stern trenches 1 and 3, dredge bag from above ceiling planking. A and B are two small lumps of solidified tar.

06-017 A–E. Hickory nutshell fragments and acorn. Stern trenches, between frames. The shell fragments are 1.9 centimeters (¾ in.), 1.3 centimeters (½ in.), 1.6 centimeters (⅝ in.), and 1.7 centimeters (¹¹⁄₁₆ in.) long. The acorn is 1.4 centimeters (⁹⁄₁₆ in.) long.

06-018. Seeds. Stern trenches 2 and 3, between frames. Measurements not recorded.

Appendix C

*Principal
Dimensions and
Scantlings of
the Horse Ferry*

HULL

Length: between perpendiculars, 18.4 meters (60 ft., 4 in.); on keel, 16.7 meters
(54 ft., 10 in.)

Breadth: molded, 4.6 meters (15 ft.); maximum, 4.6 meters (15 ft., 2 in.)

Length to beam ratio: 4:1

Height: from rabbet to sheer, amidships, 1.4 meters (4 ft., 8 in.)

Depth of hold: from top of floors to underside of deck beams, 1.2 meters (3 ft., 10 in.)

Draft: estimated, 60 centimeters (2 ft.)

Keel: red elm, molded 20.3 centimeters (8 in.); sided 12.7 centimeters (5 in.)

Stem: white oak. Four pieces (forefoot, upper and lower main posts, apron) sided
7.6 centimeters (3 in.) forward; 12.7 centimeters (5 in.) at the bearding line; and
24.1 centimeters (9½ in.) at the apron

Stern: white oak. Two pieces, sternpost and stern knee, sided 5.7 centimeters
(2¼ in.) aft; 12.7 centimeters (5 in.) at the bearding line; and 20.3–23 centimeters
(8–9 in.) at the apron

Frames: white oak and red oak (twenty-eight frame timbers sampled, of which twenty-
two were white oak and six red oak). Hull contained thirty-eight full frames, two
floors without futtocks, twelve pairs of cant timbers in the bow, and thirteen pairs of
cant timbers in the stern. Square frames on 38.1-centimeter (15 in.) centers, floors
and futtocks molded and sided 10.2 centimeters (4 in.). Square frame futtocks (two
per frame) sawn, steamed, and bent to shape

Keelson: white ash, length 15.2 meters (50 ft.), molded 11.4 centimeters (4½ in.),
sided 19 centimeters (7½ in.)

247

Hull planking: hardwood, probably oak. Width 20.3–35.6 centimeters (8–14 in.); thickness 2.5 centimeters (1 in.)

Wales: hardwood, probably oak. One wale strake per side; width 16.5 centimeters (6½ in.); thickness 7.6 centimeters (3 in.)

Ceiling: white pine. In forward and after ends of the hull, four to five strakes on each side of the keelson; hull planked to clamps amidships. Width 22.9–33 centimeters (9–13 in.); thickness 1.3 centimeters (½ in.)

Clamps: hardwood, probably white oak. Two strakes per side; upper strake maximum width 26.7 centimeters (10½ in.), tapering to a point fore and aft; thickness 2.5 centimeters (1 in.); lower strake width 17.8 centimeters (7 in.), thickness 2.5 centimeters (1 in.)

DECK

Length: 19 meters (62 ft., 5 in.)

Breadth: 7.2 meters (23 ft., 8 in.)

Deck beams: Twenty-eight; aftermost (and probably forwardmost) of white oak, all others white pine. Paddle and treadwheel beams (3) molded 15.2 or 22.9 centimeters (6 or 9 in.), sided 22.9 centimeters (9 in.). Forward- and aftermost beams molded 15.2 or 22.9 centimeters (6 or 9 in.), sided 30.5 centimeters (12 in.). All other beams molded and sided about 22.7 centimeters (5 in.)

Deck stringers: two pairs. Inner pair of white oak, length 7.9 meters (26 ft.), molded and sided 12.7 centimeters (5 in.). Outer pair, with king-post trusses, of white oak and white pine, length 5.8 meters (19 ft.), molded 20.3 centimeters (8 in.), sided 16.5 centimeters (6½ in.). King posts of white oak, length 1.4 meters (4 ft., 6 in.); width 19 centimeters (7½ in.); thickness 10.2 centimeters (4 in.). Truss braces of white ash, length 2.9 meters (9 ft., 8 in.) forward, 2.6 meters (8 ft., 6 in.) aft; width 15.2 centimeters (6 in.); thickness 10.2 centimeters (4 in.)

Guards: wood type not known, probably oak. Maximum width 31.8 centimeters (12½ in.); thickness 5 centimeters (2 in.)

Deck planking: softwood, probably pine. Width 17.8–22.9 centimeters (7–9 in.); thickness 2.5 centimeters (1 in.).

Notes

1. A BRIEF HISTORY OF THE ANIMAL-POWERED MACHINE

1. Agostino Ramelli, *The Various and Ingenious Machines of Agostino Ramelli* (1588), trans. Martha Teach Gnudi (Baltimore, Md.: Johns Hopkins University Press and Scholar Press, 1976), 569; Charles Singer, E. J. Holmyard, A. R. Hall, and Trevor I. Williams, eds., *A History of Technology* (New York and London: Oxford University Press, 1956), 2:589–608, 614–16; J. G. Landels, *Engineering in the Ancient World* (Berkeley and Los Angeles: University of California Press, 1978), 16. Technological historian Eugene Ferguson dates the earliest known description of the water wheel to the first century B.C., and the earliest widespread use of windmills to the twelfth century A.D.

2. Ramelli, *Ingenious Machines,* 570; Singer et al., *History of Technology,* 2:637, 660.

3. David H. Shayt, "Stairway to Redemption: America's Encounter with the British Prison Treadmill," *Technology and Culture* 30, no. 4 (October 1989): 912–13.

4. Singer et al., *History of Technology,* 2:110–11; Landels, *Engineering,* 15.

5. Singer et al., *History of Technology,* 2:111; Landels, *Engineering,* 15. Landels has suggested that elderly, blind, or broken-down horses were favored for use on Roman rotary mills.

6. Robert Stuart, *Historical and Descriptive Anecdotes of Steam Engines* (London: Wightman and Cramp, 1829), 97; Landels, *Engineering,* 15–16; Singer et al., *History of Technology,* 2:606–7.

7. Richard Shelton Kirby, Sidney Withington, Arthur Burr Darling, Frederick Gridley Kilgour, *Engineering in History* (New York, London, Toronto: McGraw-Hill, 1956), 247; Stuart, *Steam Engines,* 97. According to Stuart, a Roman army was once

transported to Sicily on ox-powered paddleboats, but this story has not been confirmed by any other sources.

8. Ibn al-Razzaz al-Jazari, *The Book of Knowledge of Ingenious Mechanical Devices,* trans. Donald R. Hill (Dordrecht, the Netherlands, and Boston: D. Reidel, 1974).

9. Mariano Taccola, *De Ingeneis,* ed. Frank D. Prager and Gustina Scaglia (Cambridge, Mass., and London: MIT Press, 1972).

10. Charles Gibbs-Smith and Gareth Rees, *The Inventions of Leonardo da Vinci* (Oxford: Phaidon Press, 1978), 36–37.

11. Ramelli, *Ingenious Machines,* 570, pl. 123; Shayt, "Stairway," 913.

12. Georgius Agricola, *De Re Metallica,* ed. Herbert Hoover and Lou Hoover (New York: Dover Publications, 1950), 162–63.

13. Charles Singer, E. J. Holmyard, A. R. Hall, Trevor I. Williams, *A History of Technology* (New York and London: Oxford University Press, 1957), 3:81–84.

14. Denis Diderot, *A Diderot Pictorial Encyclopedia of Trades and Industry,* ed. Charles C. Gillispie (New York: Dover Publications, 1959), 1:pls. 133, 134, 163; Kirby et al., *Engineering,* 156; Singer et al., *History of Technology,* 3:82; David Crossley, *Post-Medieval Archaeology in Britain* (London, Leicester, and New York: Leicester University Press, 1990), 123–24; Michael W. Flinn, *The History of the British Coal Industry* (Oxford: Clarendon Press, 1984), 2:99–100, 105–6.

15. Singer et al., *History of Technology,* 3:322.

16. Diderot, *Pictorial Encyclopedia,* 1:pls. 142, 201, and 2:pls. 351, 386; Singer et al., *History of Technology,* 3:45, 162, 170, 176, 342, 351, 581. Whims employed in manufacturing were typically powered by one to four horses.

17. Alexander Jamieson, *A Dictionary of Mechanical Science, Arts, Manufactures, and Miscellaneous Knowledge* (London: Henry Fisher, 1827), 666–67; Charles Singer, E. J. Holmyard, A. R. Hall, and Trevor I. Williams, *A History of Technology* (New York and London: Oxford University Press, 1958), 4:151; Oliver P. Hubbard, "The Treadmill in America," *Magazine of American History* 18 (July–December 1887): 523.

18. Michael Partridge, *Farm Tools through the Ages* (Boston: New York Graphic Society, 1973), 203; Diderot, *Pictorial Encyclopedia,* 1:pl. 23 and 2:pl. 421; Crossley, *Post-Medieval Archaeology,* 125–26.

19. Richard S. Dunn, *Sugar and Slaves: The Rise of the Planter Class in the English West Indies, 1624–1713* (New York and London: W. W. Norton, 1973), 192–94, 199; Diderot, *Pictorial Encyclopedia,* 1:pl. 38.

20. Michael Peter Goelet, *The Careening and Bottom Maintenance of Wooden Sailing Vessels* (master's thesis in anthropology, Texas A&M University, 1986), 168–72; Shayt, "Stairway," 914; Crossley, *Post-Medieval Archaeology,* 123; Ramelli, *Ingenious Machines,* 570; Singer et al., *History of Technology,* 2:685–88.

21. George S. Keyes, *Mirror of Empire: Dutch Marine Art in the Seventeenth Century* (Cambridge and New York: Cambridge University Press and the Minneapolis Institute of Arts, 1990), 235–36; Singer et al., *History of Technology,* 4:638–40, pl. 45b.

22. Singer et al., *History of Technology,* 4:639–40, pl. 46a.

23. "Description of a New Invented Machine, for Deepening and Cleansing Docks," *Pennsylvania Magazine or American Monthly Museum* (Philadelphia: R. Aitkin,

May 1775), 206; Robert C. Keith, *Baltimore Harbor, A Pictorial History* (Baltimore: Ocean World, 1982), 164.

24. Singer et al., *History of Technology,* 2:651.

25. Gibbs-Smith, *Leonardo da Vinci,* 78–80; Kirby et. al., *Engineering,* 247–48.

26. George Henry Preble, *A Chronological History of the Origin and Development of Steam Navigation* (Philadelphia: L. R. Hammersly, 1883), 2–3. Other inventors of this period were also experimenting with human-powered paddle wheels; see: Henry Dircks, *The Life, Times, and Scientific Labours of the Second Marquis of Worcester* (London: Bernard Quaritch, 1865), 407–11.

27. Stuart, *Steam Engines,* 96–98.

28. *Journal of the Franklin Institute of the State of Pennsylvania and American Mechanics Register* 10 (1830): 279–80; Jean-Baptiste Marestier, *Memoir on Steamboats of the United States of America* (Paris: Royal Press, 1824; reprint, Mystic, Conn.: Marine Historical Association, 1957), 24; Jon Ewbank Manchip White, *Marshal of France: The Life and Times of Maurice, Comte de Saxe, 1697–1750* (Chicago, New York, San Francisco: Rand McNally, 1962), 72.

29. Marestier, *Memoir,* 1–5, 62–65; Stuart, *Steam Engines.*

2. THE HORSEBOAT COMES TO NORTH AMERICA

1. Balthasar Henry Meyer, *History of Transportation in the United States before 1860* (Washington, D.C.: Peter Smith, 1948), 50–64; Archer B. Hulbert, *The Paths of Inland Commerce* (New Haven: Yale University Press, 1920), 52–53. For an entertaining description of the rigors of traveling early American roads, see John M. Duncan, *Travels through Part of the United States and Canada in 1818 and 1819* (Glasgow: Hurst, Robinson, 1823), 2:3–28.

2. John Palmer, *Journal of Travels in the United States of North America and in Lower Canada, Performed in the Year 1817* (London: Sherwood, Neely and Jones, 1818), 60–61.

3. Meyer, *Transportation,* 37–50; Hulbert, *Inland Commerce,* 46–47.

4. Careless boatmen and the hazards of currents, storms, ice, and overloaded or unstable boats took an annual toll of goods, livestock, and lives at early American ferry crossings; see: John Perry, *American Ferryboats* (New York: Wilfred Funk, 1957), 31–32.

5. François Alexandre Frédéric, duc de La Rochefoucauld-Liancourt, *La Rochefoucauld-Liancourt's Travels in Canada, 1795,* as quoted in George A. Seibel, *The Niagara Portage Road* (Niagara Falls, Ont.: City of Niagara Falls, 1990), 120.

6. Moreau de St. Méry, *Moreau de St. Méry's American Journey,* ed. Kenneth Roberts and Anna Roberts (Garden City, N.Y.: Doubleday, 1947), 65–66, 310.

7. Ibid., 96–97.

8. Ibid., 115.

9. Ibid., 118.

10. Ibid., 119–20. St. Méry updated his journal sometime after 1812 and remarked that four of the five ferries he took in 1794 had been replaced by bridges, and the fifth, the Paulus Hook–New York sail ferries, had been replaced by capacious and dependable steamboats.

11. Meyer, *Transportation*, 131.

12. K. Jack Bauer, *A Maritime History of the United States* (Columbia, S.C.: University of South Carolina Press, 1988), 132–36; Alexander Crosby Brown, "The Patowmack Canal: America's Greatest Eighteenth Century Engineering Achievement," *Virginia Cavalcade* 12 (1963): 40–47; John Seelye, *Beautiful Machine: Rivers and the Republican Plan* (New York and Oxford: Oxford University Press, 1991); Meyer, *Transportation*, 37–46.

13. Paul Forsythe Johnston, *Steam and the Sea* (Salem, Mass.: Peabody Museum of Salem, 1983), 13–14.

14. Joe J. Simmons III, "Steamboats on Inland Waterways: Prime Movers of Manifest Destiny," in George F. Bass, ed., *Ships and Shipwrecks of the Americas* (London: Thames and Hudson, 1988), 189–90; Johnston, *Steam*, 14–19.

15. John Fitch, *The Autobiography of John Fitch*, ed. Frank D. Prager (Philadelphia: American Philosophical Society, 1976), 118–20, 201; Mortimer Dormer Leggett, ed., *Patents for Inventions Issued by the U.S. Patent Office, 1790–1873*, vol. 2 (Washington, D.C.: Government Printing Office, 1874).

16. Fitch, *Autobiography*, 120, 201.

17. Archibald Douglas Turnbull, *John Stevens, An American Record* (New York: American Society of Mechanical Engineers, 1928), 126.

18. Ibid., 124–25.

19. Ibid.

20. Ibid., 126–28.

21. Johnston, *Steam*, 19.

22. Leggett, *Patents*, vol. 2.

23. Fortescue Cuming, *Sketches of a Tour to the Western Country* (Pittsburgh: Cramer, Spear and Etchbaum, 1810), 239–40; reprinted in Reuben Gold Thwaites, ed., *Early Western Travels, 1748–1846*, vol. 4 (Cleveland: Arthur H. Clark, 1904).

24. Charles Cist, *The Cincinnati Miscellany or Antiquities of the West* (Cincinnati: Caleb Clark, 1845), 142.

25. Emerson W. Gould, *Fifty Years on the Mississippi: or Gould's History of Navigation* (Columbus, Ohio: Longs College, 1951), 40; Cuming, *Sketches of a Tour*, 240. At least thirteen horses had walked the treadmill on Brookhart's *Horse Boat* by the time it approached Louisville in 1808.

26. Preble, *Steam Navigation*, 50.

27. Johnston, *Steam*, 22.

3. "WE CONGRATULATE THE PUBLIC": THE AGE OF THE
HORSE-POWERED BOAT BEGINS

1. Simmons, "Steamboats on Inland Waterways," 190; Robert Greenhalgh Albion, *The Rise of New York Port* (New York and Boston: South Street Seaport Museum and Northeastern University Press, 1939, reprint 1984), 143–145.

2. St. Méry, *American Journey*, 166–170, 173.

3. Charles H. Winfield, *Hopoghan Hackingh* (New York: Caxton Press, 1895), 30–34.

4. Turnbull, *John Stevens*, 309–11.

5. Ralph Nading Hill, *Sidewheeler Saga* (New York and Toronto: Rinehart, 1953), 40–42; Harry J. Smith, *Romance of the Hoboken Ferry* (New York: Prentice-Hall, 1931), 29–30; Turnbull, *John Stevens,* 340.

6. Isaac Newton Phelps-Stokes, *The Iconography of Manhattan Island* (New York: Robert H. Dodd, 1918), 485–486; Johnston, *Steam,* 22–23; S. Bayard Dod, "The Evolution of the Ferry-boat," *Harper's Weekly* 33, no. 1672 (5 January 1889): 18.

7. Smith, *Hoboken Ferry,* 31; Turnbull, *John Stevens,* 347.

8. Turnbull, *John Stevens,* 348, 350.

9. Marestier, *Memoir,* 22–23.

10. Dumas Malone, *Dictionary of American Biography,* 8:106–7; Frank O. Braynard, *S.S. Savannah: The Elegant Steamship* (New York: Dover Publications, 1963).

11. Leggett, *Patents;* Braynard, *Elegant Steamship,* 18–19; Perry, *Ferryboats,* 60–61; *Columbian,* no.1363 (7 April 1814): 3.

12. *(Brooklyn, N.Y.) Long Island Star,* as quoted in the *Columbian,* no.1363 (7 April 1814): 3.

13. *Niles Weekly Register* 6, no. 9 (30 April 1814): 152.

14. Joan M. Payzant and Lewis Payzant, *Like a Weaver's Shuttle: A History of the Halifax–Dartmouth Ferries* (Halifax: Nimbus Publishing, 1979), 12; Preble, *Steam Navigation,* 60; Henry E. Pierrepont, *Historical Sketch of the Fulton Ferry and its Associated Ferries* (Brooklyn: Eagle Job and Book Printing, 1879), 31. The *Nassau* made its first trip across the East River on 10 May 1814 (the chief engineer was caught in the machinery and fatally injured on the same day). This ferry required five to twelve minutes for each crossing.

15. Marestier, *Memoir,* 23; Payzant and Payzant, *Weaver's Shuttle,* 18.

16. Winfield, *Hopoghan Hackingh,* 44; Smith, *Hoboken Ferry,* 32–33; Turnbull, *John Stevens,* 348; Charles H. Haswell, *Reminiscences of an Octogenarian of the City of New York* (New York: Harper & Brothers, 1897), 84–85. Haswell dates the beginning of Stevens's Hoboken horseboat service to August 1817, but this is not correct.

17. *Columbian,* no.1409 (4 June 1814): 3.

18. New York and Brooklyn Steam Ferry Boat Company, *A Statement of Facts, with Remarks, etc. in Answer to a Pamphlet, Published at Brooklyn, in Relation to the Steam Boat Ferry* (Brooklyn, N.Y.: A. Spooner, 1822), 5, 15.

19. Ibid., 7, 10, 30.

20. Pierrepont, *Historical Sketch,* 32

21. *New York Commercial Advertiser* 23 (25 and 26 June 1819); Haswell, *Reminiscences,* 39, and Thomas H. Poppleton, "Plan of the City of New York (1817)" (foldout map bound into the back of Haswell's book); Charles Burr Todd, *In Olde New York* (Long Island, N.Y.: Ira J. Friedman, 1907; reprint, 1968), 50; ferry lease (copy), Grand Street Ferry, 12 August 1814, Charles Watts Jr. Papers, New-York Historical Society.

22. Ferry lease (copy), Walnut Street Ferry, 1817, Watts Papers.

23. Phelps-Stokes, *Manhattan Island,* 486.

24. Todd, *Olde New York,* 50.

25. Preble, *Steam Navigation,* 61. Steam ferry boilers did burst from time to time, with fatal results. The 24 July 1824 edition of the *Niles Weekly Register* reported a boiler explosion on a New York ferry that killed a nineteen-year-old woman and scalded two or three other people.

26. Smith, *Hoboken Ferry,* 35–36; Winfield, *Hopoghan Hackingh,* 44.

27. Ibid., Smith, 36–39; Winfield, 45.

28. Ibid., Smith, 40.

29. Ibid., Smith, 40; Winfield, 49.

30. Ibid., Smith, 43–48; Winfield, 49–50.

31. Ibid., Smith, 51–57; Winfield, 50, 53. Robert R. Livingston died in February 1813 and Robert Fulton died in February 1815.

32. Brian Cudahy, *Over and Back: The History of Ferryboats in New York Harbor* (New York: Fordham University Press, 1990), 38–39; Perry, *Ferryboats,* 84–85; Hill, *Sidewheeler Saga,* 75–78; Albion, *New York,* 151–53.

33. Haswell, *Reminiscences,* 188.

34. Leggett, *Patents.*

35. Payzant and Payzant, *Weaver's Shuttle,* 11.

36. Ibid., 12.

37. Ibid., 11–13.

38. Ibid., 14, 16.

39. Ibid., 18.

40. Ibid.

41. Ibid.

42. E. M. Ruttenber, *History of the Town of Newburgh* (Newburgh, N.Y.: E. M. Ruttenber, 1859), 170; *Niles Weekly Register* 10, no. 25 (17 August 1816): 414.

43. *Niles Weekly Register* 11, no. 13 (31 August 1816): 13.

44. William Gardner to John Thomson, 6 April 1817, Box 3, "Ferry Correspondence/Ferry Accounts, 1817–1839," John A. Thomson Papers, New York State Archives, Albany.

45. Moses Rogers to Benjamin Dwight, 29 March 1817, Thomson Papers.

46. Raymond Beecher, "Greene County's Horse Ferries," *Greene County Historical Journal* (N.Y.) 8, no. 2 (summer 1984): 12.

47. James Rodgers and Charles Kenyon to John A. Thomson, 3 March 1817, with enclosure "Statement of Expenses of the Albany Team Boat in 1817," Thomson Papers.

48. *Montreal Herald,* 24 July 1819; *Le Spectateur Canadien (Montreal),* 14 August 1819; *Canadian Courant (Montreal),* 13 October 1819, courtesy of Frank Mackey, Pointe Claire, Quebec; George Parkin de Twenebroker Glazebrook, *A History of Transportation in Canada* (Toronto: Ryerson Press, 1938), 72.

49. George Macbeath and Donald F. Taylor, *Steamboat Days: An Illustrated History of the Steamboat Era on the St. John River, 1816–1946* (St. Stephens, N.B.: Print'n Press, 1982), 16.

50. Lorenzo F. Fisler, *A Local History of Camden* (Camden, N.J.: Francis A. Cassedy, 1858), 32; E. T. Hamy, *The Travels of the Naturalist Charles A. Lesueur in North America, 1815–1837,* ed. H. F. Raup, trans. Milton Haber (Kent, Ohio: Kent State University Press, 1968), 17.

51. *Alexandria (Va.) Gazette and Daily Advertiser* 17, no. 4963 (10 July 1817): 1.

52. Ulrich Bonnell Phillips, *A History of Transportation in the Eastern Cotton Belt* (New York: Octagon Books, 1908; reprint, 1968), 73–74.

53. Adrian G. Ten Cate, ed., *A Pictorial History of the Thousand Islands of the St. Lawrence River* (Brockville, Ont.: Besancourt, 1982), 171.

54. James Flint, *Letters from America* (Edinburgh: W. & C. Tait, 1822), 124; reprinted in Thwaites, *Early Western Travels*, vol. 9.

55. Adlard Welby, *A Visit to North America and the English Settlements in Illinois* (London: J. Drury, 1821), 64; reprinted in Thwaites, *Early Western Travels*, vol. 12.

56. *Niles Weekly Register* 10, no. 25 (17 August 1816): 414.

57. *Niles Weekly Register* 16, no. 26 (21 August 1819): 431.

58. Frederic Trautmann, "New York through German Eyes: The Travels of Ludwig Gall, 1819," *New York History* 62, no. 4 (October 1981): 461.

59. *Niles Weekly Register* 16, no. 26 (21 August 1819): 431.

60. Polygraphisches Institut, *Schweizerische Dampfschiffahrt* (Zurich), no. 11 (1907): 740; Edouard Meystre, *Histoire imagée des grands bateaux du lac Léman* (Lausanne: Payot Laussane, 1967), 7. Courtesy Jean Di Marzi, Gargenville, France.

4. THREE EARLY HORSEBOAT VENTURES

1. Payzant and Payzant, *Weaver's Shuttle*, 19.

2. Ibid., 21.

3. Ibid., 23–25.

4. Ibid., 25.

5. Ibid., 29.

6. Ibid., 41.

7. Ibid., 44.

8. Ibid., 48–50.

9. Agnes Wallace, "The Wiggins Ferry Monopoly," *Missouri Historical Review* 43, no. 1 (October 1947): 1–3.

10. Corine Hachtman, *The History of the Wiggins Ferry Company* (master's thesis, History Department, Washington University, St. Louis, 1931), 9–10; Agnes Mary Wallace, *The Wiggins Ferry, 1795–1902* (master's thesis, St. Louis University, 1945), 17–18.

11. John F. Darby, *Personal Recollections* (St. Louis: G. I. Jones, 1880), 2–4, as quoted in Wallace, *Wiggins Ferry* (1945), 24–25.

12. Frederic L. Billon, *Annals of St. Louis in Its Territorial Days from 1804 to 1821* (New York: Arno Press and *New York Times*, 1971), 322.

13. Wallace, "Wiggins Ferry" (1947), 4.

14. *Missouri Historical Review* 51 (April 1957): 330.

15. Wallace, "Wiggins Ferry" (1947), 4; Wallace, *Wiggins Ferry* (1945), 229.

16. *Missouri Historical Review* 32 (January 1938): 229.

17. Billon, *Annals of St. Louis*, 322–23; Hachtman, *Wiggins Ferry*, 18–19.

18. Moses Meeker, "Early History of the Lead Region of Wisconsin," *Wisconsin Historical Collections* 6 (1908): 292.

19. Wallace, *Wiggins Ferry* (1945), 26; Hachtman, *Wiggins Ferry*, 16; Gottfried Duden, *Report on a Journey to the Western States of North America* (Columbia, Mo., and London: State Historical Society of Missouri and University of Missouri Press,

1980), 51. Duden crossed the Mississippi at St. Louis in October 1824 on a "large boat propelled by wheels and two horses." This suggests that the *Sea Serpent* was probably a horizontal-treadwheel horseboat, a type described in Chapter 5 of this book.

20. Wallace, "Wiggins Ferry" (1947), 5.

21. Quoted in Hachtman, *Wiggins Ferry,* 17–18.

22. Roger L. Nichols, "Army Contributions to River Transportation, 1815–1825," *Military Affairs* 33 (April 1969): 243–44.

23. Ibid., 244–45.

24. Grant Foreman, "River Navigation in the Early Southwest," *Mississippi Valley Historical Review* 5, no. 1 (June 1928): 35–38.

25. Hachtman, *Wiggins Ferry,* 20–21; Wallace, *Wiggins Ferry* (1945), 26.

26. Ibid., Hachtman, 22.

27. "Internal Improvements in South Carolina," *North American Review* 13 (July 1821): 150–52.

28. *Niles Weekly Register* 16, no. 26 (21 August 1819): 431.

29. "Horse Boat Golden Fleece," memo book dated January 1818, in a file box of miscellaneous papers titled "Ships," Manuscripts Section, New-York Historical Society. Courtesy of Morris F. Glenn.

30. *Columbian Museum and Savannah Gazette* 25, no. 4028 (18 April 1820): 2. Courtesy of Judy Wood.

31. Ibid., vol. 25, no. 4068 (6 June 1820): 2.

32. Ibid.

33. Ibid., vol. 25, no. 4046 (9 May 1820): 3; vol. 25, no. 4064 (30 May 1820): 2; vol. 25, no. 4067 (3 June 1820): 3.

5. BARNABAS LANGDON AND THE HORIZONTAL-TREADWHEEL HORSEBOAT

1. Rufus Porter, "Porter's Portable Horse Power," *New York Mechanic* 1, no. 6 (6 February 1841): 1.

2. Gerald W. Sutphin and Richard A. Andre, *Sternwheelers on the Great Kanawha River* (Charleston, W.Va.: Pictorial Histories, 1991), 8.

3. Agricola, *De Re Metallica,* 163; J. Kenneth Major, *Animal-Powered Engines* (London: B. T. Batsford, 1978), 25; Ramelli, *Ingenious Machines,* 570, pl. 123.

4. Patent Drawings Nos. 2684x and 2862x, Record Group 241, National Archives.

5. Elinor Stearns and David N. Yearkes, *William Thornton, a Renaissance Man in a Federal City* (Washington, D.C.: American Institute of Architects Foundation, 1976), 39.

6. Leggett, *Patents.*

7. Marestier, *Memoir,* 79.

8. Arthur J. Breton, *A Guide to the Manuscript Collections of the New-York Historical Society* (Westport, Conn.: Greenwood Press, 1972), 1:259–60, 305–6.

9. Report of Common Council of New York City on Petition of Philip Earle for a Ferry Lease, 29 March 1819; contract for horseboat patent rights, Moses Isaacs and Charles Watts Jr., 10 February 1819, Watts Papers.

10. Watts to Mr. Conklins, 12 April 1819, Charles Watts Jr. Letterbook, New-York Historical Society, New York; Edmund Platt, *The Eagle's History of Poughkeepsie from the Earliest Settlements* (Poughkeepsie, N.Y.: Platt & Platt, 1905), 95.

11. Watts to William Thornton, 8 April 1819, Watts Letterbook.

12. Stearns and Yearkes, *William Thornton*, 40.

13. Watts to Nathaniel Green Pendleton, n.d. (between 21 and 25 May 1819), Watts Letterbook.

14. Watts to John D. Dickinson, 29 May 1819, Watts Letterbook.

15. Statement, Sayre & Force to Watts, 14 June 1819; statement, E. Hitchcock to Watts, 20 June 1819; statement, Jacob Halsey to Watts, 15 August 1819; receipts, *New York Commercial Advertiser* to Watts, 24 June and 3 July 1819, Watts Papers.

16. *New York Commercial Advertiser* 22 (26 June and 9 July 1819).

17. Charles Sellers, *The Market Revolution: Jacksonian America, 1815–1846* (New York and Oxford: Oxford University Press, 1991), 131–139.

18. Statement of ferry operations, 8 September 1819, Watts Papers.

19. Statement, Noah Brown to "Horseboat and owners," 23 September 1819; statement, Charles Meighan to Watts, November 1819, Watts Papers; Watts to William T. Farsand, 6 November 1819; Watts to John Maynard, 30 December 1819, Watts Letterbook.

20. Moses Isaacs to Watts, 20 February 1820; H. Jones to Watts, 30 March and 29 April 1820, Watts Papers.

21. Isaacs to Watts, 20 February, 14 and 29 March 1820, Watts Papers.

22. Daniel Robert to Watts, 28 April 1820, Watts Papers.

23. Hellen F. Jones to Watts, 22 March 1820, Watts Papers.

24. Jones to Watts, 12 May 1820, Watts Papers.

25. Jones to Watts, 13 April 1820, Watts Papers.

26. Jones to Watts, 30 March 1820, Watts Papers.

27. Sidney Wright to Watts, 17 May 1820; Thomas Kittera to Watts, 12 May 1820, Watts Papers.

28. Watts to John M. Scott, 14 August 1820; Watts to Fine and Hasbrouck, 3 February 1821, Watts Letterbook.

29. Patent Drawing No. 3112x, National Archives. Langdon appears to have resubmitted his patent drawings after the Patent Office fire in the 1830s, presumably because his treadwheel was still in general use.

30. First Federal Census (1790), state of Vermont; Second Federal Census (1800), state of Vermont, courtesy of Elizabeth R. Baldwin and Richard Ward; C. E. Holden Notebooks, 7:149, 170, 212, 228, New York State Archives, Albany. Courtesy Morris F. Glenn.

31. Patent Drawing No. 2743x, National Archives.

32. *(Troy, N.Y.) Northern Budget* 22, no. 1130 (1 June 1819).

33. Benjamin Silliman, *Remarks Made on a Short Tour between Hartford and Quebec in the Autumn of 1819* (New Haven, Conn.: S. Converse, 1820; 2d ed., 1824), 74–76. A review of Silliman's book in the *Lexington (Ky.) Western Review and Miscellaneous Magazine* 3, no. 4 (November 1820): 207–8, quoted the professor's observations on the Troy ferry and added: "the description of the singular horse ferry-boat may not

only gratify our readers, but may be of practical use to some of them on western waters."

34. Arthur James Weise, *Troy's One Hundred Years 1789–1889* (Troy, N.Y.: William H. Young, 1891), 84.

35. Horatio Gates Spafford, *A Gazetteer of the State of New York* (Albany: B. D. Packard, 1824; reprint, Interlaken, N.Y.: Heart of the Lakes Publishing, 1981), 525–27.

36. Scott Belmont, "Starbuck Brothers, Iron Founders and Machinists" (undergraduate term paper, Rensselaer Polytechnic Institute, 1988), 1–4. Courtesy Dr. Dean Phelan, Rensselaer Polytechnic Institute.

37. Spafford, *Gazetteer*, 527.

38. Ibid., 525.

39. Deed of patent sale, Barnabas Langdon to Isaac Lovejoy and Amos Allen, 29 March 1820, Catskill Teamboat Ferry Papers, Rensselaer County Historical Society, Troy, N.Y.

40. Deed of deposit by John C. Langdon and Francis Denault, 9 May 1821, item 1208, Thomas Bedouin notary records, and protest of James Rodgers of Albany, N.Y., against Francis Denault, 16 June 1819, item 2691, Henry Griffin Notary Papers, Archives Nationales du Quebec. Courtesy of Frank Mackey.

41. Troy Common Council, *Centennial Manual of the Common Council of the City of Troy*, compiled for the Troy Common Council by Weise and Berdin (Troy, N.Y.: William H. Young, 1876), 154.

42. Weise, *Troy's One Hundred Years*, 84; Troy Common Council, *Centennial Manual*, 157.

43. *Troy (N.Y.) Sentinal*, 22 January 1830.

44. Tuttle and Gregory, *The Troy Directory for the Year 1830* (Troy, N.Y.: Tuttle and Gregory, 1830), 70.

45. *Troy (N.Y.) Budget*, 11 January 1833, 3.

46. *Journal of the Franklin Institute* 25 (1838): 270.

47. George W. Beardslee, *Rejection of the Application for a Reissue upon New and Amended Claims of the Letters Patent Issued in 1838 to Barnabas Langdon* (Albany: Weed, Parsons, 1852).

48. Troy city directories show that Barnabas continued to live there until around 1847, when he and his wife Mary moved across the river to live with William and Amanda Haywood (one of whom was presumably a grandchild of the Langdons) in West Troy. They were still living there in 1850, when Barnabas was eighty years old. In 1850, John and his wife Harriet were living in Schenectady, N.Y., where he was working as a machinist; in 1860 they were back in Troy, and John was listed as a "master machinist," but his limited personal estate suggests that he was not wealthy. John C. Langdon died in Troy on 21 February 1875 at the age of seventy-six; the date of Barnabas's death is not known. Biographical information on the Langdon family was obtained from vital statistics records in the Local History Room at the Troy Public Library and from U.S. census records provided by Elizabeth Robinson Baldwin and Richard Ward.

49. Andrew Bell (pseudonym for A. Thomason), *Men and Things in America: Being the Experience of a Year's Residence in the United States* (London: William Smith, 1838), 65–66.

50. James Stuart, *Three Years in North America* (New York: J. & J. Harper, 1833), 1: 43–44.

51. View of the City of Hartford, 1841, aquatint by Robert Havell (negative no. 120), Connecticut Historical Society, Hartford.

52. The Trautwine plan appears in Charles S. Boyer's *Annals of Camden No. 3 (Old Ferries)* (privately printed, 1921). The original plan has not been located.

53. William Avery Baker, *A Maritime History of Bath, Maine* (Bath, Me.: Marine Research Society of Bath, 1973), 1:550–51; Fannie S. Chase, *Wiscasset in Pownalborough* (Wiscasset, Me.: Southworth-Anthoenses Press, 1941), 155.

54. Anna Augusta Chapin and Charles V. Chapin, *A History of Rhode Island Ferries, 1640–1923* (Providence: Oxford Press, 1925), 69–72, 160, 168–70, 233–34.

55. Peter J. Revill, *A Short History of Rocky Hill, Connecticut* (Rocky Hill, Conn.: Rocky Hill Historical Society, 1972), 7; Charles W. Whittlesey, *Crossing and Re-Crossing the Connecticut River* (New Haven, Conn.: Tuttle, Morehouse and Taylor, 1938), 55.

56. Joseph O. Goodwin, *East Hartford: Its History and Traditions* (Hartford: Case, Lockwood and Brainard, 1879), 195–97.

57. Letters from Georgeville (Quebec) Historical Society members John M. Scott (1 August 1994) and Katherine Mackenzie (12 July 1994) to Kevin Crisman, citing documents in the society's files by George C. Merrill, Hazen Increase Bullock, William Bryant Bullock, and the Stanstead County Council (14 December 1848).

58. Silas Farmer, *History of Detroit and Wayne County and Early Michigan* (Silas Farmer, 1890; reprint, Detroit: Gale Research, 1969), 916; J. H. Beers, *History of the Great Lakes* (Chicago: J. H. Beers, 1899; reprint, Cleveland: Freshwater Press, 1972), 1:421.

59. James Cooke Mills, *Our Inland Seas* (Chicago: A. C. McClurg, 1910), 193–94; Seibel, *Niagara Portage,* 122–26, 129. The *Cossack* was replaced by a steam ferry in 1840.

60. Tyrone Power, *Impressions of America during the Years 1833, 1834, and 1835* (Philadelphia: Carey, Lea & Blanchard, 1836), 1:234.

61. Seibel, *Niagara Portage,* 110.

62. Homer Everett, *History of Sandusky County, Ohio, with Portraits and Biographies of Prominent Citizens and Pioneers* (Cleveland: H. Z. Williams, 1882), 433–434. Courtesy of Dr. Paul Johnston.

63. J. H. Beers, *History of the Great Lakes,* 1:418; Mills, *Inland Seas,* 194.

64. Stephen H. Long, *The Northern Expeditions of Stephen H. Long,* ed. Lucille M. Kane, June D. Holmquist, and Carolyn Gilman (St. Paul: Minnesota Historical Society Press, 1978), 119.

65. Gibson Lamb Cranmer, *History of Wheeling City and Ohio County, West Virginia* (Chicago: Biographical Publishing, 1902), 194–95. Mention of a subsequent four-horse treadwheel ferry at Wheeling can be found in: Maximillian, Prince of Wied, *Travels in the Interior of North America, 1832–1834,* Parts 2 and 3 (London: Ackerman, 1843), 474; reprinted in Thwaites, *Early Western Travels,* vol. 24, and in John K.

Townsend, *Narrative of a Journey across the Rocky Mountains* (Philadelphia: Henry Perkins, 1834), 12, reprinted in Thwaites, *Early Western Travels,* vol. 21.

66. Maximillian, *Travels,* 124.

67. Lloyd Vernon Briggs, *History of Shipbuilding on the North River* (New York: Library Editions, 1970), 199–201. Courtesy of Sheila Clifford.

6. HOOFBEATS ACROSS THE HUDSON

1. Ruttenber, *History of Newburgh,* 170–71.

2. Beulah Baily Thull, "Troy Developed around Ashley's Ferry," *Troy (N.Y.) Times Record,* 6 January 1973, B-20.

3. Weise, *Troy's One Hundred Years,* 82–84.

4. William Dunlap, *Diary of William Dunlap* (New York: New-York Historical Society, 1930), 2:544.

5. Arthur James Weise, *History of Lansingburgh, N.Y.* (Troy, N.Y.: William H. Young, 1877), 132–33.

6. Weise, *Troy's One Hundred Years,* 106–7.

7. Ibid., 84; Nathaniel Bartlett Sylvester, *History of Rensselaer County, New York* (Philadelphia: Everts & Peck, 1880), 164.

8. Freeman Hunt, *Letters about the Hudson River and Its Vicinity* (New York: Freeman Hunt, 1837), 82.

9. J. P. Benjamin, *Benjamin's New Map of the Hudson River* (1848), framed print in the Local History Room, Troy Public Library, Troy, N.Y.

10. *Troy from Mount Ida* (1825) and *View of Troy* (1848), lithographs in the print collection of the Rensselaer County Historical Society, Troy, N.Y.

11. *View of Troy, New York* (1845), lithograph in the print collection of the Rensselaer County Historical Society, Troy, N.Y.

12. Arthur James Weise, *The City of Troy and Its Vicinity* (Troy, N.Y.: E. Green, 1886), 125.

13. "Expenditures for the Horse Ferry Boat Established by the Committee," 1817, Thomson Papers.

14. A. Levasseur, *Lafayette in America in 1824 and 1825,* trans. John D. Godman (Philadelphia: Carey and Lea, 1829; reprint, New York: Research Reprints, 1970), 112–13; a mention of the Albany–Greenbush ferry in 1817 may be found in Jacques Milbert, *Picturesque Itinerary of the Hudson River* (Ridgewood, N.J.: Gregg Press, 1968), 42.

15. Arthur James Weise, *The History of the City of Albany, New York* (Albany: E. H. Bender, 1884), 455. Courtesy of Joseph Cozzi.

16. Isaiah Townsend Papers, DC 10441, Box 3, Albany and Bath Ferry Company Records, New York State Archives, Albany.

17. Report of the Construction Committee, 24 March 1821, and various stock certificates, Townsend Papers.

18. Invoice from Hand & Kenyon, 19 May 1821, Townsend Papers.

19. Samuel Rezneck, *Profiles out of the Past of Troy, New York* (Troy, N.Y.: 1970), 48–52; Blydenburgh, "Mr Burden's New Steam Boat," *Boston Mechanic* (March 1834): 89–93; Tim O'Brien, "Troy, an Early Manufacturer of Experimental

Steamships," *Albany Times Union,* 13 February 1989. Henry Burden's Troy Iron and Nail Factory would prosper until his death in 1871 at the age of eighty; under the management of his sons the concern gradually deteriorated and finally shut down in the twentieth century.

20. Order to pay Henry Burden $300, 18 May 1821; invoice from Henry Burden, 21 September 1821; order to pay Henry Burden, 26 June 1822, Townsend Papers.

21. Albany and Bath Ferry Company account with Isaiah and John Townsend, no date; invoice to Jeremiah B. Jewell, 18 May 1821, Townsend Papers.

22. Invoice for advertising, 21 May 1821, Townsend Papers; *Albany Gazette* 38, no. 3600 (25 May 1821).

23. "Albany and Bath Ferry Association," no date, Townsend Papers.

24. Receipt for payment of John Van Vorse, 1822, Townsend Papers.

25. Albany and Bath Ferry Company account with Isaiah and John Townsend, no date; "General Statement of the Cost and Expenses of the Bath Ferry Boat Establishment," no date, Townsend Papers.

26. Untitled document, 18 March 1825, Townsend Papers.

27. Joel Munsell, *The Annals of Albany* (Albany: J. Munsell, 1857), 8:84.

28. Ibid., 101.

29. Petition signed by Joseph Finch, no date, Townsend Papers.

30. Munsell, *Annals of Albany,* 8:96.

31. "Report of the Ferry Committee," 25 May 1824, Townsend Papers.

32. James Stuart, *Three Years,* 1:43–44.

33. Basil Hall, *Travels in North America in the Years 1827 and 1828* (Edinburgh: Cadell, 1829), 2:66–69.

34. George Rogers Howell and Jonathan Tenney, *Bicentennial History of Albany* (New York: W. W. Munsell, 1886), 490–91.

35. Harriet Martineau, *Retrospect of Western Travel* (London: Saunders and Otley, 1838; reprint, New York: Greenwood Press, 1969), 109.

36. Munsell, *Annals of Albany,* 8:350.

37. Spafford, *Gazetteer,* 209.

38. Ibid., 135.

39. Beecher, "Horse Ferries," 13.

40. Ibid., 14–15.

41. Ibid., 15.

42. Photograph of *W. V. B. Hermance* by C. C. Wells, loaned to the authors by Raymond Beecher, Coxsackie, N.Y.

43. Spafford, *Gazetteer,* 32–33, 240–43.

44. Beecher, "Horse Ferries," 11–12.

45. Stephen B. Miller, *Historical Sketches of Hudson, Embracing the Settlement of the City, City Government, etc.* (Hudson, N.Y.: Bryan & Webb, 1862), 20.

46. Ibid.

47. Ibid., 12; New York Public Library to Allen Penfield Beach, 10 April 1952, Allen Penfield Beach Papers, Basin Harbor Club, Basin Harbor, Vermont.

48. Hall, *Travels,* 1:98.

49. Beecher, "Horse Ferries," 13.

50. The painting is located in the Murdock Collection (under "Ferries") at the New-York Historical Society (negative number 16763), where it is mislabeled "First Horse Ferryboat on Hudson River between Newburgh and Fishkill." The same illustration appears in Jessie Van Vechten Vedder's *History of Greene County* (Catskill, N.Y.: 1927), 27.

51. Beecher, "Horse Ferries," 13.

52. Spafford, *Gazetteer*, 90.

53. Jessie Van Vechten Vedder, *Historical Catskill* (Catskill, N.Y.: 1922), 78; Frederick L. Beers, *History of Greene County, New York* (New York: J. B. Beers, 1884), 19.

54. Beecher, "Horse Ferries," 16.

55. Moses Rogers to Benjamin W. Dwight, 29 March 1817; William Gardner to John A. Thomson, 6 April 1817; James Rodgers and Charles Kenyon to John A. Thomson, 3 March 1817; Expenditures for the Horse Ferry Boat [Albany–Greenbush], 1817, Thomson Papers.

56. Henry Burden to John A. Thomson, 7 November 1821, Thomson Papers.

57. Beecher, "Horse Ferries," 17.

58. Burden to Thomson, 7 November 1821, Thomson Papers.

59. Burden to Thomson, 3 January 1822, Thomson Papers.

60. Burden to Thomson, 18 March 1822, Thomson Papers.

61. Burden to Thomson, 20 and 25 April 1822, Thomson Papers.

62. Burden to Thomson, 15 June 1822, Thomson Papers.

63. Receipt for the Horseboat, June 1822, Thomson Papers.

64. Burden to Thomson, 29 June 1822, Thomson Papers.

65. Frank A. Gallt, *Dear Old Greene County* (Catskill, N.Y.: 1915), 212.

66. Deed of Patent, Barnabas Langdon to Isaac Lovejoy and Amos Allen, 29 March 1820; Agreements Relating to the Sale of Patent, Lovejoy and Allen to John A. Thomson, John R. Hallenbeck, and Henry Van Gorden, March 1822, Catskill Ferry Teamboat Papers.

67. Catskill horseboat, various receipts and statements, 1822–28, Thomson Papers.

68. Ferry receipts for 1828, Thomson Papers.

69. Beecher, "Horse Ferries," 17.

70. Ibid., 18, 20.

71. Ibid., 18.

72. Platt, *History of Poughkeepsie*, 95–96; Frank Hasbrouck, *The History of Dutchess County, New York* (Poughkeepsie, N.Y.: S. A. Matthieu, 1909), appendix: "Milton Ferry."

73. Ibid., Hasbrouck.

7. MOUNTAIN TEAMBOATS: THE HORSE FERRIES OF
LAKE CHAMPLAIN

1. William Slade Jr., comp., *The Laws of Vermont to 1824* (Windsor, Vt.: Simeon Ide, 1825).

2. *(Vergennes) Vermont Aurora*, 19 October 1826.

3. Gordon C. Sherman and Elsie L. Sherman, *An Illuminating History of the Champlain Valley and Adirondack Mountains* (Elizabethtown, N.Y.: Denton

Publications, 1977), 2:61; William Wallace Higbee, *Around the Mountain* (Charlotte, Vt.: Charlotte Historical Society, 1991), 281–82; Zadock Thompson, *History of Vermont* (Burlington, Vt.: Chauncey Goodrich, 1842), 51.

4. Ogden J. Ross, *The Steamboats of Lake Champlain 1809 to 1930* (Albany: Champlain Transportation, 1930), 46; Morris F. Glenn, *The Story of Three Towns* (Alexandria, Va.: Published by the author, 1977), 216.

5. Ross, *Steamboats*, 46; *Burlington (Vt.) Free Press*, 7 December 1827.

6. *Keeseville (N.Y.) Argus*, 22 May 1833, 3.

7. Ibid.; "Horse Boat Eclipse," advertising broadside dated 1844, Shelburne Museum, Shelburne, Vt.

8. Higbee, *Around the Mountain*, 282–83.

9. Thompson, *History of Vermont*, 51.

10. Higbee, *Around the Mountain*, 282; William Wallace Higbee, "Around the Mountain," copy of Higbee's original manuscript in Special Collections, Bailey-Howe Library, University of Vermont, 28. The original manuscript contains some material on the *Eclipse* not included in the Charlotte Historical Society's 1991 book.

11. Higbee, "Around the Mountain," 51.

12. Thompson, *History of Vermont*, 51.

13. Higbee, *Around the Mountain*, 46, 285–86.

14. Ibid., 285.

15. Ibid., 286.

16. Oscar H. Leland, "1834 Journey to Lewis," *Reveille* (quarterly journal of the Essex County [N.Y.] Historical Society) 2, no. 14 (November 1958): 1.

17. Higbee, *Around the Mountain*, 46, 285.

18. Glenn, *Three Towns*, 189–221, 339–54; Spafford, *Gazetteer*, 165.

19. Charles McNeil to Orson Spear, 13 March 1840, Orson Spear Papers, Special Collections, Bailey-Howe Library, University of Vermont, Burlington.

20. Higbee, *Around the Mountain*, 287.

21. Ibid., 45.

22. Henry Ross to Spear, 14 July 1847, Spear Papers.

23. Enrollment papers for the steamboat *Boquette*, "Ship Registers," Record Group 41, National Archives, Washington, D.C.

24. Glenn, *Three Towns*, 346; Ross, *Steamboats*, 13; Higbee, *Around the Mountain*, 287.

25. Higbee, "Around the Mountain," 29.

26. Higbee, *Around the Mountain*, 287.

27. Morris F. Glenn, personal communication, 30 March 1996.

28. *(Vergennes) Vermont Aurora*, 13 November 1828 and 2 July 1829; Peter Thomas, Prudence Doherty, and Charles Paquin, *Kingsland Bay Fish Hatchery, Archaeological Reconnaissance Survey* (Burlington, Vt.: Department of Anthropology, University of Vermont, 1984), 40–42. An entertaining fictional account of the Grog Harbor–Hawley's Bay horse ferry can be found in Rowland E. Robinson, *Uncle Lisha's Outing* (Rutland, Vt.: Tuttle, 1934), 177–78.

29. *Middlebury (Vt.) Free Press*, 7 November 1832; *Keeseville (N.Y.) Argus*, 22 May 1833; Caroline Halstead Royce, *Bessboro: A History of Westport, Essex Co., New York* (Published by the author, 1902), 172–73, 416–17.

30. *Keeseville (N.Y.) Herald*, 15 July 1835.

31. *Keeseville (N. Y.) Argus,* 22 April 1833; *Keeseville (N. Y.) Herald,* 15 July 1835.

32. *Essex County (N. Y.) Times and Westport Herald,* 10 November 1841.

33. *Essex County (N. Y.) Times and Westport Herald,* 17 November 1841; Ross, *Steamboats,* 45–46; Royce, *Bessboro,* 417.

34. *Essex County (N. Y.) Times and Westport Herald,* 3 May 1843.

35. Zadock Thompson, in *Guide to Lake George, Lake Champlain, Montreal and Quebec* (Burlington, Vt.: Chauncey Goodrich, 1845), 21, mentions the ferry, but there is no certainty that the *Eagle* was running in 1845.

36. Allen L. Stratton, comp., *History Town of Alburgh, Vermont* (Barre, Vt.: Northlight Studio Press, 1986), 1:161–62.

37. Abby Maria Hemenway, *The Vermont Historical Gazetteer* (Burlington, Vt.: A. M. Hemenway, 1871), 2:502–3.

38. Sherman, *An Illuminating History,* 74–75; William Haswell, publ., *Acts Passed by the Legislature of the State of Vermont* (Bennington, Vt.: Clark and Doolittle, 1824), 107–8.

39. *(Vergennes) Vermont Aurora,* 26 June 1828.

40. *Keeseville (N. Y.) Argus,* 22 May 1833.

41. *Westport (N. Y.) Patriot and Essex County Advertiser,* 29 April 1847; *Westport (N. Y.) Courier,* 27 September 1849.

42. *Vergennes (Vt.) Citizen,* 30 October 1857.

43. *Vergennes (Vt.) Citizen,* 14 April 1858.

44. *Vergennes (Vt.) Citizen,* 16 May 1859.

45. Ralph Nading Hill, "Champlain Ferries," *Vermont Life* 16, no. 4 (summer 1962): 5.

46. Ibid.

47. Sherman, *An Illuminating History,* 75–76.

48. Higbee, *Around the Mountain,* 75–76.

8. "PORTABLE HORSEPOWER": THE TREADMILL MECHANISM

1. Patent Drawing No. 9756x, National Archives.

2. A human-powered internal vertical treadwheel can be seen in a painting by Charles Wilson Peale titled "Exhuming the First American Mastadon," in the collection of the Peale Museum in Baltimore, Md.; it is reproduced in Major, *Animal-Powered Engines,* 39. A saw powered by a similar device can be seen in a painting of the Smith and Dimon shipyard at New York City in the collection of the New York Historical Association, Cooperstown, N.Y.

3. William H. Brown, *The History of the First Locomotives in America* (New York: D. Appleton, 1874), 138.

4. Holland Thompson, *The Age of Invention* (New Haven: Yale University Press, 1921), 120.

5. *New England Magazine* 1 (August 1831): 177.

6. Patent Drawing No. 7888x, National Archives.

7. Patent Drawing No. 9149x, National Archives.

8. *New York Mechanic* 1, no. 6 (6 February 1841): 1.

9. The *Journal of the Franklin Institute* contains many descriptions of horse machinery patents and indicates the trends in treadmill development in the 1830s and 1840s.

10. *Journal of the Franklin Institute* 20 (1835): 155.

11. Paul C. Johnson, *Farm Power in the Making of America* (Des Moines, Iowa: Wallace-Homestead, 1978), 20.

12. Ibid., 21.

13. The monthly farm journal *Cultivator*, edited by J. Buel and Luther Tucker and published in Albany by Packard and Van Benthuysen, contains many references and advertisements relating to animal-powered farm machinery, often illustrated with woodcuts.

14. Johnson, *Farm Power;* Frank F. Rogers, "Green Mountain Horsepower," *Vermont Life* 13, no. 2 (winter 1953–54): 2–7.

15. J. Buel, ed., *Cultivator* 4 (1837–38): 52; Luther Tucker, ed., *Cultivator*, new series, 4 (February 1847): 56.

16. Luther Tucker, ed., *Cultivator*, new series, 4 (November 1847): 344; Johnson, *Farm Power*, 16–18.

17. *American Mechanic* (28 May 1842): 1.

18. Major, *Animal-Powered Engines*, 92.

19. Brown, *First Locomotives*, 123–24.

20. *Journal of the Franklin Institute* 26 (1838): 143.

21. Brown, *First Locomotives*, 155.

22. *Journal of the Franklin Institute* 20 (1835): 155.

23. Jean Lipman, *Rufus Porter Rediscovered* (New York: Clarkson N. Potter, 1968), 32; *American Mechanic* 2, no. 37 (24 September 1842): 1. It is likely that other tread-mill boats were built before 1842, but Porter's is the earliest we could find.

24. James Croil, *Steam Navigation and Its Relation to the Commerce of Canada and the United States* (Toronto: William Briggs, 1898), 29; "Horseboat Operated on Lake Winnepesaukee, N.H. from 1878–1890 by Capt. Leander Levalee," photographic postcard in the collection of K. J. Crisman; Ten Cate, *Pictorial History,* 144; stern-wheel horseboat *General Harrison*, photograph no. 9691, and sternwheel horseboat *Tilda-Clara* (no photograph number), Way Collection, Public Library of Cincinnati and Hamilton County, Cincinnati.

25. W. W. Cox, "My First Trip to Omaha," *Proceedings and Collections of the Nebraska State Historical Society* 10, 2d series 5 (1902): 81.

26. "Mississippi River Ferry, run by horsepower [Cassville]," photograph WHi(F4) 320 3884, State Historical Society of Wisconsin.

27. "Horse Ferry, Cassville, Wisconsin," photograph no. 9695, Public Library of Cincinnati and Hamilton County, Cincinnati; Joseph Shafer, "Ferries and Ferry-boats," *Wisconsin Magazine of History* 21, no. 4 (June 1938): 432–33.

28. Sue Deppe, "Ferries in Tete Des Morts Township," *History of Jackson County, Iowa*, prepared by the Jackson County Historical and Genealogical Society (Dallas: Taylor, 1989), 48.

29. *Missouri Historical Review* 30, no. 3 (April 1936): 298–99; Floyd Calvin Shoemaker, *Missouri and Missourians* (Chicago: Lewis, 1943), 1:585; George A. Root, "Ferries in Kansas," *Kansas Historical Society* 2, no. 1 (February 1933): 7–8, 11, 117, 118; Ralph Gregory, *A History of Washington, Missouri* (Washington Preservation, 1991).

30. Ibid., Root, 7–8.

31. Sternwheel horseboats *General Harrison* and *Tilda-Clara,* photographs, Special Collections, Public Library of Cincinnati and Hamilton County.

32. *Waterways Journal* (22 September 1951): 11.

33. Anonymous account written on the back of the *Tilda-Clara* photograph in Special Collections, Public Library of Cincinnati and Hamilton County.

34. *Waterways Journal* (22 September 1951): 11.

35. Dorothy Heckmann Shrader, *Steamboat Legacy* (Hermann, Mo.: Wein Press, 1993), 117.

36. Robert H. Ruby and John A. Brown, *Ferryboats on the Columbia River* (Seattle: Superior, 1974), 13.

37. Edward Blackstone, *Farewell Old Mount Washington* (Staten Island, N.Y.: Steamship Historical Society of America, 1969), 17; Paul H. Blaisdell, *Three Centuries on Winnepesaukee* (Concord, N.H.: Rumford Press, 1936), 19–21; horseboat photographs in the collection of the Wolfeboro, N.H., Historical Society. Courtesy of Ralph T. Malmgren. The remains of Levallee's boat, or one like it, may have been found recently in 9.1 meters (30 ft.) of water off Bear Island in Lake Winnepesaukee. The sidewheels and treadmill are gone. See: "Diver-preservationist alliance to save wrecks, eyed by state," *Boston Sunday Globe,* 28 July 1991, New Hampshire ed., 1NH, 6NH.

38. Gordon A. Meader, "The Lake Winnepesaukee Horseboat," *Mariner* (quarterly journal of the Ship Model Societies of Rhode Island and New York) 6, no. 4 (October 1932): 121–25. Courtesy of Ralph Malmgren, Wolfeboro, N.H., Historical Society.

39. Ibid., 123.

40. Sutphin and Andre, *Sternwheelers,* 8.

41. Two watercolor paintings of the Quebec City horse-whim ferry dating to 1829 appear in: Christina Cameron and Jean Trudel, *The Drawings of James Cockburn* (Canada: Gage, 1976), 50–51. Courtesy of Daniel Laroche. Two drawings of this ferry, one by A. Ducote (c. 1832) and the other by W. H. Bartlette (c. 1840) are in the collections of the Royal Ontario Museum. Courtesy of Phillip Gillesse.

42. *Journal of the Franklin Institute* 25 (1838): 270, and 26 (1838): 76; *New York Mechanic* 1, no. 14 (3 April 1841); *Cultivator,* new series, 1 (1844): 377.

43. Johnson, *Farm Power,* 14–21; John Didsbury, "Horse Power," *Chronicle of Early American History* 1 (March 1968): 20–21, 31.

44. *Waterways Journal* (13 October 1951): 11.

45. Lake Memphremegog horseboat photographs courtesy of Katherine MacKenzie, Georgeville Historical Society, Georgeville, Quebec. Descriptions of the Hayeater are from manuscripts by Theodore Clark Smith and Gladys Norton Evans in the archives of the Georgeville Historical Society, courtesy of John M. Scott.

46. Ruby and Brown, *Ferryboats on the Columbia River,* 14, 71.

47. Ferry photograph in the collection of the Umatilla County Historical Society, Pendleton, Oregon.

48. Ruby and Brown, *Ferryboats on the Columbia River,* 88.

49. A ferry similar in design to the St. Mary's horse-whim-propelled boat operated on the Mississippi in the southeastern corner of Missouri at Caruthersville in the late nineteenth century. See: *Waterways Journal* (16 February 1957).

50. Tony Holmes, "The Last Eight Ferry Boats in Tennessee—Frontier Mainstay Rapidly Disappearing, Part II," *Tennessee Historical Quarterly* 46, no. 3 (fall 1987): 132.

51. Lorraine Bandy, "Louisville's Horse-drawn Ferry," *St. Lawrence County (N. Y.) Historical Association Quarterly* 15, no. 1 (January 1970): 20; Phillip Gillesse, personal communication to Kevin Crisman, 2 June 1995, quoting the Tweedsmuir History of Aultsville, Ontario, and including a photograph of Robert Donnelly's horseboat found in the Ontario Archives.

9. THE WRECK IN EIGHT FATHOMS

1. Kevin Crisman, *"The Singular Horse Ferry-boat": A Report on the Archaeology of the Burlington Bay Horse Ferry Wreck* (Montpelier, Vt.: Vermont Division for Historic Preservation, 1990).

2. For a detailed summary of the 1990–92 excavations, see Kevin J. Crisman and Arthur B. Cohn, *The Burlington Bay Horse Ferry Wreck and the Era of Horse-Powered Watercraft* (Basin Harbor, Vt., and College Station, Tex.: Lake Champlain Maritime Museum and Institute of Nautical Archaeology, 1993).

3. Ibid., Appendix D, Gail Erwin, "Conservation of the Burlington Bay Horse Ferry Artifacts."

10. PIECES OF THE HORSEBOAT PUZZLE: THE ARTIFACTS

1. James P. Stevens, "Last Days of the Ship Caulking Trade," *Wooden Shipbuilding & Small Craft Preservation* (Washington, D.C.: National Trust for Historic Preservation, 1976), 92–96.

2. John R. Bratten, "Identification of Pollen and Other Plant Remains Recovered from the Burlington Bay Horse Ferry Wreck," Appendix C in Crisman and Cohn, *Horse Ferry Wreck.*

11. HOW IT ALL WORKS: THE HULL AND MACHINERY OF THE HORSE FERRY

1. William Hookey, "Improved Method of bending Timber for building large Ships of War," *The Repertory of Arts, Manufactures, and Agriculture,* 2d series (London: J. Wyatt, 1816), 28:37–42.

2. William Annesley, "Specification of the Patent granted to William Annesley, of Belfast, Ireland, Architect; for certain Improvements in constructing ships, boats, and other Vessels," *Repertory of Arts,* 35:18–30. See also patent drawings submitted to the U.S. Patent Office by William Annesley dated November 1830. Patent Drawing No. 6230x, National Archives.

3. Dunlap, *Diary,* 2:569. Dunlap was read a letter from Annesley to his wife dated 18 August 1820 and observed in his diary on 18 October of the same year: "The letter is a plain, sensible, excellent letter from a Husband who has been long seperated [*sic*] from his family & struggling for a great object against power, prejudice and the

interest of many individuals." For further discussions of Annesley's trials and tribulations, see Linda McKee Maloney, "A Naval Experiment," *American Neptune* 34, no. 3 (July 1974): 188–96.

4. Troy Common Council, *Centennial Manual of the Common Council of the City of Troy,* compiled for the Troy Common Council by Weise and Berdin (Troy, N.Y.: William H. Young, 1876), 157. With special thanks to Richard Ward and Morris Glenn.

5. Personal communication from architectural historian John V. Butler, June 1990. See also G. Lister Sutcliffe, ed., *Encyclopedia of Timber Framing and Carpentry* (Harrisburg, Pa.: National Historical Society, 1990), 382.

Bibliography

PUBLISHED SOURCES

Agricola, Georgius. *De Re Metallica*. Ed. Herbert Hoover and Lou Hoover. New York: Dover Publications, 1950.

Albion, Robert Greenhalgh. *The Rise of New York Port*. New York and Boston: South Street Seaport Museum and Northeastern University Press, 1939; reprint, 1984.

Annesley, William. "Specifications of the Patent granted to William Annesley, of Belfast, Ireland, Architect; for certain Improvements in constructing ships, boats, and other Vessels." *The Repertory of Arts, Manufactures, and Agriculture*. 2d series, vol 35. London: Printed for J. Wyatt, 1819.

Baker, William Avery. *A Maritime History of Bath, Maine*. Vol. 1. Bath, Me.: Marine Research Society of Bath, 1973.

Bandy, Lorraine. "Louisville's Horse-drawn Ferry." *St. Lawrence County Historical Association Quarterly* (N.Y.) 15, no. 1 (January 1970).

Bass, George F., ed. *Ships and Shipwrecks of the Americas*. London: Thames and Hudson, 1988.

Bauer, K. Jack. *A Maritime History of the United States*. Columbia, S.C.: University of South Carolina Press, 1988.

Beardslee, George W. *Rejection of the Application for a Reissue upon New and Amended Claims of the Letters Patent Issued in 1838 to Barnabas Langdon*. Albany, N.Y.: Weed, Parsons and Company, 1852.

Beecher, Raymond. "Greene County's Horse Ferries." *Greene County Historical Journal* (N.Y.) 8, no. 2 (summer 1984).

Beers, J. H. *History of the Great Lakes*. Vol. 1. Chicago: J. H. Beers, 1899; reprint, Cleveland: Freshwater Press, 1972.

Beers, Frederick L. *History of Greene County, New York.* New York: J. B. Beers, 1884.

Bell, Andrew (pseudonym for A. Thomason). *Men and Things in America: Being the Experience of a Year's Residence in the United States.* London: William Smith, 1838.

Benjamin, J. P. *Benjamin's New Map of the Hudson River.* N.p.: J. P. Benjamin, 1848. Framed print in the Local History Room, Troy Public Library.

Billon, Frederic L. *Annals of St. Louis in Its Territorial Days from 1804 to 1821.* New York: Arno Press and *New York Times,* 1971.

Blackstone, Edward. *Farewell Old Mount Washington.* Staten Island, N.Y.: Steamship Historical Society of America, 1969.

Blaisdell, Paul H. *Three Centuries on Winnepesaukee.* Concord, N.H.: Rumford Press, 1936.

Blydenburgh. "Mr Burden's New Steam Boat." *Mechanic* (Boston), March 1834.

Boyer, Charles S. *Annals of Camden No. 3 (Old Ferries).* Privately printed, 1921.

Bradbury, Anna R. *History of the City of Hudson, New York.* Hudson, N.Y.: Record Printing and Publishing, 1908.

Bratten, John R. "Identification of Pollen and Other Plant Remains Recovered from the Burlington Bay Horse Ferry Wreck." Appendix C in *The Burlington Bay Horse Ferry Wreck and the Era of Horse-powered Watercraft.* Kevin J. Crisman and Arthur B. Cohn. Basin Harbor, Vt., and College Station, Tex.: Lake Champlain Maritime Museum and the Institute of Nautical Archaeology, 1993.

Braynard, Frank O. *S.S. Savannah: The Elegant Steamship.* New York: Dover Publications, 1963.

Breton, Arthur J. *A Guide to the Manuscript Collections of the New-York Historical Society.* Vol. 1. Westport, Conn.: Greenwood Press, 1972.

Briggs, Vernon Lloyd. *History of Shipbuilding on the North River.* Boston: Coburn Brothers, 1889; reprint, New York: Research Reprints, 1970.

Brown, Alexander Crosby. "The Patowmack Canal: America's Greatest Eighteenth Century Engineering Achievement." *Virginia Cavalcade* 12 (1963): 40–47.

Brown, William H. *The History of the First Locomotives in America.* New York: D. Appleton, 1874.

Cameron, Christina, and Jean Trudel. *The Drawings of James Cockburn.* Canada: Gage, 1976.

Chapin, Anna Augusta, and Charles V. Chapin. *A History of Rhode Island Ferries, 1640–1923.* Providence: Oxford Press, 1925.

Chase, Fannie S. *Wiscasset in Pownalborough.* Wiscasset, Me.: Southworth-Anthoensen Press, 1941.

Cist, Charles. *The Cincinnati Miscellany or Antiquities of the West.* Cincinnati: Caleb Clark, 1845.

Cox, W. W. "My First Trip to Omaha." *Proceedings and Collections of the Nebraska State Historical Society* 10, 2d series 5 (1902).

Cranmer, Gibson Lamb. *History of Wheeling City and Ohio County, West Virginia.* Chicago: Biographical Publishing, 1902.

Crisman, Kevin. "A Horse-Powered Sidewheel Ferry Sunk in Burlington Bay, Lake Champlain." *Proceedings of the 1993 Conference on Underwater Archaeology.* Ed. Sheli O. Smith. Kansas City, Mo.: 1993.

————. "Horseboat, Canal Boat, and Floating Bridge: The 1992 Field Season on Lake Champlain." *Institute of Nautical Archaeology Quarterly* 19, no. 4 (winter 1992).

————. "Horsepower on the Water: The Burlington Bay Horse Ferry Project." *Institute of Nautical Archaeology Newsletter* 18, no. 4 (winter 1991).

————. *"The Singular Horse Ferry-boat": A Report on the Archaeology of the Burlington Bay Horse Ferry Wreck.* Montpelier, Vt.: Vermont Division for Historic Preservation, 1990.

Crisman, Kevin J., and Arthur B. Cohn. *The Burlington Bay Horse Ferry Wreck and the Era of Horse-powered Watercraft.* Basin Harbor, Vt. and College Station, Tex.: Lake Champlain Maritime Museum and the Institute of Nautical Archaeology, 1993.

Croil, James. *Steam Navigation and Its Relation to the Commerce of Canada and the United States.* Toronto: William Briggs, 1898.

Crossley, David. *Post-Medieval Archaeology in Britain.* London, Leicester, and New York: Leicester University Press, 1990.

Cudahy, Brian. *Over and Back: The History of Ferryboats in New York Harbor.* New York: Fordham University Press, 1990.

Cuming, Fortescue. *Sketches of a Tour to the Western Country.* Pittsburgh: Cramer, Spear and Etchbaum, 1810. Reprinted in *Early Western Travels, 1748–1846.* Reuben Gold Thwaites, ed. Vol. 4. Cleveland: Arthur H. Clark, 1904.

Darby, John F. *Personal Recollections.* St. Louis: G. I. Jones, 1880.

Deppe, Sue. "Ferries in Tete Des Morts Township." *History of Jackson County, Iowa.* Prepared by the Jackson County Historical and Genealogical Society. Dallas: Taylor Publishing, 1989.

Diderot, Denis. *A Diderot Pictorial Encyclopedia of Trades and Industry.* 2 vols. Ed. Charles C. Gillespie. New York: Dover Publications, 1959.

Didsbury, John. "Horse Power." *Chronicle of Early American Industry* 1 (March 1968).

Dircks, Henry. *The Life, Times, and Scientific Labours of the Second Marquis of Worcester.* London: Bernard Quaritch, 1865.

Dod, S. Bayard. "The Evolution of the Ferry-boat." *Harper's Weekly* 33, no. 1672 (5 January 1889).

Duden, Gottfried. *Report on a Journey to the Western States of North America.* Columbia, Mo., and London: State Historical Society of Missouri and University of Missouri Press, 1980.

Duncan, John M. *Travels through Part of the United States and Canada in 1818 and 1819.* Vol. 2. Glasgow: Hurst, Robinson, 1823.

Dunlap, William. *Diary of William Dunlap.* Vol. 2. New York: New-York Historical Society, 1930.

Dunn, Richard S. *Sugar and Slaves: The Rise of the Planter Class in the English West Indies, 1624–1713.* New York and London: W. W. Norton, 1973.

Erwin, Gail. "Conservation of the Burlington Bay Horse Ferry Artifacts." Appendix B in *The Burlington Bay Horse Ferry Wreck and the Era of Horse-powered Watercraft.* Kevin J. Crisman and Arthur B. Cohn. Basin Harbor, Vt., and College Station, Tex.: Lake Champlain Maritime Museum and the Institute of Nautical Archaeology, 1993.

Everett, Homer. *History of Sandusky County, Ohio, with Portraits and Biographies of Prominent Citizens and Pioneers.* Cleveland: H. Z. Williams, 1882.

Farmer, Silas. *History of Detroit and Wayne County and Early Michigan.* Silas Farmer, 1890. Reprint, Detroit: Gale Research, 1969.

Fisler, Lorenzo F. *A Local History of Camden.* Camden, N.J.: Francis A. Cassedy, 1858.

Fitch, John. *The Autobiography of John Fitch.* Ed. Frank D. Prager. Philadelphia: American Philosophical Society, 1976.

Flinn, Michael W. *The History of the British Coal Industry.* Vol. 2. Oxford: Clarendon Press, 1984.

Flint, James. *Letters from America.* Edinburgh: W. & C. Tait, 1822. Reprinted in *Early Western Travels, 1748–1846.* Ed. Reuben Gold Thwaites. Vol. 9. Cleveland: Arthur H. Clark, 1904.

Foreman, Grant. "River Navigation in the Early Southwest." *Mississippi Valley Historical Review* 15, no. 1 (June 1928).

Gallt, Frank A. *Dear Old Greene County.* Catskill, N.Y.: n.p., 1915.

Gibbs-Smith, Charles, and Gareth Rees. *The Inventions of Leonardo da Vinci.* Oxford: Phaidon Press, 1978.

Glazebrook, George Parkin de Twenebroker. *A History of Transportation in Canada.* Toronto: Ryerson Press and New Haven: Yale University Press, 1938.

Glenn, Morris F. *The Story of Three Towns.* Alexandria, Va.: Published by the author, 1977.

Goodwin, Joseph O. *East Hartford: Its History and Traditions.* Hartford, Conn.: Case, Lockwood & Brainard, 1879.

Gould, Emerson W. *Fifty Years on the Mississippi: or Gould's History of Navigation.* Columbus, Ohio: Longs College, 1951.

Gregory, Ralph. *A History of Washington, Missouri.* N.p.: Washington Preservation, 1991.

Hall, Basil. *Travels in North America in the Years 1827 and 1828.* 2 vols. Edinburgh: Cadell, 1829.

Hamy, Ernest Theodore. *The Travels of the Naturalist Charles A. Lesueur in North America, 1815–1837.* Ed. H. F. Raup. Trans. Milton Haber. Kent, Ohio: Kent State University Press, 1968.

Hasbrouck, Frank. *The History of Dutchess County, New York.* Poughkeepsie, N.Y.: S. A. Matthieu, 1909.

Haswell, Charles H. *Reminiscences of an Octogenarian of the City of New York.* New York: Harper & Brothers, 1897.

Haswell, William, publ. *Acts Passed by the Legislature of the State of Vermont.* Bennington, Vt.: Clark and Doolittle, 1824.

Hemenway, Abby Maria. *The Vermont Historical Gazetteer.* Vol. 2. Burlington, Vt.: Published by the author, 1871.

Higbee, William Wallace. *Around the Mountain.* Charlotte, Vt.: Charlotte Historical Society, 1991.

Hill, Ralph Nading. "Champlain Ferries." *Vermont Life* 16, no. 4 (summer 1962).

———. *Sidewheeler Saga.* New York and Toronto: Rinehart, 1953.

Holmes, Tony. "The Last Eight Ferry Boats in Tennessee—Frontier Mainstay Rapidly Disappearing, Part 2." *Tennessee Historical Quarterly* 46, no. 3 (fall 1987).

Hookey, William. "Improved Method of bending Timber for building large Ships of War." *The Repertory of Arts, Manufactures, and Agriculture.* 2d series, vol. 28. London: Printed for J. Wyatt, 1816.

Howell, George Rogers, and Jonathan Tenney. *Bicentennial History of Albany.* New York: W. W. Munsell, 1886.

Hubbard, Oliver P. "The Treadmill in America." *Magazine of American History* 18 (July–December, 1887).

Hulbert, Archer B. *The Paths of Inland Commerce.* New Haven: Yale University Press, 1920.

Hunt, Freeman. *Letters About the Hudson River and its Vicinity.* New York: Freeman Hunt, 1837.

Ibn al-Razzaz al-Jazari. *The Book of Knowledge of Ingenious Mechanical Devices.* Trans. Donald R. Hill. Dordrecht, the Netherlands, and Boston: D. Reidel, 1974.

Jamieson, Alexander. *A Dictionary of Mechanical Science, Arts, Manufactures, and Miscellaneous Knowledge.* 2 vols. London: Henry Fisher, 1827.

Johnson, Paul C. *Farm Power in the Making of America.* Des Moines: Wallace-Homestead, 1978.

Johnston, Paul Forsythe. *Steam and the Sea.* Salem, Mass.: Peabody Museum of Salem, 1983.

Keith, Robert C. *Baltimore Harbor, A Pictorial History.* Baltimore: Ocean World, 1982.

Keyes, George S. *Mirror of Empire: Dutch Marine Art in the Seventeenth Century.* Cambridge and New York: Cambridge University Press and the Minneapolis Institute of Arts, 1990.

Kirby, Richard Shelton, Sidney Withington, Arthur Burr Darling, and Frederick Gridley Kilgour. *Engineering in History.* New York, London, Toronto: McGraw-Hill, 1956.

Landels, J. G. *Engineering in the Ancient World.* Berkeley and Los Angeles: University of California Press, 1978.

Leggett, Mortimer Dormer, ed. *Patents for Inventions Issued by the U.S. Patent Office, 1790–1873.* Vol. 2. Washington, D.C.: Government Printing Office, 1874.

Leland, Oscar H. "1834 Journey to Lewis." *Reveille* (quarterly journal of the Essex County [N.Y.] Historical Society) 2, no. 14 (November 1958).

Lemieux, Paul-E. "Les bateaux à manège (Horse Boats)," *Saguenayensia* (journal of the Société Historique du Saguenay, Quebec) 38, no. 1 (January–March 1996).

Levasseur, A. *Lafayette in America in 1824 and 1825.* Trans. John D. Godman. Philadelphia: Carey and Lea, 1829. Reprint, New York: Research Reprints, 1970.

Lipman, Jean. *Rufus Porter Rediscovered.* New York: Clarkson N. Potter, 1968.

Long, Stephen H. *The Northern Expeditions of Stephen H. Long.* Ed. Lucille M. Kane, June D. Holmquist, and Carolyn Gilman. St. Paul: Minnesota Historical Society Press, 1978.

Macbeath, George, and Donald F. Taylor. *Steamboat Days: An Illustrated History of the Steamboat Era on the St. John River, 1816–1946.* St. Stephens, N.B.: Print'n Press, 1982.

Major, J. Kenneth. *Animal-Powered Engines.* London: B. T. Batsford, 1978.

Malone, Dumas. *Dictionary of American Biography.* Vol. 8. New York: Scribner, 1936.

Maloney, Linda McKee. "A Naval Experiment." *American Neptune* 34, no. 3 (July 1974).

Marestier, Jean-Baptiste. *Memoir on Steamboats of the United States of America.* Paris: Royal Press, 1824. Reprint, Mystic, Conn.: Marine Historical Association, 1957.

Martineau, Harriet. *Retrospect of Western Travel.* London: Saunders and Otley, 1838. Reprint, New York: Greenwood Press, 1969.

Maximillian, Prince of Weid. *Travels in the Interior of North America, 1832–1834.* Parts 2 and 3. London: Ackerman, 1843; reprinted in *Early Western Travels, 1748–1846.* Vol. 24. Ed. Reuben Gold Thwaites. Cleveland: Arthur H. Clark, 1906.

Meader, Gordon A. "The Lake Winnepesaukee Horseboat." *Mariner* (quarterly journal of the Ship Model Societies of Rhode Island and New York) 6, no. 4 (October 1932).

Meeker, Moses. "Early History of the Lead Region of Wisconsin." *Wisconsin Historical Collections* 6 (1908).

Meyer, Balthasar Henry. *History of Transportation in the United States before 1860.* Washington, D.C.: Peter Smith, 1948.

Meystre, Edouard. *Histoire imagée des grands bateaux du lac Léman.* Lausanne: Payot Laussane, 1967.

Milbert, Jacques. *Picturesque Itinerary of the Hudson River.* Ridgewood, N.J.: Gregg Press, 1968.

Miller, Stephen B. *Historical Sketches of Hudson, Embracing the Settlement of the City, City Government, Etc.* Hudson, N.Y.: Bryan & Webb, 1862.

Mills, James Cooke. *Our Inland Seas.* Chicago: A. C. McClurg, 1910.

Munsell, Joel. *The Annals of Albany.* Vol. 8. Albany: J. Munsell, 1857.

New York and Brooklyn Steam Ferry Boat Company. *A Statement of Facts, with Remarks, etc., in Answer to a Pamphlet, Published at Brooklyn in Relation to the Steam Boat Ferry.* Brooklyn, N.Y.: A. Spooner, 1822.

Nichols, Roger L. "Army Contributions to River Transportation, 1815–1825." *Military Affairs* 33 (April 1969).

O'Brien, Tim. "Troy, an Early Manufacturer of Experimental Steamships." *Albany Times Union,* 13 February 1989.

Palmer, John. *Journal of Travels in the United States of North America and in Lower Canada, Performed in the Year 1817.* London: Sherwood, Neely and Jones, 1818.

Partridge, Michael. *Farm Tools through the Ages.* Boston: New York Graphic Society, 1973.

Payzant, Joan M., and Lewis Payzant. *Like a Weaver's Shuttle: A History of the Halifax–Dartmouth Ferries.* Halifax: Nimbus, 1979.

Perry, John. *American Ferryboats.* New York: Wilfred Funk, 1957.

Phelps-Stokes, Isaac Newton. *The Iconography of Manhattan Island.* New York: Robert H. Dodd, 1918.

Phillips, Ulrich Bonnell. *A History of Transportation in the Eastern Cotton Belt.* New York: Octagon Books, 1908. Reprint, 1968.

Pierrepont, Henry E. *Historical Sketch of the Fulton Ferry and its Associated Ferries.* Brooklyn: Eagle Job and Book Printing Department, 1879.

Platt, Edmund. *The Eagle's History of Poughkeepsie from the Earliest Settlements.* Poughkeepsie, N.Y.: Platt & Platt, 1905.

Polygraphisches Institut. *Schweizerische Dampfschiffahrt* (Zurich), no. 11 (1907).

Porter, Rufus. "Porter's Portable Horse Power." *New York Mechanic* 1, no. 6 (6 February 1841).

Power, Tyrone. *Impressions of America During the Years 1833, 1834, and 1835.* Vol. 1. Philadelphia: Carey, Lea & Blanchard, 1836.

Preble, George Henry. *A Chronological History of the Origin and Development of Steam Navigation.* Philadelphia: L. R. Hammersly, 1883.

Ramelli, Agostino. *The Various and Ingenious Machines of Agostino Ramelli (1588).* Trans. Martha Teach Gnudi. Baltimore: Johns Hopkins University Press and Scholar Press, 1976.

Revill, Peter J. *A Short History of Rocky Hill, Connecticut.* Rocky Hill, Conn.: Rocky Hill Historical Society, 1972.

Rezneck, Samuel. *Profiles out of the Past of Troy, New York.* Troy, N.Y.: N.p., 1970.

Robinson, Rowland E. *Uncle Lisha's Outing.* Rutland, Vt.: Tuttle, 1934.

Rogers, Frank F. "Green Mountain Horsepower." *Vermont Life* 8, no. 2 (winter 1953–54).

Root, George A. "Ferries in Kansas." *Kansas Historical Society* 2, no. 1 (February 1933).

Ross, Ogden J. *The Steamboats of Lake Champlain 1809 to 1930.* Albany: Champlain Transportation, 1930.

Royce, Caroline Halstead. *Bessboro: A History of Westport, Essex Co., New York.* Published by the author, 1902.

Ruby, Robert H., and John A. Brown. *Ferryboats on the Columbia River.* Seattle: Superior Publishing, 1974.

Ruttenber, E. M. *History of the Town of Newburgh.* Newburgh, N.Y.: E. M. Ruttenber, 1859.

Seelye, John. *Beautiful Machine: Rivers and the Republican Plan.* New York and Oxford: Oxford University Press, 1991.

Seibel, George A. *The Niagara Portage Road.* Niagara Falls, Ont.: City of Niagara Falls, 1990.

Sellers, Charles. *The Market Revolution: Jacksonian America, 1815–1846.* New York and Oxford: Oxford University Press, 1991.

Shafer, Joseph. "Ferries and Ferryboats." *Wisconsin Magazine of History* 21, no. 4 (June 1938).

Shayt, David H. "Stairway to Redemption: America's Encounter with the British Prison Treadmill." *Technology and Culture* 30, no. 4 (October 1989).

Sherman, Gordon C., and Elsie L. Sherman. *An Illuminating History of the Champlain Valley and Adirondack Mountains.* Vol. 2. Elizabethtown, N.Y.: Denton Publications, 1977.

Shoemaker, Floyd Calvin. *Missouri and Missourians.* Vol. 1. Chicago: Lewis, 1943.

Shomette, Donald G. "Heyday of the Horse Ferry." *National Geographic* 176, no. 4 (October 1989).

Shrader, Dorothy Heckmann. *Steamboat Legacy.* Hermann, Mo.: Wein Press, 1993.

Silliman, Benjamin. *Remarks Made on a Short Tour between Hartford and Quebec in the Autumn of 1819.* New Haven, Conn.: S. Converse, 1820; 2d ed., 1824.

Simmons, Joe J., III. "Steamboats on Inland Waterways: Prime Movers of Manifest Destiny." In *Ships and Shipwrecks of the Americas,* ed. George F. Bass. London: Thames and Hudson, 1988.

Singer, Charles, E. J. Holmyard, A. R. Hall, and Trevor I. Williams, eds. *A History of Technology.* Vols. 2–4. New York and London: Oxford University Press, 1956–58.

Slade, William Jr., comp. *The Laws of Vermont to 1824.* Windsor, Vt.: Simeon Ide, 1825.

Smith, Harry J. *Romance of the Hoboken Ferry.* New York: Prentice-Hall, 1931.

Spafford, Horatio Gates. *A Gazetteer of the State of New York.* Albany: B. D. Packard, 1824. Reprint, Interlaken, N.Y.: Heart of the Lakes Publishing, 1981.

St. Méry, Moreau de. *Moreau de St. Méry's American Journey.* Ed. Kenneth Roberts and Anna Roberts. Garden City, N.Y.: Doubleday, 1947.

Stearns, Elinor, and David N. Yearkes. *William Thornton, a Renaissance Man in a Federal City.* Washington, D.C.: American Institute of Architects Foundation, 1976.

Stevens, James P. "Last Days of the Ship Caulking Trade." *Wooden Shipbuilding & Small Craft Preservation.* Washington, D.C.: National Trust for Historic Preservation, 1976.

Stratton, Allen L., comp. *History Town of Alburgh, Vermont.* Vol. 1. Barre, Vt.: Northlight Studio Press, 1986.

Stuart, James. *Three Years in North America.* Vol. 1. New York: J. & J. Harper, 1833.

Stuart, Robert. *Historical and Descriptive Anecdotes of Steam Engines.* London: Wightman and Cramp, 1829.

Sutcliffe, G. Lister, ed. *Encyclopedia of Timber Framing and Carpentry.* Harrisburg, Pa.: National Historical Society, 1990.

Sutphin, Gerald W., and Richard A. Andre. *Sternwheelers on the Great Kanawha River.* Charleston, W.Va.: Pictorial Histories, 1991.

Sylvester, Nathaniel Bartlett. *History of Rensselaer County, New York.* Philadelphia: Everts and Peck, 1880.

Taccola, Mariano. *De Ingeneis.* Ed. Frank D. Prager and Gustina Scaglia. Cambridge, Mass., and London: MIT Press, 1972.

Ten Cate, Adrian G., ed. *A Pictorial History of the Thousand Islands of the St. Lawrence River.* Brockville, Ont.: Besancourt Publishers, 1982.

Thomas, Peter, Prudence Doherty, and Charles Pacquin. *Kingsland Bay Fish Hatchery, Archaeological Reconnaissance Survey.* Burlington, Vt.: Department of Anthropology, University of Vermont, 1984.

Thompson, Holland. *The Age of Invention.* New Haven: Yale University Press, 1921.

Thompson, Zadock. *Guide to Lake George, Lake Champlain, Montreal and Quebec.* Burlington, Vt.: Chauncey Goodrich, 1845.

———. *History of Vermont.* Burlington, Vt.: Chauncey Goodrich, 1842.

Thull, Beulah Baily. "Troy Developed around Ashley's Ferry." *Troy (N. Y.) Times Record* 6 (January 1973).

Thwaites, Reuben Gold, ed. *Early Western Travels, 1748–1846.* Vols. 4 (1904), 9 (1904), 12 (1905), 21 (1905), and 24 (1906). Cleveland: Arthur H. Clark.

Todd, Charles Burr. *In Olde New York.* Long Island, N.Y.: Ira J. Friedman, 1907. Reprint, 1968.

Townsend, John K. *Narrative of a Journey across the Rocky Mountains.* Philadelphia: Henry Perkins, 1839. Reprinted in *Early Western Travels, 1748–1846.* Vol. 21. Ed. Reuben Gold Thwaites. Cleveland: Arthur H. Clark, 1905.

Trautmann, Frederic. "New York through the German Eyes: The Travels of Ludwig Gall, 1819." *New York History* 62, no. 4 (October 1981).

Troy Common Council. *Centennial Manual of the Common Council of the City of Troy.* Comp. for Troy Common Council, Weise and Berdin. Troy, N.Y.: William H. Young, 1876.

Turnbull, Archibald Douglas. *John Stevens, An American Record.* New York: American Society of Mechanical Engineers, 1928.

Tuttle and Gregory. *The Troy Directory for the Year 1830.* Troy, N.Y.: Tuttle and Gregory, 1830.

Vedder, Jessie Van Vechten. *History of Greene County.* N.p.: Catskill, N.Y., 1927.

———. *Historical Catskill.* N.p.: Catskill, N.Y., 1922.

Wallace, Agnes. "The Wiggins Ferry Monopoly." *Missouri Historical Review* 43, no. 1 (October 1947).

Weise, Arthur James. *Troy's One Hundred Years 1789–1889.* Troy, N.Y.: William H. Young, 1891.

———. *The City of Troy and Its Vicinity.* Troy, N.Y.: E. Green, 1886.

———. *The History of the City of Albany, New York.* Albany: E. H. Bender, 1884.

———. *History of Lansingburgh, N.Y.* Troy, N.Y.: William H. Young, 1877.

Welby, Adlard. *A Visit to North America and the English Settlements in Illinois.* London: J. Drury, 1821; reprinted in *Early Western Travels, 1748–1846.* Vol. 12. Ed. Reuben Gold Thwaites. Cleveland: Arthur H. Clark, 1905.

White, Jon Ewbank Manchip. *Marshal of France: The Life and Times of Maurice, Comte de Saxe, 1696–1750.* Chicago, New York, San Francisco: Rand McNally, 1962.

Whittlesey, Charles W. *Crossing and Re-crossing the Connecticut River.* New Haven, Conn.: Tuttle, Morehouse & Taylor, 1938.

Winfield, Charles H. *Hopoghan Hackingh.* New York: Caxton Press, 1895.

NEWSPAPERS AND PERIODICALS

Albany (N.Y.) Gazette 38, no. 3600 (25 May 1821).

Albany (N.Y.) Times Union, 13 February 1989.

Alexandria (Va.) Gazette and Daily Advertiser 17, no. 4963 (10 July 1817).

Alexandria (Va.) Herald 7, no. 894 (13 August 1817).

American Mechanic (New York and Boston) (28 May 1842); 2, no. 37 (whole no. 89) (24 September 1842).

Boston Sunday Globe, 28 July 1991.

Burlington (Vt.) Free Press, 7 December 1827.

Columbian (New York), no. 1363 (7 April 1814); no. 1409 (4 June 1814).

Columbian Museum and Savannah (Ga.) Gazette 25, no. 4028 (18 April 1820); no. 4046 (9 May 1820); no. 4064 (30 May 1820); no. 4067 (3 June 1820); no. 4068 (6 June 1820).

Cultivator (Albany, N.Y.), ed. Luther Tucker. New series, 1 (1844); 4 (February and November 1847); 9 (June 1852).

Cultivator (Albany, N.Y.), ed. J. Buel. 4 (1837–38).

(Utah) Deseret News, 6 July 1854.

Essex County (N.Y.) Times and Westport Herald, 10 November 1841; 17 November 1841; 3 May 1843.

Journal of the Franklin Institute of the State of Pennsylvania and American Mechanics Register 10 (1830); 20 (1835); 25 (1838); 26 (1838).

Keeseville (N.Y.) Argus, 22 April 1833; 22 May 1833.

Keeseville (N.Y.) Herald, 15 July 1835.

Middlebury (Vt.) Free Press, 7 November 1832.

Missouri Historical Review 30, no. 3 (April 1936); 32 (January 1938); 51 (April 1957).

(Montreal) Canadian Courant, 13 October 1819.

Montreal Herald, 24 July 1819.

New England Magazine 1 (August 1831).

New York Commercial Advertiser 22 (25 and 26 June, 9 July 1819).

New York Mechanic 1, no. 6 (6 February 1841); 1, no. 14 (3 April 1841).

Niles Weekly Register 6, no. 9 (30 April 1814); 10, no. 25 (17 August 1816); 11, no. 13 (31 August 1816); 16, no. 26 (21 August 1819); 26, no. 671 (24 July 1824).

North American Review 13 (July 1821).

Pennsylvania Magazine or American Monthly Museum (Philadelphia: R. Aitkin, May 1775).

Le Spectateur Canadien (Montreal), 14 August 1819.

Tennessee Historical Quarterly 46, no. 3 (fall 1987).

Troy (N.Y.) Budget, 11 January 1833.

Troy (N.Y.) Northern Budget 22, no. 1130 (1 June 1819).

Troy (N.Y.) Sentinal, 22 January 1830.

Vergennes (Vt.) Citizen, 30 October 1857; 14 April 1858; 16 May 1859.

(Vergennes) Vermont Aurora, 19 October 1826; 26 June 1828; 13 November 1828; 2 July 1829.

Waterways Journal (St. Louis, Mo.), 22 September 1951; 13 October 1951; 16 February 1957.

Western Review and Miscellaneous Magazine (Lexington, Ky.) 3, no. 4 (November 1820).

Westport (N.Y.) Courier, 27 September 1849.

Westport (N.Y.) Patriot and Essex County Advertiser, 29 April 1847.

UNPUBLISHED PRIMARY SOURCES

Beach, Allen Penfield. Papers. Basin Harbor Club, Basin Harbor, Vt.

Bedouin, Thomas. Notary Papers. Archives Nationales du Quebec.

Catskill Teamboat Ferry Papers. Rensselaer County Historical Society, Troy, N.Y.

Evans, Gladys Norton. Manuscript. Georgeville Historical Society, Georgeville, Quebec.

Fulton, Robert. Manuscript Book. "Propulsion of Vessels." U.S. Patent and Trademark Office Scientific Library, Arlington, Va.

Gardner, Hester. Typescript. "Early Fairlee Boats." Fairlee Historical Society, Fairlee, Vt.

Griffin, Henry. Notary Papers. Archives Nationales du Quebec.

Higbee, William Wallace. Manuscript. "Around the Mountain." Special Collections, Bailey-Howe Library, University of Vermont, Burlington.

Holden, C. E. Notebooks. Vol. 7. New York State Archives, Albany, N.Y.

"Horseboat Golden Fleece." Memo Book. File Box "Ships." Manuscripts Section, New-York Historical Society.

Patent Drawings. Record Group 241. National Archives, Washington, D.C.

Ship Registers. Record Group 41. National Archives, Washington, D.C.

Smith, Theodore Clark. Manuscript. Georgeville Historical Society, Georgeville, Quebec.

Spear, Orson. Papers. Special Collections, Bailey-Howe Library, University of Vermont, Burlington.

Thomson, John A. Papers. Box 3. "Ferry Correspondence/Ferry Accounts, 1817–1839." New York State Archives, Albany.

Townsend, Isaiah. Papers, Box 3. Albany and Bath Ferry Company Records. New York State Archives, Albany.

Watts, Charles Jr. Papers and Letterbook. New-York Historical Society, New York, N.Y.

Way Collection. Public Library of Cincinnati and Hamilton County, Cincinnati, Ohio.

UNPUBLISHED SCHOLARLY PAPERS AND THESES

Belmont, Scott. "Starbuck Brothers, Iron Founders and Machinists." Undergraduate term paper for Dr. Dean Phelan, Rensselaer Polytechnic Institute, Troy, N.Y., 1988.

Goelet, Michael Peter. *The Careening and Bottom Maintenance of Wooden Sailing Vessels.* Master's thesis in anthropology, Texas A&M University, 1986.

Hachtman, Corine. *The History of the Wiggins Ferry Company.* Master's thesis, History Department, Washington University, St. Louis, Mo., 1931.

Wallace, Agnes Mary. *The Wiggins Ferry, 1795–1902.* Master's thesis, St. Louis University, 1945.

Index